# Race to Equity

*Race to Equity* is a wonderful and moving addition to the literature on anti-oppression education. McCaskell's account of the work of activist educators, trustees, parents, communities and students is inspirational; his analysis of the events, activities, and movements that make a difference is insightful; and his belief that school change involves both internal and external forces points the way towards a more equitable future for all students.

— **Tara Goldstein**, Department of Curriculum, Teaching and Learning, OISE/UT

This is "history of the everyday" at its best, with a rich cast of characters. Tim McCaskell writes from the double perspective of an insider-outsider; someone who was in the system, but not of it, and who was always alert to the need for community leadership and activism as a precondition for change. Sober, lucid and yet passionate, this book is a must read for people working for institutional change in Canada and beyond.

— **Alok Mukherjee**, Vice Chair, Toronto Police Services Board

McCaskell's telling of this story, in which he was a central actor, does it justice. It is resolutely personal *and* political, without a shred of jargon or rhetoric, and is always aware of the larger economic and social forces shaping action on the ground. It is a history progressive educators everywhere can be grateful for.

— **George Martell**, School of Social Sciences, Atkinson College, York University

*Race to Equity* provides a valuable institutional ethnography of major educational bodies. In the process it depicts successes and frustrations of the many actors in projects of social transformation. It is a tribute to those who struggle to change our everyday life but are often forgotten in the passing of time.

— **Himani Bannerji**, Sociology, York University

McCaskell's careful and succinct capturing of key developments and moments from the vantage point of someone "positioned to know" brilliantly illuminates the complex nature of school board politics and community activism. A must read text for every anti-oppression worker.

— **George J. Sefa Dei**, Department of Sociology and Equity Studies, OISE/UT

# Race to Equity

## Disrupting Educational Inequality

Tim McCaskell

Between the Lines
Toronto, Canada

**Race to Equity**



First published in Canada in 2005 by
Between the Lines
720 Bathurst Street, Suite #404
Toronto, Ontario
M5S 2R4
1-800-718-7201
www.btlbooks.com



**Library and Archives Canada Cataloguing in Publication**

McCaskell, Tim, 1951-
Race to equity : disrupting educational inequality / Tim McCaskell.
Includes bibliographical references.
ISBN 1-896357-96-2

1. Educational equalization – Ontario – Toronto. 2. Educational change – Ontario – Toronto. 3. Toronto Board of Education. 4. McCaskell, Tim, 1951- 5. Schools – Ontario – Toronto. I. Title.
LA419.T6M32 2005 379.2′6′09713541 C2005-900626-9

Cover design by David Vereschagin, Quadrat Communications
Interior design and page preparation by Steve Izma
Printed in Canada
Second printing July 2017

Between the Lines gratefully acknowledges assistance for its publishing activities from the Canada Council for the Arts, the Ontario Arts Council, the Government of Ontario through the Ontario Book Publishers Tax Credit program and through the Ontario Book Initiative, and the Government of Canada through the Book Publishing Industry Development Program.

# Contents

# Preface

THIS BOOK IS A SERIES OF REFLECTIONS on my involvement with the experiments, successes, and mistakes of twenty years of equity initiatives at the Toronto Board of Education. For almost three decades the Toronto Board's efforts to reshape an education system to provide truly equitable education for a hugely diverse student body garnered national and international attention. My motivation for writing this book was to try to preserve the memory of what I believe was a period of significant social struggle, cultural transformation, and deep learning.

I have used the trajectory of my personal involvement with anti-racism and anti-homophobia education and the evolving links to issues of gender, class, and disability to trace some narrative threads in this "booming buzzing confusion" of institutional and social transformation. In order to round out my admittedly biased and faulty memories, I have also integrated interviews with key participants and consulted twenty-five years of Board minutes, as well as several academic theses on different aspects of the work, and a number of the important documents produced along the way. Unless otherwise noted, all quotations in the book are from the interviews.

I hope that my still admittedly partial account can at least dimly reflect the enormous work of the activist educators, trustees, parents, communities, and students who propelled this process in the belief that education should play a key role in creating a more equitable world.


## Thanks

I need to thank a number of people for inspiring and helping with this book. The first is my partner, Richard Fung, who shared many of these experiences with me and whose own activism and artistic practice have been so fundamental to my own understanding of questions of race. The advice, medicines, and humility of my doctor, Philip Berger, helped me survive through the darkest days of the AIDS epidemic, which spanned much of the period covered by this book. Between the Lines and especially Robert Clarke provided invaluable editorial advice in turning my often rambling memories into a much more readable story.

Those who consented to be interviewed – Nora Allingham, Domenic Bellissimo, Keren Brathwaite, John Campey, Pat Case, Olivia Chow, Vern

Douglas, Marg Evans, Carolyn Goossen, Tam Goossen, Marlene Green, Hari Lalla, Ruby Lam, Geoff MacDonald, Susan McGrath, Marsha Melnik, Alok Mukherjee, Fatema Mullen, Charles Novogrodsky, Myra Novogrodsky, Gail Posen, Vanessa Russell, Tony Souza, Kristen Swartz, Alice Te, Barb Thomas, Margaret Wells, Sandy Wong, Ya Ya Yao, Terezia Zoric – all provided invaluable insights without which this book could not have been written.

The many others whom I could not interview and whose stories I could not tell but who played a role in fighting for change at the Board must also be credited. Thanks too to those who persevered in reading my much-too-long first draft and offered their comments and suggestions. They include Glen Brown, Kari Dehli, Bob Gardner, Tara Goldstein, and Lisa McCaskell.

Finally there are the thousands of young people I worked with over the years. Their enthusiasm, honesty, experiences, ideas, and courage made this whole experience immensely rewarding and exciting. I may have been their facilitator, but they were truly my best teachers.

# Chapter 1

# Back Story

IN BEAVERTON, THE LITTLE SOUTHERN ONTARIO TOWN where I grew up in the 1950s, the range of social and cultural difference stretched from Protestant to Catholic. The only Indians I ever saw were on television, although some apparently lived on a reservation not far away, near Orillia. For a while a Jewish family, the Roses, owned a clothing store on Main Street, but they moved away. The only Chinese family in town, the Chus, ran Dan's Café. My family's church, like many others across the country, raised money to support missions in the less fortunate, heathen areas of the world. Those were the days of "Eat up your vegetables. Children in China are starving."

When I was eleven, and my family drove down to Florida for a holiday, I learned that Black people didn't really look like the ones portrayed in the Beaverton Lions' Club Minstrel Show. The Southern U.S. service-station washrooms were designated "Men," "Women," and "Colored." My mother explained that in America, Black people were often not treated very well. This, I was told, was not properly Christian. When the civil rights movement began, I learned in Sunday School that it was just like Moses leading the Israelites out of slavery in Egypt. By the time I was in high school, "Black Power" was in the news. My friends and I sympathized, and remarked that we were lucky there was no racism here. Of course, apart from the presence of Lilly Chu, Brock District High was an all-white school.

I left Beaverton for university in Ottawa in 1969 but quickly became immersed in left-wing anti-Vietnam War politics and soon dropped out, opting instead for a mixture of travel to India, unskilled labour, and communal living in Toronto. Then I spent two years living in South America, learning Spanish in the process. By 1974 I was working at Toronto's Centre for Spanish Speaking Peoples, an advocacy centre for Latin American immigrants. Student power, the anti-Vietnam War movement, national liberation struggles around the globe, and two years of living in the social upheaval of South America had turned me into a young Marxist. Still, when my new comrades in Toronto's Marxist Institute proposed a lecture series on racism in Canada, I was puzzled. Racism wasn't really a problem here in Canada, was it?

John Saul, a professor of political science at York University, led off the series with an analysis of racism as an ideology spawned by Western imperialism to justify slavery, genocide, and colonialism. Other speakers gave first-hand accounts of the abuse, humiliation, and discrimination they faced in Canada. Still others debated "theory" – how racism was a strategy to divide and conquer the working class to prevent it from organizing for socialism; how racism's role was to produce different strata in the labour force, which served to generate superprofits from low-wage labour; how racist scapegoating and blaming everything on immigrants got capitalists off the hook in times of economic crisis; or how racial identity was either a distorted or a legitimate form of class-consciousness. The series opened my eyes to a whole new world.

That same year opened my eyes in another way. I came out of the closet. I had been deeply in love with a man for almost four years – in fact, I had followed him to South America – but I was always too terrified to tell him or anyone else about it. The only thing I knew about gay people beyond my own suppressed desires was a sordid picture of bitchy drag queens mired in guilt and shame. Growing up in Beaverton in the 1950s and 1960s had not exactly provided me with positive gay role models. In the summer of 1974, finally recognizing that I had to deal with my sexuality, I nervously dragged myself off to a gay pride march and duly discovered yet another whole new world, the vibrant milieu of gay liberation. Gay lib, I learned, was revolutionary. Gay activists were, it seemed, the vanguard in the creation of a new, sex-positive, polymorphously perverse society that would liberate the sexual capacities of humanity.

I soon began writing for *The Body Politic*, a national gay liberation magazine published in Toronto. Crowning the paper's masthead was a 1921 quote from early gay rights pioneer Kurt Hiller – "The liberation of homosexuals must be the work of homosexuals themselves" – and for me that statement marked an epiphany. An appropriation from Marx, the quote expressed an important truth: oppressed people must speak for themselves and be the driving force in ending their own oppression. It also meant that people had to be more careful about speaking on behalf of others. The recognition shaved a little of the arrogance off of my initial revolutionary pretensions. Perhaps gay liberation was more about overcoming our own oppression than it was about liberating gay desire in everyone else.

In the following year I helped to organize a course in Marxism and gay liberation at the Marxist Institute. In that course I met the man who would become my partner. Richard Fung was Chinese Trinidadian and had recently immigrated to Canada. That brought racism back into the picture. For Richard, racism was not an abstract social phenomenon but a concrete personal experience. Sometimes subtle, sometimes blatant, the experience of racism intimately, and regularly, located his position in a white Canada.

## A Political Context

The 1970s were a time when the world was in great turmoil and the future seemed exciting and promising. American imperialism, as my friends and I unapologetically called it, was suffering its most serious historical defeat ever, at the hands of the plucky people of Vietnam. The power of the people was proving to be greater than "the man's" technology. "Liberation" was the word of the day. All around the globe national liberation movements were challenging colonialism and racism, and oppressed people were standing up to end poverty and exploitation and to demand true democracy and self-determination. Women's liberation was confronting traditional gender roles. The civil rights movement in the United States had given way to the more radical critiques of Black liberation. Gay liberation had emerged.

In the Soviet bloc too, sullen bureaucrats were under increased pressure to permit true democratic reform. In China the Cultural Revolution (still unblemished by later revelations of vicious sectarian infighting and abuse) appeared to offer an example of millions of people, sweeping away oppressive backward thinking and opening up the world's most populous nation to a new culture of equality, co-operation, and liberation.

Even in traditionally stodgy Canada things were changing. The Trudeau Liberals' promise of social security, human rights, and an independent foreign policy firmly established the political centre far to the left of anything conceivable before, or later.

Only in 1958 had the right to vote in Toronto municipal elections finally been extended to non-property owners. For the first time the majority of the city's residents had a democratic right to help choose their municipal government. As Toronto overtook Montreal to become Canada's largest and most multicultural city, reformers began to be elected – people who would encourage community development and oppose the corporate gutting of neighbourhoods and the indiscriminate building of high-rises and expressways. The notion of "community" was soon extended to racial and cultural groups, and new social movements began to assert themselves and flex political muscle on the municipal scene. The city's conservative Anglo protestant establishment was losing its traditional dominance.

The Toronto Board of Education, as I would soon find out, was part of this changing political context.[1] The Toronto Board was governed by just over twenty locally elected trustees who oversaw a complicated bureaucracy managing some 30 secondary and 120 elementary city schools.

In the elections of late 1969, reformers became a significant voice at the Toronto Board of Education for the first time. The genie was out of the bottle. The days when trustees were expected to do little more than attend a Board meeting once a month to rubber-stamp administration recommendations were over. Unlike most of their predecessors, these new reform trustees understood their positions as full-time jobs. They were in close contact with schools in their area and well acquainted with various local school and parent communities.

Not surprisingly, the reform trustees began to champion the interests of their working-class and immigrant constituencies who knew that their children were often being poorly served by the educational status quo. One of the reformers' strategies was to set up liaison committees, usually representing different ethnic groups, as a means of bringing community concerns to the attention of the institution. When sufficient momentum had been built up in a liaison committee, progressive trustees could then carry the concerns raised forward to the more formal standing Board committees. Under the influence of the reformers, the Board began to experiment with real democracy. In 1970, for instance, after lobbying from the Italian and Portuguese communities, the Board struck a Special Committee on Educating New Canadians. The committee focused on "new Canadian" students who were facing particular challenges and succeeded in establishing an infrastructure of social workers, interpreters, and counsellors.

In September 1971, inspired by the community schools movement in New York City,[2] a small group of Toronto activists began publishing a newsletter called *Community Schools*. They were part of a growing movement in Canada, also evidenced in a parallel national publication, *This Magazine is About Schools*, which saw reforms in the education system as pivotal in the struggle for fundamental social change. Over the next four years *Community Schools* expressed eclectic interests: the "reading crisis" in downtown schools; the streaming of working-class kids into vocational programs; "alternative schools"; Third World liberation; bias in the curriculum; discrimination against women teachers; student rights; administrators' refusal to allow gay speakers to address students; sex education; new ideas of "child-centred" education; demands for "full-time" trustees; education in China; and calls for greater democracy and community control of schooling to involve parents, students, and teachers. The newsletter articles reflected a range of constituencies that were becoming increasingly interested in education issues in Toronto: the Third World solidarity movement; organized labour; parents interested in alternative schools; working-class and immigrant communities; the women's movement; and progressive academics.

The education activists at *Community Schools* and *This Magazine* soon realized that by organizing to bring these constituencies together, they could have a huge impact on the outcome of local school board elections. As time went on, the Toronto Board of Education would become a stronghold of community-based politicians, many of them associated with the New Democratic Party. Relatively poor by party standards, the NDP based its election strategy on volunteer, labour-intensive door-to-door canvassing rather than on the more expensive media-based campaigns favoured by the major parties. This strategy was especially effective in the relatively low-profile school board elections.

More reformers were elected in December 1972. Thereafter, and throughout the decade, a continuing series of work groups and committees and reports would sift through issues of immigrant status, culture, class, and gender. By the end of the decade the Toronto Board of Education would have set in motion a series of initiatives, experiments, and struggles that would carry through into the next century. Much to my own surprise, too, I would eventually end up working there for some twenty years.

Chapter 2

# Beginnings

JANUARY 1977: THE STREET CAR LUMBERED through the dark of the early evening, over the Don River bridge and into the east-end Toronto neighbourhood of Riverdale. I got off and walked through the snow to the Queen Street Presbyterian Church, where I was to be interviewed for the position of co-ordinator, and only employee, of a new organization called the Riverdale Intercultural Council (RICC).

At the church I settled into a question and answer session with Reverend John Robson, two police community liaison officers, and a local social worker. My biggest asset, other than (like all the interviewers) being white and male, was that I had just returned from my second overland trip to India. I was thus expected to be an expert on all things Indian, and, as I found out that day, RICC's main concern was an ongoing "cultural conflict" between the community's older, well-established white working-class majority and its new "East Indian" population.

The early 1970s had seen the construction of Gerrard Square several blocks north of the church. The large indoor mall bled the life out of the traditional storefront businesses along Gerrard Street. Then a floundering local movie theatre near Gerrard and Coxwell was taken over by a South Asian entrepreneur who renamed it the Naz and began to show Bollywood movies. The Naz acted as a magnet, drawing new South Asian immigrants from across Toronto. The low rents of the depressed business area meant that the theatre was soon surrounded by small "East Indian" clothing stores and restaurants catering to the rush of weekend business. A Sikh Temple opened up just south of Gerrard Square. Toronto's "Little India" was born.

The shift in the nature of local business activity – from catering to the largely white working-class residents to attracting South Asians from across the city – produced "problems." Quiet residential streets became congested. Driveways were blocked by parked cars. Tempers flared. Exchanges took on a racist tone. The same years had already seen a pattern of high-profile and violent "Paki-bashing" across the city. Swastikas and "Paki Go Home" were daubed on the doors of the Sikh Temple. Cars were vandalized. People were harassed. The government needed to been seen to be doing something to calm the situation. So in late 1976 the provincial Ministry of Culture and Recreation decided to fund the Riverdale Intercultural Council, the brainchild of Reverend Robson, long-time minister at the Queen Street Presbyterian Church.

I have little recollection of what I said to the interview team that day, but it was obviously nothing too alarming. Soon after, armed with a cursory knowledge of Indian sweets, a hodge-podge of leftist theories, and a little second-hand experience with racism, I had a new job.

## The Riverdale Intercultural Council

Reverend Robson was a remarkable man – down to earth, open to new ideas, and with a solid commitment to social justice. If there had been a liberation theology among Presbyterians he would have been in the forefront. He enjoyed pushing the envelope. I will never forget the impish twinkle in his eye when he announced his plan to rent the second floor of the church offices to the Jesuit Centre for Social Justice. He mused aloud on how that was going to go over with his board of elders, a conservative anti-Catholic group.

Reverend Robson and the handful of RICC members had a soft spot for multicultural festivals. They thought that what was happening in Riverdale was the result of cultural misunderstanding. After a few weeks on the job, I became convinced that there was a quite particular, and concrete, irritant: parking. For me, fresh from the Marxist Institute, that was the "material basis" of the neighbourhood conflict. As long as Little India had street congestion and blocked driveways, the result was going to be friction that would manifest itself in racism. The solution to racism in Riverdale, it seemed to me, was a parking lot.

Miraculously, the neighbourhood's Roden Public School had just such a lot for teacher parking, directly behind the business area. When the school was closed on weekends and evenings, the high-volume time for businesses, the lot was empty; but it was also always chained shut. Getting rid of that chain, I reasoned, would relieve much of the parking pressure, and the problem of racism would abate.

I soon found myself speaking about this issue to the relevant committee of the Toronto Board of Education. That was, I believe, my first visit to the high-modernist seven-storey building just west of University Avenue on College Street. The building's front lobby had soaring two-storey glass windows looking north to the University of Toronto. The second-floor panelling above the entrance was carved with various depictions of student endeavour. Off to the left was the entrance to the trustee offices, with a list of all the Board's chairs chiselled into the marble wall. To the right, behind the information desk with its gruff custodian, was the inner sanctum: the main committee room, the boardroom, and the trustees' lounge. This was an intimidating and powerful institution, a site of state power.

The committee that I appeared before did not show much evidence of the radical new trustees I had been reading about in local newspapers. It seemed mostly to be made up of rather sour-looking old men in suits. They gave the impression of having much better things to do than listen to someone from the Riverdale Intercultural Council, whatever that was. I made my request awkwardly, explaining that tensions around parking were leading to racism in the area, but that the Board could help to solve the problem by opening up the public school parking lot. The school trustee for Riverdale looked down his nose at me and sniffed. Who was I to say that there was racism in *his* community? This was just scaremongering to try to get the Board to subsidize a group of businesses. If the Board opened one parking lot to benefit one group, where would it end? What about liability? Who would supervise it? It was just too much trouble. Request denied.

Back at the church, Reverend Robson and I strategized. He would use the Christian angle to get support from neighbourhood churches, and talk to the community cops on the Council to get police backing for the idea. I would try to mobilize the East Indian Business Association and other community representatives to make a more formal proposal. To help make our case, we also needed to find allies in the Board.

I arranged to have lunch with one such possible ally, Tony Souza. Our meeting would prove to be the beginning of a long friendship.

## Allies

Tony, I found, was a frenetic bundle of energy, always racing to keep up with the thoughts and ideas that danced through his mind. He was one of the twenty-four school community advisors in the Board's new School Community Relations (SCR) Department, set up within the Curriculum and Programs Division in 1976 after the Board's multiculturalism report had identified the need to build bridges between schools and Toronto's new "multicultural" communities. The SCR Department worked with three levels of parent groups: local school parent groups, area councils, and city-wide groups based on either ethno-racial identity or on particular issues.

Tony was Indian, from Calcutta, and had been hired to work with the East Indian community. His experience in community development led him to believe that he needed to be more than just a liaison to the schools. He decided he had a responsibility to organize the community to press for change. By this point he had learned the Byzantine workings of the Board. He too was gay.

When he first came to Canada, Tony's understanding of racism was limited to what he knew about the U.S. civil rights movement and stories of the treatment of Indian immigrants in Britain. But his first community development job in Canada had introduced him to the "brutal policing" faced by Black youth in Toronto. He personally experienced mysterious apartments, available over the phone but always "just rented" when he showed up in person. For a time, he said, he found himself without a name for his experiences.

Tony introduced me to Marlene Green, his direct supervisor, the school community relations officer in Area 5. Marlene had grown up in the island nation of Dominica in the Caribbean. She did have a name for what was going on – racism – and she had an analysis of what was causing it. Her understanding of racism had developed through the anti-colonial struggle that was sweeping the West Indies in the 1950s. She saw race as power. In Dominica and elsewhere, "White people meant the Brits, and it was clear they wanted to hang onto their colonies for economic benefit to themselves."

In Canada Marlene had become involved in solidarity work. It was the early 1970s, the time of the "Black Power" uprising in Trinidad and the beginning of the New Jewel Movement in Grenada. She was soon working with African students supporting liberation movements in Southern Africa, and then with Caribbean students facing deportation because of their involvement in the 1968-69 anti-racist protests at Montreal's Sir George Williams University.

The experience made her keenly aware of what she saw as Canadian hypocrisy. "We would be watching news reports of the U.S. civil rights struggle and seeing the dogs attacking people, and the Canadians would say, 'That's so horrible.' But at the same time they wouldn't want to deal with anything having to do with racism in Canada. It was always somewhere else." She said that this was as true for the traditional white left as for anyone else. Her analysis continued to develop after she started teaching an upgrading program to immigrant and working-class students at George Brown College in downtown Toronto. She began to make more connections between the experiences of those students in Canada and her own anti-colonial work – to see how people used racism to maintain power.

Another of the idealistic young Black students who were streaming into the Canadian university system was Keren Brathwaite, who came from Antigua as a graduate student in 1967. Shocked at the lack of representation she found within the University of Toronto, she was soon working to help set up the university's Transitional Year Program. She was inspired by the potential of the program's recruits – young people who had dropped out of the public school system and been denied the opportunity to advance themselves and their communities. Clearly, she saw, the problems the Black community was facing began in the public school system, long before students even began to think about university. As a result, in the early 1970s she was part of a group of Black university students who founded the Black Education Project. Full of the energy of committed youth, BEP worked with youngsters in danger of dropping out and failing. One of its goals was to help kids find their place by learning more about their own histories.

Marlene Green became BEP's first executive director. As well as setting up after-school tutoring programs, the group advocated for Black students and their parents. BEP also faced a growing demand to present workshops for teachers. For Marlene those workshops became a "treadmill" that went nowhere. "You'd expend an enormous amount of energy preparing a workshop and going out and talking for two hours so that they could say, 'We've done race and culture.'" Meanwhile, from Marlene's perspective, the schools were "freaking out." They were saying, "Oh my god, we have all these weird Black kids coming in from Jamaica. We don't understand what they're saying." A disproportionate number of Black students were being suspended or expelled. One day a principal called Marlene and asked if BEP could develop a tutoring program for all his school's Black students during the school day. It was basically an attempt "to get rid of them," to push them all off to one side, out of the way.

After five years at BEP Marlene was hired as one of the new school community relations officers and became more intimately acquainted with the attitudes and practices permeating the school system. One day, for example, a principal began talking about "chinks." When Marlene challenged him, he backtracked. She went to the area superintendent, who in the end did "absolutely nothing" about the remarks. One of her first priorities at the Board was to set up training programs for the school community advisors to ensure that they had an analysis of racism that they could apply to their work.

## Understanding Racism in Riverdale

Tony and I found ourselves launched on a steep learning curve. We had finally managed to get the school parking lot open, but racism had not gone away. One night in the basement of a church on the Little India strip, as we waited for the arrival of the South Asian business representatives for a community meeting, we were chatting with an older white woman, a pillar of the local church. "You know," she remarked innocently, "one of the big problems is the cockroaches they bring in."

"From the garbage?" I offered. We had been trying to encourage the city to increase its garbage collection to meet the increased demand from the many new restaurants.

"No, no." She shook her head. "It's their culture, you know. They encourage them. Whenever an East Indian couple move into a new house, their friends give them a pair of cockroaches to let loose and breed. They think that cockroaches are a sign of prosperity. It's part of their religion." She smiled sweetly at us, seemingly proud of her cultural competency.

"I've never heard that before," I managed to say, giving Tony a quick glance. "Where did you hear that?"

"My brother," she replied. "He owns a little apartment building in Scarborough and he rents to East Indians. He says there are so many cockroaches that the white people have all moved out, but there isn't any use fumigating or anything, because the East Indians like the cockroaches and they would just bring more in anyway."

I made a mental note – racism as "interested knowledge." When you hear that kind of story, one thing you can do is ask: who benefits?

We clearly needed to know more about what was going on in people's minds. Reverend Robson gave me a list of community movers and shakers and sent me out on a fact-finding mission. I was to call these people up, introduce myself and the RICC, and see what they thought needed to be done. It turned out that the Riverdale Intercultural Council did not have a high profile. "Agricultural council? I didn't know there was agriculture in Riverdale." Nor did most people on Reverend Robson's list seem to be very interested.

Still, some of the exchanges did prove to be seminal in my growing understanding of the community and the issues. In the course of one conversation, a middle-aged white woman living in a public housing development launched into an attack on unions, paraphrasing the contents of any number of right-wing editorials about unions having too much power. I listened, uncomfortably, and diligently took notes. Soon she began complaining about how hard it was for people to make ends meet, and the importance of working people sticking together to fight for their rights.

"Isn't that what unions are for?" I asked. "Yes," she agreed. Then she began recounting her husband's experiences in the workplace.

I left the conversation feeling puzzled. The woman was bright, articulate, and informed on current events. Yet she was also full of contradictions. Then I remembered the term "bifurcated consciousness." The woman had two contradictory sources of information about the world: the official version, which she heard and read about in the media; and the personal version, which she drew out of her own immediate experience. The conclusions that she formed from these two sources of information were contradictory, impossible to integrate. Depending on context, or how a question was phrased, she would draw on whichever seemed appropriate. My role as an educator and community organizer, I realized, was to strengthen her understanding of the world based on her own real-life experience.

But what happened when experience itself was shaped by perceptions that in turn had been shaped by "dominant ideological forms"?

"Indians are all drunks," another respondent explained. "We need more police to get them out of the parks. Send them back to the reserves. A decent family can't enjoy themselves there [in the parks] anymore. I was there with my kid just the other day and these guys were screaming and swearing. I had to take my daughter home. It was awful."

Most of the First Nations population of Riverdale were neither drunk nor in the park, but the Aboriginal people who owned their homes and went to work every day blended into the neighbourhood and were probably not even visible as "Indians." But here racist conclusions were being grounded in personal perception. How was I to pull that one apart?

On another occasion, a woman who identified herself as Native started complaining about the "Vietnamese immigrants." She said, "They take all the good jobs. I was born here and I can't get a job no matter how hard I try because they're all taken by Vietnamese. And they're all on welfare. When I have to go down to the office to get something done with my cheque, I have to wait in line for hours. The place is full of Vietnamese."

The irony of her perception – that the same group that was taking all the jobs was simultaneously all on welfare – did not dawn on her. It was another clear contradiction, and easy enough to point out, but getting her to choose one stereotype over the other hardly seemed a solution.

I found that "consciousness-raising" was a complicated business. I began to think about what might happen if these people – the woman who wanted Indians to go back to the reserves, the Native woman, and some Vietnamese immigrants – came together in an environment where they could talk to each other, and share and compare their experiences. Would they be able to come to understand what was shaping their perceptions and discover what they had in common?

After many calls I managed to find enough people willing to attend a workshop. Then I realized that I didn't really know how a workshop was supposed to work. Tony suggested I talk to Barb Thomas, who had helped to organize the workshops on racism that Marlene Green had set up for the SCR Department. Barb was working at the Cross Cultural Communications Centre (CCCC), an organization founded at the beginning of the 1970s when returning volunteers from CUSO (Canadian University Service Overseas) had set up a network of "learners centres" across the country. While most of the centres concentrated on the world outside of Canada, Cross Cultural focused more on "colonial relations" in the city itself. It joined the smattering of other progressive organizations that dotted the Toronto landscape in those days: Development Education Centre, Toronto Committee for the Liberation of Southern Africa, Latin American Working Group, the Black Education Project.

At age twenty-two Barb had wanted to see something more of the world, and in 1970 she went to teach in Barbados. "It was part of that colonial thing that a white person from Canada could go to Barbados and teach without a diploma," she explained. Barbados began Barb's political education. She found it "pretty humbling" trying to teach high-school students who had a deep experience of colonial history when she came from a completely different background.

By the time she returned to Toronto in 1972 the city had become a very different place. All around her were children like those she had taught in the Caribbean. When she went to the Black Education Project to volunteer, she met Marlene Green. She also went to teachers' college, but afterwards, during a time of impending layoffs, she couldn't get a job as a teacher. Instead she collected readings on development and education that would make up an orientation package for CUSO volunteers. She began asking herself about the role of educators in social change: "What kind of thinking did you have to do about yourself and your own location in the world, and the location of people you were working with?" Finally she got a job with CCCC and met Fran Endicott at the Ontario Institute for Studies in Education (OISE). Together they began studying the Toronto Board's newly published "Every Student Survey," which correlated school success with factors such as first language, ethnicity, race, and social class. They also began to look at how class and race played out in the classroom in practical ways: the teacher's glance, who got attention, who got disciplined, expectations. The Board's 1975 report on multiculturalism gave Barb and Fran a context in which they could contact teachers and co-sponsor workshops on the situation of West Indian students. Together they struggled with the question of how to deliver workshops in ways that didn't reinforce stereotypes.

By the time I arrived seeking advice, Barb was a driving force behind the CCCC, with years of experience in curriculum development and popular education around issues of race and class. Her first question was, "What do you want to achieve?" I was not quite sure how to respond. I couldn't very well say "world revolution." Even "an end to racism in Riverdale" suddenly seemed a little vague. "Finding out what the issues in the community are" seemed better, so I tried that. But I knew I didn't just want information, I wanted to "raise consciousness."

Barb demonstrated that one of the most important qualities of a facilitator was patience. Out of my confusion, bit by bit she extracted goals for the workshop: to help people get to know one another, to share information and perspectives, to identify key issues, to investigate steps RICC could take to resolve those issues. If some of the participants became active in the organization, so much the better.

An unexpected problem arose on the afternoon of the first workshop. The two police community liaison officers who sat on the Council decided to show up. They were two large, assertive white men. In their private conversations with me, several of the participants had mentioned police harassment of minority youth as an issue. When the two officers introduced themselves, there was palpable tension in the room and it only got worse. When an Aboriginal woman tried to raise the issue of how the police had treated her son, the officers began to argue with her, questioning her version of the facts and pressing for details, names, dates. She quickly clammed up. Even the mostly white social work types seemed intimidated. I tried to carry on with a discussion of less contentious issues, but the tone had been set. I was learning something about the exercise of power in groups.

The next day I met with Reverend Robson and told him that we had to do something about the police in the workshops. I proposed that we ask them not to come back. The reverend was ambivalent. He had worked in the neighbourhood long enough to understand the widespread distrust of the police among the poor and marginalized. But RICC's goal was to bring everyone together, and the two officers were members in good standing. He said they were good people. They had been helpful. He wondered if we could just ask them "to tone it down a little." I argued that as long as the other people knew there were cops at our meetings, they were not going to open up. We could suggest that the police participation was really important in our general meetings, but not in the community discussions. Reverend Robson finally agreed, and the next day I phoned the cops and asked them not to come to the meetings. They put up an argument for their continued attendance, but I didn't back down.

The workshops went on without the police officers, but I began to notice something else. Although participants were all drawn from the Riverdale "community," the mix included two different kinds of people: working-class residents of different backgrounds and "service providers," professionals who represented different community agencies. Over and over again, when residents would talk about their experiences, the service providers would jump in to provide ready-made interpretations of those experiences – usually conceptualizing the problem as "cultural miscommunication." They often saw the poor treatment that people received as a result of their not knowing or following proper procedures: their difficulties were a result of being "new" to the country; once they assimilated a little more, everything would be fine. Racism was never a factor.

Since the service providers tended to be better educated, more fluent in English, and more used to talking in groups than the community people, they dominated the conversation. They were also much more likely to be white. "It's the dictatorship of the bourgeoisie," I explained earnestly to Reverend Robson as we drove to a community meeting. He gave me a worried glance.

"Marx said that the ruling ideas of any period are the ideas of the ruling class," I went on. "It's not just in the media. You can see it happening in those meetings. The middle-class people who have learned the dominant ideas in social work school always have the approved answers ready. They can talk circles around the rest of us. We lose track of what our own experience means. A dictatorship isn't just somebody giving orders. It happens all the time, in the course of a million different conversations, in who dominates a million different discussions. It's more subtle than what the police were doing, but it's the same thing."

"You don't want to ask them to leave too?" Reverend Robson asked.

"No, I don't think we can do that. But it's just interesting to see how it works."

Later, after I had read Gramsci, I learned to describe the phenomenon as a manifestation of "hegemony." But in those days, when the left was still trying to figure out how the "dictatorship of the proletariat" could be democratic and not degenerate into a repressive system of purges and show trials, I thought this was an important insight. If the bourgeoisie could exercise its "dictatorship" with a minimum of repression, dominating every little community gathering with its kindly police officers or army of social workers, why couldn't the working class do the same?

## If You're Brown, Turn Around

Clearly, parking lots were not enough. We needed to do some education work. I proposed that the Council apply for funding to develop a slide-tape show on the East Indian community. We could take people's pictures at work, in their homes, on the street, and combine the slides with recordings of them talking about their experiences of racism and discrimination and how it felt. We could use the show in community meetings, church gatherings, schools, wherever people wanted to discuss the issues. We got a small grant from the Ministry of Culture and Recreation and hired Pat Murphy as RICC's second employee, though just for the summer of 1977.

Pat had the soft drawl of the Southern states and had worked with the Development Education Centre and other community groups after coming to Toronto. Together we decided that the slide-tape show would look first at the history of the Indian subcontinent and how its economy had been undermined by British imperialism (after all, that was why people had to emigrate), and then at the experiences of East Indians who had come to Riverdale. Pat suggested that we call the show, "If You're Brown, Turn Around," from a poem she knew from her childhood: "If you're White, all right. If you're Brown turn around. If you're Black, step back."

Our reference group was IPANA, the Indian People's Association of North America, which, as the name suggests, was somewhat to the left of centre. We also met Alok Mukherjee, who was working with Indian Immigrant Aid Services and had just produced "East Indians, Myths and Realities," a report on the representation of South Asians in Ontario social studies textbooks. Alok introduced us to people in the community with stories to tell, and I made use of the slides that my partner Richard and I had taken on our overland trip to India. We photographed historical pictures from library books and scenes from the neighbourhood. Reverend Robson and the Council were happy with the script. The police liaison officers were silent.

For my part, the interviews for the slide show led to new insights about racism and its impact. The notion that racism was a "natural" reaction to an unfamiliar group was still an important strand in our understanding. People are afraid of difference because they don't understand it, the theory went, and people dislike what they fear. This was the foundation for the multicultural approach. Familiarize them with the new group, a taste of their food, and some ethnic dances, and the problem will go away.

I was talking to a middle-aged South Asian woman when she mentioned that when her family had first arrived in Canada in the 1960s they had moved to Lindsay, Ontario. My interest perked up. Lindsay isn't far from Beaverton, where I had grown up. I knew it as the epicentre of small-town Ontario WASP identity, deeply conservative and almost entirely white. "That must have been difficult," I said to the woman. "You must have been the only Indians in town."

Yes, she said, but added that it hadn't been difficult. In fact, it was the time in Canada when she had experienced the least racism. People would see her in a sari and would be curious and want to ask questions. It was almost like being a celebrity. It wasn't until her family moved to Toronto in the 1970s that they were even aware of any kind of problem around their race.

It was obviously impossible to attribute the difference between this woman's experience in rural Ontario in the 1960s and in the much more cosmopolitan, worldly Toronto in the 1970s to ignorance of South Asian culture. Toronto was both far more familiar with South Asians and far less welcoming. I realized that other factors must be more important than familiarity. In Lindsay, as the only Indians in town, the family was treated with benign, if patronizing curiosity. But the intervening years had seen a major recession, a deluge of media portrayals of immigrants stealing jobs, and a federal Green Paper on the problems caused by immigration. The latent racist stereotypes and prejudices did not spring from cultural ignorance, but from economic and political developments that turned South Asians into a threat.

Another of our interviews was with Krisantha Sri Baghyaddatha, a Sri Lankan who was a common fixture around the Queen Street church that summer. A budding poet and writer, Krisantha was helping out on a small community newspaper that Reverend Robson had installed in an unused back room of the church. He was slight, dark-skinned, with an unruly head of jet-black hair, a tempting target for anyone interested in "Paki-bashing."

"I always wait at the front of the subway platform," he explained to me matter of factly. "That way I can see all the cars as they come in, and choose the one that has the most Black and Brown people on it. So if anything happens there is more likelihood that someone will cover my back. Strength in numbers." For Krisantha, racism was woven into the intimate texture of day-to-day experience.

Unfortunately, when the slide-tape show was completed we found that Riverdale was not quite ready for our anti-imperialist, anti-racist message.

The all-white mothers' group at a local library said we were too hard on the British. After all, Canada was a British country. This was just going to stir up bad feelings. Even the East Indian Business Association was lukewarm and wondered: did we really need to spend so much time talking about history? An Indian consultant for the Ministry of Culture and Recreation didn't like the talk about poverty in India, and suggested we look at some Bollywood movies to see how happy people were there. Why were the people all talking about unpleasant experiences like racism? Why be so negative?

The following summer we decided to get funding for a second slide-tape project, but perhaps my currency at the Ministry had become seriously devalued by the politics of "If You're Brown, Turn Around." The grant proposal was rejected on an administrative technicality. Reverend Robson and I, scrambling, managed to rescue the project at the last minute. The result was "Blue Canadian Sky," a slide-tape show about the history of Canadian immigration through the eyes of people who had arrived as children. Starting with a ninety-year-old Ukrainian great-grandmother who had arrived before the turn of the century, we interviewed a number of people about their first memories of coming to Canada. A Portuguese woman spoke of being punished by the teachers for speaking her language at school. A South Asian mother described how her young daughter had painted a picture of "my family" for school, portraying everybody in the picture as blond and blue-eyed. The show culminated with a group of West Indian youngsters talking about police harassment.

That was the last straw for the police community liaison officers, who demanded that the segment be removed. I stood my ground, and Reverend Robson backed me up. The section stayed in. The cops stopped attending meetings soon afterwards, and I was not unhappy to see them go. By that time I had become convinced that the police were not exactly allies in the fight against racism.

Once, at a community meeting focusing on the role of the police, several South Asian participants spoke about their experiences of trying to report incidents of racial harassment. They had been told that in cases in which there had been no physical injury, the police could not intervene. The person who had been victimized had to go to a police station and lay charges personally – but the officers also "didn't have the power" to force the harassers to identify themselves, thus making it impossible for charges to be laid. When confronted with this Catch-22, the officers on the panel shook their heads sadly and advised everyone there that they should be lobbying the government for wider police powers, which would help them to be more effective in such cases.

Yet only two weeks before that meeting I had been speaking to an unemployed, disabled Latin American man who had been stopped by two officers at a subway station. They were looking for illegal immigrants and demanded to see his identification. When he could produce none, he was given two choices – be accompanied home by the officers and show them his passport, or go to the station and stay in a cell until someone could bring him his documents. It appeared that police already had unlimited powers when identifying racially profiled immigrants, and that they only ran into difficulty when it was a matter of identifying white racists.

At another meeting, Black youth from the Regent Park Housing Development complained that they were constantly being stopped by police when they were riding their bicycles in their neighbourhood. The police officers at the meeting said something about how a good many bicycles were being stolen, and that the police interventions were part of an effort to track down stolen property. But I knew that I bicycled through the heart of the same neighbourhood twice every day on my way to and from work, and had never been stopped. Slightly older white riders, it seemed, were not suspected of bicycle theft. The police enforced, and thus reinforced, the dominant ideas of guilt and innocence on the streets.

## A Report on Race Relations

By the mid-1970s public consultations organized by the school board's Work Group on Multicultural Programs were raising the issue of racism in schools. In 1977 a subcommittee of the Race Relations and Multiculturalism Committee, with the encouragement of reform trustees Bob Spencer and Dan Leckie, began to compile a report on this issue. According to Marlene Green, who co-authored the report, Spencer and Leckie, both long-time allies of BEP, had started by looking at working-class students with the group of people around *This Magazine is About Schools*. What they saw were differential experiences and unfair treatment based very much on class background, and that finding got them interested in the question of vocational schools. What they saw there was a hugely disproportionate number of Black kids compared to their representation in other schools across the Board. At the same time the researchers were seeing a growing agitation and advocacy within the Black community itself.

As part of its public consultations the Subcommittee on Race Relations distributed issue papers to the system, students, and the community, translating the papers into fifteen languages. The SCR Department mobilized parent groups to bring forward their concerns. In fourteen months of consultations the subcommittee visited nineteen schools, held eight public meetings, and received forty-three formal briefs, including input from social service agencies as well as community groups. The Board's new liaison committees, especially the Black and South Asian committees, were at the forefront of the consultations.[1] In essence the Board both "encouraged and set up an avenue for communities to talk about what was happening," Marlene

Green recalled, and that made a huge difference. "The images that stick in my mind about the consultations were of parents giving accounts of bad experiences, but another memory is a feeling of hope." Though the process was difficult, something had been started that people could engage in.

The May 1978 *Draft Report of the Subcommittee on Race Relations* concluded that while racism might not be "rampant," it did exist in the school system. The report cited a "chain of events" involving racially motivated crimes of violence that had recently shaken the city, and listed a wealth of contemporary local studies that identified racism in both the school system and in society. It noted that the communities' viewpoint in general "was that the system's response to visible minority students, teachers and parents is insensitive and negative." The writers attributed this finding to a mixture of "racial discrimination and ignorance of the cultures and traditions of visible minority people."[2]

According to the report, the communities consulted expressed wide-ranging concerns: biased and Eurocentric curriculum and standard achievement tests; the disproportionate streaming of minority children into vocational schools; the lack of effort to communicate the long-term significance of placement decisions to immigrant and non-white parents; teachers' failure to deal with or report racial incidents; and teachers' participation in racist banter. Visible minority employees reported that they were often overlooked when it came to promotion, that they received little support or mentoring, and that, as a result, few role models existed for non-white students.

In its preface, the *Draft Report* conceptualized the problem as one of "racial bias" and expressed the hope "that once people get used to the fact that racist behaviour will not be tolerated, the appropriate attitude change will follow." But the report's definition of racism moved well beyond a consideration of attitudes.

> Racism then can be defined as any attitudes, actions *or institutional structures* which subordinate a person or group because of their race or colour. It's not only a matter of actions; institutional structures and attitudes can also be racist. For that reason, we considered not only situations of openly prejudiced personal actions *but also those more subtle organizational programs and practices which provide encouragement and support for racism, albeit unwittingly.*[3]

The report characterized the responses that it had received from within the school system, including teachers, as "generally defensive" and went on to say that "one compelling reason" for this response "is that many local schools felt that an admission that racism existed in their schools would be taken as a sign of failure in leadership. . . . Consequently, we found it necessary to assure many school staffs that we were conducting an objective inquiry and not engaging in a 'witch hunt.' "[4]

The *Draft Report* made 159 recommendations, including a review of curriculum materials, the replacement of biased resources, mandatory teacher training, the development of guidelines for the discussion of "racially biased great literature," and the inclusion of a wider range of literature from different parts of the world. The study of race relations should be included in social studies and values education. Special funding should be provided to supplement school library collections, and schools should encourage the formation of ethnic and multicultural clubs. There should be more research on the placement of visible minority students in the system, a review of assessment methods, translation of information sheets for parents, and regular communication of the right to appeal placement decisions.

The report called on the Board to condemn and refuse to tolerate expressions of racial bias in any form by its trustees, administration, staff, or students. Staff witnessing verbal exchanges between students should be required to intervene immediately. Racial slurs during sports events should result in the immediate suspension of students from games. Graffiti should be cleared from washrooms at least once per day. Race relations representatives should be appointed in all schools. A special advisory committee should be set up to investigate reports of racial incidents involving staff, and staff found to be racially biased towards students, either in attitude or behaviour, should be considered incompetent and subject to standard disciplinary procedures.

There was more: principals should be trained to screen for racial bias in employment interviews; a survey should be conducted to determine the actual numbers and percentages of visible minority employees; and the Board should seek permission from the Ontario Human Rights Commission to initiate "positive recruitment and hiring measures designed to remedy the underemployment of visible minority teachers." The Ministry of Education should be consulted to review policies regarding the accreditation of foreign teachers. The Board should also consider incentives for early retirement, the establishment of term appointments, and changes to the seniority system, to encourage the entry and mobility of visible minorities in its workforce.

Finally, the report recommended that the Board establish an equal opportunity position to advise the director of education and oversee implementation of all the recommendations.

As the *Draft Report* began circulating, the system dug in its heels. When meetings were held to discuss the report's findings and recommendations, parents would complain about how their children were being treated; but teachers at the meetings would continue to insist, "There is no such thing as racism. We treat everybody the same." Administrators would "try to paint a rosy picture of their schools." Board representatives would try to be careful not to upset the teachers and administrators.[5]

Marlene Green remembered that even her own superintendent thought that the document was "off base and extreme" – though she believed it "was really wishy-washy" compared to the input that the subcommittee had received. "We even had some Black teachers and administrators who were in total denial," she said. "They were trotted out on a regular basis to counteract what the community was saying." While a few people in the system recognized the problems and saw the need for change, "generally the community lined up on one side and people in the system lined up on the other."

Pat Case, recently elected on a Communist Party ticket, was one of Toronto's first Black trustees. For him, the opposition to the report from teachers and administrators began a long process of re-evaluation of the role of teachers and their unions in the workings of the system. He began to recognize that "sometimes teachers' interests could become diametrically opposed to the interests of parents and students." Teachers did need to defend their economic and union interests, but they were still part of the general education machine. "A lot of them had a great analysis of the misdeeds of the Board as an employer, but none of what they were doing as educators."

## The Final Report on Race Relations

The *Final Report of the Subcommittee on Race Relations*, published in May 1979, noted, "Whereas the bulk of responses during the first round of consultation had come from the community, by far the majority of responses to the Draft Report came from within the system – from teachers, administrators, board departments etc."[6]

As a result the Board had directed that the report had to be softened. Most of the original introduction, including the definition of racism that included "institutional structures" and "subtle organizational programs and practices," disappeared from the *Final Report*. So too did the recounting of the "chain of events" of serious racial incidents in the city, mention of supporting studies, characterization of the system's "defensive" response, and the community's evaluation of the system as being "insensitive and negative" towards visible minorities.

The list of recommendations was reduced to 119. The items dealing with term appointments and seniority that sought to make more space for visible minority staff were withdrawn, as was the recommendation that the Board seek approval from the Ontario Human Rights Commission for adopting recruitment and hiring measures that would address the underemployment of visible minority teachers. That item was apparently interpreted as an attempt to institute a "quota system."

Not all the criticisms had been simply defensive. Some argued that the focus on race was "too narrow," and the *Final Report* affirmed: "We expect the spirit and intent of the recommendations on racial/ethnic relations to apply (wherever appropriate) to all forms of discrimination and prejudice." The subcommittee also bowed to concerns that its previous recommendations on discipline were "too prescriptive" and "insensitive to particular conditions in particular schools or grades – particularly in primary grades." It amended many of those recommendations. But it did reiterate its conviction "that one option not open to teachers, administrators, etc., is the option to do nothing when racial incidents occur." With these changes, the Board soon approved the final report *in toto* – all 119 recommendations – and it now became the Board's race relations policy.

Marlene Green was deeply disappointed with the final results. She realized, though, that the Board had gone as far as it was willing to go. "For all the good will that there was among certain people, I saw it was going to take Herculean efforts to move the weight of the institution." She resigned two months later, in July 1979.

Tony Souza was more philosophical. He believed that the report was a "really brave" first step. "At least it was some kind of an acknowledgement that gave us an in. When it became policy, we could say to the schools, you have to do this."

From a community perspective, Keren Brathwaite agreed. For her, the approval of the final report was a breakthrough and an important stage in the struggle for equity. The Toronto Board of Education, she said, was the first in Canada to take a stand. "Even if the final report was watered down, the document was groundbreaking. . . . A Board was finally acknowledging the need for something to be done." The document was something tangible, something education activists could "wave around" and ask, "When is the Board going to deliver on this?"

## Women Hold up Half the Sky

Issues of race and culture were not the only ground covered by the reform-minded trustees. Women's liberation was also shaking up the system. But unlike community concerns about multiculturalism and racism, much of the impetus for dealing with women's issues came from *within* the institution, and particularly from women teachers who were dissatisfied with the glass ceiling they faced around promotion.

In 1972 a high-powered group of women appeared before the Board to speak in support of a motion by reform trustee Graham Scott, who had called for the Board to ensure that the sex ratio in positions of responsibility reflect the proportion of males and females in the system as a whole. Although women made up a majority of the Board's teachers, especially in elementary schools, the higher up the system the greater the dominance of males. In secondary schools, at the assistant head level, for example, men outnumbered women four to one. At the department head level the ratio was eight to one. Among vice-principals it was fourteen to one, and among principals twenty-eight to zero.

Laura Sabia, a member of the 1970 Royal Commission on the Status of Women, excited the press and shocked stodgier members of the Board by saying, "And when God made the heaven and the earth, She . . . " The debate continued well into the night, and in the end the Board unanimously passed two motions: to develop an affirmative action program to eliminate the imbalance of women in positions of responsibility; and to consider "what changes might be made to avoid the appearance or fact of channelling girls into inferior or lower-status jobs or educational objectives."[7]

The Board struck a committee, originally called the Select Committee on Positions of Responsibility, which included members from the teachers' federations and the provincial Women's Bureau. Soon known as the Status of Women Committee, it pushed a series of recommendations through the Board, including the introduction of recruitment and career development programs for women, procedures to identify women employees with management potential, the adoption of permanent part-time employment, and the development of day-care facilities for employees. It also began to examine bias in hiring practices.

As the original 1972 recommendations indicated, there was also growing concern with what was happening to young women in the classroom. Marg Evans, a consultant in the Board's Language Studies Centre, helped to produce a film on the stereotypical depiction of women in the curriculum; it became widely used in teacher training. In 1975 a Women's Studies Consultant position was created in the Curriculum Division. The first consultant, Dr. Patricia Kincaid, encouraged women's programs in the schools, developed curriculum guidelines, and facilitated International Women's Year activities in the system.

The committee's early successes proved to be its own undoing. Different Board departments, including management bargaining groups dominated by men, were soon demanding a place at the table. The result was committee members sitting alongside their supervisors, and a pervasive sense of intimidation. According to researcher Janet Louise Sheffield, "Some members now believed that if they criticized the Board in front of outsiders, they might be labelled disloyal employees and thus jeopardize their own careers. Certain new members appeared to have an interest in obstructing the committee by spending time on questions of procedure."[8]

When trustee Fiona Nelson left the Status of Women Committee to become chair of the Toronto Board in 1974, the resulting vacuum worsened the situation, and work ground to a halt. In November 1976 the committee was formally disbanded. But a Pandora's box had been opened and was not about to be closed. The committee was quickly replaced with a Women's Liaison Committee that was less structured, more open to the public, and less vulnerable to the control of vested interests in the organization. The Women's Liaison Committee provided an opportunity for women within the Board to work with the city's feminist community to regroup and plan future strategy. In addition a staff group made up of administrators and employees, the Affirmative Action Task Force, continued the work of analyzing the challenges facing women employees in the Board workforce.

The task force soon issued a report focusing on such problem areas as job ghettoization, lack of career counselling for women, promotion criteria, sex bias in Board language, and child care. Task force member Sue McGrath recalled that the report "reflected the current thinking about voluntary programs for improving the position of women in the workforce." In March 1977 the Board adopted its recommendations. Administrators were trained to implement the recommendations, and each school and workplace was instructed to develop a local affirmative action plan. The Board also established an Affirmative Action Reference Committee, which in June 1978 joined with a new Race Relations Committee to call for the hiring of an equal opportunity advisor.

The first equal opportunity advisor was hired in January 1979 and given responsibility for both women's and race issues – two separate and enormously demanding assignments.

## A Crisis at Eastdale

After Marlene Green left in July 1979, Tony Souza suddenly found himself the SCR Department's point person on the new race relations policy. He ended up doing the training and answering questions about the report. One day he got a call from Eastdale Collegiate.

Eastdale Collegiate Institute, on Gerrard Street East near Broadview, drew most of its students from the nearby Regent Park public housing development. Regent Park had a history of racial tension, but the Eastdale administration, in keeping with the general trend of high-school administration, had always maintained that the school was one big happy family. Then, "out of the blue," a serious altercation occurred between two students, one Black, the other white. One boy got his jaw broken. Revenge was threatened. A gun was seized in the school. At lunch all the white kids were on one side of the cafeteria, all the Black kids on the other, and all hell was threatening to break loose. As "race relations expert," Tony was called to come into the school to fix things.

Tony knew it would be suicidal to try to intervene alone as a person of colour. He needed someone white there with him, and he called me at RICC. We got together and began to work out strategy for an emergency program. We decided to do workshops in every class in the school, but first we had to clarify our objectives. I argued that we needed to help students understand the roots of the underlying conflicts. Tony was more concerned about communicating to the students how much racism hurt. I countered that they didn't care if it hurt – they wanted it to hurt. Tony said he couldn't believe people worked that way. Later, looking back, Tony described his thinking at the time. "It was part of the human relations model that we had in those days. We felt it was a matter of teaching people how to communicate and get along with each other better." But in hindsight my Marxist search for underlying contradictions was not all that useful either. We were hardly going to convince a group of high-school kids that their problems were the result of capitalists trying to divide and conquer the working class.

In the end we both let go of our preconceptions and opted for exploratory workshops, similar to the one that Barb Thomas had helped us develop at RICC. Meeting with the students class by class, we began by explaining that although we knew there was a problem with the atmosphere in the school, and that it was making everyone's life more difficult and dangerous, we didn't claim to understand what was going on. They were the experts. We needed their help. We encouraged them to talk about their experiences and what they were feeling.

We ran workshops class by class through the end of 1979 into February of 1980, and what emerged was a complex picture that could not be reduced to any simple schema. We found that widespread and unchallenged stereotypes portrayed non-white students as immigrants, and immigrants as freeloaders and job stealers. Racist banter, name-calling, and teasing were common. The all-white staff tended to ignore such "minor" racial incidents and sometimes even participated themselves. Students were left to deal with difficult situations on their own. The curriculum did not include the histories and experience of non-white students, which made it all that much harder, if not impossible, to break down the racial barriers.

There was little happening in the school to bring students together. The Student Council was not functioning, and extracurricular activities were rare. Students generally felt disenfranchised and powerless. In this context, turf wars emerged over access to little privileges such as the "best" seats in the cafeteria. These turf wars further encouraged students to group themselves along racial lines for support, and personal conflicts often took on a racial character. The staff saw groups of Black students as potential gangs, and regarded any non-white gatherings with suspicion. While Black students believed that they were often unfairly targeted for discipline and were always under surveillance, staff interpreted their complaints of racism simply as a way of evading the consequences of bad behaviour. The staff saw talk about race and ethnicity as divisive, which meant there had never been any forum for open or frank discussion of such issues. Students were not aware of each others' feelings. Communication between groups had broken down.

I remember thinking to myself, "So this is what Lenin meant when he said the heart and soul of Marxism is the concrete study of concrete conditions." Listening to the students, we began to see the many institutional issues identified in the race relations report played out. But how was this complex social reality to be changed? The students had many suggestions, but as students they had little power to make the necessary institutional changes.

Tony wrote up our findings and consulted with the school administration, who were now under the spotlight. The passage of the race relations policy helped reinforce the staff's recognition of their responsibilities. As well, the airing of pent-up grievances and the communication that had occurred in our workshops reduced some of the tensions in the school. Our process also served as a model for teachers who wanted to engage in further discussions and more proactive intervention. There were no more serious incidents.

## An Equal Opportunity Office

In January 1980, in an attempt to give women's concerns equal institutional clout to those of the new Race Relations Committee, the Status of Women Committee was re-established as an official standing committee. (The Women's Liaison Committee petered out soon afterwards.) This time, however, the women had learned from their previous problems. Although its membership was drawn from broad employment categories, such as secondary and elementary school teachers, educational assistants, and caretakers, openings in the committee were filled by a relatively closed system of nominations, and members were expected to be committed to women's issues.

Around the same time both Tony Souza and I were ready for a change. I decided I would go back to school full-time to finish the three-year general B.A. that I had begun in 1969 before wandering off to India. But although I left the Riverdale Intercultural Council, I remained involved in the Riverdale community and anti-racism work. The Klan had opened an office in the neighbourhood, and my replacement at RICC, Bobby Siu, was central to a huge community organizing effort to drive them out. I ended up managing security for massive anti-Klan demonstrations.

Tony was likewise unable to extricate himself. The man hired as equal opportunity advisor had resigned in April 1980, and the Race Relations and Status of Women committees and the NDP trustees were now determined to see action on their various policy recommendations. It was decided that the Board's Equal Opportunity Office would be expanded to two advisors, one for race relations and the other for affirmative action.

When the race relations advisor position was advertised, Tony was reluctant to apply, assuming that it would go to a superintendent or principal.

He had already decided to leave the Board and go to chef's school. But colleagues put pressure on him, and the NDP trustees liked his activist credentials. He got the job. At the same time, Myrna Mather was hired as affirmative action advisor. Both positions were two-year appointments, which perhaps reflected the Board's optimism that whatever problems existed, they would be solved in short order. Myrna's teaching credentials and Tony's community links both contrasted and complemented one another, and also reflected the main constituencies driving their respective issues.

Although the two new advisors held parallel positions in the same office, their mandates were significantly different. Tony was responsible for overseeing the implementation of all of the race relations report's 119 recommendations, which ran the gamut from curriculum issues such as bias in textbooks and student placement, to personnel issues such as hiring and promotion of visible minorities. Indeed, because the race relations recommendations had been generated by community complaints about the treatment of visible minority students, much of Tony's focus would be on school curriculum and teacher-training. As affirmative action advisor, Myrna almost exclusively dealt with the issues of hiring and promoting women. A women's studies consultant in the Curriculum Division took responsibility for questions of curriculum.

According to Tony, despite such differences the two new advisors found themselves working together in the face of a common challenge."We were just dropped into these positions. We had nobody to talk to. There was nobody else who had done this kind of thing before. We were trail-blazing."

# Chapter 3

# Utopia

CAMP KANDALORE SEEMED ABOUT AS FAR as you could get from downtown Toronto. High on the Canadian Shield, a three-hour drive north of the city, a dirt road abruptly left the highway and snaked through the forest to a ramshackle collection of buildings on the edge of a little lake. We were alone. The silence of the forest was broken only by the occasional call of loons or the wind in the trees. Sometimes at night we heard the howls of wolves.

The facilities were, to say the least, rudimentary. Central meeting areas were kept warm by old oil stoves and stone fireplaces that often belched as much smoke into the room as up the chimney. The sleeping cabins were heated by cantankerous clanking electric wall-heaters that puffed a Sahara-like wind to desiccate anyone nearby, while leaving the nether reaches of the room on par with the outside weather conditions – which could be just about anything in late October and April, the unpredictable times when our camp sessions took place. For most of the fifty or so students who attended each session at Camp Kandalore, it was as if they had been transported to the ends of the earth.

The task of running the camps had fallen to Tony Souza after a number of teachers had returned from a province-wide Ministry of Education leadership retreat for students and suggested that the Toronto Board of Education could do similar camps. As the Board's new race relationship advisor, Tony, working with Barb Thomas, agreed to lead one of four teams of students in a pilot project on leadership in April 1981. Tony chose Kandalore as the site for the program mainly because the camp's skeleton staff shared some understanding of co-operative education and knew how to organize recreation activities for free time. He assured everyone concerned that this remote location would provide a unique environment for the project, and rationalized the often abysmal conditions as a bonding experience for pampered city kids. The camp was to be an austere utopia in the wilderness.

Somehow, magically, it worked. The site, a universe away from the conveniences of the city, was also far from its stresses and complications. The totally different environment helped open participants to new experiences and ideas. Shared hardship did generate camaraderie. Eating the same food, bunking in the same cabins, and coping with the same conditions were levellers that established the necessary atmosphere of equality, trust, and honesty.

At the first camp, Barb and Tony's group took on a very different shape from the back-to-back leadership games that characterized the other three teams' activities. Using a model based on popular education and community development, they built a framework to help kids talk about their experiences. They used some of the experiential games, but only to set the stage for the conversations that they really wanted to happen. They got an enthusiastic response from the students.

With the pilot project declared a success, a second camp was planned for October 1981, and Tony asked me to take time off from my university classes to help facilitate a group. By that time Tony had taken control of the project. The camp was to be fundamentally different from other student leadership experiences. Not content with simply building skills or hoping that a shared experience would encourage diverse students to learn to like each other more, its goal was to forge a social analysis out of the collective sharing of experience. Students were to leave not only with an understanding of the dynamics of personal and institutional racism, but also with an action plan that they could use to help change their schools. This was not to be a utopia restricted to one campsite. It was to be infectious.

Tony tightened up the criteria for participants. Each school delegation consisted of five to ten students in their second or third year of high school, accompanied by one or two teachers. Schools throughout the Board were to send a rough balance of males and females, and the participating students were supposed to represent the racial and cultural mix of their schools. All students were volunteers who had demonstrated some sort of leadership potential and had expressed interest in race relations issues. The teachers attending came on a volunteer basis.

Each of the thirty secondary schools in the Board was to participate once every two years. The ongoing cycle ensured that new students would always be trained to replace those who were graduating and there would always be a group of experienced students in each school. Schools were rotated on a schedule so that every camp would not only have representation from the centre of the city, the east, the west, and the north, but also a blending of collegiates (academic, university-bound), technical and commercial (community-college-bound) programs, basic-level (directed to the semi-skilled labour force) programs, and alternative schools. The idea was that each camp should as much as possible be a microcosm of the diversity of the city as a whole.

When I joined in at the fall 1981 session, my experience was limited to running relatively short workshops with classrooms of students at Eastdale, and the discussions at RICC, and I had questions about how to sustain that kind of work with a group for almost a week. I knew the camp program was loosely modelled on Paulo Freire's work around *conscientização,* a process based on the belief that, given a chance to think through and work out the dynamics of their own and others' experiences, people would be able to see through the mystifying veils of "false consciousness." Freire asserted that with this clearer view of the world, learners would be motivated to challenge systems of discrimination and injustice that they were experiencing in their lives. This kind of education was not about the transmission of knowledge from adults to children or from teachers to students. It was an attempt by students, teachers, and facilitators to work together to create knowledge about their connected social worlds.

When we arrived in the middle of nowhere that first grey October evening, facing fifty disoriented teenagers, all this theory seemed a little fanciful. We started with ice-breaking exercises meant to both display participants' many commonalities and differences and help them learn one another's names. After a great deal of confusion, hooting and hollering, laughing and moving around, the students were assigned to five "family groups." Each of the five groups was led by two facilitators, one from the Board and one from the community, and each group would consist of representatives from all of the participating schools (which might include a teacher), and were balanced so that there would be equal numbers of boys and girls and a range of racial backgrounds.

With the opening exercise and administrative tasks completed, we brought out the ropes. Students in each family group were tied together by one wrist. Each group received a map of the campsite, where a number of stations had been set up, and were told to locate each station in a predetermined order. At each station the participants had to complete instructions before going on to the next station.

For example, one station played on the old aphorism, "Before you judge someone, try walking a half-mile in his moccasins." The participants had to exchange a shoe with somebody else in the group and walk to the next station. The response was predictable. "You've got to be kidding! It's not sanitary!" someone said. Another wailed, "They won't fit!" A more co-operative kid said, "Just hurry up. The sooner we get this done the sooner we can get back inside and get warm." The facilitators, tied up just like everyone else, took mental notes of potential allies, leaders, and resisters.

After the excitement of "Rope Orienteering" and the calming effect of food, even camp food, the evening group sessions were genuinely placid. Each group made its meeting area as comfortable as possible, employing odd pieces of furniture, old mattresses, whatever was available. As facilitators we explained that we were not teachers, we didn't know all the answers, and that our role was to help people share, discuss, and think things through. When it came to their own lives, their own schools, their own neighbourhoods, the students themselves knew best. Their experiences were the "raw material" that would form the basis of what happened at the camp. But since everyone had fragments of knowledge, the whole picture depended on all of us sharing our expertise.

The goal of this approach was to extend respect to students and to transform traditional adult/student relationships. As much as possible, we wanted to establish a rough equality between participating youth and adults. Everyone was on a first-name basis and accommodation, facilities, and food were the same for all. We all shared the labour of meal clean-up and set-up. Still, this was an equality tempered by the reality that the adults were legally responsible for the students but the students bore no such corresponding responsibility for the adults.

There did, of course, have to be rules. Even egalitarian utopias have to have rules. But where school rules tend to be about arbitrary restrictions that adults impose on youth, this camp tried to be different. The rules we had were necessary to reasonably guarantee the safety and comfort of participants: everyone participates, no smoking in the sleeping or meeting areas, no alcohol or drugs, keep off the ice or water (depending on season), no visitors in the sleeping cabins, lights out at midnight. Students interested in the program had discussed the rules before they signed up. Once at the camp they found little of the policing and regulation often associated with school life and field trips. Anyone who couldn't live by these agreements was sent home. The ultimate sanction was banishment – and during the thirty-odd camps that took place over fifteen years, students had to be sent home on only two occasions. When major issues arose, they were discussed and resolved by everyone. Our utopia was an experiment in democracy.

The family groups also set their own operating principles. Facilitators asked students to think of a time when they had felt comfortable, accepted, and valued in a group. Together we went on to identify what it was that had made that group work, and to develop ground rules to try to ensure that our present group functioned in a similar way.

The sharing of experience continued into free time and long into the night, long after the formal groups concluded – in the cabins, in the smoking areas, along forest paths.

In the regular meeting times exhaustion would occasionally set in, and when it did facilitators had a stable of "Energizers" to call on. One of the best loved was "Spaghetti." A group of ten to fifteen students would form a tight circle with hands stretched into the centre. Everyone would grab two other hands, forming a tangled lattice of arms. Then they had to untangle without letting go. With patience, sometimes considerable patience, crawling over and under one another, the participants would unsnarl the latticework and somehow finally produce a large open circle, or sometimes two linked circles. The activity was physical, fun, and required stretching, concentration, and co-operation. For anyone looking for deeper meaning, it could represent the camp project of using co-operation to sort out an apparently chaotic situation to reveal underlying patterns.

The energy generated by that kind of closeness was infectious. After pairing off for introductory interviews, each participant introduced her or his partner to the group and described that person's experiences with stereotyping, prejudice, or discrimination. Students slowly began to come out of their shells and tell stories of name-calling, harassment, exclusion, or violence. They would talk about unfair treatment and feelings of isolation, rejection, and tension. The recording facilitator duly noted these experiences on large sheets of flip-chart paper and eventually the walls would be papered with the results.

Some participants would insist they had nothing to report. Perhaps they were still checking out the group, not yet ready to share possibly painful experiences and make themselves vulnerable in this strange new setting, or perhaps they had actually lived privileged lives. Others had made a habit of forgetting such things; sometimes it would take time before the memories began to flood back. But the activity always yielded enough raw material to produce further revelations when the group members found themselves gazing at the flip-chart notes on the walls all around them. Suddenly their experience was no longer isolated, individual, or uncommon.

The groups then began to organize their material, physically rearranging the notes on the walls. This could take a thematic form: examples of racism, examples of sexism, for example. After several camps I learned to prefer grouping by the actual activities described, such as name-calling, stereotyping, discrimination, and violence, which helped us to explore what different forms of oppression had in common. Often the result was a mix of conceptual categories. What was important was that the students felt comfortable with the categories they produced.

The next crucial moment in the process was setting priorities for a discussion of what we had come up with. Where would our discussion start?

Here I found a bit of a pitfall to avoid. Some students, who had experienced international travel or taken "advanced" programs that covered weighty international issues – such as apartheid in South Africa – would identify the clear and blatant injustice of organized, state-sponsored discrimination as the key issue. Surely our discussion should start there.

The problem with that approach was that many of the participants did not read the newspapers and had only the vaguest appreciation of what was happening on the other side of the world. Most of those who did were the more academically successful or advantaged. There was a danger, then, that a certain expertise would take over the discussion, led by privileged participants who might have the most limited personal experience with racism. Starting with international questions could also reinforce the notion that racism was something "out there." By comparison, what was happening in our local schools would seem unimportant and trivial.

As a facilitator I learned to affirm the importance of what was going on in places such as South Africa, but to suggest that we *begin* our discussion with experiences a little closer to home. Starting with examples of direct personal experience equalized the expertise within the group, and even privileged the voices of students who, because of their class or racial backgrounds, were usually least likely to be heard.

## Sticks and Stones: Name-calling and Power

An experience all students knew about, we found, was name-calling, and it was an experience we could use to get at larger questions.

When we asked who got called names at school and around the neighbourhood, an immediate answer was usually "everybody." When we asked whether some people got called names more often than others, we heard about "people who aren't popular" or "people who are different" or "people who are weak and can't fight back." The responses gave us an opening into a discussion of social power. "What does it take to be popular? Different from who? What does it take to be able to fight back?"

"Being able to buy cool clothes."

"Being like everybody else."

"Different from everyone else."

"You need friends to cover your back."

"Being big."

"Having power."

So then we'd ask, "How do you get power? What gives people power?" The answers would range from "having money" to "being in a group" or "being able to talk good." The kids might mention "muscles" or "being in the majority." Gender would sometimes come into it – "I mean, like being like a man." It might be "having an education" or "having a weapon" or "having a uniform" or even just "having a position."

The students recognized that people "with power" did not get called names, at least not directly (it could happen, of course, behind their backs). It was too dangerous – a teacher called a name "could fail you," or a cop "could arrest you." Or "If they're really rich, they never even have to see you."

When we asked about the names that people were called, after an initial hesitation a torrent of abusive names would soon fill the room, producing a variety of responses, from giggles to obvious extreme discomfort. They would cover the waterfront, everything from racist to sexist and homophobic to just plain obscene. Taken all together, written down and postered up on the wall, they made a disturbing picture for everyone in the room.

Looking at the words written up on the wall, we'd ask if all of them carried the same weight – were they all equally heavy?

Some were "just stupid." Others would be laughed off. The heaviest would cause a "rumble," one person said. "Big time. Especially when it happens all the time. You get so mad it feels like you're going to explode."

We considered the racist words on the list one by one. "Which ones are the heaviest? Let's call the really heavy ones fives and the really lame ones zeros, and you can figure out the numbers for the ones in between."

While the participants might disagree on the nuances, they were usually able to reach a consensus on the power of each word. If they had any serious disagreements, we would leave the final determination of the grading to members of the group most likely to be called the name in question. When we finished the grading we grouped the words according to their scores, usually with quite surprising results. The long list of "heavies" – fours and fives – generally referred to people of colour – nigger, chink, Paki, for example. The twos and threes were largely terms applied to "ethnic" Europeans – wop, spick, kike. The ones and zeros, almost always the smallest list, were mostly names that white Anglo Canadians could be called – white bread, mangecake, honky.

Now we were into a discussion of social power. The question was: "Why do some groups have so many heavy names getting thrown at them, but if you're white and born here, there's not a lot racist names you have to worry about?"

The exercise was not without its challengers. "You can't rate words like that," someone might say. "It depends on how they say them." Whether the word was screamed out or said sweetly, with a smile, made a difference – though sometimes a word said sweetly could be even worse, someone once said.

Someone – perhaps a teacher in the group – might assert that any kind of name-calling was bad. Others noted that the harm of name-calling depended on who was doing it.

"Yeah. Black people call each other nigger all the time. How come if I call somebody 'nigger' it's bad, but if a Black person does it it's okay?"

"If somebody else Black calls me nigger it's not like they're saying they're better than me. It's like we've got something in common. If a white person says it, it's different."

"So what's a teacher supposed to do? You can't punish white kids for using the word "nigger" and then turn around and let Black kids get away with it."

"That's why nobody should use it."

"But my friends and I use it. It doesn't mean anything 'cause we're all Black. It doesn't hurt anybody. It means you're part of the group."

"You're putting yourself down. I don't like it when anybody uses it. I won't let anybody use it on me, even other Black people."

The object of the discussion was not to come up with a definitive ruling on the use of a word. It was to develop an understanding of the context of social power. The students would maintain, for instance, that teachers should never use a word like "nigger" or any of the other pejoratives – "because a teacher's got power."

Occasionally a white participant wanted to rate "white bread" a five. Given that our process put experience front and centre, who could say that in that person's experience "white bread" wasn't a damaging putdown? If no other white person was willing to challenge the assertion, as a facilitator, and a white person, I could draw on my own experience to do so – strategically display my whiteness. The concept of power could help participants understand the dynamics of racial name-calling.

While names like jerk, asshole, or fuckhead can be returned in kind, racial name-calling quickly escalates. "If they call you a nigger, you hit them," a student would say.

"Why?" I asked.

"What are you going to call them back? Whitey? That doesn't mean anything. When they call you nigger they're not just insulting you, they're insulting your family and everybody that's like you. Even if you don't want to fight for yourself, you have to fight for them."

"So what happens if you haul off and hit somebody?"

"You probably get suspended. . . . And then they say that Black kids are all violent."

"And what if you don't have much of a fist? What if they're bigger?"

"Then you get your posse."

"Yeah, that's why you need friends. That's why people hang with their own."

"And then what do they say?"

"They say that you're always in gangs, that you're criminals."

Questions of social power were not always straightforward and often took a great deal of teasing out. Local school or community-based power relations could be quite different from those in the broader society. In some schools, people of colour might even be in the majority. White students could report feeling themselves a marginalized minority. As well, from a youth perspective, the popularity of "Black" style in clothing, music, and sport meant that the determination of just what was the socially dominant group was a complex matter. As a facilitator I learned that I had to respect each student's lived experience when working through the issues and conflicts. These groups were no place for dogmatism – and they called for enormous patience, all in the hope that at the end of the day each one of us would have a little better understanding of how the world immediately around us was working.

## Stereotypes and Discrimination

From name-calling to stereotyping was a short step. Starting with what we had already heard in the conversation about name-calling – "Black kids are always violent" – the list of stereotypes that the student campers could come up with in a short session was always lengthy:

"Chinese are good in math."

"East Indians smell like curry."

"White people are all racist."

"If you're Black you're from Jamaica."

"White men can't jump."

"Black people are good at basketball."

"Vietnamese are all in gangs and can't speak English."

"And are fresh off the boat."

"Arabs are terrorists."

"Indians are drunk and on welfare."

The students could also come up with a list of people who were often being stereotyped: minorities; people of colour; teenagers; poor people; people who have less power; sometimes even white people. Most the stereotypes had harmful effects. "You know when they say how Black people are criminals?" one young Black woman said. "Every time I go into a store they follow me around. Like if you're Black you can't have any money and they all think you're trying to steal." But some of the stereotypes, like "Chinese are good at math," were positive. Still, someone asked, if you were Chinese, and lousy at math, did that mean you weren't a "proper Chinese"? Even positive stereotypes were limiting.

Stereotypes could do more than just hurt feelings. They could cause damage to people's prospects in life. Teachers thinking you were stupid, police saying you were criminal, employers rejecting you: all of these could have a heavy impact. Stereotypes led to discrimination. One student told her story: "My dad, back in Vietnam he was educated. He had a business. But here he can't get a job here except for working in a restaurant. The people treat him so bad. He's just a dirty Vietnamese, a dirty Chinese, a chink. And he works so hard. All the time till late at night for next to nothing. It's all because of us being Vietnamese. It makes me so mad. I just want to hit somebody. I want to scream."

Stereotypes could have other effects. "You can begin to believe them," a student said. That, that's who you are. That you're no good."

"You can want to be someone else."

"Sometimes I tell people I'm a Canadian Indian."

"But you're Vietnamese."

"In a new school they don't know. I don't sound Vietnamese. That's why I wear my hair long."

Students pinpointed "the media" as a place that helps to produce stereotypes. "Every time a Black person commits a crime they mention his colour," one student said. "But if it's a white person, they're just a person." Someone said stereotypes get passed on from parents. Another said they come from watching basketball games (most players are Black) and hockey games (most players are white). It seems reasonable to think that Black guys are made for basketball and white guys are made for hockey. Those attitudes could lead to a discussion of where basketball players come from. "What's the situation in the States for many Black people? Where do they live, for instance?"

"In the ghetto."

"Are they rich in the ghetto?"

"No. Poor."

"Why?"

"Cause people have stereotypes. They don't want to give them good jobs."

"Discrimination."

"And the schools aren't as good."

"All those kinds of reasons. So if you're young and ambitious and want to get out of the poor part of town, what do you need?"

"Money."

"And how do you get money?"

"Sell drugs?"

"Till you get busted."

"An education?"

"Okay. And to get a good education, to go to university, what do you need, especially in the States?"

"To be smart?"

"And what else? Do you have to pay to go to university?"

"You need money. It's expensive there. You need a scholarship."

"But your schools aren't very good. It's hard to compete with people from rich schools for academic scholarships. What kind of scholarship are you going to try for?"

"An athletic scholarship."

"So you're going to choose a sport. What do you need to have to play hockey?"

"Pads, skates, helmet, ice time in an arena . . . "

"And what do you need to get that?"

"More money."

"What do you need to play basketball?"

"A ball, a hoop, sneakers, a floor, empty lot . . . " Not so expensive.

"So is it surprising, that so many young Black men get drawn to basketball?"

"It's their best choice."

"Given the results of discrimination. So you put a group of people in a similar situation and a lot of them are going to react in the same way."

"And then everybody else thinks that they're all the same and just like that."

"And you've got a stereotype."

"So a racist, when he looks at the NBA will say, 'Black people are good at basketball, it's their nature, it's their biology, it's their bones.' But an anti-racist will say, 'What's the situation that produced this? How did this get to be part of this group's culture? What do we need to do to change it so that everybody has the same kind of chances and the same kind of choices?"

"It may be hard to change the situation."

"Right. But it's impossible to change biology. Racism says, we're stuck with the way things are. People who are against racism say, it may be hard, but there's hope if we work at it. You can't change biology but you can change the world."

"What about the one that Chinese people are good in math? Where do you think that comes from?"

"You can see it in math class. You can see it when they hand out the math awards."

"That would lead to a stereotype, but why should that be the case?"

"In Chinese culture parents really push their kids to study hard."

"But why math? Why not history or geography, for instance?"

"Maths and sciences get you lots of jobs, the best jobs."

"So a new community trying to establish itself in a new country might encourage its kids to study something that will help them make money."

"Yeah, you get a degree in history and you'll end up unemployed."

"Or being a history teacher."

"That's no future." (Laughter.)

"Anything else about being in a new community? When you come here from another country what's the first thing you have to do?"

"Learn the language."

"Right. And what do you have to do to get good marks in history or geography or English?"

"Write essays, in English."

"What about math?"

"Numbers are the same everywhere."

"So math might be an easier subject for you to do well in."

"And if your parents are on your back, that's where you'll concentrate."

"And when you see everybody else in your group doing it, you think, that's where I belong."

"So whenever you see a group of people acting in a particular way you always have to try to figure out what puts them in that situation. You've got to know something about their history, the problems that they're facing. It may be easy to say, 'That's just what they're like, that's just what they're good at.' But when you do that you're starting to stereotype."

Stereotyping can take other forms as well. One student said: "My parents are so old-fashioned. Like they still think they're living in India. My brother? He can stay out till nine, ten o'clock. But me I have to be in by dark, just cause I'm a girl."

"But it's because they care about you. It's more dangerous for girls," a fellow student interjected.

"Why? Things can happen to boys too. Boys are more likely to get into trouble."

"Boys can't get pregnant."

"Just because I'm out after dark doesn't mean I'm going to get pregnant. And why should it just be the girl that's in trouble if she's pregnant. You need a boy for that too."

"It's the same in my family," said another student. "Girls just do housework. That's how the Portuguese are. I can stay in school 'til I'm sixteen but then I'm just expected to get married and do housework for somebody else. I don't get to do anything. Nobody ever listens to me. Even teachers. They think, she's just a Portuguese girl. She can't do anything. She doesn't have anything important to say."

"I used to hang with these guys. And one night we didn't have any money and somebody said let's go roll somebody, and he goes let's go roll a queer because they can't fight."

"A gay person."

"Yeah. So we went over to this bar that we knew was for gays and we went inside and there was all these big guys with black leather jackets and stuff, it wasn't what we expected at all."

"So you learned that your stereotype about gay people was wrong."

"We decided not to mess with them."

Somewhere in the discussion questions of identity would surface. "Why do people think it's so important to be Black or Italian or whatever?" said one young white woman. "Why can't we all just be people?"

"Yeah," another white student chimed in. "Isn't all this multicultural stuff racist? I'm just a human being. I never think about what colour I am. Why is it important? If people didn't always stick together we wouldn't have all this stereotype stuff."

We went around the group and asked each student to describe what her or his culture meant to them. While almost all the "minority" students had something clear to say about identity, the importance of history or language or family, many Anglo Canadian students suddenly found themselves at a loss. Some made weak jokes about hamburgers or that Canadians had no culture. After more discussion most of them, though, recognized that they too had a sense of identity – it just came from a different starting point – and they came to understand the importance, for those excluded from or misrepresented by an indifferent majority, of developing a sense of identity. They began to develop new insights about why groups might want to "stick together."

In the mid-1980s we added a new exercise. Students met in same-race groups to explore the similarities and differences among people within their group in terms of immigration history, culture, and language. They listed the major stereotypes that their group faced, and the different ways that individuals both benefited and were disadvantaged by their group membership. They talked through other factors that influenced these benefits and disadvantages, such as gender, age, and class. They talked about being asked to group themselves in this way, given that the process could often be uncomfortable in a culture where identification by race, although universally recognized, is often officially discouraged. Each group prepared a report on their discussions for the whole camp.

The different "racial" groups that students organized were often different from camp to camp. Sometimes groups of mixed-race students formed; at other times such students joined a group that they thought they were most likely to be associated with. Sometimes Jewish students formed a group; sometimes they were invisibly integrated into the white group. The same was true for Aboriginal and Latin American students. Although some students were clear and proud of their "racial" identification, for others the exercise was the first time they had seriously confronted how they were seen in a racist society.

White students were the most unused to being defined by their "race" and often found the "segregation" inherent in the process disturbing. Finding themselves in a white-only group produced feelings of guilt and anxiety about what others might be saying about them. The white facilitators had to work hard to challenge this defensiveness and lead students into a deeper investigation of the discomfort of being associated a group that was seen as privileged.

At one family group session the conversation turned to police harassment of Black youth. A white male student whose family lived on public assistance in a housing development was quiet throughout the discussion. There was anger in his voice when he did finally speak out. "The cops hassle me too. They hassle everybody – not just Blacks. But the Blacks can always scream racism, so the cops let them get away with stuff. But not me. What am I supposed to say? I'm white."

Some race relations theory would have characterized the outburst as defensiveness, an unwillingness to admit to privilege – white guilt. But to do that would have been to dismiss this young man's experience. As a white person he couldn't claim discrimination in the context of a discussion on race. But he did face discrimination because of who he was, how he looked, how he dressed, how he sounded, where he lived – his class combined with his age.

It was a crucial moment in the discussion. The conversation had helped the Black students talk about oppression, but it had not addressed similar issues facing this young man. As a result, instead of being able to see himself and Black people facing a common problem of police harassment, he was experiencing resentment at the ability of Black people to articulate and have validated what was happening to them, all while he felt silenced. If our work focused exclusively on racial power and powerlessness, ignoring or silencing other forms of oppression, this young man had little stake in becoming an ally. The process would produce his resistance.

We managed to identify the class character of what the young man was facing and to give him a way of articulating it, not in opposition to what the Black youth were describing, but as a parallel process. Rather than blundering into the swamp of hierarchies of oppressions, and flaunting victimhood ("Look at me, I'm most oppressed"), we were able to talk about the real similarities and significant differences in the experience.

In the course of the work it became clear that validating all forms of oppression together was a *practical* necessity of anti-racist work. The common denominator of class oppression, racism, sexism, and heterosexism is that they are all expressions and practices of power. They may manifest themselves differently and have different histories and kinds of impact, but they also have many of the same effects.

Guilt, denial, and the resistance of those who experience some form of privilege, whether it is around race or gender or wealth or sexual orientation, does exist and must be confronted. But to ignore indices of power other than race (or sex, class, or sexuality) makes this guilt and resistance insurmountable. Those defined into the power group in a particular context can find no common ground with those they are oppressing (and who may in turn oppress them in another context). To effectively challenge oppression we had to understand that power shifts and twists, and that people can simultaneously be oppressor and oppressed in the complex web of racial, gender, and other hierarchies.

The camp discussion focused on race, not because race was the only significant determinant of identity or experience, but because racism could be an important door to understanding the range of unjust power relations.

## Systems and Simulations

Slowly we were able to weave together the threads of individual experience into a coherent tapestry. The experiences themselves displayed the impact of racism on individuals. But facilitators also needed to help participants develop a picture of racism's systemic nature. This was the culmination of the family group process.

Systemic and institutional racism are not simple concepts. The notion of bad people, or people with bad ideas who treat other people unfairly, corresponds with popular narrative structures familiar to everyone who has read a fairy tale or watched a Hollywood movie. But the concept that the dynamics and constraints of the operation of an institution or a system can result in discrimination, without anyone being particularly prejudiced or malicious, can be more difficult to grasp.

We used a role play to help students understand some of the dynamics of institutional racism in their schools. The scenario was a meeting in the principal's office. A South Asian girl has been roughed up by a number of white students. She and her Sikh father are at the meeting with a teacher, the principal, and one of the harassers. The father will not be satisfied until he sees that the culprits have been punished severely. The teacher, who witnessed the incident, is worried that she is going to be blamed for her failure to act. The harasser, a star on the school's hockey team, feels that "Pakis" are taking over the school and comes from a home where racist comments are commonplace. The daughter is afraid and wants to change schools. The principal wants to play down the incident to preserve his school's reputation and not disrupt the hockey team that is in line to win the championship.

On one occasion I was more than a little concerned about potential stereotyping when a young Black man who offered to play the father, wrapped a towel around his head to simulate a turban. The "father" faced an exceptionally adept principal who smoothly downplayed the incident. His sultry tone sought to reassure everyone how hard the school was working to resolve "personal conflicts" among students, and how it would be in no one's advantage to blow this little incident out of proportion. The principal's performance was being roundly enjoyed by other group members, when the "father" suddenly ripped the turban off his head and shouted, "Stop laughing! This isn't funny! It's not just a game! This is what always happens. They never take it seriously. They never do anything about it!"

It was an exceptionally rich moment. We discussed why this particular pattern was being followed. As we began to explore motivations, the group began to see how institutional constraints and interests, more than individual prejudices, were shaping the outcome. Certainly the harasser had a racist motivation. But about the principal? Would a clearer institutional policy on dealing and reporting racial incidents have made a difference?

We also needed to sort out another aspect of systemic racism, which was how treating people in an apparently neutral or equal fashion could result in discrimination.

We had a few stock examples to prime the pump. Toronto police at the time still had "height and weight" restrictions for candidates. Although the restrictions applied equally to everyone, it was clear that they disproportionately hurt the employment prospects of women and those who came from parts of the world where people tended to be of slighter stature. Did you really have to be big and heavy to belong to the police? Popular kung fu actor Bruce Lee probably couldn't meet the requirements. Couldn't he handle himself with criminals?

We would try to focus the discussion on school-based examples. Did school textbooks include the history and contributions of everybody or just certain groups? How did that reinforce ideas that some groups were less important. People wrote literature in English all over the world, reflecting the experience of many different cultures. Why were almost all the books studied in English class written by white men from England or North America?

We brought out different world maps. It was the first time for many students to realize that the commonly used Mercator projection expanded the northern European and American parts of the globe. How did it compare to the equal-area approach of the newer Peters projection? And which countries were placed in the centre of the map? That often depended on when and where the map was made. When I was in elementary school, the world maps always had England at the centre with North America to the left and Europe and Asia to the right. Now most school maps have North America in the centre with the European part of Eurasia on the right and the Asian part on the left. What other subtle biases were hidden in our everyday ways of doing things? How did they influence our views of ourselves and others?

Our message was: analyze everything. Criticize everything you have been taught. Look for subtle biases. Don't accept anything at face value. Challenge authority.

## School Groups and Action Plans

Now we were ready for action planning. The heterogeneous family groups representing the range of racial, cultural, gender, and class differences were the laboratory to develop an understanding of the world based on an analysis of diverse experiences. But the goal of the camps was to mobilize students to push for change in their schools. That work had to fall to the group of students from each school.

Schools were located in different parts of a city that included rich and poor neighbourhoods, white and non-white communities, new immigrant and old settler areas. Most schools drew from their immediate neighbourhoods, which meant that their student bodies reflected the makeup of their neighbourhoods. Collegiates, technical schools, and basic-level schools also drew students according to their academic aspirations. School groups, then, tended to be more homogeneous. Participants often brought back different lessons from their family groups.

A transitional exercise to bridge family and school groups was to take the school group out on a silent walk through the forest. Each student was asked to find something there that represented an important thing they had learned in their family group. One time I facilitated this exercise with students from a largely white, middle-class school. One by one, the students presented pretty pieces of foliage of one sort or another: a flower "representing humanity," a stick that might look dead now but given warmth and light it could produce beautiful leaves – "you can't judge by first impressions"; two plants that looked really different, "but they all belong in the forest, just like different kinds of people do, and they all need the same things to grow."

Then a young Asian man, the only person of colour in the group, dropped a mud-covered shard of a broken bottle into the centre of the circle. The group stared at it, uncomprehending. "This is a dirty piece of broken glass," he said slowly. "It cuts and infects like a racial slur."

The action plans devised by school groups to tackle the identified issues demonstrated varying degrees of sophistication. They ranged from commitments to talk about the issues with friends and setting a good example, articles in school newspapers and yearbooks, through various kinds of school clubs and international or multicultural festivals and concerts. Some of these festivals were little more than the usual ethnic food and dance fairs; others included workshops and challenging speakers.

Students in schools where ethno-specific "cultural" clubs did not exist often attempted to establish them, and those attending schools where such clubs already existed often tried to increase communication and co-operation between them. Some groups hoped to communicate the content of the intensive four-day process in speeches at school assemblies. Others recognized the limitations of such forums, but thought they could still be useful for at least raising issues, informing their peers about the Board's race relations policy, and identifying the teacher race relations rep that each school now required. Others worked to have such information included in student handbooks. Buddy systems for ESL students were established in a number of schools. Students spearheaded discussion groups and film viewings. Others ensured that morning announcements noted festivals of importance to different cultural and religious groups. Some managed to change school policy that required all announcements be made only in English.

Groups made presentations to school staff, outlining the problems that they saw, and encouraged the administration to provide ongoing training for teachers on cultural sensitivity and dealing with incidents. Some tried to facilitate and support student complaints of racism or sexism. They met with heads of departments to call for the inclusion of world literature and non-European history in the curriculum, with librarians to demand inclusive resources in school libraries, and with English teachers to ask for creative writing assignments on student experiences with racism and other forms of discrimination. Coaches were asked to make an effort to involve a wider range of students in school teams. They reported graffiti and helped caretaking staff clean it up. Groups took over control of student councils and established executive positions to focus on race relations issues or represent ESL students. Often uncomfortable administrators were told they needed to hire more minority teachers and take racist incidents more seriously.

Students from the camps acted as watchdogs, bringing issues to light that might otherwise have been suppressed. One young man, a Vietnamese boy who attended the camp when he was in Grade 9, and whose frenetic energy must have been enough to drive a dozen teachers to Valium, even managed to secure a public apology from his school principal and a police community liaison officer for their thoughtless and stereotypical remarks about "Asian gangs" in a school assembly.

## Personal Impact

The young men and women who attended the camps encompassed an enormous range of racial and cultural differences. Some were privileged by their race, gender, or class. Others were struggling to survive in a world from which they could expect few opportunities. Some knew it, some didn't. They often arrived shy, suspicious, angry, or arrogant. Most left more sensitive, open, and empowered. The days of sharing experiences of pain, confusion, anger, resistance, joy, and pride produced remarkable personal transformations. Some of them developed the self-confidence to speak out against what they knew was wrong. Some of them recognized the importance of their own identities and cultures or those of others. Some of them learned important new skills. One young man explained that coming home "was like coming back to a different planet." All of a sudden he saw racism and sexism and discrimination happening everywhere. That heightened awareness of injustice and a common commitment to challenging oppression was often the basis of friendships and networks formed across racial, cultural, and class divides.

One young woman of mixed race described her experience of the discussions. "I began thinking about the memories of childhood and particularly the dynamics between my mom and us – going to the park and people thinking that my mom was our nanny, or my mom getting spit at. Going to the camps allowed me to really get these ideas that were all over the place and talk through them in an environment that was really comfortable." She said that the mixed-race group she was involved in was the first time she had ever thought about mixed race as a potential identity category.

Pat Case, who attended many camps as a facilitator, saw "kids for whom the light just went on." The camps helped him "to see that racism was not the natural state of affairs." For him the sense of comradeship that built among people at the camps would not often be replicated.

When Tony offered me a job working with youth who had been through the camps a few years after my first facilitating experience, the task I saw facing me was to nurture those fragile relationships and insights into a force that would actually be capable of transforming the education system. The elation of realizing what was possible was now to confront the sobering reality of an obstinate world.

# Chapter 4
# Beachhead

THE NEW DECADE BROUGHT WITH IT signs of a sea change in the world. The optimism that the left had shared during the 1970s began to seriously fray around the edges. The Soviet intervention in Afghanistan, conflict between the former allies Vietnam and China, and the revelation of the Cambodian killing fields dominated international news. In Iran a revolution toppled the despotic Shah, but ended up producing a repressive, socially conservative regime, soon locked in a fratricidal war with neighbouring Iraq. The political right seemed resurgent everywhere. In 1980 Thatcher was elected in the United Kingdom and Reagan assumed the presidency of the United States. Even the once impregnable Trudeau Liberals were defeated by the Tories in 1979. The victory of the Sandinistas in Nicaragua, the revolution in Grenada, and the increasingly active anti-apartheid struggle in South Africa brought some solace, but in general things did not look as promising as they had five years before.

The shift to the right was also felt on the municipal level in Toronto. John Sewell, the city's progressive mayor, was defeated in the fall 1980 elections. Sewell had been outspoken in his defence of minorities and calls for police accountability, and his loss was widely attributed to his support of the gay community after police raids on the offices of *The Body Politic*. George Hislop, an openly gay candidate for City Council, also went down to defeat. The same elections undermined the progressive majority at the Toronto Board of Education.

## Against the Current

While the passage of the race relations report had created a certain momentum, the new political atmosphere did not make Tony Souza's work any easier. Tony and Myrna Mather were responsible for setting up and conducting the workshops that were to take place on the new policies in all of the Board's 132 schools in 1980. Given the defensive response of the teachers during the consultations on the policy, Myrna and Tony were not allowed to bring in resource people from the outside – they had to do it all themselves. The Board higher-ups "didn't want to do anything that might upset the teachers," Tony recalled. "There had already been enough controversy and we weren't to rock the boat."

Not upsetting the teachers was harder than it sounded. The race relations report was a lightning rod. Tony found he couldn't get beyond the first part of the report before teachers "started saying it was all lies." Most of the few teachers of colour didn't feel strong enough to contradict their colleagues. "And then there were always those people of colour who did get up and say, to much applause, 'I've never experienced racism, it doesn't exist.' So then what were we supposed to do?"

## Case and Endicott: Board Politics

The situation was not completely bleak. Fran Endicott had been elected to the Board in 1980. She joined Pat Case, first elected in 1978, as the new Board's second Black trustee. Although Pat and Fran came from very different backgrounds, they soon became fast friends and allies.

Pat had come to Canada as an eighteen-year-old in 1968. Although he had faced discrimination growing up in England, it wasn't until he stumbled across Red Morning, an anarchist/Maoist group with a commune just up the street from where he was living in Toronto's largely immigrant west end, that he began to really think about how his skin colour located him in the world. Soon afterward he came across the Third World Books and Crafts store and read Bobby Seale's *Seize the Time*. The bookstore owner, Toronto's legendary Lenny Johnson, took him under his wing. Pat couldn't afford to buy a lot of books, and Lenny gave him some on loan. For Pat, the store and Johnson's stories about his life as a sleeping car porter were a "revelatory experience." After Johnson convinced him that he would never learn anything about the working class in Canada outside of the Communist Party, Pat joined the Young Communist League.

The CP convinced Pat to run for municipal office as its token candidate in 1974. After two losses, he was elected school trustee in 1978. Like the other reformers, Pat saw the streaming of racial minority and working-class kids as a key issue, recognizing it as part of his own experience in England. The reform trustees' willingness to confront the Board's senior administrative staff impressed him. "The senior staff hated that, but at the end of the day I think they recognized that the whole process was unique. There was a push-back from the trustees that didn't exist in other boards. It had a lot of useful effects since it did actually wrest some power away from the superintendents." Pat's first motion at a Board meeting was to reinstate a popular ESL teacher who had been laid off because of cutbacks at one of the schools in his ward. The director was "apoplectic," but the motion carried.

Ironically, the Communist Party found Pat's concerns for practical solutions to issues such as streaming or school day cares "reformist," and when he voted to save the jobs of 104 teachers working in inner-city schools by taking money out of the teachers' contract, it was the beginning of a parting of ways. When he was re-elected in 1980, it was as an independent.

If Pat was a working-class scrapper, Fran Endicott was the epitome of cultured West Indian literary society. Her father, Vic Reid, was a Jamaican novelist, and she gained first-hand experience as a high-school student in Toronto after he came to Canada on scholarship, bringing his family with him. After graduating from the University of the West Indies in history and English in 1968, Fran returned to Toronto's Ontario Institute for Studies in Education to work on a Masters thesis analyzing the history of Canadian investment in Jamaica. Her work at OISE's Third World Project led to her engagement with issues facing inner-city Caribbean youth, such as the teaching of Black and West Indian history in Ontario schools. She immersed herself in community work with the Immigrant Women's Centre and Black Education Project and joined the boards of the Development Education Centre, Learnx Foundation, and *Tiger Lily* magazine. Friends of her new husband, long-time NDP activist Giles Endicott, convinced her to run for school trustee in the largely working-class and increasingly immigrant Ward Seven. At the Board, as a voracious reader with an encyclopedic knowledge of literature and history, Fran soon charmed the intellectual elite of the upper management with her ability to engage in conversations ranging from literary theory to pedagogy.

Although close allies, Pat and Fran sometimes found themselves on different sides in the caucus of NDP trustees that regularly met to discuss strategy. Pat was not an NDP member, but attended meetings and was often at loggerheads with a "doctrinaire core" that tried to impose party discipline. There were "endless, endless meetings" around the internal politics of the party, and Pat thought that the caucus often spent so much time on such debates that it failed to provide real leadership to the Board staff. One substantive issue that split the caucus was the idea of "term appointments," which had been raised in the draft race relations report. The plan was to put principals back in the classroom after five years. Pat believed that the resultant turnover would open up positions of responsibility to women and visible minorities. Most of the NDP caucus, including Fran, refused to support such a radical approach, which they knew would stir up a hornet's nest among the principals.

Pat found committee work more rewarding. As chair of the Race Relations Committee he focused on curriculum issues and the review of classroom materials for bias. Part of his job was contacting publishers to ask for changes, and that work held a certain satisfaction. Action on other issues, such as student streaming and the hiring and promotion of visible minorities, remained more elusive. Although white women were climbing up in the organizational apparatus, little or no progress was being made on the race front.

## A Splash in the Baths

For Tony and the NDP caucus, the first major crisis after the 1980 election was around another other issue altogether – homosexuality.

As the downtown gay presence had grown and matured, the revolutionary pretensions of early gay liberation had given way to a quasi-ethnic notion of gay identity and gay community, and that community had emerged as a significant voting bloc in downtown Toronto. Gay activists within the NDP had also become an important force in the labour-intensive municipal campaigns. John Argue, one such NDP gay activist, also happened to work as a swimming instructor for the Board. Stereotyping, isolation, and harassment in schools were common memories for most lesbians and gay men, and the race relations report stated that the spirit of its recommendations should apply to other marginalized groups. Argue believed that it was time to make that happen. An ad hoc committee began meeting, and soon asked the Board to set up a Gay Liaison Committee, modelled on those already established for many immigrant communities.

Tony met with part of the NDP caucus to go over the issues. Although Fran was supportive, he found many others "personally terrified of gay people" and astounded to learn he was gay. "I had to sit them down and talk with them and say I had no interest in fucking young children. You can't convert someone to being gay. This is who you are. All of that stuff. I remember they were shocked, but did get it together to pass the motion to study setting up a liaison committee."

*The Toronto Sun* went wild. Left-wing trustees were going to give homosexual predators access to children. The right-wing Board trustees sensed a hot issue and did their best to fan the flames. At the Board meeting in August 1980, trustee Alex Chumak tried to have the subcommittee studying the possibility of a liaison committee disbanded. The motion failed, but generated a new round of publicity. By September, with the election only three months away, the left was feeling the heat. A group of progressive trustees issued a statement of concern about the "misunderstandings surrounding the establishment of a subcommittee to investigate a possible link with homosexual groups." The real issues, they maintained, were human rights and academic freedom, not the espousal of homosexuality for young people.

To try to frame the issue as a matter of human rights, the left moved to have sexual orientation included in the general statement on bias that had been passed with the race relations report. The new statement read, "The Toronto Board of Education condemns and will not tolerate any expressions of racial/ethnic bias, nor bias on the basis of sex or sexual orientation, in any form by its trustees, administration, staff or students." The right countered by attaching an amendment that the Board "will not countenance the proselytization of homosexuality within its jurisdiction," and instructed the new subcommittee that before it deliberated on the need for any ongoing mechanism of communication with the homosexual community it should come up with a report on whether evidence of discrimination and prejudice against homosexuals existed in the system.

As the fall election approached, the jockeying continued. In October the left moved that the new Equal Opportunity Office be asked to include an analysis of anti-gay incidents in its yearly report. The right instructed the director to seek "legal interpretation and clarification of the Board's policy relating to discrimination on the basis of sexual orientation."

When the election campaign began, Pat included his support for the Gay Liaison Committee in his campaign literature, perhaps naively not realizing how heavy the backlash would be. About a week before the election, a leaflet headlined "Pat Case Communist," with a diatribe about his support for the Gay Liaison Committee, was dumped in his ward. Then *The Toronto Sun* published a centrefold with photos of the trustees who had voted to allow homosexuals into classrooms. Pat's picture was set against a red background with the word "Communist" underneath.

Panicking, Pat phoned the printer who was preparing his second piece of campaign literature to ask them to remove the reference to his support for the Gay Liaison Committee. His campaign committee, though, demanded that he stand his ground, and the gay liaison reference stayed in. Pat not only won the election but also increased his share of the vote. "It taught me a very important political lesson," he said. "Do not run."

The new Board was split down the middle. The new chair, Irene Atkinson, "came on with a vengeance," Tony said. "She was going to get rid of all this stuff, especially the gay stuff."

In February 1981 a new crisis exploded. On the evening of February 5 police simultaneously raided all of Toronto's gay baths. They smashed down doors, ripped open lockers, verbally and physically abused patrons, and arrested all of the 286 men they found inside. It was Canada's largest mass arrest since the War Measures Act in 1970. Tony was on his way to a school when he opened the morning paper and saw the report of the raids. He quickly arranged a permit for the Right to Privacy Committee, the group leading the response to the raids, to hold an evening public meeting the following week at downtown Jarvis Collegiate. The meeting drew over 1,200 people. "It was all over the media," Tony remembered, "and the right-wing on the Board just blew up because a school had been used."

A few days later Tony spoke out at another meeting at City Hall. "How many Black people need to be killed, how many gay people need to get arrested before we put some controls on the police? People are going to revolt," he said. "How long do you think people are going to take this shit?" *The Toronto Sun* reported that the new race relations advisor for the Board of Education was calling for revolution in the streets. Irene Atkinson had found her opportunity, Tony said. "She told the director that she was going to move to get me fired."

On February 23 a special Board meeting was called to hear delegations on the inclusion of sexual orientation in the Board's discrimination policy, consider the lawyer's report on the matter, and deal with a private personnel matter – Tony's firing. On the first issue the Board's right-wing members held sway. Although a majority of the over forty deputations on the policy supported the inclusion of sexual orientation, the Board lawyer reported that he believed the Board had exceeded its authority because the issue was not covered by the Ontario Human Rights Code. Sexual orientation was removed from the bias statement in a fourteen to twelve vote.

But even some of the right-wing members realized that the reaction had gone too far. Trustees and senior officials knew that a number of teachers had been caught up in the bath raids. Without any kind of non-discrimination policy referring to sexual orientation, these teachers were completely vulnerable. The *Sun* was threatening to publish the names of all those arrested. By a large majority, the Board moved that it would not tolerate discrimination "in its employment practices" on the basis of sexual orientation. At least teachers did not have to fear for their jobs.[1] When the attention turned to Tony, Fran Endicott managed to convince a majority of trustees that his remarks had been taken out of context. He escaped with a reprimand and was told by the associate director to restrict himself to race relations and keep being gay out of the equation.

Tony went back to work, but the issue of sexual orientation did not go away. It was impossible to talk to students about racism without the conversation leading into other issues. At one Camp Kandalore session students raised stereotypes about gay people, and Tony asked them how much of their list applied to him. His coming out sparked "a really good discussion." After he got back to the city, a superintendent called to say a parent had complained and warned him to keep things on a low-key basis.

A few months later, at a student reunion, a young woman from Tony's group apologized for causing him trouble. After the camp she had challenged her father at the dinner table about his homophobia. The father went to the school principal, who turned out to be in the closet himself and was afraid to deal with the issue. He passed the father on to the area superintendent. "There was so much closetry in those days," Tony said later. "Everybody knew who was gay but nobody ever talked about it." Gay people rarely got either support or acknowledgement. The prevailing belief was that "if you didn't talk about it, it would go away." It was much the same as the response to questions of racism. It was the activism of Tony Souza and many others that finally made the authorities deal with the issue.

## Parent Organizing and Institutional Change

The independent parent movement was still going strong. Largely organized on the basis of ethnicity, language, and race, with the help of the School Community Relations Department, these parents were no longer content with traditional "home and school" activities. Armed with the "Every Student Survey," which confirmed that schools were failing to provide equal opportunities for all students, they worked to influence policy and pressed the Board on questions of curriculum, student assessment, and the provision of heritage language classes.

In spring 1979 the SCR Department organized a large city-wide parent convention and parents began to organize groups in schools across the system. A school-by-school parent council survey of staffing needs, released in 1981, argued that the Board needed to hire 427 additional elementary school teachers to improve the quality of teaching and learning.[2] In May, eight hundred parents descended on the Board and forced trustees to pass a motion calling on the provincial government to provide $12 million in emergency funding. A second parents' convention in March 1982 demanded that the Board more widely publicize and translate the race relations policy and develop a timetable for implementation. The convention also called on the Board to consult with parents to "develop appropriate measures to eliminate the streaming of students from low income background or from certain immigrant families, into programs which are inappropriate to their potential and which may limit their future career options."[3] With this kind of mobilization nipping at their heels, even conservative trustees were not about to meddle with programs associated with multiculturalism and racism.

Facilitated by the SCR Department, liaison groups of Black parents had formed around the Black cultural heritage programs that were part of heritage language efforts in a number of schools. Keren Brathwaite, now a parent of school-age children, was an active participant. "We used to come together as Black parents to talk about how the programs were progressing. We were really excited about them, even though they were after school. We felt if we could show how important this content was in the after-school program, it would move into the school system."

According to Brathwaite, the consultations and the race relations report convinced these parents that it was time to form a city-wide organization. With Board and SCR Department support, the Organization of Parents of Black Children (OPBC) was founded at a conference in May 1980. It would be a powerful voice for change at the Board for the next twenty years.

It was not only "ethnic" parents who took advantage of the new democracy sweeping the Board. A Labour Education Liaison Committee was formed after a parent who was an active member of his union came to the Board to complain about the anti-union perspective in a text used in his child's secondary school economics course. The new liaison committee, made up of union activists, parents, and teachers, soon became a think-tank looking at how schools were teaching about work, workers and labour issues.

## Equal Opportunity Work

Around the same time Tony Souza was struggling to find effective affirmative action strategies to transform the unrepresentative composition of Board staff. Among other things, he recognized the need for a "Visible Minority Survey" that would provide statistics on the makeup of the organization. That required asking employees about their race, which in turn required permission from the Human Rights Commission. The unions and administration needed to be brought onside to set up a Race Relations Employment Task Force. At every step he met with opposition.

Tony also worked to bring together progressive teachers to write curriculum and figure out ways of getting the material into classrooms. In this at least, Tony was not without support from the top. Don Rutledge, the associate director of Program, and thus in charge of curriculum, made it clear that things had to change. Indeed, although Tony reported to the director's office through Ron Halford in Operations, he depended on Rutledge to make things happen when muscle was needed in curriculum and training issues. Tony remembered a science consultant complaining that there was no way to introduce "race relations" into the science curriculum. Rutledge told him, "We all have to do it." The trick in science, Tony said, was "using different kinds of names in examples, and talking about different cultures' contributions to scientific development, and bringing examples of people of colour who were important scientists, and that kind of thing."

A tool was also needed for the system-wide workshops around the policy. Once again Tony turned to Rutledge, who managed to find $40,000 to make a movie. Jennifer Hodge, a young Black filmmaker, was hired. She interviewed a number of people who reminisced about their experiences as visible minorities in the education system. The film looked at bias in the curriculum and the importance of a culturally sensitive and supportive school system for minority youth.

Tony was also working on building a network. He began to organize regular parties at his home and invited sympathetic people from across the system so that they could get to know each other. More formally he and Myrna worked to ensure that each school appointed both a race relations and an affirmative action representative. The goal was to give people more support to take action in their schools. With Fran's support, after a year Tony was able to get release time for the race relations reps to receive training, and permission to hire Barb Thomas to deliver the workshops.

While the idea of race relations reps looked good on paper, it was much more problematic on the ground. Barb wondered what the new reps were really getting out of the sessions. The reps were usually a teacher, sometimes a volunteer, possibly even a principal or vice-principal. A few of them, Barb said, "really wanted to do something, but others had just been appointed because they weren't doing anything else, and some were actively opposed to the whole effort." The people most interested in doing the work were often already overextended – perhaps already serving on four or five other committees. The reps worked without a structure in place for reporting back to the school or for gathering information from the school to bring to meetings. "They didn't have any power or influence," Barb said. "I remember feeling how much work it was going to take to make this effective. But, on the other hand, I didn't have a better idea. We did need somebody in each of the schools."

The student camps also continued to go on twice a year. Students returned to try to put their action plans into place, but, just as important, the camps were an opportunity for Tony to find out what was really going on in the schools. The camps brought issues to light. At one camp, for instance, students from Central Tech mentioned how a film company shooting a movie on the Terry Fox cross-country run had arranged with the school to provide extras. When the students arrived to fill the roles, the film producers pulled out all the Black students and just filmed the white kids. When he came back from the camp, Tony called the principal, who "just flew into a rage" that Tony would even bring this up. After passing on the complaint to the Human Rights Commission, Tony received a call from the school's vice-principal, "who was big on affirmative action for women." The vice-principal complained that Tony was causing trouble. Tony told her that he was required to act on complaints. "One of the key things in the race relations report that I used to no end was that any racial incident that had been reported had to be acted on. There was a principle of mandatory response. Eventually all of those kids got an apology."

## New Strategies for the SCR Department

In 1982 a change of command occurred in the SCR Department. Charlie Novogrodsky, a colleague of Barb's from the Cross Cultural Communications Centre, was hired to lead the department.

Charlie and his wife Myra were part of the generation who had cut their political teeth on the civil rights movement, and had come to Canada from the United States as part of their resistance to the war in Vietnam. They quickly settled into life in Toronto, qualifying as teachers and having two children. Charlie became active in the Ontario Secondary School Teachers' Federation (OSSTF) in 1975, at a time when teachers first won the right to strike. His union work put him in touch with other teachers interested in developing more progressive curriculum, and he soon became involved in producing material on the histories of different immigrant and refugee groups in Canada. In 1980 he left teaching and went to work at Cross Cultural, where he came into contact with anti-racism struggles from a community perspective. Cross Cultural was also working closely with the Board at the time, and Charlie prepared the first evaluation of the race relations camps. By the time he moved to the SCR Department, he already knew many of the NDP trustees and their Board allies.

Charlie Novogrodsky saw the department as an agent for institutional change. Basing his approach on the work of Johan Galtung,[4] he argued that institutional change involved three pieces: advocacy; research and education; and policy change and implementation. While the SCR Department had a strong history of advocacy, Charlie believed that it had to pay more attention to the other areas. The department needed to work with teachers to train them in more effective communication with parent communities. It need to do direct parent education, around literacy skills, for example. It needed to do research that could be used for advocacy or for pushing institutional change. Clearly, those different kinds of work would often require different skills. People who were good at doing advocacy work would not necessarily be at home in a training room, or able to carry out negotiations with policy allies.

The SCR Department had allies among the progressive trustee majority, but others within the organization, particularly in management, were suspicious of the department's advocacy and agenda, Charlie said. They didn't like how the department was encouraging parents to ask for changes in how their kids were being schooled.

## A Student Program Worker

Tony's job – delivering workshops, handling complaints, and trying to oversee implementation of the race relations policy – was obviously too big for one person, and he somehow managed to secure funding for a new position in the Equal Opportunity Office. The new person would take over the administration and follow-up of the camps with the long term goal of establishing a city-wide anti-racist student organization.

At the time I was at the Centre for Spanish Speaking Peoples working as the legal secretary, and found myself facing a choice. I could stay there, perhaps become a community legal worker, and spend my life trying to sort out the interminable messes that people found themselves embroiled in just because they were immigrants. Or I could go into education and try to convince young people to change the world. It was not a difficult decision. I had immensely enjoyed the experience of watching students understand things and transform themselves at the camps. Visions of cultural revolution danced in my head. I would be able to do follow-up to the camps, organize young people to "bombard the headquarters," and transform the oppressive educational system. Although it was a major cut in salary, since the job at the Board was only half-time, I decided to apply.

My new job in the Equal Opportunity Office started in September 1983. Tony and I debated what my position should be called and I came up with the title "Student Program Worker." I didn't want the job to sound too professional. After all, the future belonged to the working class. I never suspected that for the next twenty years, every time I went to the United States, border guards would look at me suspiciously and ask if I was still a student.

Part of the groundwork for justifying the new position had been Charlie Novogrodsky's report on the camps. As well as calling for the hiring of someone to provide administrative support, Charlie had recommended a number of other changes, including more explicit explanations to principals about the camp program's goals and better selection of accompanying teachers.

We had had some inappropriate teachers come to the early camps. For example, in one session, we were going around the group to identify the major race relations issues in a school. When it came the teacher's turn he said, "Hygiene." Puzzled, I asked him to clarify.

He explained, "The Vietnamese and Greek kids all eat so much garlic and they don't wash. They stink so bad it's hard for anyone to concentrate in class."

In a classic understatement Charlie's report recommended, "A reputation for fair-mindedness, openness and an ability to listen should be minimum requirements for teachers attending the camp."

Charlie also believed that students needed more time to reflect on the egalitarian atmosphere of the camps in contrast to their "normal" school experience, and that teachers needed more opportunity to talk with other adults about the process. The camps' family groups needed to clarify their goals. Were they sensitivity sessions or an opportunity for a course on race relations? If the goal was simply to help students share and become more sensitive, then we needed some other vehicle to raise the issues and histories of specific groups. If the intent was more of a course, then facilitators needed to be better trained to deliver analytical material on economic, psychological, and cultural theories of racism. Finally, the camps' school groups needed to be given more time to develop their plans, and students needed to be better prepared to face the culture shock of returning to their schools. My role was to try to incorporate these suggestions in the camp process.

My first task was to help Tony organize the camp that October. I soon found that getting a half-dozen schools to pull together a handful of students was a complicated task. Being more explicit with principals on the purpose of the camp was not easy. Many of them didn't read their mail or return phone calls. We were usually happy if we could convince them to appoint a contact teacher. So we concentrated on explaining the purpose of the camps to the contact teachers and getting them to advertise for students in their schools. Then we had to make sure that they selected a representative group. "No," I explained to one male teacher. "Eight good-looking blond girls that you personally choose from one of your classes is not really the kind of diversity that we had in mind."

We encouraged the teachers to advertise as widely as possible. Then I would come to the school, armed with a slide-tape show, to explain the program to students who expressed interest. I tried to weed out students who were clearly just interested in a holiday. We also had to train the teachers who were going to attend, and then we had to select the facilitators. We tried to have one experienced and one new facilitator in each group. One of these two had to be a person of colour, one white. One had to be from the Board, one from the community. One had to be female and the other male. All of that took some juggling. Then they too had to be trained.

Then there was administrivia. Permission forms had to be collected from all the students, sent back when they were improperly filled out, duplicated so that in emergencies we had proof that we were not kidnappers, and located at the last minute when they became lost in the Board mailroom. We had to arrange an orientation session for participating students to remind them what to bring – sleeping bags and warm clothes, yes, drugs and knives, no. We had to assemble a week's supply of materials: flip charts, markers, handouts, and exercises.

We needed to organize the family groups so that they had a balance of boys and girls and people from a range of schools and backgrounds. We had to prepare and duplicate family group lists, school group lists, and cabin lists and stuff them into participant kits with policy brochures, name tags, and daily schedules.

After the camp was over, I had to type up and copy the outlines of the school action plans, organize reunions, and do follow-up in the schools to help the students implement their plans. Education wasn't all fun and games.

## A Facilitators' Handbook

My second major task was to write a handbook for camp facilitators. The handbook set out the camp's goals and outlined expectations for facilitators. It provided a snapshot of our current understanding of racism: as not just a matter of violence or legal segregation, but rather a pervasive part of everyday culture that had an impact on everyone's lives in different ways. Structural and institutional racism shaped groups' access to power and privilege.

Racism was usually seen as a matter of people holding attitudes that led to discriminatory behaviour; the handbook argued that attitudes were the *result* of discriminatory structures and institutions. "Doing something about racism is not only a matter of changing attitudes. It is also a matter of changing how our lives and institutions are organized."

I reprised the popular definition of racism as prejudice plus power. Racism was a "white problem" because, although any group could be prejudiced, it was white people who held power in Canada. My assumed simple correspondence between whiteness and power – an important part of anti-racist theory at the time – tended to obscure other indices of power, but, to be fair, the reduction of power to race parallelled similar reductions in other progressive movements. Feminists tended to see everything as the effects of patriarchy, reducing power to maleness. Socialists tended to see everything in terms of class. Still, perhaps struggling to escape this essentialism, I added that this formulation did not mean that people who had white skin had something "naturally" racist in their makeup. Given similar situations, other groups were just as capable of developing racist attitudes and practices.

The camp's goal was the development of "anti-racist" rather than "non-racist" people. Being anti-racist meant being committed and empowered to do something to combat racism; and doing something was the best way of deepening our understanding. "We learn to think differently from doing new things. We learn to do things differently when we understand new ideas." To inspire action we had to debunk common explanations of racism that led to complacency – that racial differences in aptitude were real, that racism was just human nature, that it was the result of unfamiliarity, and therefore that it was a stage that would just go away if minorities would put up with it long enough.

The next section laid out the camp process. Facilitators were asked to conceptualize "consciousness-raising" using an industrial metaphor. The first step was to obtain "raw materials," the experiences of the participants. Since all students had life experiences, everyone should have something to offer. The next stage was to "refine" these materials, grouping experiences according to theme, followed by discussion of the themes in more detail. The final product was a "map" of the social organization of racism and other forms of discrimination, which made evident how they were achieved and who was benefiting. The final step was to use this product to change the world, to develop an action plan that students could take back to their school, or use in their own lives. Such action would deepen and reinforce what they had learned at camp and stop them from being reabsorbed into their old habits and ways of seeing and living in the world.

Facilitators were expected to be "a combination host, teacher, organizer and recording secretary." As hosts, facilitators should ensure that everyone felt safe to participate. They should monitor participants' energy levels and be prepared to change formats and call for breaks. As teachers, they should ask questions, clarify and validate people's comments, draw connections, and provide information if necessary. They should model constructive expression of feelings, giving feedback, and dealing with conflict, and be prepared to diffuse guilt and defensiveness and bring speculation back to earth. As organizers they should remind the group of the different stages of the process, keep people on track, and help them avoid dead ends.

Writing the handbook gave me the opportunity to think about some of the issues that Charlie had raised about the program. He had been questioning whether the camp was sensitivity training or a course, and I became firmly convinced that the appropriate model was neither of those. Students were not just becoming more sensitive; they were learning about the world around them. But they were doing it from studying their own experiences, not course work. More analytic work around particular group issues, history, or academic theories of racism could only be taken up after students had a solid analysis based on the sharing of experiences.

The danger of the handbook was that although it might help to harmonize the week's work within groups and be a useful training tool for new facilitators, it might also appear to be prescriptive and to encourage the group process to become "curriculum driven" rather than emerging from the needs and experiences of participants. What was important at the camps was the processing of experience – letting experience talk – rather than the completion of "lessons." For many teachers this approach could be profoundly unsettling. What if we didn't cover everything we were supposed to? What if the analysis that emerged was wrong? At some point don't we need to give them the correct answers? Facilitators had to learn to trust that the processing of experience would lead to social analysis. Some groups might cover everything, other groups might not. How much any group covered was not as important as the grounding of whatever they had learned, and were learning, in real life.

## Following Up

As I began to do post-camp follow-up work in the schools, I also began to identify several general problems. Asked to select students with "leadership potential," schools had often interpreted that as students who were already in positions of leadership – in student councils or athletic associations, for example. When it came to choosing between receiving praise for non-controversial, high-profile activities compared to butting heads with the principal about the way racial incidents were dealt with, for example, the traditional activities usually won out.

Nora Allingham attended camps as both a teacher and a facilitator, and she found a "systemic resistance to continuing the work after the groups returned to their schools." She blamed it on "the inertia of the system." The students, and teachers, who wanted to bring action back to the schools quickly came up against roadblocks and found few allies beyond their own small group. "The system was just too big and entrenched."

In schools in which teachers were enthusiastic, things generally went well. In schools in which teachers were less than enthusiastic, the follow-up was less successful. I began to wonder if some principals' selection of teachers for the camp was problematic. One time two teachers told me in no uncertain terms that they were not interested in doing anything when they returned to school – that they had only come to the camp because the principal had ordered them to, and they didn't believe in any of this stuff anyway.

The integration of student plans into their school's official race relations action plans also presented problems. Although all schools were required to submit a plan to the race relations advisor through their race relations reps, in practice most didn't bother. Tony was stretched far to thin to hunt them down. I found that many of the reps were less active than the teachers who had attended the camp. Those schools that did submit a plan often made no mention of student involvement. Kandalore action plans often hung in an administrative limbo without official mandate or backup.

Still, sometimes, in schools with supportive teachers and administrations, groups did manage to put their action plans into practice. I organized regular reunions to try to keep everyone enthusiastic, attended meetings in the schools to help with planning, and found resources to support student activities. In the summer of 1984 Tony hired Debbie Douglas and Chris Jones, two students who had attended the camps, to write a handbook for participating students to help consolidate their learning and share successful action plan strategies. It wasn't exactly "bombard the headquarters," but things were happening.

## A Strange Country

There was another thing I had to learn about when I arrived at the Board of Education: its labyrinthine structure. The elected trustees were supposedly in charge. The full Board, consisting of twenty-six trustees, met once a month, and between those meetings various layers of committees worked to vet and prepare material before it went to the Board for final decision. The major committees, such as Personnel and Organization, School Programs, or Educational Finance, were made up of trustees and senior administrative staff. More issue-specific committees, which over time came to include Race Relations, Status of Women, or Heritage Languages (HELACON), had additional representatives from the communities they were related to. Less formal liaison committees focused on reaching out to different communities, and from time to time other shorter term advisory committees were formed to accomplish specific tasks.

Under all this lurked an even more complicated bureaucratic hierarchy, largely white, male, conservative, and territorial. The apex of the organization in 1983 was the director, Ned McKeown. Below him were the associate director, Operations, Ron Halford, and the associate director, Curriculum and Program, Don Rutledge. This division represented the great fault-line that ran through the institution. The Operations Division was in charge of the mechanics of sustaining a huge organization – buildings, staff, payroll. Curriculum and Program managed what was taught.

Below Rutledge was Charlie Taylor, superintendent of Curriculum and Program. Taylor supervised areas such as special education, continuing education, the Language Studies Centre, and the different subject area co-ordinators and consultants. On the other side, reporting to Halford, was Helen Sissons, superintendent of Personnel, who dealt with staffing issues such as hiring, promotion, and seniority.

Away from the Education Centre, the city was divided into four areas: East, West, North, and Central, each of which had an area superintendent in an area office, in charge of three or four school superintendents who managed different "families of schools." Each school had its principal, who managed vice-principals, teachers, non-teaching staff, and ultimately students. All these fiefdoms had their own politics, rivalries and histories, which constantly had to be negotiated in order to get anything done. It was no wonder that pushing for change often felt like trying to nail Jell-O to a wall.

## Gail Posen

By the time I came on as student program worker, Myrna Mather had been replaced as affirmative action advisor by Gail Posen. Gail had grown up in Windsor, Ontario, in a left-wing Jewish family. At the time Windsor had a significant Black community, and some of Gail's earliest memories were of the blatant discrimination that Black students faced in her public school. But Gail also had her own problems. When she was in school in the 1950s, she said, "The Catholic Church was still promoting the idea that the Jews killed Christ." One day when she was still "just a little kid," a pupil from the Catholic school in her neighbourhood yelled out to her, "You killed Christ." Gail had to go home and ask her mother who Christ was, because she had no idea. "I knew I hadn't killed anybody."

Gail had taught at Central Commerce, a largely immigrant working-class school in Toronto. She became involved in OSSTF and was branch president of her school during the bitter 1975 teachers' strike, but even as a "union radical" she had not made connections between labour and women's issues. Then her principal, one of the first women promoted after the passage of the affirmative action policy, suggested that she take on a women's studies course to give the girls an opportunity to recognize that they had options beyond being a secretary or a homemaker. Resistant at first – why would she want to do something just for women? she wanted to politicize all the students, not just the girls – Gail eventually warmed to the idea, and when she plunged into the course she was surprised to discover a new level of engagement on the part of her students. "We spent a lot of time talking about issues that came up in their families and how some of these made them feel, and we would strategize about how they could handle situations differently. The students in the class were finally relating to something." They would ask why they had never learned about women's history or literature in other courses. Why had they never learned anything about unions? The classes gave Gail a new sense of energy. She started to incorporate some of the same topics in her business communications course.

Later, after doing a year of research on women and the curriculum in an M.A. program at York University, Gail, along with a colleague, went to the Board's Status of Women Committee and asked to be released half-time to write a new business education curriculum on technology and women and work. Gail had never been entirely comfortable teaching business education. "It always seemed so much from the perspective of the employer. It taught girls to go out and be little sheep, to do exactly what they were told, never to question anything." The request was unprecedented, but the committee managed to convince associate director of curriculum Don Rutledge to come up with the money. They wrote eleven units of curriculum for use across the whole Board. The units included women's issues such as sexual harassment and unionization, and also material on working in computerized offices and related issues of occupational health and safety and the nature of work – and especially how there were going to be rapid changes in the way offices were organized in the future.

She did meet with a certain resistance. The Board's computer staff objected to the analysis of the impact of computers on the workplace. She came up against business communications teachers in the Board who just didn't want to do anything new. At one point her department head forbade her to show a film about sexual harassment or even talk to students about the issue. Together with the other women in the department, she just ignored him.

In 1982 Gail applied for and got the affirmative action position at the Board. Like Tony she found herself "flying by the seat of her pants." She had two reference committees, the reconstituted Status of Women Committee and the less formal Women's Liaison Committee. At first she simply carried on with the goals of "the white women's community of liberal feminists who seemed to have charge of women's issues at the Board": goals and timetables for the advancement of women teachers, equal pay for work of equal value, the sexual harassment policy. But she also gravitated to the Labour Studies Committee, and one of her first initiatives was to set up a retreat to bring teaching and non-teaching women together to combat "the sense that teachers were the more important people in the system" and to give recognition to the importance of the work of non-teaching staff. She noticed that few women of colour were coming to these retreats: questions of race and culture were still peripheral to the mainstream women's movement. Even though they worked out of the same office, her relationship with Tony was at best distant.

## Gaining Momentum

In the early 1980s other groups that had traditionally been given short shrift by the school system had begun to come forward. "All of a sudden people began to see the Equal Opportunity Office as a way of being able to get information out into the schools," Tony recalled. "There was a Ukrainian guy who wanted to talk about the Ukrainian famine. Armenians raised the question of the Armenian genocide. Myra Novogrodsky spearheaded the 'Facing History and Ourselves' approach to studying the Holocaust." Tony's relationship with Don Rutledge was instrumental in his ability to find out where and how these requests could be integrated into the school curriculum.

In October 1983, representatives of Canadians Concerned About South Africa (CCSA) approached the Race Relations Committee, requesting that the Board organize a conference for students on apartheid in South Africa. Tony seized on the idea. "Apartheid was a perfect example of institutional racism. By this time our understanding had evolved a lot. We saw institutional racism as the final step, from stereotyping and prejudice to discrimination to enshrining that discrimination in the way institutions or governments operated."

Lynda Lemberg, a teacher and CCSA member, took a lead role and brought the OSSTF onside. The Toronto Committee for the Liberation of Southern African Colonies (TCLSAC) soon got involved as well. The planning group pulled together speakers, materials, and films. The conference took place in April 1984 with close to five hundred students from across the city attending. It was to become an annual event.

## Tony Bows Out

Less than six months after I began, Tony announced that he would be leaving at the end of his contract in the fall of 1984. His four years in the position had taken their toll. He felt himself being caught between community activists who wanted him to do more and push harder for change and the administrators saying, "Don't go so fast. Don't push so hard. Don't rock the boat."

The Race Relations Committee was often a battleground. Keren Brathwaite of the Organization of Parents of Black Children remembered the tensions that came with the new work of dealing with race. "Some committee members had a gradualist approach, but others of us younger ones felt that wouldn't work. There was an impatience for something to happen." Schooled in the civil rights movement and the Black consciousness struggle, influenced by the political writings of Frantz Fanon, the activists saw the work as "serious and deep stuff" and believed that the issues were being watered down. Karen recognized that it must have been very difficult for someone like Tony Souza who was working within the system.

Tony was also frustrated by his inability to get information. He came to believe that information was being held back because the administration was afraid he would cause trouble. Fighting against the Board's institutional culture was an uphill battle. One of his biggest disappointments was the Board's lack of progress on the issue that would later come to be called "employment equity." Despite the results of the "Visible Minority Survey," which demonstrated that less than 8 per cent of the Board staff were people of colour, little seemed to be changing.

He also had his personal issues. "One of the things you constantly got was, 'Don't take this personally, this is not about you.' What do you mean it's not about me? I'm a person of colour. I'm gay. Somehow I was supposed to separate who I was from the job, because in the job I should have an 'objective' view."

## A Plan for the Future

Tony's frustrations indicated that the advisor's position and the race relations program needed to be reconceptualized. As he prepared to leave, he turned to Barb Thomas to analyze the difficulties he had experienced and to come up with recommendations for change in the position.

By that time Barb was compiling her own list of frustrations with the education system. For one thing she was finding was that people pushing for change in the climate and culture of a school would, time and again, come up against hostile conditions, and eventually they would back away from the problems. "The nature of teaching is that when teachers get too discouraged and don't have the heart or the energy to take on their colleagues in the school or the area anymore, they can just close their doors and concentrate on their classroom." Mechanisms for change were clearly needed – serious structural changes.

After a series of interviews with Tony and others who had been involved in the race relations program, Barb produced a discussion paper that began circulating in March 1984. In it she proposed a number of indicators of an "ideal system."

Her vision was both a goal and a pedagogical device for focusing discussion and evaluating the effectiveness of the recommendations of the original race relations report. It was also an important foundation for Barb's subsequent contention that the work of transforming the school system was far too extensive to be the responsibility of the race relations advisor alone.

She noted that Tony reported to the director's office (which consisted of the director and the associate directors of Operations and Program). This had the advantage of giving him independence and a direct line of communication to the top, but left him outside of the Curriculum and Personnel departments, the two major areas he was trying to influence. It was the familiar contradiction of an organization hiring someone to push for change but locating him in a way that limited his effectiveness.

While it was important to have an independent department to do "the prodding, piloting, pushing and mobilizing," Barb argued, racism in the education system could only be challenged through long-term, system-wide strategies embedded in regular institutional functions involving all departments and people in authority. Curriculum and Personnel needed to be made accountable and responsible for the work. She concluded, "Personnel must be convinced that countering racism is in everyone's best interest so that they can hold themselves and others accountable for constructive action."[5]

The idea that countering racism was in "everyone's best interest" was a striking assertion given the resistance that both the development and the implementation of a race relations policy had encountered over the previous five years. Although the idea was consonant with assumptions of a well-meaning and benevolent education system, it did not take into account the nature of the opposition that the small race relations staff constantly faced. It discounted the possibility that racism might actually benefit particular groups or individuals within the system or within society at large, a notion that was certainly part of the discussion at the student camps. Even a facilitator with Barb's depth of analysis and experience found herself constrained by hegemonic assumptions when preparing a document that would be acceptable for circulation within the system.

The final report, *Race Relations Program: Phase II Report,* went to the Board in June 1984. The six pages of recommendations essentially called on the Board to reaffirm its commitment to improve race relations and to continue and broaden discussions on the indicators of an ideal system. The system should be held accountable for implementation of the policy through annual reports to the director from school superintendents on behalf of their schools, and from the Personnel and Curriculum departments. The Race Relations Committee itself needed to re-examine its mandate, role, and composition. The responsibilities of the race relations advisor should be split, with a new position of curriculum advisor on race relations created to facilitate the integration of race concerns in the curriculum. The original advisor's position should be seconded half-time to the Personnel Division to focus on developing a coherent policy on equal opportunity employment and staff development programs for both teaching and non-teaching staff. There should be a systematic evaluation of the status of all 119 recommendations of the race relations report.

Phase II promised a new focus in the struggle for change. But there were dark clouds on the horizon as well. During the last years of Tony's tenure the parent movement, which had been the motor of the Board's race relations efforts, was facing serious challenges.

## The SCR Department and Institutional Change

When he took over the SCR Department, Charlie Novogrodsky inherited two major political issues: the integration of heritage languages and the struggle against Bill 127.

Immigrant parents organized by the SCR Department were fighting for the integration of heritage languages and Black cultural programs into the regular school day, rather than having those programs relegated to after-four or weekend time slots. They argued that integration was vital to improve the educational experience of immigrant children by moving "minority" languages and cultures towards a more central position in the school curriculum.[6] But such a change, which would extend the school day by a half-hour, was opposed by teachers, who also argued that it would fragment classroom activities. The alliance between immigrant parents and teachers that had been forged in the fights to increase staffing in downtown schools came under serious stress. Some white middle-class parents, and particularly parents in the "north end" – generally more wealthy than the working-class and immigrant neighbourhoods downtown – also opposed integration.

Tam Goossen, a Chinese Canadian parent activist, experienced the tension when her children's downtown school began to consider introducing integrated heritage languages. She saw a split between the Anglo parents and the Chinese and Portuguese parents. The usual "civil and friendly" atmosphere of parent meetings had become "hostile" and "sometimes outright nasty," Goossen said. "People were sitting in different groups and Anglo parents were asking tough questions about what was going to happen to their kids." The result was divisive – indeed, so divisive that some north-end parents walked out of the second parents' convention held in March 1982. They ended up sending a delegation to a subsequent Board meeting to complain that the convention had been a "political rally where open discussion was discouraged."

But the struggle around the integration of heritage language education did also generate an important sense of unity among immigrant groups. Keren Brathwaite was a member of the Heritage Languages Committee during much of the struggle for integration of the programs into the school day and spent many long evenings at Board meetings, once getting home at three in the morning. She found different communities coming together – the Italians, Greeks, Portuguese, Spanish. There was a sense of a broad, unified struggle that was not simply limited to one group and was not just about heritage languages but also about Black cultural heritage programs, curriculum changes, and parent involvement.

Although Charlie remembers the fight around heritage languages as "bloody," for him the main opposition was not the wealthier white parent groups but the internal dynamics of the Board as an organization. He heard about secret meetings of trustees who wanted to defeat the integrated day. Other opponents were the publishers of *The Toronto Sun*, some of the school principals, and the local executive of the elementary teachers' federation. All of them "sincerely hated the idea of integrating heritage languages into the regular program," and together they made for a powerful force. "We had stories of teaching assistants in particular elementary schools, in the downtown and central part of the city, being told by their principals that if they wanted to retain their jobs, they were to go out on the playground on the lunch hour and at recess and find parents . . . and tell them that if the integrated day program happened, their children would fail to learn English and become school dropouts." For Charlie, the conflict "was the last institutional gasp of Anglo Canadian privilege in the school system. And boy, it gasped. But it lost."

The issue continued to fester. By 1984 the Board found itself facing not only a boycott of extracurricular activities by elementary school teachers opposed to integration but also a legal challenge by the teachers' union (which lost its case). Special Board meetings were held on the issue in February and a compromise was finally reached that exempted teachers from any requirements around direct involvement in the program. Integrated programs would only be offered in schools in which a majority of parents requested them. Although in the spring of 1984 only three schools opted in, integrated programs were now a fact of life, and over the years more and more immigrant parents fought for and won integrated programs in their children's schools.

According to Charlie Novogrodsky, the political victory, even if it initially involved only a few schools, "penetrated into the heart of the school day." Principals had to reschedule timetables. Black people came into the schools to talk about their histories in Canada. "It was a fight about the nature of our society and what kind of space it was going to make for different cultural and ultimately different racial identities."

The second major struggle was around organizing opposition to Bill 127. In May 1981 the Conservative provincial government reacted to the demand by Toronto parents and trustees that more teachers be hired to meet the needs of inner-city students. It introduced Bill 127, which restricted the rights of local boards of education to raise local taxes to hire teachers above their provincial allocation and limited local bargaining with teachers over working conditions.

This was an issue that could once again unite parents and teachers against a common enemy, the provincial government. The SCR Department threw its weight into organizing parents to fight the bill, and had what Charlie saw as a partial success. The main issue around Bill 127 was local democracy and the local financing of education, and as a result of the campaign against the bill, a brake was applied to some of the worst elements of the legislation, however temporarily.

In their analysis of the early work of the SCR Department, however, researcher Kari Dehli and her co-writers concluded that the struggle had unintended consequences.

> From the point at which [Education Minister Bette] Stephenson introduced Bill 127, the organizing agenda in Toronto and at Metro switched from staffing and programs to blockage of the bill. For the first time, the Toronto parent movement became directly engaged in a fight with the province and its allies at Metro. At the same time, the organizing of parents around local concerns – both in Toronto and in the boroughs – came to a standstill.[7]

The same writers also argued that the media and lobby-centred campaign aimed at forcing Queen's Park to back down favoured the domination of more affluent conservative north-end parents, and that by the time Bill 127 passed in February 1983, the popular base of parent organizing had become dispirited and weak.

Other parts of the first wave of parent organizing were in decline from internal conflict. As the Board finally began to put more resources into teacher training, curriculum, and the Black heritage programs, Marlene Green noted a growing "difference of perspective" emerging within the Black Education Project. Some members believed that Black kids were "getting so screwed in the regular system" that the group needed to be working to establish an alternative school for Black kids. Others believed that such a move would lead to ghettoization and that the fight should be to make regular schools meet the needs of Black students.

"That debate made it difficult to agree on what direction programming should go, and what we should apply for money for," Marlene said. "We just couldn't get it together to agree on what to do next." The Black Education Project went into a terminal decline.

Chapter 5

# Taking on the System

ALOK MUKHERJEE BECAME RACE RELATIONS ADVISOR in the fall of 1984. It would be hard to imagine someone with a more different personality from Tony's. If Tony was often like a bee in a bottle, Alok was a quintessential philosopher: contemplative, calm, academic. Alok grew up in Bengal as part of a "very political family." His grandmother, "the first feminist" he knew, was a Communist Party activist, always leading rallies and protests. He learned about North American politics through opposition to the Vietnam War.

When he and his wife Arun came to Canada in the early 1970s to finish their doctorates, they encountered "blatant racism" in the academic world. Later, as vice-president of the Graduate Students' Union and president of the Indian Students Association at the University of Toronto, Alok found himself speaking out against the differential fee for visa students and began developing an understanding of systemic racism – "how something that may not have been intended to be discriminatory could have a discriminatory impact." But trying to explain that to the university senators or the minister of education was a challenge. "I think the understanding of the time was that if you didn't intend to discriminate it was not discrimination," he remembered. A visit to an elementary school gave him direct experience with popular misunderstandings. Apparently, when the children heard Indians were coming to the class they expected someone "dressed in feathers," not wearing a jacket and tie. When it was established that Alok was from India, he was peppered with questions about why the people in his country didn't eat all the cows to solve the hunger problem. After that experience he put together a funding proposal – "East Indians, Myths and Reality" – to look at how South Asians were portrayed in Ontario school texts. In a political climate where South Asians were a major target of racial harassment, the 1976 report attracted a lot of attention. The Toronto Board's South Asian Liaison Committee and the SCR Department organized a press conference to publicize the work, which brought it to the attention of the Ministry of Education. *The Toronto Sun* attacked the findings in an editorial entitled "Curried History."

By 1980 Alok had lost interest in his Ph.D. studies – English literature seemed increasingly irrelevant in the context of his community work. When

Tony had left the SCR Department to become the race relations advisor, Alok replaced him as the South Asian worker in the east end. Now, a little over four years later, he was replacing Tony once again. With Barb Thomas's *Race Relations Program, Phase II Report* approved by the Board, and with a larger budget to handle the cost of its implementation, Alok met with Anne Marie Stewart, an ally in the Staff Development Office, to set priorities. They identified four areas: developing the Board's understanding of the issues, building stronger community linkages, establishing student programs, and dealing with employment issues.

Alok saw the first two areas as interlinked: the Board's understanding would deepen as a more vocal community held it accountable. He met with parent and community groups to convince them to use the Equal Opportunity Office and the Race Relations Committee to bring their issues to the Board. He also continued to provide training for Board staff, recognizing that in a large organization with its constant turnover, it was necessary to do the same kind of training over and over again.

Alok took another important step. Dealing with complaints of discrimination until then had generally fallen to Tony to manage. Since people came to the office for counselling, support, and to learn about their rights, the advisor was being asked to play simultaneous and conflicting roles of advocate, counsellor, investigator, and judge. As well, in the end, the advisor had no organizational authority over anyone to enforce decisions, since he was neither a principal nor a superintendent. Alok tried to reshape the complaints process by shifting responsibility back to administrators in the system – usually principals or superintendents. "We could assist them and provide training and resources, but they had to do the investigations."

## Hari Lalla

In January 1985 the Board filled the second position recommended in the *Phase II Report*, the curriculum advisor on race relations.

Hari Lalla, an English teacher at Bloor Collegiate, had come to Canada from Trinidad in 1964 to do a degree in psychology with plans to go into medicine. Instead he ended up getting married and went into teaching. At first he was oblivious to racism in Canada. "When I was dating my first wife, who was white, some people looked at us with disgust or were insulting, but we didn't pay much attention. The incidents were rare, so we didn't feel threatened." But when he went to the Department of Manpower to apply for a job as a counsellor, and was told that clients wouldn't want to be interviewed by a person of colour, he began to recognize that something more serious was going on.

In his first teaching job, at Danforth Tech, Hari found himself making "Paki jokes" in the staffroom to fit in with the rest of the staff – something he eventually came to see as "legitimizing racism." As the 1970s progressed, "Paki bashing" made headlines. In the growing racist atmosphere Hari began to curtail his movements and watch where he went. He stopped going to pubs and avoided public transit – "There were so many incidents of racial harassment in the subway it became a kind of phobia."

When he transferred to Bloor Collegiate in the early 1980s Hari began, reluctantly at first, to accompany students to the Camp Kandalore retreats. Over time his trips to the camps as a facilitator led to changes in his teaching style. He had been taught to give lectures, but now began to use more participatory group techniques. He joined the Race Relations Committee as the OSSTF representative, although his primary role was to be on the alert against any attempt to revive the idea of "quota" hiring.

Hari felt unprepared for his new position as curriculum advisor, and the Curriculum Division seemed even more unprepared for him. The position had been created from above by Board fiat. Nobody seemed to know what he was supposed to do. His job description was a long list of vague goals. He was supposed to advise teachers on how to improve race relations through the curriculum, but he wasn't sure exactly how to go about doing that. He immersed himself in literature from New York's Council on Interracial Books for Children, trying to find practical strategies to insert "race relations and multiculturalism" into the regular curriculum. At first he found himself floundering in the face of resistance. It was the same old thing: teachers and principals in the schools would say, "What are you doing here? We don't have any problems." Others attacked him over Board policy calling for the removal of "racist" books from classroom use.

Slowly Hari began to find his feet. His presence in Curriculum Division meetings was changing the atmosphere. Just because he was there, people were thinking more carefully about the language they used. They were beginning "to discover for themselves the discomfort they were feeling discussing racism and its impact on curriculum." A structural element also came into it: "People also wanted to impress their superintendents by talking about how they were going to be working with me. They had ambitions in terms of promotion, and when they began to see the writing on the wall that race relations was important, they began trying to get my attention." Hari's cautious approach – he admitted later that he didn't push too hard – helped to earn trust. "They realized that I was not going to accuse them of racism right away. I became a part of the team." Most teachers, he thought, were not ready to accept that they had a major role in challenging racism.

## Myra Novogrodsky

Working with Hari in Curriculum also put me in much closer touch with Myra Novogrodsky. After she and Charlie came to Canada, Myra soon gravitated to the women's movement, specifically in the struggle for the establishment of community-based child-care facilities at the University of Toronto. She went on to become managing editor of *Community Schools Magazine*, which introduced her to thinkers who saw schools as a place to work for social change.

A.S. Neill's *Summerhill: A Radical Approach to Child Rearing*[1] was something of a Bible for education radicals at the time, and Myra soaked up the theory about non-hierarchical, student-focused education. In 1974 she got her first teaching job at SEED, a small downtown alternative school. In 1980 she and three other teachers from SEED founded City School, an alternative school more directly committed to social justice.[2] Getting City School set up acquainted her with the workings of the Board, and she soon became active in the Labour Education and Women's Liaison committees.

As a history teacher, Myra found herself teaching about fascism and Naziism. "Although I had a good political idea of what I wanted to do, at first I probably did a lot of damage, or at least I didn't do any good. A couple of my crazy students probably identified with Naziism more after I did my work than before, which was certainly not my intent. So I started to back away from it. That was unusual for me. It wasn't often that I backed away from teaching controversial issues. But I just thought that I needed to think a lot more about how to do it."

At some point she came across a small non-profit organization based in Boston. "Facing History and Ourselves" was looking at ways of using the Holocaust as a case study of extreme racism. She was particularly impressed with how the group brought teachers and scholars together to develop ideas about the relationship of the Holocaust to other historical experiences. "Facing History" also took adolescent development into account. Myra realized that the chronological study of history was "almost inevitably going to be a bust with kids." Students were interested in their own issues. It would be more effective to connect historical experiences with the moral issues that students were facing in their everyday lives. It might also better help them to become active citizens. Thanks to a small grant, the City School staff was able to go to Boston for a summer training program, which they then made the basis of the school's annual interdisciplinary course.

The approach was very much the kind of thing that Tony had been trying to promote in his race relations work. In 1983 he scraped together money and arranged for Myra to be seconded half-time to begin working with teachers in yet more schools. She would now do work around racism and anti-Semitism in the whole system. In 1984 she left City School and moved to the Board to work full-time as assistant co-ordinator focusing on women's and labour studies in the Curriculum Division.

Despite similarities in our interests and approach, Myra and I regarded each other warily. While I supported the struggle of the Palestinian people for national liberation against Israeli occupation, Myra believed that the left's position on Israel often reflected a deep-seated anti-Semitism. I, and most anti-racism activists, focused on racism directed against people identified by their skin colour. Myra saw anti-Semitism as a template for understanding racism. Myra was a teacher, and some of my experiences at camp had made me suspicious of teachers. Convinced that if nobody rocked the boat it wasn't going to move, I wanted to organize students to demand change. Myra believed that confrontation could be irresponsibly provocative. She preferred to work with teachers to convince them to broaden the curriculum.

## Anti-Racist Education

The early 1980s saw an explosion of theory around racism and education. In Canada the polemics often came down to whether you believed in multiculturalism or anti-racism. For multiculturalists, the problems between groups were fundamentally grounded in misunderstanding and miscommunication. "Race relations" would improve when people got to know more about each other. Anti-racist education, on the other hand, conceptualized the issue of racism not as a human failing, a misunderstanding, or a lack of awareness, but as a problem of ideology, of a worldview that categorized people on the basis of "race" and justified and reinforced power imbalances between groups. If the task at hand was to challenge racism, that required a critique of Eurocentric culture, a rereading of history, and affirmative action to redistribute social power.

Immersing himself in the new literature, Alok condensed the differences in "From Racism to Anti-racist Education: A Synoptic View." The document compared traditional, multicultural, and anti-racist education in three areas: theory, practice, and the relationship of students, teachers, and parents in the learning process.

Traditional education, he argued, grew out of the nineteenth-century Anglo-American imperialist view of the world with its ideology of social Darwinism and survival of the "fittest." Multicultural education was rooted in modern, liberal-reformist circles and asserted that "fit" individuals were to be found in all cultures. Anti-racist education emerged from the struggles of racial minorities against imperialism, colonialism, and racism.

Traditional education was essentially conservative, elitist, and Eurocentric. It assumed the superiority of Western culture and supported existing power relations.

Multicultural education saw the need for reform, and aimed at improving race relations by counteracting individual prejudices through sensitization and the provision of information about minorities. Anti-racist education asserted that the problem was one of racist thought and practices, not cultural difference. It proposed an education that would be critical of the status quo, aimed at challenging and altering existing power imbalances.

The three approaches led to very different educational practices. While traditional education glorified Western achievements, and multiculturalism tried to add on celebratory and exotic aspects of other cultures, anti-racist education promoted a critical examination of all cultures and recognized that experience was shaped by race, class, and gender.

Traditional education refused to recognize the different needs generated by a variety of experiences shaped by race, class, and gender. It therefore opposed equity programs and placed the full responsibility for success or failure on the individual. Multicultural education did recognize difference but failed to address issues of power and powerlessness. It explained differences in success with reference to cultural or home factors. Anti-racist education saw racial and, by implication, class and gender differences as central, and strongly supported system-wide equity programs to address issues of power and historical inequities. While not ignoring the effects of social and economic factors, anti-racist education saw institutional racism as the main cause of group differences in student success.

Traditional education also tended to be subject- and teacher-centred, and promoted individual competition as the best way of determining success. Parents were expected to leave education to the experts. Multicultural education saw learning as more open-ended, with the inclusion of teacher-facilitated co-operative strategies and the recognition of parent cultures. While anti-racist education was student-centred, it was not completely open-ended because it included clear goals of encouraging active, anti-racist individuals. The teacher was an active participant and guide in the construction of knowledge through collective and co-operative strategies. Anti-racism promoted strong partnerships between parent and school and emphasized the daily life experience of parents.

A second milestone for anti-racist education in Canada was the special fall 1984 issue of *Currents*, the journal of Toronto's Urban Alliance on Race Relations. Subtitled, "The Fourth R? Racism and Education," the issue put the notion of anti-racist education on centre stage. A number of articles, including "Multiculturalism as an Assimilative Ploy" by veteran civil rights activist Wilson Head, critiqued notions of multicultural education. A key article in the issue was Barb Thomas's "Principles of Anti-racist Education."

Barb's piece used multiculturalism as a foil to display the more radical implications and principles of anti-racist education. She saw multiculturalism as an attempt to make the discussion of diversity and unequal treatment "palatable to dominant-group Canadians." While multiculturalism might deplore the existence of stereotypes and prejudice, anti-racism examined not only the history of those ideas but also the practices and power structures they supported. Multicultural notions of "equal opportunity" might aim at levelling the playing field in the competition for scarce resources, but anti-racist education would equip learners to work collectively to change the conditions of scarcity that pit people against each other.

While everyone had a role in the struggle, a fundamental principle of anti-racism, Barb asserted, was that leadership had to come from those who suffer most of racism's effects: people of colour.

## Making Connections

By 1985 Alok Mukherjee, as race relations advisor, and Gail Posen, as affirmative action advisor, had noticed a certain peculiarity of their work: most of the people of colour who came to Alok's office were men, and most of the women involved in Gail's programs were white. That realization marked the beginning of a major shift in the affirmative action program. Working together, Alok and Gail launched the Visible Minority Women Employees' Group, a pilot project for women of colour in the education system.

Like most innovations at the Board, the joint project was controversial. A few administrators were threatened by this new, tightly focused formation, and members of the target group had their criticisms too. The first meeting was rocky. "We're glad you are doing this," one of the participants said. "But make a note that of the three facilitators, one is a man and two are white women." Alok and Gail's "liberal desire to do the right thing" and their approach to the new terrain would have to be refined.

"You do things for a while and then you realize from talking to people and from incidents, that maybe that's not the best way, so you try to do it differently," Gail said. "Alok and I were constantly rewriting the script and trying to address issues that people raised with us." But they did find that the group met an important need. For several women of colour, Gail said, the group "was a real eye-opener." The women could now "bring up issues of racism without fearing that somebody was going to dismiss them."

The other major breakthrough for Gail was Myra Novogrodsky's appointment to the women's and labour studies position in the Curriculum Division.[3] Both women's studies and affirmative action had separate sets of reps in the schools. The two offices began to hold joint meetings for their reps and to run them in a far more participatory way: getting the reps' input and responding to it, working together to implement the Board's policies in their schools. Both Myra and Gail were also assigned as staff to the Board's Status of Women Committee, with its twin responsibilities, employment issues and curriculum. The employment side covered not just women teachers, but also support staff, which brought up issues of non-traditional work. The curriculum side took in women's studies and questions of bias in the curriculum. The committee had input in the Curriculum Division's process for reading and critiquing new curriculum materials. According to Sue McGrath, a veteran member of the committee, "We talked about how much of the curriculum was taught – math being the big example – and how that was not the way a lot of young women learned. As a result, boys dominated in the maths and sciences. We felt that if somehow we restructured the curriculum, we would be able to get girls to be just as good in math and science as boys. There were also issues of equity in sports, the limited access female students had to the school playing fields, and the unfair distribution of students' fees to male activities."

Trustees such as Pam McConnell, Fiona Nelson, and Fran Endicott, and senior Board staff such as Associate Director Ron Halford guided the group through the Board bureaucracy. After its rocky start in the mid-1970s, the reconstituted committee was becoming a force to be reckoned with.

## Affirmative Action Policy Review

In 1983, Fran Endicott, who was chairing the Status of Women Committee, convinced the Board to embark on a review of the affirmative action policy. Although the promotion of women on the teaching side had met with some success, the situation for non-teaching employees had not significantly changed. The review ended up going beyond affirmative action to investigate the impact of Board policies and practices on both women and visible minorities. Continuing until 1988, it was to be one of the longest and ultimately most expensive review processes in Board history.

Co-ordinated by an umbrella group called the Affirmative Action Review Group, the review included five or six major projects. Principals, vice-principals, area superintendents, and Board administrators were represented on all the review committees. Experience had shown that if these stakeholders weren't involved in discussions, they would be neither committed to the project nor able to explain or implement the decisions once the process was finished. Despite cumbersome consultations, one of the first reports from the Review Group in June 1984 was withdrawn because it "may have implied disapprobation of staff in the Personnel Division." The Group duly apologized for "any distress this may have caused staff."[4]

At the time, for me, the Review Group's approach to women's issues seemed cautious and bureaucratic. The fear of expressing "disapprobation" was the furthest concern from my mind: it was right to express disapproval of a system that was racist and sexist, or of anyone who worked to make it function in that way. At one point I asked Gail why she didn't organize student camps for young women to encourage them to challenge sexism and push for change, much in the same way as we were doing around racism. She said that type of project would be a Curriculum Division responsibility. Her office was more interested in working with teachers. I concluded that anti-racism must be somehow more fundamentally "revolutionary" than women's liberation. In my radical naïveté, I failed to appreciate that the area of race relations was equally subject to the same practical institutional pressures that were shaping the struggles around women's issues.

## Hitner Starr

Barb Thomas's *Phase II Report* had recommended a detailed examination of progress on the implementation of the race relations report's 119 recommendations. A consulting company, Hitner Starr Associates, was commissioned to do the research. Trevor Hitner had been involved in the City of Toronto's Mayor's Committee on Race Relations and was considered to be highly qualified for the job. His firm set out to do research and conduct interviews with senior Board personnel who had been charged with implementing the recommendations of the 1979 report.

"Trevor was like a bull in a china shop," Alok recalled. "He rattled people. He went to people right up to the director and asked them what they had done with particular recommendations. Often the answer was, 'Was I supposed to do something about that?' One very senior official used swear words and described the race relations office as people in jack boots or something like that. Hitner's report quoted people by name and in their own words."

The report was released in December 1985 – by happenstance in the middle of a session on human rights that Alok was conducting with the director's office and superintendents.[5] Hitner was involved in the session and had already antagonized the group with his "acerbic" style. When participants began leafing through the report, the first things to catch their eye were the "juicy" quotes and accusations of the system's negligence, incompetence, and racism. There was an uproar. The director, Ned McKeown, demanded a rewrite.

Alok and associate director Ron Halford were assigned the task of meeting with Hitner, who said that changing the report was against his personal ethics. Halford explained that the director didn't want him to tone down the message, but that the report had to follow a certain etiquette. He had to remove the swear words and make sure that comments were anonymous. After a "difficult" meeting, Hitner agreed to a rewrite, but the damage among the senior officials had already been done. From Alok's perspective, the report "strengthened the suspicion" that the race relations office was "up to something" and that its staff was looking for ways of tripping the other administrators up.

Even with the revisions, the Hitner Starr report was a damning indictment of the system's inaction five years after the approval of the race relations report. Indeed, it found that many of the Board's staff had failed to take on the appropriate responsibility for implementing the recommendations.[6] The report identified five factors that had "adversely affected" implementation, collegial culture, management by crisis, unfocused organizational objectives, dysfunctional reporting lines, and ineffectual communication.

The Board's collegial culture had evolved from the nature of the teaching system. Teachers worked behind closed doors; the system therefore counted on their professionalism and integrity in exercising their responsibilities. While this gave teachers control over their working environment, when extended to the organization as a whole, and especially in times of changing expectations and new policies, it was an approach that did not ensure accountability, monitoring, or evaluation. It also made it difficult if not impossible to ascertain how many, if any, recommendations had been fully implemented throughout the system. For example, in response to the recommendation that guides be produced to help teachers and students identify material containing racial/ethnic bias, Curriculum had issued *Identifying Bias in Educational Material: A Guide*. The Board had distributed four copies of the document to each school in the system, but without monitoring and evaluation there was no way to determine if anyone used it.

The collegial culture led to management by crisis. In the absence of monitoring and evaluation, managers assumed that everything was going well unless they heard something to the contrary, which usually occurred in a crisis situation. The failure of managers to ensure that staff fulfilled their obligations led to "ad hoc, inconsistent, and in many cases, superficial implementation." The report cited a recommendation directing that a counselling program be established to provide encouragement and information to visible minority employees seeking promotion. That recommendation was not implemented until 1985, after number of complaints had been received from minority teachers.

Given unfocused organizational objectives, staff tended to use their discretion about implementing or modifying particular recommendations. For area and school superintendents, with their "endless list of things to do," the report found, "the Race Relations Program was not perceived as having high priority."[7] The report noted that until 1985, the director of education's annual priority-setting remarks to principals and superintendents had failed to even mention the race relations program. The director had also failed to submit the required annual report to the Board on the progress of equal opportunity in the system.

But, in an example of the effect of dysfunctional reporting lines, the Advisory Council on Bias in Curriculum had no authority over the schools or school superintendents. Without functional reporting lines, no one took responsibility for such monitoring and, not surprisingly, it never did take place.

Hitner also criticized the very organization and presentation of the race relations report itself, noting that it combined an excessive number of recommendations that were poorly organized and ambiguously worded, making comprehension difficult. The critique then sifted through the 119 recommendations to determine which had been fulfilled, and which had been partially fulfilled or ignored.

Looking first at curriculum-related recommendations, Hitner found: "The overwhelming consensus among interviewees was that if the Race Relations Program has had any impact at all, then this impact has been most evident in the production of bias-free curriculum materials."[8] This was faint praise. The report noted the Board's failure to produce the required guides on racial bias in "great literature," and pointed out that only new materials had been checked for racial bias while older material continued to be used without review. None of the school superintendents had formally assessed materials used in their schools. While the Library Services Department had prepared bibliographies on reading materials available in English from the home countries of many immigrant students, there was no way of knowing how much of this material was actually available in school libraries. There had been no system-wide training for teachers on bias since Tony's first efforts in 1980–81.

Issues of student placement and assessment had been a major bone of contention between minority communities and the school system. Recommendations that parents of new students entering the system receive information on placement and assessment procedures had been ignored, and it was impossible to determine if parents were being informed of their right to appeal such decisions. Hitner concluded, "The Board does not appear to have provided sufficient information to parents which would allay the fears they might have about 'racial streaming.' "[9]

Hitner saved some of his harshest language for the recommendations concerning racial incidents in schools – an area of the program that "has been largely ignored by those persons responsible for ensuring its implementation."[10] Superintendents had not formally encouraged principals to convey Board policy on dealing with incidents. There was no system to monitor how incidents were resolved. Principals were unaware of their responsibility to discipline staff demonstrating racial or ethnic bias. There was even little agreement among senior staff as to what constituted an incident. "One School Superintendent for example did not consider racial name-calling to be a racial incident."[11]

In the area of extra-curricular activities, Hitner noted that none of the school superintendents indicated that they had followed recommendations to encourage schools to organize cultural exchange programs or form multiracial clubs and associations. Only one of four athletic associations had introduced a clause that racial slurs would not be tolerated at sports activities. The potential impact of the Kandalore Program had been undermined by lack of school support.

Although the original race relations report put a great deal of emphasis on sensitivity training for staff, Hitner concluded, "Under the present organizational structure, there is nothing to *ensure* that all Board staff will receive race relations training," noting that the Board's Staff Development Office did not include specific workshops on race relations in its professional development calendar.

Few of the original recommendations concerning employment and promotion issues aimed at attracting and promoting more visible minority staff had been fully implemented. "For example, although the Board states in public advertisements that it is an 'equal opportunity employer,' it has not addressed those recommendations which involve developing strategies to meet the needs of visible minority employees. When asked why these recommendations had not been implemented, one senior personnel officer commented that it would be perceived as reverse discrimination if the needs of a particular group were addressed."[12]

The Board had also failed to identify and counsel specific "promotable" visible minorities. The committee set up to provide candidates for employment with a vehicle to appeal employment decisions "had never been operational," and there had been no monitoring of any changes in Personnel Division procedures that might have an impact on the racial and ethnic composition of staff.

The race relations report had recommended that the Board take an active role in encouraging teacher-training institutions and the Ministry of Education to offer and extend courses in race relations, multiculturalism, and human rights and to develop practices that promoted the participation of visible/ethnic minorities. Since the Board had no authority over such institutions, Hitner pointed out, the only impact it could have would be to advise all faculties that race relations training would be considered an asset in the selection of applicants. But the Board had not acted upon this critical recommendation.[13] Hitner's report concluded:

> Successful implementation of any organizational change program also requires senior staff to accept ownership of that program. This element too seemed to be lacking with respect to the Board's Race Relations Program. The result has been a series of mandated race-related activities which have been conducted to one degree or another, or simply ignored in certain instances. If the Race Relations Program was designed to present a cohesive plan of action in order to achieve some measurable goals or objectives, then the Program to date has fallen short of its intention.[14]

The Hitner Starr report was "powerful," Hari said. "It taught us all a lot about how systems and structures should work." The report laid bare the responsibilities of administrators, especially superintendents, and "revealed the gaps in Board operations.... The report clearly outlined the failures of the Board, where the weaknesses were, and where opposition to the work of race relations resided."

With its exposure of the inaction of many of the Board's senior officials, the report did shake up the system, but it also revealed the practical difficulty of challenging hegemonic assumptions and practices in a huge and complex institution. Hitner recommended a traditional management approach to monitor and ensure that changes were implemented – while recognizing that such an approach would run counter to the education system's institutional culture. He pointed out that a number of his interviewees had praised the "soft-sell approach" of the new race relations advisor. The challenge that Alok faced was reconciling his soft-sell approach with the more hard-edged management techniques that Hitner recommended.

## Race Relations Committee

Both the *Phase II* and Hitner Starr reports agreed that the Race Relations Committee needed to be reorganized and revitalized. Deciding that the committee should be expanded to include not just trustees but all major stakeholders, Alok invited representatives of the teaching and non-teaching unions, the Principals' Association, other Board committees (Labour Education, Heritage Language, ESL, and the ethnic liaison groups, for example), and parent groups such as the Organization of Parents of Black Children.

Race relations was a major interest of newly elected NDP Trustee Olivia Chow. She believed that institutional change required both inside and outside pressure, and saw the Race Relations Committee's lack of integration into the workings of the Board as a serious limitation. To make the expanded committee more manageable, and to mirror the Board's organizational structure, the committee members decided to divide into two subcommittees, one focused on employment issues and the other on curriculum. Each subcommittee would meet separately, and the Race Relations Committee would continue to meet as a whole.

Alok worked directly with the employment subcommittee to tackle issues identified in the 1984 Employment Task Force Report and the Hitner Starr report. The goal was to ensure that the Board's staff composition reflected the racial makeup of the city. A key strategy was to provide training and skills development for visible minority employees seeking promotion to positions of responsibility.

Hari became staff to the curriculum subcommittee, which focused directly on the challenges of ensuring that what was taught in schools reflected anti-racist principles. With Olivia Chow as chair, the committee looked at the Hitner Starr report's curriculum findings to see what needed to be done, and it came up with timelines for completing the work.

As a whole, the Race Relations Committee had its limitations. According to Nora Allingham, by this time the OSSTF representative on the Race Relations Committee, the presence and involvement of trustees on the committee were "often sporadic." The community representatives had limited knowledge of how the Board worked, and Alok's attempts to have training and workshops for members proved frustrating. "In some cases," Nora said, the committee became "little more than a sounding off opportunity for individuals." The theory and practice of letting all the members have their say and represent their constituencies were sound, but it often seemed that all the meetings and talk were wasting time and energies that could have been directed in more productive directions. Still, the committee did make things happen. "It was a kind of moral monitor," Nora said. "It could make people feel uncomfortable enough that it would help to get things done that wouldn't have been done otherwise." Alok, she said, had set it up as a committee that had political clout through the trustees sitting on it. "Senior staff were not going to do anything, and we all knew that." Change had to come through political channels.

## Organizing for Change

By the end of 1985 the Board had what must have seemed to any casual onlooker a morass of groups and committees engaged in overlapping issues: Race Relations Committee, Holocaust Studies Advisory Committee, Anti-Apartheid Conference Planning Committee, Japanese Canadian Conference Planning Committee, Black Studies group, various ethnic liaison committees, Heritage Language Consultative Committee, and a Cross Cultural Studies group working out of the Social Studies Department. These bodies were generally unconnected and their members in danger of burnout. They were, perhaps, the most obvious sign of the need to push for change within the institution. But there were others: despite their training, the race relations reps were still marginal when it came to challenging racism in their schools. New models had to be developed for training and supporting advocates in the system.

Alok decided to try to build on existing training programs for teachers to create an activist cadre of anti-racist educators across the Board – people who could then move into leadership positions. Following a January 1986 workshop, "Towards an Anti-Racist Curriculum: Let's Work Together," which attracted over fifty participants, a racially mixed group of fourteen made up primarily of teachers and a few administrators came together to form an independent group, the Committee of Anti-Racist Educators (CARE).

As CARE met and organized activities over the next sixteen months, several tensions emerged in the group. Some members wanted to remain small, working as a closely knit group that could develop a clear analysis to support themselves in their work. Others wanted to expand into a larger, more powerful network of progressive educators. The group debated its focus: whether it should be about raising consciousness or changing structures and behaviours. While some members had grown weary of talking about white people's feelings about racism, others argued that since the dominant culture controlled decision-making in the organization, whites needed to be convinced of the need for change.

Even the relationship with the Equal Opportunity Office was grist for discussion. CARE was heavily dependent on Alok and the office for administrative support and co-ordination: booking rooms, keeping minutes, sending out meeting notices. Some members argued that to effectively challenge the system the group needed to be more independent; others believed that the Board had a responsibility to take such leadership.

One particularly tense discussion occurred after a public presentation by British anti-racist educator S. Sivanandan, director of London's Institute for Race Relations. Sivanandan, a guru of anti-racism in Britain, was scathing in his critique of anything that he believed smacked of multiculturalism. From Hari's point of view he was arrogant and belittling of any practical attempts to make change, however small. After Sivanandan's presentation CARE members seemed to be trying to outdo one another over how radical they could sound. When Hari asked them what kind of revolution they were talking about, "No one answered. Everybody was struck dumb, as if to say what's the matter with him?"

Nora Allingham, also a member of CARE, had the opposite reaction. "I loved listening to Sivanandan. He was so angry and articulate. He said things that were absolutely right. But I knew that his approach was just going to die in that environment. He was just far too radical. I know that Hari found him absolutely incomprehensible. A lot of other people were outraged. That was probably the kind of thing that led to CARE not going too far."

CARE did manage to develop a ten-day facilitator-training program, "Challenging Racism in Our School System," the first such program to be structured around the concept of anti-racism as opposed to race relations. This program went beyond consciousness-raising, beyond identifying individual instances of racism. It focused on preparing teams of activists to recognize and challenge systemic forms of racism and discrimination. Its projected outcomes included pools of trained teacher-facilitators available to families of schools, and the development of new anti-racist leadership workshop models to challenge the weaknesses in the implementation of the race relations report.

The ten-day program, held in the fall of 1987 and based on democratic adult education principles, stressed collaborative work and frank discussion of the dynamics of building mixed-race teams. Participants were encouraged to look at their own discomfort around their racial identities, whether that involved white guilt or the anger and frustrations of participants of colour. Effective advocacy would require not only a knowledge of the history and impact of racism, but also a recognition and analysis of its individual, systemic, and ideological forms. Using a technique called the "learning cycle," participants started by sharing experiences and went on to analyze those experiences for patterns and themes; developing a theory based on the analysis, they then applied the learning to action, which would lead to new experiences.

That first program became an annual event that continued for Alok's term as advisor. Significantly, within five years, more than a half-dozen of the original participants had become vice-principals, principals, or senior officials.

Alok also brought together a group called the Visible Minority Employees Network. Primarily an advocacy group, it also provided individual counselling, mentoring, and training. Successful administrators of colour came to talk about career planning and how to move up through the system. The group organized a retreat, inviting the director, the associate directors, and senior superintendents to attend, thus creating an unusual possibility: visible minority employees questioning the upper bureaucracy, raising issues, and lobbying for long-term work around employment equity.

## Strategies and Conflicts

Hari and Alok reflected two very different approaches to organizational change. Through the lens of left theory I saw Hari as more of a social democrat. He was more cautious and less confrontational. He wanted to keep the widest possible group on side and avoid ruffling feathers. He wanted to change the system through slow, incremental change. Alok, despite his laid-back style and ability to play the system, was more of a Leninist. He wanted to organize the most advanced elements to confront the system and prepare them to take over positions of power in the institution.

The lines of responsibility between Alok's and Hari's positions were blurred, both in common perceptions and on paper. Administrators on the curriculum side tended to be sensitive about anything that appeared to be interference in curriculum matters by the Equal Opportunity Office. According to Alok, one of the superintendents of curriculum, for instance, was "very territorial" and on a number of occasions complained to the director about race relations activities. The ambiguity in roles encouraged a "mischievous gossip culture" in the Curriculum Division. The fuzzy organizational division of labour seemed designed to pit the two advisors against each other. But despite their differences in approach, the two men shared a solid commitment to transforming the education system. Sometimes the ambiguity could even be useful. In the curious world of the Board hierarchy Alok reported directly to the associate director, but Hari reported to a superintendent who reported to the chief superintendent of curriculum who then reported to the associate director. For Hari, getting permission and money to do anything took some time. "Often when I wanted to get something done, and didn't have the money or permission to do it," Hari said, "I would ask Alok, who always complied. It wasn't strictly by the book."

I too was learning to take a more pragmatic approach in my work. If I had initially understood anti-racist work as a potentially subversive activity, I had come to admit that the prospects for fundamental change were becoming more and more dim. All the frantic "party-building" activity of the late 1970s and early 1980s had come to naught as the Marxist-Leninist left in Canada imploded and the remaining fragments drowned themselves in ever more arcane sectarian infighting. The Vietnam War was now a distant memory, and the apparently crucial issues of the Cultural Revolution appeared increasingly irrelevant as a more complete picture of its abuses, manipulations, and careerism were revealed. In the 1970s I had been inspired by *Fanshen*, William Hinton's first-hand account of the revolution in a Chinese village just after liberation, but his publication of *Shenfan*, a follow-up account of the factional twists and turns of the Cultural Revolution in the same village, was more than sobering.

Rather than as a means to an end, I began to see anti-racist work as an end in itself. If, as it appeared, we weren't contributing to the revolution, at least we might be able to make the system less abusive to marginalized groups. Maybe institutional change was more than just "bombard the headquarters." Certainly, although difficult in themselves, incremental changes in the education system now seemed more feasible than a total reshaping of society's power relations.

## Community Work

As Alok and Hari jockeyed to press the system wherever they could find openings, the School Community Relations Department was continuing to educate, involve, and mobilize parent and community groups. It worked, for instance, with parents in the Korean and Vietnamese communities, building knowledge of the Toronto school system and of the struggles taking place against racism. Its interpretation and translation budget went up to almost a million dollars, according to Charlie Novogrodsky, and the department was part of the city's general success story in work on settling and integrating newcomers. "We had people coming from England and Australia to watch us work with immigrant communities," Charlie said. "We developed a real craft around running such meetings." The work of the SCR Department was far from non-controversial, though. Its campaigns for heritage language integrating and against streaming had seriously ruffled the feathers of conservative principals and administrators. The right-wing at the Board saw it as a Trojan Horse promoting the partisan politics of the left. The municipal election of late 1985 was to dramatically change the balance of forces in the institution and challenge the impetus of the movements for educational change.

Chapter 6

# Backlash and Response

IN THE TORONTO BOARD ELECTION OF 1985 right-wing candidates, cheered on by *The Toronto Sun*, were triumphant by a narrow margin, ending a decade of progressive leadership at the Board. Both the new chair, Anne Vanstone, and vice-chair, Nola Crewe, were openly hostile to initiatives associated with the NDP and aimed their guns at the SCR Department.

The resurgent right-wing had the support of much of the educational establishment, including principals, who, according to Alok Mukherjee, saw the SCR Department as "their biggest enemy and a major cause of trouble in their schools." At the first Board meeting of the year Crewe asked for a report on the department. Charlie Novogrodsky duly submitted an "Establishment Review Report" in March, highlighting some of the department's successful campaigns, including the preservation of adequate classroom staffing and the winning of amendments to Bill 127, worth $1.5 million annually to the Board. The report cited research illustrating the link between parent involvement and student achievement. Some eighty pages of appendices illustrated the staff's work with dozens of parent groups on issues such as school funding, curriculum implementation, streaming, and heritage languages.

At a series of hearings and special Board meetings, parents and community groups packed the boardrooms to support the department. Nevertheless, at a Board meeting on April 14, by a majority vote, the co-ordinator and all four SCR officer positions were terminated. Although Charlie and several of the others launched ultimately successful wrongful dismissal suits, the department was dismantled.

With no co-ordinator or officers to report to, the department's community workers were left in administrative limbo. Those who stayed on the job were eventually reclassified as school community advisors (SCA), reporting directly to individual school superintendents. The support for independent oppositional community organizing was gone in the blink of an eye.

Alok saw it as the beginning of the loss of momentum of the race relations effort. "By then there were different groups active within the Board so that anti-racist work was not entirely dependent on community pressure. But there was a danger in that. As long as those internal groups remained vocal, things would be okay. But what would happen if they didn't? I think eventually the inside people got promoted and shut up, and when that happened, and the outside pressure had disappeared, there was nothing left." Still, according to Hari Lalla, not all was lost. Although the school community advisors "lost political flexibility," he said, they now "became more integrated with other educators, like the consultants in the area offices, and were able to work more closely with them." The SCAs, he said, became more of "an in-group" rather than being "an outsider group" as before.

Clearly, the loss of the SCR Department had a strong impact on anti-racist projects, particularly as many of the parents who had been mobilized around race relations issues drifted away and as progressive voices in immigrant communities were replaced by more conservative and insular forces. The department "had unusual levels of skill to reach and educate new communities," Charlie Novogrodsky said. "Not to have us there to help educate, mobilize, train and identify people who would be a more equitable voice was a big loss." The loss had a ripple effect on other equity issues such as homophobia and women's rights.

## Biting Back

In the spring of 1986 the right-wing Board members took aim at yet another subversive conspiracy masquerading as education: the plans for a fourth Anti-Apartheid Conference, scheduled to be held during the 1986-87 school year. At the May Board meeting, a recommendation from the Race Relations Committee to hold the conference was defeated. Instead, trustee Ron Marks moved to hold a conference on "Civil Rights in Africa."

The campaign against the conference had been stirred up by a letter that had arrived from the South African Ambassador complaining about the Anti-Apartheid Conference, and not surprisingly the arguments made by the right-wing trustees coincided with those being promoted by apologists for the racist South African regime at the time. Marks cited "tragic" human rights abuses in independent African states with Black majority governments, and the intervention of Cuba and the Soviet Union in neighbouring Angola. "South African racism has to be placed in an African perspective," he argued. "Having done that and having looked at racism in a continental African context, I would submit that the year after that we look at another continent, because there is certainly lots of racism to deal with around the world."[1]

Vice-chair Nola Crewe proposed that as a case study for understanding violations of human rights, South Africa was not a good example. "It happens to be the very light-skinned tribe against the very dark-skinned tribe and that makes it very simplistic and easy to look at. And it's very easy to say, you know, that's what racism is, it's whites against blacks."[2]

This time, though, the right had overreached itself. Support for the anti-apartheid movement had become a worldwide phenomenon, and Toronto was hosting a major Arts Against Apartheid festival. The day after the cancellation was announced, Bishop Desmond Tutu of South Africa was addressing the Ontario Legislature. The NDP trustees immediately issued a press release declaring the cancellation of the conference an "outrageous action" and a "devastating blow to the Board's long-standing policy of opposition to Apartheid." Students, parents, and teachers involved in the conference planning committee quickly began to contact the substantial list of supporters of the arts festival.

A letter to the Board from Professor John Saul of York University demolished the right-wing arguments.

> We are faced in South Africa with virtually the only regime in the world which premises its political system on unabashed and unapologetic institutionalized racism. . . . It is this fact which, quite correctly, has made South Africa a target of virtually unanimous world opprobrium. It is this fact which also makes the issue of apartheid a particularly appropriate one for our young people. . . . In focusing on a society in which white racism has, literally run amok, they can also learn something important about the urgency of the fight against racism in our own multi-racial society.

Youth Against Apartheid, a group formed by activist students from the conferences and anti-racism camps, became a key player in the campaign. The group collected thousands of signatures in support of the conference, including those of Bishop Tutu, Harry Belafonte, and Stephen Lewis. An ad hoc coalition called on community members to appear at a School Programs Committee meeting scheduled for June 16.[3] Nearly sixty people registered as deputants. Youth Against Apartheid took over the Board lobby. Senior officials advised trustees to move to the main boardroom to accommodate the raucous crowd. Supporters of the conference demanded that the Board reopen the motion. The number of speakers to the motion was so great that the meeting continued until midnight – with still a long lineup of speakers waiting – at which time chair Anne Vanstone moved that the meeting would be adjourned. Vanstone made a remark about the many young people in the room and that "they all must be tired because it was so late." The participants protested. One young woman stood up and said, "This lady wants to send us home. Are we tired?" The crowd yelled "No," and the chair had to continue the meeting. The committee voted to ask the Board to reopen the question of the conference.[4]

*The Toronto Sun* put a right-wing spin on the fracas, claiming that Marks and Crewe were only trying to "expand" the conference and that they had been "jeered and cursed" by angry members of Youth Against Apartheid. The article said that Crewe stated that she "felt physically threatened" and that Marks described the meeting as "politics by intimidation." A few days later, *Sun* columnist Judi McLeod characterized the meeting as "Terrorist Tactics."[5]

The next morning on the CBC's popular radio program *Metro Morning*, when he squared off against Youth Against Apartheid's Liz Gold, trustee Marks was already backpedalling. "Well, there will still be a conference on apartheid, that will still be discussed. It is simply a matter of bringing in lots of other civil liberties abuses in Africa, so that people will begin to realize that racism is bigger than simply one country."[6] Pressure continued to build over the following week, and on June 26, at the full Board meeting, the motion to cancel the anti-apartheid conference was rescinded.

The dramatic about-face on the conference proved to be a turning point in the right-wing bloc's campaign against the Board's NDP legacy. The Labour Education Committee, which the right-wing trustees had planned to disband, was merely suspended. It took over a year to kill off a peace education movement and its Thinking and Deciding in a Nuclear Age Committee, which was closely linked to the city-wide Parents for Peace group.[7] Throughout the fall of 1986 and spring of 1987 several initiatives begun under the NDP were approved. A new Modern Languages Department was created to encourage and monitor the expansion of third-language credit courses in secondary schools. Saturday-morning credit classes in Korean, Cantonese, Mandarin, and Greek were renewed, and consultations to integrate heritage languages were initiated in six more elementary schools.

The Board also gave the go-ahead for a second student conference that I was organizing on redress for Japanese Canadians interned during World War II. Funds were allocated to ensure that all school libraries contained literature and materials about racial and ethnic minorities. The Equal Opportunity Office was authorized to collect information on the racial, ethnic, and gender composition of the Board's workforce every three years. The positions that Hari and I held were both renewed. Finally, when the report on the Fourth Anti-Apartheid Conference was received at the Board the following September, trustee Olivia Chow successfully moved that the conference continue to be held annually "until there has been significant progress in the dismantling of apartheid."

## Homophobia

The Arts Against Apartheid Festival was not only instrumental in saving the Board's anti-apartheid conference, but also an opportunity to reassert the "expansive" notion of anti-racist struggle.

I had been compiling the international news shorts for *The Body Politic* early in 1985 when I came across an enigmatic, one-paragraph article in a Scottish gay paper that referred to a gay anti-apartheid activist being held in prison in South Africa. When I phoned friends in Johannesburg, I found out that Simon Nkodi[8] and twenty-one other members of the United Democratic Front were being tried for treason as a result of their political activities. If convicted, they potentially faced the death penalty. In prison Simon had decided to come out and publicly speak about the similarities in the prejudice and discrimination faced by South Africa's Black majority and its lesbian and gay minorities. The case had been completely ignored by South Africa's white gay media.

Within months Simon was corresponding with me from his prison cell. A number of us formed the Simon Nkodi Anti-Apartheid Committee (SNAAC). During the Arts Against Apartheid Festival we organized a cultural evening to raise awareness about Simon's case. Unfortunately, the festival organizers did not quite know what to do with us and "forgot" to mention our event in the official list of activities. Still, our banner proclaiming "Lesbians and Gays Against Apartheid" took its legitimate place with other anti-apartheid organizations at the front of the Festival's huge march.

After the defeat of the proposal for a Gay Liaison Committee in 1981, the gay and lesbian community had withdrawn to lick its wounds. Other issues such as defending those arrested in the bath raids, lobbying for the inclusion of sexual orientation in the Human Rights Code, and the growing AIDS epidemic seemed more pressing to community activists.

In spring 1985 Kenneth Zeller, an elementary school librarian, was murdered by a group of queer-bashing high-school students. Later, at their trial, the boys' defence attorney described them as "average, normal kids" – raising the question of what was going on in schools that would lead "average normal kids" to stalk and kill a gay man in a park. Not long afterwards, Western Technical-Commercial School, which those boys had been attending, asked me to come in to talk to some students. The issue was racial name-calling in a particular class. The teacher had tried everything he could think of to address the issue, but to no avail.

I began by asking the students to list the derogatory names they had heard – a throwback to the "name-calling" sessions we did at Camp Kandalore. We went on to talk about the origins of the terms and the stereotypes they conjured up, the long-term impact on individuals, and the potential for escalation of conflict between groups. Things went well; the students seemed focused on the issues. At the end of the session a young Black man stood up to thank me for coming in. He said he thought everybody understood what I was getting at. "We thought it was just funny but it's really a lot more serious. Personally I'm not going to use those kinds of words any more. Even if people don't admit it, they can really hurt." As an afterthought he added, "But what about the queers? That's different isn't it? We can still call people queer, can't we?"

Taken aback, I stammered something about there being similarities between name-calling that was racist and name-calling that attacked gays. The bell rang just then, the class ended, and I went away thinking that if a thoughtful, bright kid could come to that kind of conclusion at the end of one of my workshops, it was time for me to seriously reconsider what I was doing. I was growing impatient with the education system's reluctance to deal with the issue of homophobia. If a Black South African man considered the issue important enough to speak out about from jail, in the midst of his people's titanic struggle against apartheid, why did gay and lesbian kids have to suffer in silence in Toronto?

Trustee Olivia Chow's downtown ward included much of Toronto's "gay ghetto." In response to the Zeller murder she began an ad hoc investigation of homophobia in the school system, concluding that "considerable abuse" towards those suspected of being gay was taking place unchecked in Toronto schools. Her concerns echoed those of Mary Templin, president of the local district of the OSSTF, who called on the Board to "investigate the possibility of implementing programs that would sensitize students to the basic human rights of homosexuals in our society and counteract the homophobia which is found in their overall social environment." In April 1986 Olivia tabled a report calling for the inclusion of discussion about sexual orientation in sex education classes, the establishment of counselling services for lesbian and gay youth, the development of curriculum materials, in-service training programs for all teachers, and prohibition of discrimination on the grounds of sexual orientation in the Board's anti-discrimination policy.

After considerable discussion and many amendments to amendments, the Board adopted Olivia Chow's report – except for the inclusion of sexual orientation in the Board's anti-discrimination statement. Even the unprovoked murder of a respected staff member could not convince the right-wing-dominated Board to go that far. That notwithstanding, a reluctant Board bureaucracy began to consider recommendations for a counselling program for gay and lesbian youth and a new curriculum document on sexual orientation for secondary school physical education teachers.

The profile of lesbian and gay issues was changing. By the end of 1986, after a long public struggle, sexual orientation was finally added to the Ontario Human Rights Code. Through my work in the schools and the community I found myself in touch with more gay and lesbian youth. I began reading material from the United States that outlined the impact of homophobia, from depression and dropping out to drug abuse and suicide. But although we received more and more requests for workshops around homophobia from alternative schools, most mainstream schools still seemed oblivious to the issue.

## Identifying Bias

The destruction of the SCR Department was a serious blow, but the lesson of the anti-apartheid conference was that a strong student and community response was still capable of shaking loose sufficient votes from the right-wing majority to win decisions at the Board.

The 1979 race relations report had emphasized the importance of identifying bias in curriculum material, and Hitner Starr had pointed out how little had been implemented around the issue. In fall 1986 I came up with the idea of an "Identifying Bias Contest" to encourage students to identify biased material in their schools on the basis of race, culture, religion, sex, sexual orientation, age, handicap, or class. What better way to involve students in the implementation of the policy?

Alok took a flyer announcing the contest to Halford for approval and got permission to send it out. Copies went to English teachers across the system, asking them to distribute it to students. A cover letter to teachers clarified that winners would be chosen based on the quality of their analysis. The letter encouraged teachers to use the contest as the basis for class projects, and it invited them or individual students to contact the Equal Opportunity Office if they wanted background material.

Although Hari warned us that we could expect some resistance, neither Alok nor I was ready for the reaction that the contest quickly provoked. The Office was deluged with angry letters and calls.

"This exercise puts me in mind of people who wish to ban books and justify their position by pointing out a few passages from a book which they have not read in its entirety."

"As a teacher-librarian, I am appalled at the implication of turning students into 'thought police.' I believe that all responsible educators must oppose prejudice but not by such means. They are totally unacceptable to me. Surely context and culture, time and place must be considered when reading any material. Are The Bible, Shakespeare, Twain and many other culturally significant writings to thus be targeted for bias by these latter-day Savonarolas?"

"I have received numerous telephone calls from secondary school teachers who are affronted by this extraordinary method of removing biased materials from our schools. The attitude of these callers has been extreme anger that students should be encouraged by a prize (especially a monetary prize) to seek out biased material. Several teachers have asked if they should start by removing The Holy Bible from their shelves."

Confronted with the overwhelming opposition from teachers, librarians, and the Curriculum Department, the director ordered that the contest be scrapped. It seemed that only teachers were qualified to identify bias – not the Equal Opportunity Office and certainly not students. The contest had touched a nerve because it challenged an educational culture based on teacher expertise. It would empower students to begin to do the work that the system was failing to do.

We were more successful in the next skirmish, which took place the following spring.

In 1985 one of the last legacies of the Trudeau era, the Canadian Charter of Rights and Freedoms, came into effect. In the midst of the neo-conservatism of the Mulroney years, the Charter provided legal backing for an understanding of the commonalities among different minority struggles and a broader interpretation of rights. Alok and Gail Posen were sent to a national conference on the Charter, and together with the Curriculum Department they organized a conference for Board staff to explain the impact of equality rights on the education system. That October 1986 staff conference, though generally well received, ran aground on the shoals of the new identity politics that was becoming increasingly important by the mid-1980s. In an embarrassing oversight, the conference panel had four white women and no people of colour, and the organizers came under justified criticism.

When Hari Lalla took on responsibility for organizing a follow-up conference for students, issues of representation were fresh in everyone's mind. The planning committee agreed that the day should begin with a panel to talk about the issues facing key equality-seeking groups. To avoid the kind of criticism that had emerged at the teachers' conference, I argued that all the opening panellists needed to be members of groups protected by the Ontario Human Rights Code. The planning committee, made up of teacher reps and volunteers from Curriculum, agreed. It appeared that only I remembered what the rest of the committee had apparently forgotten: that members of one of the equality-seeking groups, the gay community, had been expressly forbidden to address students by the 1981 Board policy prohibiting the "proselytization of homosexuality." My strategy was to have the committee challenge that policy.

When the Curriculum superintendent in charge of the conference heard about the proposal to invite a gay speaker, he immediately told the committee that the plan was unacceptable. To my surprise and dismay, the committee, despite past rhetoric about human rights, agreed to withdraw the invitation. When I confronted them, they all expressed their personal support for the rights of gay people, but were still not willing to buck the bureaucracy. Policy was policy. That was a matter for trustees. I decided to resign from the planning process.

As it turned out, Alok had scheduled a luncheon date with the conference's keynote speaker, Mark Nakamura of the Ontario Human Rights Commission. The Ontario Human Rights Code had been amended six months before to include sexual orientation, and Nakamura agreed that he could scarcely open a conference that was openly discriminating against one of the designated groups he was charged to protect. He informed the Board that unless the decision was reversed, he would have to withdraw.

In the meantime I apprised Lesbian/Gay Youth Toronto of the situation, and they prepared to set up a picket line and contact the media. The Board's showcase conference to highlight its commitment to human rights was shaping up to be a public relations disaster. At the last minute, the associate director intervened, issuing a memo "clarifying" Board policy. He asserted that the proselytization clause was never intended to ban gay speakers; the policy only required a teacher to be present to supervise activities. The position amounted to a complete reversal of practice. The day of the conference, John Argue, who had spearheaded the unsuccessful attempt to set up a Gay Liaison Committee in 1981, took the stage to address more than three hundred students, recounting his struggles as a gay youth in high school. He was warmly received. With the associate director's memo on file, the six-year ban on gay community speakers was effectively over.

## Committee on the Education of Black Students

In June 1987 the Board received a draft of the "Report on the Education of Black Students." The document illustrated the changes that had taken place since the 1985 election – the shift in the balance of power away from community activism and the reassertion of the traditional paradigms of the entrenched educational bureaucracy.

The process had begun promisingly enough. Representatives of OPBC had met with the associate director in November 1985, just before the elections, to forcefully raise once again the litany of complaints about what was happening to many Black students in Toronto schools. Several months later, Keren Brathwaite was attending one of the regular meetings of the HELACON committee as the Black parent representative. After hearing yet another report emphasizing the continuing problems that Black students were disclosing to their heritage teachers, Brathwaite proposed a comprehensive study on the education of Black students in Toronto schools. The committee unanimously passed her motion.

When HELACON brought its motion to the Board in March 1986, it reminded trustees of concerns expressed by Black parents as far back as 1975 and cited the results of repeated Grade 9 student surveys, which showed that almost a third of Black students were registered in lower level programs, a higher percentage than for any other racial group except for students of Native Canadian ancestry. It pointed out that a 1982 study showed that a third of Black students were placed in Special Education classes. This was not simply a matter of the transitional difficulties faced by new immigrants. The draft report pointed out, "While the majority of Grade 8 students who identified themselves as Blacks in 1982 were not born in Canada,

34.6% were born here and appear to be subject to the same concerns as immigrant students."[9] The Board agreed to set up a consultative committee on the education of Black students.

From an anti-racist perspective, the failure of the educational system to meet the needs of Black students was a demonstration of institutional racism. But an education system that had just shifted decisively to the right was not about to take responsibility for the difficulties faced by Black students or for the resulting racist stereotypes associating Black youth with school failure.

The makeup of the Consultative Committee on the Education of Black Students in Toronto Schools was the first indication of how things would turn out. The committee consisted of fourteen Board staff, including principals' association and teachers' federation representatives, two trustees, but only four parent representatives, and no students. It was hardly a committee that would provide a solid platform for parent or student concerns. While most of the Board staff on the committee were ostensibly sympathetic to the complaints of the OPBC, they were also acutely aware of the organizational and political context in which they were operating. The system's reaction to the Hitner Starr report was still fresh in everyone's mind, as was the outcome of the "confrontational" tactics of the SCR Department.

The committee was headed by superintendent Ouida Wright. The only Black person at a superintendent's level in the Curriculum Division, Wright had risen rapidly in the system through a combination of hard work and a devoted allegiance to the institution's point of view. She was, according to Barb Thomas, "a complex character." At an early superintendents workshop about the race relations policy, in the midst of a discussion about how racism plays out in everyday life, Ouida Wright had remarked, "I've never experienced racism in my whole life." Not surprisingly, Wright was often given responsibility for controversial issues, especially those touching on questions of racism or discrimination. She would get the work done and could be counted on not to rock the boat in the process. From the left-wing point of view, it was more difficult to criticize the results when they were the responsibility of a Black woman.

According to Alok, the issues that came up in the work of the committee were "quite a revelation to Ouida." Still, the draft report – written entirely by Ouida Wright – was masterful in "not getting backs up." It asserted that the Board had done its best "to provide effective education opportunities for all its students." To achieve that goal it had "expended an enormous amount of time, effort and money to investigate and respond to parental concerns by developing and implementing procedures and programs."[10] Incredibly, the concept of institutional racism did not appear in the report.

After it had put past Board performance in the best possible light, the draft report went on to deal with concerns raised by the parents, but consistently described their ideas and observations as "views," "feelings," or "perceptions" as opposed to facts. Of the report's thirteen recommendations around streaming, seven concerned strategies for providing better information to parents to help establish the necessary "partnership between home and school." The others called on teachers and principals to review and scrutinize present evaluation and guidance procedures. Such reviews, conducted by the very people who had traditionally been in charge of such procedures and who accepted them as neutral and unbiased, were unlikely to produce substantive change. The report did not call for any significant changes to the Identification, Placement and Review Committee (IPRC)[11] procedures, which so often resulted in the placement of Black children in special education classes. Instead principals and local school teams were asked "to find ways of creating *a more reassuring experience for parents* and develop and implement procedures to address the parents' concerns."[12]

Recommendations on the Board's Employment Equity Policy called for a review of the policies and asked administrators to make an effort "to provide students with Black role models by calling on the human resources within the Board." They stopped well short of suggesting the kind of affirmative action programs that were already in place for women.

The final section on "Curriculum Issues and Black Cultural Studies" was slightly more substantial, at least in the number of recommendations offered. The Modern Languages Department was asked to review the Black cultural studies courses, and schools were asked to review their curriculums "to determine the degree to which the cultural backgrounds of the students in Toronto are integrated . . . and take the necessary corrective steps."[13] The report also asked secondary schools "having a significant number of Black students" to consider offering an optional Black studies credit course. The Curriculum Division was asked to develop suggestions for teachers on how to include Black studies at all grade levels, and Library Services was asked to provide lists of books reflecting the Black experience.

The committee's most innovative element was to set in place student consultations initiated by school community advisor Ian Jeffers. Despite resistance from some principals, who complained that they were unable to identify which of their students were Black, two hundred Black youth from secondary and elementary schools across the system met for consultations with experienced Black facilitators leading small focus groups. Similar focus groups were organized for smaller numbers of recent graduates and dropouts. Unfortunately the concerns of the students – stereotyping, patronizing or unfair treatment, racist comments, Black invisibility in curriculum, unsympathetic guidance counsellors, insensitivity to their cultures, and intolerance of the use of West Indian English – were relegated to an appendix in the committee's report.

Ouida Wright concluded, "The parents' concerns speak for themselves.

Politely, but insistently, the parents are saying, 'Despite the Board's policies, despite the considerable efforts of some Board staff, our children are hurting. Please do something. Help us to help you to help them.' "[14]

From Alok's perspective, the major thing that came out of the draft report was the annual Black Student Conference, inspired by the experience of the student consultations. The Board also started sending more teachers to the National Alliance of Black School Educators' Conferences in the United States. Keren Brathwaite saw the report as an "important step" and "the most specific report about Black students after generations of complaints from the parents' communities." Pat Case was more blunt in his assessment of the report: "I thought it was a waste of time." For him the report failed to "grapple with the issues." While it spoke out against streaming, its recommendations did little or nothing to deal with the systems that caused the problems. The report avoided questions of power and decision-making. It avoided issues of employment.

The Board's top administration dragged its feet on implementation of the recommendations. According to Keren Brathwaite, many administrators were "suspicious of the whole effort." From her point of view, the need for different approaches for different groups, depending on history, current position, or what wrongs needed to be made right, was never sufficiently understood. After years of effort, she said, the Board had still "not delivered to Aboriginal People. That is a disgrace. I'm surprised at their patience. Similarly it has not delivered to African Canadians."

## Taking Stock: Anti-Racism in One School

These experiences made me begin to think more about the interaction between the major players involved in anti-racist institutional change. The original race relations policy had overcome resistance in the schools because of a strong alliance between communities and a majority of trustees, and at least passive acquiescence by the central administration. The student camp program could also weather opposition in the schools because of community, trustee, and central administration support.

Although the SCR Department had functioned successfully for more than a decade, with a weakened community and parent movement, hostile school principals, an indifferent central bureaucracy, and the loss of the progressive majority on the Board, it was doomed. The Anti-Apartheid Conference, with strong support from the community, the schools, and the central administration, was able to overcome even trustee opposition. Without an independent power base outside the system, however, an initiative such as the Bias Contest didn't stand a snowball's chance in hell when faced with strong opposition from the schools and the Curriculum Division. In the case of the Equality Rights Conference, changes in human rights law and the threat of bad publicity were enough to convince the system to "reinterpret" its policy. The Black students' report seemed an example of the bureaucracy's ability to domesticate criticism and let a community blow off steam, while ensuring that the broader system and its now conservative political masters were not antagonized.

A growing appreciation of the complexity of institutional transformation convinced Alok Mukherjee that a new approach was necessary. He saw a need to break away from what "had essentially been a scattergun approach" – and instead turn the focus onto one school alone, using that school "to demonstrate what a systematic anti-racist approach would look like in terms of curriculum, community interaction, staffing, and all the rest of it."

For a pilot project his team chose Lord Dufferin, an elementary school located in a predominantly low-income, working-class community in downtown Toronto. Half the school's students were born outside Canada, and just less than a third spoke a language other than English at home. More than half of the school population were students of colour. While the teaching staff was predominantly white, nine of the forty-five were people of colour, as were three of the fourteen educational assistants: a much higher percentage than the 7 per cent employment rate for people of colour across the Board as a whole. Although the administration was exclusively white, the principal and several teachers were members of the Committee of Anti-Racist Educators, and the school superintendent was supportive.

The school was also an "inner-city project school," which meant that the Board was already providing extra resources to assist regular teachers with enriched language and math programs. Alok provided additional money for anti-racist resources and hired Barb Thomas to work as consultant for one day a week over the 1986–87 school year. Barb's role would be to facilitate teacher groups, be a resource for classroom teachers, help develop an anti-racist school plan, and make herself available for professional development and training.

When she arrived in September, Barb found that her first task was to get the rest of the staff onside. Although the principal and a core activist group had committed the school to the project, the staff as a whole had not been privy to the decision. Many saw the project as being imposed, and distrusted an outside consultant. They worried that it would involve additional burdens beyond the "real" mandate of teachers. Others believed that racism had already been adequately dealt with in previous school workshops, and that further work was irrelevant in a school in which "racial incidents" were rare.

Only twenty-three of the school's sixty-five office and teaching staff attended an initial introductory after-school workshop, and most of the teachers of colour stayed away. According to Barb, the teachers of colour in particular "had been through years of this shit. They were not going to make themselves vulnerable, and then find themselves asked to carry most of the weight and then finally maybe be punished for doing it."

At that first workshop Barb began with a clarification of why the school had been chosen, to allay fears that Lord Dufferin was considered especially racist. The group then began to look at why and how racism was an issue in the school. Through discussion, and responses to a checklist on anti-racist education practices, the teachers identified a number of issues – learning materials had never been assessed for racial, class, or gender bias, guidelines for the selection of new resources were far from clear, and assistance was needed in recognizing, confronting, and talking frankly with students about racism.

Perhaps the most touchy issue that emerged in that initial workshop was assessment and placement. In a school with a large new-immigrant population, testing was administered in English only. There were also no reliable statistics on student representation in different programs on the basis of race or gender. Although 30 per cent of the students moved into basic-level programs in secondary school, no one knew what proportion of these belonged to different racial groups. Some pieces of the puzzle were obvious: a much higher percentage of Asian students were registered in the gifted program, and Asian children received most of the prizes on Awards Night.

The teachers were prepared to acknowledge that in general anti-racist concerns were considered additional and often marginal to the "regular business" of the institution. Barb's report noted, "Anti-racist skills, knowledge and experience are not valued commodities. Structurally, this is reflected in the absence of any consideration of these in informal or formal teacher performance reviews. Nor are these skills and knowledge valued elsewhere in the Board in hiring or promotion."[15]

As an inner-city project school, Lord Dufferin did have a developing tradition of teamwork; but most teachers expressed complaints about the fragmentation of the school day, a lack of time for professional development, isolation in their classrooms, and overwhelming policy directives from the Board and the Ministry. Participation of minority parents in the parent-teacher association was low despite a few efforts to provide interpreters. Written communication to parents was primarily in English, a language that many parents were unable to understand. PTA meetings, not surprisingly, were dominated by more middle-class parents.

The meeting also heard about how there had been a decline in racial name-calling among students since the school had taken a firmer stance on racial incidents; but non-Asian students continued to mimic Asian students' languages, made disparaging comments about their food, and generally considered them "teachers' pets." Aboriginal students often denied their backgrounds.

By the end of this initial three-hour workshop, eight teachers had agreed to take release time to develop a plan for future work based on the key issues. As time went on, this group increasingly took responsibility for organizing weekly noon-hour workshops on different themes. Some thirty-five such workshops were held over the course of the year. Attendance at the sessions continued to grow as time went on.

A key turning point in building a more collegial environment – one supportive of learning and making mistakes – took place in November, when an experienced Grade 4 teacher described a "disaster" that had happened the day before. She had introduced her class to material suggested by Barb: two poems written by Black children about racism. The exercise had produced obvious discomfort among her Black students. Barb's response was that she herself had also had her share of awkward experiences over the years and could only try to learn something from them each time they happened. The conversation turned to how to do anti-racist work without putting children on the spot. Another teacher said that it was important to work through discomfort. Someone added that minority kids were already experiencing racism, even if they were not used to dealing with such issues in class. The frank discussion helped to give courage to teachers who were more timid about taking risks.

The program continued over the following months. Teachers began to talk more freely about ways of handling problematic materials or interactions; the school's monthly newsletter carried a regular column on the issues being raised; the school community advisors worked at building community links. In December an Anti-Racist Pilot Committee was set up to plan activities for the rest of the school year. The nine-member committee included representatives from each of the school's three divisions, the librarian, the principal, the school's race relations rep, and a member of the inner-city project team.

By February the staff was ready to take on more contentious issues. A debate was held on whether *The Five Chinese Brothers* should be withdrawn from use. The children's book, written by a white American in the 1930s, was rife with racist stereotypes. After the debate the audience of almost forty teachers voted for removal. The process sensitized the most resistant teachers to the damage that even "beloved classics" could do to children. In April, during a workshop on Asian Canadians, the school librarian talked about her childhood as a Japanese Canadian in British Columbia and her experience of internment.[16] She recalled that a teacher had quietly hugged her on the last day of school before her removal to the camp, but had said nothing in the classroom. The silence had denied her experience pubic validity. "Saying and doing nothing is doing something," she said.[17]

By the end of the year the school had purchased new toys, games, skin-colour crayons, books, and other materials, and was developing a way of evaluating library and classroom materials. The Grade 8 teachers' group had produced new curriculum units; and the Grade 7 teachers had completed units on Native People. A consensus existed that the next year's program would start with children's experiences of migration and tie that material into various courses. Two Grade 4 teachers, disturbed that non-Asian students were teasing the Chinese and Vietnamese students about their breakfasts, had developed an extensive unit on food. A group of primary teachers put together a binder of strategies for creating an anti-racist environment for younger students. A clause on racial harassment was written into the school's discipline policy. Several parents volunteered to help in classroom discussions on issues such as racism and immigration, and the job description for a new vice-principal required "experience in challenging racism in schools."

The school's library had also been transformed. The librarian had discovered new sources for resources and set up displays of books to complement the noon-hour workshop series. She read new books to groups of children and co-ordinated reading and discussion with teachers who wanted to do follow-up. She developed a program on apartheid with Grade 8 students based on their reactions to the novel *Journey to Johannesburg*.

Despite these and less tangible outcomes – a heightened awareness of what racism looked, sounded, and felt like, increased teacher confidence and skill in confronting and talking about racism with students, and greater student self-esteem – many of the indicators of inequity remained entrenched. Award recipients were still not representative of the school population, and the staff remained largely white. Many teachers were still not using the new, more inclusive materials, and a high percentage of students continued to be placed in basic-level programs.

The follow-up to the project proved disappointing. A committee with broad staff involvement had been established to guide future work, and clear outcomes for measuring progress in equity had been identified for the next year; but the promotion of the principal and several other key people set the process back. Ironically, it was the display of leadership skills during participation in the program that accounted for a number of the promotions. A strong, active parent association might have been able to sustain commitment and cushion the effect of staff turnover by working with new staff, but such independent parent activity was not forthcoming, at least in part, due to the demise of the SCR Department a year before. While extensive training and workshops had begun to transform teachers' consciousness, this new awareness still had to be encoded into the policies and procedures of the school. Without such changes, as staff turned over, the lessons of the project would slowly be lost.

Implementing anti-racism in one school had built-in limitations. Important factors such as employment equity policies that influenced staff makeup, criteria for teacher and administrative performance reviews, curriculum guidelines, assessment requirements, and long-term allocation of resources to areas related to race relations, such as language teaching or booster programs, were all system-wide, and out of the control of the individual school.

Work at Lord Dufferin by no means came to a halt at the end of the pilot project in June 1987. Individual teachers continued to try to reshape their classrooms, and several persisted in experimenting with partnerships with other staff and parents. A committee of teachers interested in anti-racist work was still meeting in the early 1990s, and the school was the site of other equity initiatives during the next decade. While the project did not succeed in creating a model anti-racist school, it both answered and raised new questions about what was required to achieve such a goal, and demonstrated the large amount of work and time necessary to change a school culture.

## Affirmative Action: The Review Continues

The Affirmative Action Review set up in 1983 continued despite the rightward shift in the Board. When the Equal Opportunity Office hired consultants to review all Board personnel policies and practices, it did so from the perspective of both affirmative action and race relations – which made some of the "white liberal feminists" uncomfortable, according to Gail Posen. One of the results of the review was the adoption of the Board's Employment Philosophy Statement in April 1987. Billed as a commitment from the Board's senior administration to ensure that working for the Board would be a "valuable and productive experience for everyone," the statement committed the Board to a number of basic principles, the first of which was human rights. It reaffirmed that the Board would work to ensure that its "workforce at all levels and at all schools and offices will reflect the diversity of the population of the City of Toronto." It asserted that equal opportunity policies would be applied throughout the Board's operations "to remove possible organizational barriers to competing on an equal basis." It restated the Board's commitment to affirmative action programs for women and the pursuit of programs and policies to realize and monitor equal employment opportunity for "different cultural and ethnic groups and visible minorities."

The principle of equal pay for work of equal value, a new provincial requirement, also came into play in Board employment. The resulting review of job descriptions had the unexpected result of increasing all our salaries in the Equal Opportunity Office when our responsibilities were compared to those of others in the institution.

The work of establishing goals and timetables for hiring women teachers to positions of responsibility was also part of the review. A portion of the task was technical: looking at factors such as labour force statistics, qualifications, rate of turnover, and the number of expected hirings. Another part was political: bringing the teachers' federations on side. The notion that the Board should go out of its way to encourage the promotion of women was anathema to a vocal group of men in the OSSTF who were used to having principalships and other administrative positions as a private male preserve. By this time, however, the OSSTF had a strong Status of Women Committee and had put time and effort into developing policies that encouraged goals and timetables for change. A motion for Federation approval passed, but not before Gail Posen received a hate letter accusing her of personally ruining the lives of men at the Board.

There were other concerns as well. Union activists were suspicious of the Employment Philosophy Statement, which they saw as akin to the "feel good, do nothing" statements used by corporations to weaken unions. The length of time it was taking to complete the review also generated criticism. Many upwardly mobile white women continued to grumble that the linking of affirmative action for women to questions of racial equality was slowing down the process.

In the last year of Gail Posen's tenure the issue came to a head at an advisory committee meeting when a number of women began questioning why Gail was working so closely with race relations instead of concentrating on the goals that were originally tied to her job as affirmative action advisor. The women questioned why the Affirmative Action Review was taking so long. "Finally," Gail said, "they asked when I was leaving." It was obvious to her that the group had planned the attack ahead of time.

When the report of the Affirmative Action Review Group finally came to the Board it pointed out that the experience of monitoring promotion for the previous three years had shown that the goal of equality appeared to be achievable "in spite of declining enrolment, extension of funding to the Separate schools and twinning of schools." It went on to say, however, that the unevenness of the record underscored "the need for the adoption of formal goals and timetables."

In April 1988 the Board officially passed its "Goals and Timetables for the Employment and Promotion of Women in the Teaching System."[18] The ten-year goal for women's representation for elementary vice-principals was 68 per cent. For elementary principals it was 64 per cent. Secondary vice-principals and principals should reach 41 per cent. Achieving these goals in practice meant that in elementary schools six out of every ten vice-principalships and five out of every ten principalships would have to be filled by women; in secondary schools, four women would have to be hired for every ten openings for vice-principal and three out of ten for principals.

The establishment of formal goals and timetables was a huge victory in the struggle for women's rights and a benchmark for what the Board needed to do for other target groups. But it also put in stark relief the Board's resistance to taking similar steps for visible minorities, an issue that was to exacerbate distrust along racial lines over the next two years.

With goals and timetables in place, Gail Posen decided that she had done as much as she could and left the Board. Contemplating her accomplishments during six years as affirmative action advisor, she reflected, "If you ask others they'll probably say the goals and timetables were the most important thing, and it was great that we developed all these policies. But it wasn't just the formal changes that were important. It was also the informal things, relationships, the growing confidence of women at the Board."

## A New Student Program Worker

Both the network of people involved in CARE and the Lord Dufferin project brought increasing numbers of elementary school teachers into the debates around anti-racism. It was inevitable that this group would begin to question why student programs to challenge racism had largely been confined to secondary schools. The problem was that as the only student program worker, I had been hired to work on the secondary camps and was already swamped with their follow-up.

It seemed unlikely that the right-wingers on the Board would be much inclined to expand the race relations program, but Alok Mukherjee, always a superb tactician, saw an opening. During 1986 and 1987 the local media had widely publicized a number of incidents of violence between students. The story was generally constructed around narratives of "Asian gangs." In response the Board struck a committee to produce a report on safety in secondary schools. As the discussions wormed their way through the system, they became the site of ideological skirmishes between the left and the right. The right, always partial to law-and-order issues, framed the problem as one of security and discipline. The left talked about root causes, alienation, and difficulties facing immigrant youth.

Alok used the discussion of safety to deftly stickhandle a proposal for a second student program worker through the relevant committees. The new worker would concentrate on younger students who were at risk of being swept into gang activity. That pleased the left, while the right could scarcely object to a program framed as part of an anti-violence initiative. The Board approved a hiring in January 1988.

As he left to conduct the interviews, I reminded Alok that the new student program worker needed to be a person of colour. He smiled enigmatically and continued to fiddle with his pipe. When he returned, he announced that Domenic Bellissimo had been selected. "He's white. He's male. He's probably straight too," I whined.

"He's Italian."

"That's still white."

"He was by far the best candidate. You'll just have to make do as best you can," Alok said.

Despite my initial misgivings, Domenic turned out to be a excellent student worker. Down to earth, funny, and charismatic, he had grown up in the multicultural west end of Toronto in a tightly knit working-class immigrant family. In his late teens he had developed a left-wing analysis through neighbourhood work against the Klan with the Committee for Racial Equality (CRE), one of the family of organizations connected to the Communist Party. We had met at that time, but I hardly remembered since we had been on opposite sides of a political divide. CRE had been pushing the slogan "Ban the Klan," while those of us with Maoist tendencies considered that revisionist – since it implied reliance on the bourgeois state – and instead proposed "Smash the Klan" as the correct slogan to mobilize the masses.

But all that was in the past. Now we were faced with the task of organizing an anti-racist camp for grades 7 and 8. Alok, Domenic Bellissimo, and I first tried modifying the Kandalore program to make it suitable for younger students, but then the Curriculum Department got involved. Its staff pointed out that we were not teachers and insisted that what we needed was a "process" to develop a truly "excellent" camp program. That didn't seem like a bad idea, and as a result we ended up inviting a group of interested elementary school teachers to what turned out to be several full days of discussions facilitated by the Staff Development Department. Months later, after much pulling of teeth, we had a cobbled-together plan that was not much different from the original program that Alok, Dom, and I had devised. I grumbled about touchy-feely process queens with too much time on their hands.

The person who made the new program happen was Marg Wells, who had been appointed acting curriculum advisor while Hari Lalla took a year's leave. Marg was a long-time teacher who had been involved in setting up Contact and The Student School, two alternative schools aimed at providing working-class students with a different educational experience. While at Student School, she attended Kandalore as an accompanying teacher, and had argued that facilitators needed to pay more attention to issues of class. She was aware that while the more middle-class kids often had the language to be able to say the right, liberal things, working-class students would sometimes get into trouble within their groups because they would say something that was racist or sounded like it might be.

But Marg's years as a secondary school teacher, Domenic's degree in social work, and my experience at Kandalore had still not prepared us for the first elementary school camp. It may have been the numbers – we had over eighty kids – but we also weren't equipped to handle their energy level, what Marg later recalled as "their waking up at 6:00 a.m. and raiding each others' cabins and that sort of thing." Younger students required different facilitating skills. Keeping them focused, making sure they paid attention, dealing with a higher level of disruptive behaviour all presented new challenges. Elementary school pupils in the two grades also had a wider range of maturity levels – especially with girls and boys. An intense argument between two facilitators also did not help matters. "It just happened that one of them was a Chinese woman and the other was Black, and their conflict embodied what was going on in the school they were working with, which had a significant Chinese and Black population," Marg said. "So the kids saw the conflict in their school being enacted in front of them."

It was a humbling experience. To me it felt like trying to herd hamsters on horseback. But although the seasoned facilitators emerged from the camp in a state of shell shock, the elementary teachers who had accompanied us were ecstatic. Domenic dove into follow-up work with the participating schools, and we began the long process of transforming the program to meet younger students' needs based on experience rather than theory. As Marg pointed out, "With equity work in general, you can't refine it until you do it. That first experience probably made future experiences with the Grade 7 and 8 that much better." Correct ideas came from practice and practice alone.

The metaphor that I was using at the time to describe the experience of facilitating a secondary school camp was riding like a surfer on the wave of energy released by student experiences. Younger students had far fewer life experiences to draw on. With them I felt like a surfer on a calm sea. Younger students required a more directive approach from the facilitator, a role that seemed uncomfortably like that of a traditional teacher. Slowly we groped our way towards a more structured approach, a program focused on bite-sized exercises and activities. I changed my metaphors. With Grade 7 and 8 students I was no longer a surfer, I was more like a cook tending a pot. My job was to be stable, regulating the heat, measuring and adding ingredients, patiently stirring to stop it from burning or spattering out of control.

Domenic Bellissimo found that the follow-up work was also different. A first step was to try to form clubs in as many of the schools as possible. But while high-school students can be "assertive and mature enough to gather together and push for institutional change, Grade 7 and 8 students just don't have that ability," Domenic said. "Even if they had the commitment to continue to work on equity issues, younger students were just not able to do it on their own." A staff advisor, or a teacher who was willing to continue the work, was a key ingredient. Domenic also found that many of the teachers we worked with relied on us "on a year-to-year basis to keep them energized and committed and to give them the strength to challenge administration when they weren't encouraged to do it."

A second new initiative during that year was a conference on First Nations issues. Because "Indians" were part of the senior public school curriculum, the conference was also pitched at a grades 7 and 8. We had involved Aboriginal people in the planning but "didn't really know how to do a conference that would be sensitive to Native culture," Marg Wells recalled. "Here we were, these white people running this thing with our agenda, and the Native elder who was the keynote speaker was totally insulted that there would be a time limit put on him to speak, and went on and on." The auditorium was full of squirming kids, and the conference went hopelessly behind schedule. "When the students finally got into their small group workshops, there were more problems with kids asking resource people if they lived in tepees." The afternoon program ran out of time. "Instead students returned to the gymnasium to dance to a Native drumming group. It wasn't exactly a great day for the undermining of stereotypes."

## Susan McGrath

In 1988 Susan McGrath replaced Gail Posen as affirmative action advisor. Sue had grown up in the conservative small-town atmosphere of Barrie, Ontario. Her father was a doctor and her mother was a long-time feminist who grew up in a working-class family. As a teenager Sue was already reading Simone de Beauvoir and Betty Friedan. Her father died when she was seventeen, and the resulting financial struggle for her and her sister to go to university led to an interest in socialist politics. When she was hired as a librarian in the Board's reference library in 1972 she gravitated to union politics and ultimately became a member of the executive and negotiating committees of the Canadian Union of Public Employees local, which organized much of the Board's non-teaching staff. She was also one of the earliest members of the Status of Women Committee.

When she took on the job of affirmative action advisor, Sue had to give up her union activities because the advisor's position was part of management. She remained suspicious of "state feminism": "There was a lot of criticism at the time about how affirmative action positions were just stepping stones for ambitious individuals. There was also a theoretical criticism about the difficulties of reforming organizations from within, and whether employees who are paid to do that could really be effective. If the organization is no longer supportive, the staff who survive become a form of window dressing and apologists for the system."

After she got the job she was asked to take an "etiquette session." Perhaps she had sounded too aggressive or flaky at the interview, she said. "I gather that I did not speak proper 'Boardese,' and they were afraid I might upset some of the principals and superintendents with my approach." In a hierarchical and class-structured board, she said, "I always found one was expected to adopt an air of deference."

As affirmative action advisor, Sue was interested in playing a stronger role in the issues faced by the Board's non-teaching workforce. Her union experience in dealing with grievances made her keenly aware of the importance of working on complaints of sexist harassment and discrimination.

## The Proof of the Pudding: Race vs. Gender

The impact of race relations efforts on teacher attitudes and classroom atmosphere tended to be subjective and hard to measure; but the impact – or lack of impact – on the employment of visible minorities could be seen through statistical analysis. The figures clearly showed that the number of visible minorities in the Board's workforce lagged far behind their representation in the city as a whole. Using the muscle of the Race Relations Committee, Alok began to press for reports on who was applying for jobs and who was getting them. Despite the suspicions of many school administrators, the Equal Opportunity Office was finally given clearance to collect information and the race and gender makeup of the institution every three years.

A study released in 1987 showed less than encouraging results. In 1,082 staff changes in 1986 the Board had gained only 39 additional visible minority workers.[19] A second report released that same year was even more damning. It compared the rates of application for non-teaching positions by visible minority candidates to their success rates in being hired or promoted. Although the proportion of visible/racial minorities seeking appointments with the Board was consistent with estimates of visible minority populations in the Metro Toronto area (19 per cent), and although visible minority candidates tended to have higher levels of formal education and more specialist qualifications than white candidates, their rate of hiring was significantly lower than that of their white counterparts. The gap between the application rate and the success rate was even wider for external candidates than it was for those applying for promotion within the Board.[20]

Clearly the Board's various strategies – holding training sessions for principals on how to conduct bias-free interviews, advertising in ethnic media, and making statements that it was an equal opportunity employer – were not sufficient. Especially when compared to affirmative action programs for women, programs for "visible minorities" were hardly on the radar. Indeed, "affirmative action" had generally come to be understood as referring to programs concerned with encouraging the hiring and promotion of women.

Several competing explanations tried to address the question of why employment equity on the basis of race had lagged behind efforts around gender. For some, it was a simple matter of racism being more pernicious, fundamental, and widespread than sexism. The white men who controlled the system were more willing to share power with white women than with people of colour. Pat Case believed the difference had to do with family. It was easier for white men in power "to get their heads around" programs for women because they had white women in their families and the benefits were immediate in their family income. "The resistance to employment equity came from white people wondering if their children would get jobs or if [the jobs] would all be taken by visible and racial minorities."

The impetus for the Board's anti-racism efforts largely came from outside the institution – communities concerned about what was happening to their children in schools. The focus therefore tended to be on issues such as teacher attitudes, curriculum, and student assessment. Pat noted that from the outside, "It's hard to put your finger on what the problem is, other than to say it's racism, because you're not in there and you can't figure out the blockages."

Women were already inside the organization. They knew how the system worked. Workforce data was more accessible. It was relatively simple to determine how many women teachers, principals, and vice-principals there were, and to adopt an appropriate goal: that the percentage of women administrators in those positions should reflect the percentage of women teachers. For visible minorities the process of identification was much more complicated, because employees were often reluctant to identify themselves in terms of race or ethnicity. Once they were identified, should the goal be parity with the general population, with the workforce, or with the qualified workforce?

Marg Evans, a long-time Board activist around women's issues, agreed that the argument for equity was easier to make for women because white women were at least already on the inside. Achieving equity for visible minorities meant looking outside the Board and changing hiring practices, which "was a long hard struggle," Evans said. "All sorts of things were done to try to get visible minority candidates from teachers' college, but even there it wasn't easy because they weren't coming into teacher training institutions in numbers that would allow us find them."

This major discrepancy – the increasing success of white women in achieving positions of responsibility versus the abysmal results for people of colour – set the stage for a growing suspicion that would feed into the shift towards a narrow identity politics. Moreover, it would provide the fuel for yet another crisis that would shape the struggle for equity in education.

Chapter 7

# Power, Pedagogy, Curriculum

IN 1985 I WENT BACK TO SCHOOL PART-TIME to do a Masters in Education, in part because I wanted a chance to think through the meaning of anti-racist education, and in part because I wanted to puff up my credentials and credibility in the eyes of the system. Happily, the very first course I took allowed me the opportunity to begin to think through a question raised at the Committee of Anti-Racist Educators: "Is anti-racism just a slogan or a kind of pedagogy?" The professor, Garnet McDiarmid, had developed a kind of taxonomy of curriculum approaches based on three sets of variables.

*Content-focused* and *student-focused* education marked the two poles of his first axis. Traditional approaches to education tend to be content-focused. Students are seen as little more than empty vessels to be filled with pre-determined knowledge. Student-focused approaches, on the other hand, are grounded in student experience and encourage learners to explore their own worlds at their own pace and according to their own interests. Different approaches to pedagogy can be placed at different points along this axis depending on how content- or student-centred they are.

*Teacher-directed* and *student-directed* are the two poles of the second set of variables, which focuses on the role of the teacher in the educational process. Does the teacher take a directive, didactic role or a process-oriented approach that facilitates student exploration? Is the teacher's relationship to the student one of authority or partnership?

Thirdly, McDiarmid classified curriculum goals as either *instrumental* or *developmental*. An instrumental approach is aimed at teaching a particular skill; a developmental approach seeks to make the student a better, more responsible, more rounded individual.

McDiarmid characterized conservative, traditional educational approaches as highly content-based, teacher-directed, and instrumental. He characterized progressive or "liberal" approaches as being more often student-based and developmental, with teachers playing a neutral process-oriented role. Of course, using various combinations of these variables an infinite number of possible curriculum approaches are possible.

The question for me was, where does anti-racist education fit in this analysis? By the mid-1980s I had come across a number of resources that studied anti-racist educational practice. One of them was *Challenging*

*Racism*, published by the All London Teachers Against Racism and Fascism in 1984. The book was a collection of articles by teachers and educators who had been involved in radical anti-racist work in London schools before Prime Minister Margaret Thatcher dismantled the Inner London Educational Authority. Another was Enid Lee's *Letters to Marcia: A Teacher's Guide to Anti-Racist Education*, published in Toronto by the Cross Cultural Communications Centre. Lee drew on her experience as an educational consultant to sketch out the basics of anti-racist educational practice.

Although the two books had differences in terminology, Lee and the authors featured in *Challenging Racism* generally agreed on the fundamentals that Barb Thomas had outlined in her 1984 *Currents* article on the principles of anti-racist education. Racism was not "human nature." It was a structural product of the institutional framework of society. As Lee put it, "Through anti-racist education, we come to understand that it is not because individuals act on bad faith, or are inherently unwilling to be generous to other people; but rather that historical patterns and contemporary situations give us the cues as to how we ought to treat each other."[1]

The consensus of these educators was that anti-racist education, while not unconcerned with the specific content of social and historical analysis, must start from the student's reality. To be effective in changing how students thought and acted, anti-racist education had to touch both hearts and minds. Anti-racist education, then, was fundamentally but not exclusively *student-focused*.

McDiarmid's axis on the range of roles available to the teacher revealed an interesting dilemma for anti-racist educators. Student-centred approaches are usually associated with less directive, more neutral roles for teachers. But anti-racist education had particular goals for its students. It expected them to become active agents in the fight against racism. Teachers could therefore not accept all conclusions or expressions as being equally valid. A racist conclusion is not to be accepted on par with an anti-racist one, and in a society structurally permeated with racism, teachers must expect racist opinions and conclusions to be commonplace in the classroom. In order not to reproduce common racist thinking, teachers would have to take a more directive role.

In an article published in 1985, Jean Goody and Hugh Knight warned, however, that anti-racist teachers needed to be on guard against resorting to traditional teacher-student relationships. "In all these efforts to get the content right, it was sometimes forgotten that the methodology was crucially important.... For instance, some teachers may find it difficult to take a firmer line on racism without becoming more authoritarian in their approach."[2]

Anti-racist education required teachers both to reject the authoritarian power associated with traditional educational practice and to be more than a neutral manager of a process. Another anti-racist teacher, Martin Francis, proposed that teachers could resolve this paradox by relying on the self-correcting elements present among students. A class could sort through the many contradictory views expressed to weed out the views that were "prejudiced, reactionary or just plain daft" and reinforce the ones that were "generous, thoughtful open minded [and] sorted out."[3]

The anti-racist educator only reluctantly resorted to the traditional teacher's role as a source of authority and information, but had to be willing to take on such a role when racist ideas might otherwise go unchallenged. Anti-racist education therefore found itself mid-way between student and teacher-directed approaches on McDiarmid's axis.

Anti-racist education's focus on developing leadership among learners was also often described in *instrumental* terms. Lee talked about how anti-racist education provided "the skills to work collectively to combat racism"[4] – an approach that challenged McDiarmid's notion that located instrumental and developmental goals at opposite ends of a continuum: for anti-racism, skills development and personal development were inexorably linked.

For me, these conclusions – that anti-racist education needed to be strongly student-centred without neglecting content, that it called on teachers to play the role of attentive guides and facilitators rather than authority figures in most, but not all, situations, and that it attempted to overcome the polarity between instrumental and personal development – clarified some of the resistance to our efforts. Anti-racist education ran against the grain of school culture, especially the more content- and subject-oriented cultures of secondary schools, which stressed teacher authority and instrumental learning. Anti-racist education's stress on student experience rather than "book learning" had another result: it was seen as being not properly academic. It was also feared as being potentially out of control because it discouraged teachers from taking a traditional directive role. Some critics would see it as a "frill," something non-essential, because it could not demonstrate immediate utility in achieving marketable skills. Anti-racist education didn't just challenge racism in the system, it challenged the supporting educational culture on the level of its most dearly held values, its entrenched power relationships, and its conventional goals.

This critique seemed to leave three options for anti-racist education. It could continue to operate in the cracks of the institution, talking advantage of situations in which the conventional values and power relationships were not hegemonic, perhaps becoming a thorn in the side of the system but substantially abandoning real hopes of widespread systemic change. It could become part of a much broader movement for an institutional and social transformation that could challenge conventional values, power relationships, and goals within and beyond the education system. Or it could try to accommodate itself to the existing institutional culture, seeking ways of contesting racism that did not run afoul of the mainstream institutional culture. The work of the next decade would involve all three strategies and engender many debates and conflicts among their respective proponents.

I found myself opting for the first approach. The broader movements for social change that had sparked our work seemed in serious decline and unlikely to achieve major social transformation any time soon, and personally I wasn't much interested in accommodation. The Equal Opportunity Office and the camps were both within the system and on the periphery of its central processes. I contented myself with trying to develop activities within this crack in the system's hegemony.

## Race, History, and Experience

At the student camps by the mid-1980s the limitations of a purely experiential approach were becoming more evident. As we became more adept at leading a program that used participants' experiences to develop a social analysis of racism, students were raising new questions. Once they began to understand the dynamics of racism, they wanted to know where it came from. They were increasingly asking about history. We were back to the issue of "course work" that Charlie Novogrodsky had raised in his analysis of the camps years before. The history of racism was not to be teased out of the experiences of sixteen-year-olds, no matter how skilled the facilitator. That content had to be brought in from the outside.

I was reluctant to introduce a didactic element into the camp, and our first attempt to deal with racism in history took place in a follow-up session in spring 1984. Professor John Saul, whose lecture on racism at the Marxist Institute almost a decade before had opened my eyes to racism's concrete history, spoke to the students. Although he struggled gamely to pitch his material to a high-school audience, most of the lecture was clearly over their heads.

At the following camp, on the morning of the last day, I tried to do an even more schematic talk myself. I was met with blank stares. Several students took the opportunity to doze off. After three days of intense, interactive learning, most participants simply zoned out to anything resembling a lecture, never mind a lecture on history.

Clearly, if anti-racist education was to include history, we needed to figure out a way of blending history with an experiential student-centred approach. I mulled the problem over for months. Then I remembered the "principal's office" role-play, which was a regular part of the camp curriculum. The activity gave students a simulated experience of dynamics that might be unfamiliar to them. We were already using dramatic role plays to get students to understand situations outside of their direct experience. Why couldn't those techniques be applied to history?

I also began to think about "Star Power,"[5] a simulation game that Tony had shown me several years before. The game developed an economy of winners and losers and looked at the dynamics that developed between such groups. Those who were "losing" became increasingly frustrated with the game, especially after the winners, as a "reward" for their success, were allowed to make changes to the rules, which they inevitably did to favour themselves even further. Sometimes the "losers" would try to convince the rule-makers to play more fairly. At other times they would refuse to participate or begin to cheat. The "winners" would try to enforce the rules. The groups quickly developed unflattering opinions about each other's ethics, abilities, and morality. Eventually pandemonium would ensue and the game would break down.

In practice "Star Power" was a laboratory that took participants through the experience of being winners or losers in a social situation. Afterwards, in debriefing, they were able to analyze not only their own reactions and strategies, but also those of others who found themselves with or without power in other contexts. The simulation approximated class struggle, but also could apply to groups whose unequal power and success in society were associated with race, ethnicity, or other factors. "Star Power" abstracted, compressed, and simulated the experience and the dynamics of living in an inequitable society.

It occurred to me that through combining elements of simulation and role-playing we might be able to give students an experiential appreciation of the economic and historical dynamics of racism.

The final result was "World History of Racism in Minutes" (WHORM). It could be played with as few as twenty-five participants or as many as a hundred, although in especially megalomaniacal moments I dreamed of leading it in a football stadium with a cast of thousands. The game was played on a room-sized map of the world sketched out on the floor with masking tape. Participants were divided into five geographical groups: Africa, Europe, India, China, and the Americas. If time permitted a sixth area, the Middle East, could also be added. I was surprised to realize that for many students, their physical location on this map led to their first clear understanding of the geographical relationships between different parts of the world.

Using information sheets, the students produced and performed tableaux demonstrating what was happening in their part of the world at different time periods, starting with relatively egalitarian gathering and hunting societies around 30,000 BCE. The second tableau illustrated the development of agriculture and class stratification during the period 5000 BCE to 1000 CE, a long period during which peoples in all parts of the world developed relatively permanent communities with sophisticated art, architecture, philosophy, and science. The third tableau, 1000 AD to 1300, focused on trade. To simulate trade, groups traded different kinds of cookies representing their area's products. In the next section, the voyage of Columbus provided Europe with access to the riches of America, which in turn promoted European economic and military domination of the Mediterranean and Eurasian trade routes.

For the period covering 1600 to 1820, information sheets on Europe, Africa, and the Americas focused on the impact of the slave trade. The Europeans needed cheap labour to exploit the natural riches of America, and they would think up ideas to justify the enslavement of Africans. Africa, America, China, and India all experienced the effects of European expansion. The years 1820 to 1930 represented the high point of European imperialism. Europe began to gather cookies from around the world. Participants depicted how "scientific" classification systems that were developed for categorizing and ranking animals were applied to humans, and notions of white racial superiority flourished in North America and Europe, climaxing in Nazi rule in Germany. The next presentations depicted the defeat of the Nazis, the scientific discrediting of ideas of racial superiority, and the struggle against colonialism in Africa and Asia. But by this point the cookies were all in Europe and North America. The period from 1965 to the present looked at immigration to the "developed" world – as people followed their cookies – and demonstrated how racist ideas were used to exploit immigrants. In the final section, the Future, there were no information sheets. Participants produced a tableau showing the kind of world they wanted to build.

Although WHORM's historical narrative was highly schematic, participants left with several key understandings. They recognized that all human groups contributed to science, art, and philosophy. They grasped the economic and historical roots of the gross inequality of the modern world, and understood the connection between the emergence of those inequalities and the development of racist ideas used to explain and justify them. They made the connections between the anti-colonial movements in the developing world and the anti-racist struggles in developed countries. Most groups finished their vision of the future by redistributing the cookies, implicitly demonstrating that the fight against racist ideas was part of the fight against the material reality of global inequality and exploitation.

WHORM was an immediate hit at the camps after its introduction in 1986. It was refined through experience and ended up being used in teacher training and university courses, and adapted for use at the elementary level.

## Simulating History

Following the introduction of WHORM, I went on to experiment with several other issues. The "Colonialism Game," examining the dynamics of anti-colonial struggles, divided participants in two groups, colonists and Native peoples. The colonists were subdivided into a governor representing the metropolis, settlers, and missionaries. The other team, Native people, was also subdivided, into peasants, rebels, and traders. The two groups set about trying to negotiate independence for the colony. Each subgroup had slightly different interests and would win or lose differential points depending on the results of each negotiating session. Although the goal was to score points, groups were instructed to couch their arguments in terms of what was good for the country, what civilization meant, and whether or not Native people were capable of governing themselves.

Over the years I developed three other large-scale simulation activities for use at different student conferences. At several student conferences organized during the struggle for redress, we used a fictional, role-play debate around the decision to intern Japanese Canadians. A second game explored the impact of the head tax and Chinese Exclusion Act on Chinese Canadians, and we used a game on the history of South Africa modelled on WHORM at a number of anti-apartheid conferences. Although none of these activities could substitute for a thorough study of history, they bridged the gap between "book learning" and the experiential approach, giving students a direct, immediate overview of historical material that was by definition outside their personal experience.[6]

## Peer Power and New Programs

Conferences and camps were educational vehicles that we could control and experiment with, but they could never take in more than a small fraction of the students enrolled in Toronto schools. How could we reach the thousands of other students in schools who never had an opportunity to attend such activities?

Some of the smaller alternative schools had organized successful anti-discrimination days, and the Equal Opportunity Office was able to pay for a limited number of facilitators and resource people. But for larger, mainstream schools we need to come up with a different approach. Our opportunity came at Lawrence Park Collegiate, a large north-end school. The school's Kandalore group asked English teachers to assign students the task of writing a short essay about their experiences with prejudice and discrimination. After the essays were duly marked, and student names removed, the Kandalore group poured over the hundreds of stories to identify major themes and issues. From this material they produced a collection of case studies touching on topics such as interracial dating, racist jokes, various cultural attitudes to school achievement, minority religious practices, and stereotyping. These case studies became the basis for a half-day workshop delivered to the schools' intermediate students. I trained a group of more than forty senior students as facilitators, gave them practice with group facilitation, and prepared them for some of the problems that might occur. We developed a consensus on a simple program organized around discussions of the case studies.

On the day of the program, two hundred participating students were broken down into groups of fifteen to twenty-five. Teachers were instructed to keep a low profile and to allow the student facilitators to work without assistance or interference. The groups developed basic definitions of terms such as stereotype and discrimination and spent time discussing the case studies, how the people described might feel and react, and productive ways of resolving difficult situations. Midway in the morning we had a short break, serving soft drinks and cookies to help create a relaxed, informal atmosphere. The half-day ended with a discussion of Board policy and what students could do if they found they were facing discrimination.

The program worked remarkably well, exceeding everyone's expectations. The student facilitators reported that the discussions were enthusiastic, with lots of participation and a sense of the participants "helping each other get their ideas across about something that was obviously important to them." Several facilitators announced plans to become teachers.

The experience also showed the importance of having visible minority students in each group. Based on the facilitators' reports, the best groups seemed to be the ones that included minority students, who were able to speak from their own experiences. Given that Lawrence was a predominantly white school, not all groups had such representation. Students had been assigned to their groups alphabetically, which exacerbated the situation. Some groups ended up with all the "Mcs and Macs" while others had all the "Wongs." Subsequent programs made sure that each group had a range of student backgrounds.

In a few of the groups I observed, the facilitators ended up mimicking teachers and trying to exercise didactic authority. For subsequent facilitator trainings I developed a simple activity that focused on the difference between the roles of a traditional teacher and facilitator. Using a ball of yarn, we asked the students to demonstrate the communications pattern in a traditional classroom setup by passing the ball from person to person as they spoke, starting with a student playing the teacher holding the ball. As the ball unravelled it left a record of the interactions. After a few minutes of this, the "teacher" would be clutching a fan of yarn that stretched back and forth out to students sitting in rows, rather like a stagecoach driver stretching out the reins to a large team of horses. There would be few direct connections from student to student. The teacher was centred out as the source and the evaluator of knowledge.

I asked the group to consider what a teacher had to do to produce that kind of pattern, and the students invariably knew the tricks that teachers used to maintain authority and control in the classroom. I warned student facilitators that when they were under stress they had to be careful not to find themselves trying to use such tricks, acting like the teachers that they had always hated.

The second stage was to ask students to use the yarn to display the communications pattern in a group of well-functioning peers. This time, as the yarn passed randomly among students arranged in a circle, it crossed in the centre rather than always stretching back to the hands of one authority. Knowledge was being shared and produced rather than disseminated from one source. The next question was what facilitators had to do to produce that kind of pattern.

I also learned to spend time having facilitators think about when to intervene in a discussion. They realized that when the process was going well and everyone was participating, they could draw back and take a neutral role. If the discussion was unbalanced, the facilitator might gently ask questions of quieter participants. The only time it was necessary to exercise authority was if a participant was being offensively insensitive or intimidating others.

Over the next few years the model spread successfully to a number of other large schools. Northern Secondary School developed case studies for its program based on student writings around sexism, anti-Semitism, ableism, ageism, classism, and homophobia. The guidelines of an anti-racist curriculum – that it be student-based, facilitator-guided, and provide participants with skills and knowledge to effect change – applied to effective pedagogy around all these issues, although sometimes a slightly different approach was required. For example, most schools could be counted on to have students of different races, cultures, genders, and abilities to give voice to their points of view on the case studies. But if the discussion was to focus on homophobia it was necessary to bring in openly gay students from other schools to act as resource people because most gay and lesbian students found it too dangerous to come out in their schools.

Other schools developed their own versions of such "enrichment" activities. Under the leadership of English teacher Lynda Lemberg, Oakwood Collegiate Institute began holding annual "Breaking down the Barriers" activities. Originally these activities were concentrated on a specific day on which a variety of workshops were made available. As the program developed, workshops were stretched out over a week and integrated into regular classroom periods. I would train a group of students to offer generic workshops on topics of racism or sexism. We also made outside speakers available on a variety of topics; teachers could book them into their classes.

Oakwood also took seriously the notion that curriculum was the sum total of student experiences in the school. Along with many other schools, it provided a variety of ethnically and culturally based student clubs that organized a range of activities. One of the most dynamic was its Afro Canadian Club, which organized an annual system-wide Black History Month celebration and awards ceremony for all Toronto schools. At Jarvis Collegiate Institute, "Mosaic," which spotlighted the talents of the school's ESL students, eventually eclipsed the venerable downtown school's traditional student talent night, the Red White and Blue.

Another variation of these projects to raise issues of racism and discrimination was the "Student Encounter," a program that brought students together from schools in different parts of the city. The program had the advantage of ensuring diversity, which was not always the case with the mix of students at an individual school. It also corresponded with the recommendations of the Safety in Secondary Schools Report, which had called for more co-operative activities between schools to resolve interschool tensions that could lead to violence. The first Student Encounter, held May 4, 1989, involved four schools: Lawrence Park Collegiate Institute, a relatively affluent north-end school; Harbord Collegiate Institute, a downtown academic-focused school with large numbers of Asian students; Central Technical School, a working-class institution with students from a wide range of different backgrounds; and Oakwood Collegiate, with its Italian and Portuguese majority and a strong presence of students of Caribbean background. Again, students from each school were trained as facilitators, and they developed scenarios based on relevant issues in their home schools and a program for the day. For many participants, the Student Encounter was the first time that they had come together with students from other schools other than at highly charged, competitive sports matches. It remained an annual program until the ground began to shift under equity work in the mid-1990s.

## Entering the Mainstream

Most educators did not have the privilege of working in the cracks. As teachers, they were confronted with the everyday demands of curriculum, class management, and evaluation. As head of English at Humberside Collegiate Institute in the late-1980s, Nora Allingham set out to transform the English curriculum in her school, using principles of anti-racist education.

By the time she reached Humberside as English head, Nora had years of experience behind her. She had been involved in the students camps, produced curriculum documents on how to deal with bias, and had written annotated bibliographies and book reviews to help teachers expand their resources. Her work included a major document on Caribbean, Aboriginal, and African writers.

The traditional canon taught in English classes largely consisted of monocultural fiction, poetry, and drama produced by white, male (occasionally female) British, American, and Canadian authors. Sometimes openly sexist or racist, most often such material simply ignored the significant presence of women and people of colour. But changing curriculum materials was far from simple. Most staff had only studied the white Western writers, and were unfamiliar with other literature and its social and historical contexts. They were uncomfortable dealing with unfamiliar material that raised explosive issues like race and class. Administrators worried about the cost of purchasing new materials. Vocal parents wanted their children to study the important classics.

Nora Allingham's first step was choosing new materials that provided a realistic, authentic, non-patronizing, and non-exotic portrayal of its subjects. She looked for Canadian literature that included the history and experience of visible minority communities, although the theme or central focus did not necessarily have to deal overtly with racism. She was convinced that the new material could not be presented as an add-on. It needed to be legitimated by its position at the core of the curriculum.

The next step was getting teacher buy-in. Over a two-year period Nora organized a series of in-service sessions that began with rationales for multicultural literature, discussed school culture and common expressions of bigotry, analyzed institutional racism and sexism, and finally provided small-group sessions to allow teachers to work through their own responses to the new material and to develop teaching strategies, assignments, and projects for students.

By the end of the process, the new core novel for the Grade 12 course was *The Dragon Can't Dance* by Black Trinidadian author Earl Lovelace. The conventional collection of American, Canadian, and British short stories had been replaced by the work of writers from a variety of backgrounds from Canada, the United States, the Caribbean, and South Africa, including a significant representation of Aboriginal authors. Student research topics included reading related fiction, investigating the lyrics of calypsos and reggae for social and political content, researching social agencies available for immigrants and Native people, analyzing newspapers and television reporting for bias, and writing to politicians about Native issues and Canada's relationship with the apartheid government in South Africa. Teachers were encouraged to change their teaching styles and have students work in small groups and study projects whenever possible, so that the adults would not appear to be "preaching."

As time went on, Nora recorded multiple impacts from the new curriculum. With the introduction of *The Dragon Can't Dance*, two recently arrived Trinidadian students who had previous been ignored or baited by their predominantly white classmates became the resident experts on Trinidadian society and music. Their social status moved from one of marginalization to expertise and influence. Discussions of racial conflict in Trinidad led to the identification of racist attitudes and behaviors in Canada. The students organized a trip to the Caribana festival with a group of white peers who had always been afraid to go to the "Black" carnival.

After reading two novels by Chinese Americans, a Canadian-born student of Chinese ancestry talked to her mother for the first time about her family's immigration experience. The process brought them closer and allowed her to begin to develop pride in her background, which she had previously denied. An Aboriginal student reported that he had never known there were so many Native writers and decided to study Ojibway so that he too could write about the experience and teach Native children. A middle-class white student had expressed the opinion that Black people were "overreacting" to police shootings of a number of Black youth. She returned from her interviews with the editors of local Caribbean community newspapers and several parents of Black children with a new appreciation of the anger and frustration of those who faced both violent and institutional racism as a daily fact of life.

Nora's experience showed that with determination and perseverance, anti-racist change was possible, even within the confines of a traditional high school. Anti-racist education was coming out of the cracks. But the project also underscored the extent to which institutional change still hinged on the presence of individual initiative. After Nora left Humberside the work she had introduced quickly melted away. "You need somebody to keep pushing it," she said, "and there just wasn't anybody there."

## Younger Students?

The definition of anti-racist education, with its stress on student experience and activist outcomes, raised questions around what was appropriate and possible to do with younger children. Could the much more limited experience of younger students be fruitful raw material? Were the goals of anti-racist education realistic for a younger developmental level?

Traditional child development theory, particularly as influenced by the Swiss psychologist Jean Piaget, suggested that "preoperational" kids under seven couldn't really understand the nature of groups, and that more abstract social concepts like race would not be comprehensible until children were at least eleven. Similarly, kids under seven wouldn't distinguish between natural and human laws; those between seven and eleven might have a sense of justice based on treating everyone the same, but preteens would not understand the notion that, to be fair, rules might be applied differently in different situations. The notion of affirmative action to address the results of discrimination, so central to anti-racist education, would therefore probably fall on deaf ears until the "formal operational" stage was reached after age eleven, when children could move from simple egalitarianism to grasp the importance of equity. With younger kids, it might even be counterproductive to bring up the concept of injustice, since to the child's mind bad things only happened to bad people.

Luckily, however, reality bit theory. Working with U.S. children in the 1950s, Mary Ellen Goodman had found that kids were interested "in characteristics or behaviour having to do with what adults call race, nationality or religion" as young as age four. Most of her four-year-old subjects, both Black and white, showed interest in and curiosity about race distinctions. They often used racial epithets and depreciatory terms and tended to positively value whites and negatively value Black people. When she republished *Race Awareness in Young Children* in 1964, Goodman proposed that the dawning of consciousness of self and others in terms of racial identity began after age two.[7] From ages two to four, children began to learn race-related words, concepts, and values, and by seven they were establishing full-fledged race attitudes.

The publication in English of Lev Vygotsky's *Thought and Language* also challenged Piaget.[8] Vygotsky asserted that rather than the gradual widening or decentring towards an understanding of social values, children began with social values and representations and used them to interpret their own experience and to construct their knowledge of the world. In *Mind in Society*, Vygotsky proposed that what was important was what children could do with appropriate adult guidance and help. He maintained that such learning "awakens a variety of internal developmental processes that are able to operate only when the child is interacting with people in his environment and in co-operation with his peers. Once these processes are internalized, they become part of the child's independent developmental achievement."[9] Vygotsky was turning Piaget on his head. Instead of learning being limited by development, learning was dragging development along behind itself.

The debate between different models of child development spilled into the ongoing disputes between multiculturalism and anti-racism. The "foods and festivals" approach associated with multiculturalism was often justified for younger children through the argument that the developmental level of children precluded dealing with anything as abstract as social power or injustice. For multiculturalists, the problem was that the "actual content of the curriculum material used is virtually dominated by the majority culture." Multicultural education sought to change this content to include the cultural experiences of minority students to "increase the child's security, sense of belonging, and self confidence, thereby enhancing learning."[10]

Producing confidence, overcoming ethnocentricity in classroom materials, and helping children understand diversity as a norm were understandably seen as laudable; but from the anti-racist point of view, the failure to deal directly with racism and prejudice left teachers unprepared for children's inevitable expressions of racism, and left children unprepared to be critical of the messages of the broader racist society. By ignoring questions of stereotyping and discrimination, multiculturalism failed to equip minority children to face the challenges of a racist society, and it failed to help majority children deal with the seductive power that comes with being part of a dominant culture.

The U.S.-based Council for Interracial Books for Children had already gone beyond the multicultural approach in 1980. The authors of an article in one of its bulletins, while still referencing Piaget, proposed an approach in which teachers acknowledged children's observations on racial and cultural identity, helped them sort out incorrect information and generalizations, and gave corrective feedback about unfair and untrue depictions of people.[11] Suggesting that teachers utilize children's emerging moral sense to help them perceive the "unfairness"of racism, the article called on educators to give five- to eight-year-olds the tools they needed to deal with expressions of ethnocentrism and prejudice in their immediate world. By age nine, children could be taught to "differentiate between 'majority' and 'minority' perspectives" and encouraged to engage in concrete social action projects directed towards changing particular manifestations of institutional racism in their communities.[12]

If three- to five-year-olds were ready to deal with unfair and untrue depictions of people, it followed that no developmental barriers stood in the way of dealing with racism as an ideology and practice, even with primary students. Still, very young children might need assurance that "the adult world does not condone such [racist] behavior."[13]

An anti-racist pedagogy for young children would not be identical to that used with their older siblings. For example, in a society that values power, problems can arise when, on the one hand, one focuses on questions of power and powerlessness among particular racial groups and when, on the other, one is attempting to build a positive self-image among minority children. While much of the work with older students could take place in more independent, "extracurricular" student groups, work with younger students tended necessarily to be more classroom-based. But these were practical problems that could be worked out by experienced educators; they should not be an excuse to avoid the issues.

Teachers began providing practical examples of such theory. Elizabeth Parchment described teaching her Grade 4 class about how it was safe to talk about pain, rejection, and name-calling. The class talked about fairy tales and why they didn't include all cultures, and the children took on the task of adding folk tales from different cultures to be more representative. "We talked some more about self image and how important it is to see oneself mirrored in print. We discussed the validity and the pride of knowing that others can read about your experiences. We talked about taking this for granted and about this as a new experience."[14]

Her class also talked about the often negative associations of the word "black" and what that meant for children. They focused on the achievements of non-white groups and created a program to celebrate Martin's Day.

Two years later a young girl from Parchment's class discovered racist material in a store near her school and threatened a student boycott until the store owner agreed to remove it. The child had learned both to recognize racism and the importance of confronting it.

During the anti-racist pilot program at Lord Dufferin Public School, librarian Joanne Maikawa-Roman recognized the importance of using student discussions and reactions as entry points. In a unit on stories and myths, a Black student painted a mural portraying Nyame, the African sky god, as blond, blue-eyed, and fair. The young artist explained that she hated dark-skinned people. A number of other students revealed their discomfort about their skin colour as well, generating an angry response from many of their peers.

Maikawa-Roman recognized the importance of such a volatile discussion:

> The students live in a world where they are constantly made aware of skin colour and they internalize many of these evaluations. The self-depreciation and sense of inferiority illustrated in this portrayal of Nyame [are] a reflection of the impact of racism on a child. Not to have challenged this depiction and not to have discussed skin color issues with the group would have been a denial of their experience of racism. It was important to acknowledge the painting of a White Nyame as an expression of felt racism. It was important to bring these issues into the open within the classroom where they could be constructively dealt with rather than to leave them for the schoolyards where they are hurtfully expressed. Nyame, incidentally, remained White. The student who painted it insisted it be so.[15]

Another teacher, Lisa McNair, described her approach of starting with students' own knowledge in a unit on First nations peoples.

> We began . . . by first establishing a myth list, a technique I have used many times since in a variety of circumstances. The myth list was a compilation of the 'knowledge' we thought we had about Native people in Canada. It was three pages long. Prominent on the list were the conceptions that native people had red skin and scalped enemies regularly. We displayed the myth lists at one end of the room and proceeded to gather resources (books, pictures, people) to either confirm or dispel the myths. Each time we felt convinced that we had the 'truth' about something, we marked the list with bold magic marker. By the end of the six week unit, we discovered that almost everything we had 'known' was untrue! Even I was shocked. The unit provided much food for thought, both among the seriously learning disabled children in my room and their families at home.[16]

By the late 1980s anti-racist education had taken strides both in content and pedagogy. Its principles had been distilled from the practice of educators, and new insights and new theory had emerged. Optimism and excitement balanced discomfort and resistance.

Chapter 8

# Great Leaps Forward

In the period leading up to the November 1988 municipal election, a number of valuable initiatives began to trickle through the system. Money was set aside for the purchase of multi-language library materials. Despite skirmishes concerning the percentage of parents who needed to vote for the programs, integrated heritage language classes continued to proliferate. Olivia Chow finally succeeded in having a Human Sexuality Program established in the Student Services Department. Tony Gambini, an openly gay social worker, was mandated to work part-time in that program, advising schools on issues of sexual orientation and providing direct counselling to lesbian and gay students. At a May 26, 1988, Board meeting, the 1988–89 school year was proclaimed "Year of the 10th Anniversary of the Race Relations Policy."

In June 1988 the mandate of the Advisory Committee on Bias in the Curriculum was expanded to include the review of any material referred to it. Previously the committee had reviewed only new material. The Board allotted $60,000 for each of the next three years for the implementation of the recommendations of the *Report on the Education of Black Students in Toronto Schools*, which was issued that same month. Even right-wing bastion Nola Crewe seemed to be trying to position herself more to the left, demanding the removal of "sexist" images in the Education Centre's murals. Painted in 1959, the murals portrayed women in stereotypical fashion. From my point of view, they were also racist. Indeed, I had often asked students to analyze them as an exercise in detecting bias. The resulting official report rejected Crewe's request, arguing that the work should be preserved for its "historic value."

That September I began work on setting up a third new camp program, this one aimed at English as a Second Language students in secondary schools. ESL students often attended the Kandalore program, but it had seemed to me that the camp did not meet their needs. Much of the program involved intense discussions, and it was often difficult for students still learning English to participate fully. Students new to the country also often had limited experience with the nuances of Canadian racism. They found it hard to determine whether difficulties they faced were due to racism or the result of a lack of familiarity with Canadian culture and English. Many of them wanted to believe that once they had learned fluent English all their troubles would be over. I wanted to provide an opportunity for these kids to explore issues at their own pace and in their own way. The proposal was accepted. In an election year no one in the right-wing of the Board was prepared to publicly oppose a program for immigrant students. If appearing to be more moderate was an election strategy for the right, it didn't pay off. In November 1988 the left regained control of the Board and began trying to pick up where it had left off.

A federal election was held that same month, and it was during that campaign that the dark cloud of AIDS, which had been hanging over Toronto's gay community for more than half a decade, touched the Equal Opportunity Office.

Doug Wilson had moved to Toronto with his partner Peter McGehee in 1982. Doug had gained a certain notoriety in 1976 when he laid a human rights complaint against the University of Saskatchewan after the Department of Education there had refused to allow him to supervise practice teachers because of his involvement in a gay students' group. In Toronto he had co-ordinated Mission for Peace, a social justice organization focusing on Central America, and was a founder of *Rites*, a lesbian and gay monthly that positioned itself to the left of *The Body Politic*. Tony Souza had hired Doug to do contract work in the Equal Opportunity Office, and during Alok Mukherjee's tenure Doug had become the regular editor of *Focus on Equality*, a joint publication of the Equal Opportunity Office and the Curriculum advisors. He also took on co-ordination of the student anti-apartheid conference. Although he was not a formal Board employee, he was around the office as much as anybody. In fall 1988 Doug ran for the NDP in Toronto's Rosedale riding, becoming the first openly gay candidate nominated by a major Canadian party. In the middle of the campaign, much to his own surprise, he was suddenly hospitalized with PCP pneumonia, a "marker" illness for AIDS.

There were some treatments by that point, and Doug bounced back. Although I hadn't been sick, I had also tested positive for HIV, and Doug and I became much closer as we worked together at the Board. We shared information on complementary therapies and took leadership positions in Toronto's new AIDS activist organization, AIDS Action Now! Suddenly our work at the Board took on new urgency. As friend after friend sickened and died around us, we both had to recognize that we might not be around for the long haul.

The first ESL camp was held in February 1989. It was a success, and Alok and I began to manoeuvre to establish it as a regular Board program. A new anti-racist video, *Cindy*,[1] commissioned by our office, was also nearing completion. The narrative film recounted the dilemma of a young South Asian woman trying to decide whether to run the risk of supporting a Black friend's complaint about the racist behaviour of a teacher. We were concerned that the uncomfortably accurate portrayal of school life might provoke an uproar. To head off a blow-up Nora Allingham arranged a preview for the district executive of the OSSTF, providing background information about the piece and its intended uses. The executive agreed to support the video's use, and with the Federation stamp of approval any criticism from the schools was effectively muted.

Meanwhile, Alok was concentrating on activities to mark the tenth anniversary of the race relations report. A combined celebration and concert focusing on student work were planned for the end of April, and a community banquet to honour the winners of the race relations awards would take place in June. With the left once again in control of the Board, Alok also hoped to use the anniversary to keep up the pressure for change. Two projects were planned: a major conference for anti-racist educators; and the publication of a book recording the experiences of anti-racist work in Toronto schools.

Other than *Letters to Marcia*, there was no Canadian material about the challenges of anti-racism education. In the absence of documentation about what worked and what didn't, people kept making the same mistakes. Alok set aside some money, and Barb Thomas was commissioned to pull the book together. But the project ended up on the back burner as the logistics and planning for the conference, scheduled for early November 1989, kept getting more complex.

The conference had evolved into a showpiece for the Board's anti-racism efforts, and could be no rinky-dink affair held in a school on a weekend. The Westin Harbour Castle hotel on the lakeshore was booked for what we called "A Challenge to Racism: An Anti-Racist Educators' Conference." As more and more educators from across the country expressed interest, it ballooned into a national event. The registration fee was hefty, but 150 Toronto students, teachers, and community reps were given full subsidies.

It wasn't just a matter of size. This was to be a conference with a difference, more than the usual plenary speeches and experts reading papers. It had to reflect anti-racist principles and practice, beginning with participants' experience and culminating with their active involvement in struggles for change. Some four hundred registrants had to be divided into small groups, each led by trained facilitators. That meant finding and training dozens of facilitators and developing an open-ended program that would meet a variety of needs. We had to figure out a way of recording and sharing the results of these parallel discussions. It was an immense task, and we had no models to base it on. Planning committee meetings became more tense.

In the Board itself, big changes were occurring. Ned McKeown, the long-time director of education, resigned, and the three associate directors were also retiring. In a matter of months there would be a complete changeover in the senior administration. Joan Green was appointed director, the first woman to hold the position. The position of associate director of Personnel also went to a white woman. On the eve of the conference the Board was to decide on who would fill the two other associate director positions, Operations and Program. Two people of colour had thrown their hats into the ring: Ouida Wright and Harold Brathwaite. The general feeling was that these appointments would send out a message about the institution's values – a message that would be particularly loud and clear in the context of the Anti-Racist Educators' Conference.

The night before the conference was to open, Alok received information about the two remaining associate director positions: both had gone to white applicants. Wright and Brathwaite had been overlooked. For Alok and others who had been trying to improve the Board's record on the hiring and promotion of visible minorities for years, the passing over of qualified Black candidates for these senior positions was the last straw. The next morning at seven o'clock, a small group met at Alok's home to prepare a response. They decided that the conference should be used to put pressure on the Board around employment equity. A suite at the hotel became campaign headquarters.

Alok had chosen Charlie Novogrodsky to give the conference's midday keynote address. Given Charlie's firing as head of School Community Relations three years before, it was a symbolic as well as strategic choice, demonstrating at an important Board event that the retreat of the last three years was over. Charlie's talk, "The Anti-Racist Cast of Mind," warned against focusing merely on oppressive interpersonal behaviour as the sole object of anti-racist work and affirmed the community as "an anti-racist engine that powers change in the workplace and educational institutions."[2] He called for a broad movement against racism, arguing that effective anti-racist advocates had to engage with those holding "assimilationist and multicultural outlooks." He said anti-racist advocates had to be tough when it came to initiating their organizational practice; but they also had to be sensitive to the fears, beliefs, and anxieties of other people engaged with the issue. Anti-racism had to connect with work on other issues and forge links among different struggles for equity – and avoid falling into the trap of ranking or ordering pain. Fighting racism, he said, required advocates "to challenge the system of control and privilege upon which racism rests."

Charlie's talk would have provided more than enough material for discussion over the rest of the conference, but it was almost immediately overshadowed by the Board's hiring decisions. By the time Charlie was delivering his speech, a petition was circulating calling on the Board to immediately adopt employment equity goals and timetables for visible minorities. The parts of his speech that called for tough advocacy and structural change helped fan the flames. The conference that the Board establishment had seen as a celebratory occasion to receive congratulations for their accomplishments turned into a highly charged political event focusing on the Board's shortcomings.

When his turn came to address the plenary, Board chair Tony Silipo struggled to justify the hiring, but was in a tight corner. Faced with a motion from the floor that the Board should adopt an employment equity program within six months, he had little choice but to make a commitment to that proposal.

Silipo's commitment was a substantial victory, but it came at a cost. The community, led by the Equal Opportunity Office, had humiliated the senior bureaucracy and trustees. Alok recalled that for the full three days of the conference none of the senior people would speak to him. Towards the end as people were leaving, the new director, Joan Green, emerged from the crowd and took Alok aside. She said she knew that he had done what he thought he had to do, but "in the future, things were going to be different." The Board needed to be seen as working together. "She said she would be meeting with me every week and would make that public knowledge." For Alok this meant that "the boom was coming down."

Employment equity was not the only controversial issue that bubbled to the surface at the conference. One weakness of anti-racist education that Charlie had alluded to was its focus on visible racial difference as the sole measure of oppression. Not all racialized groups defined themselves in that way. A number of Aboriginal participants angrily pointed out that the conference had no Aboriginal facilitators and made no specific mention of First Nations issues. They insisted that the issues facing Aboriginal people were unique, and that it was not appropriate to simply lump them in with those of immigrant and multicultural minorities.

Native Peoples were the group with the longest experience of institutional racism in Canada, and the struggle for Aboriginal rights was becoming increasingly militant. Yet the Board's flagship conference, organized through the Race Relations Committee and the Equal Opportunity Office, had overlooked Native issues. Some four months later, the Race Relations Committee recommended that the Board set up a Consultative Committee on the Education of Native Students.

The establishment of an independent committee to deal with Native issues in the spring of 1990 was propitious. That summer Canadians would become familiar with the image of Manitoba MLA Elijah Harper holding an eagle feather as he blocked the ratification of the Meech Lake Accord because of its failure to entrench Aboriginal concerns in the constitution. They would witness the brutal faceoff at Oka between Mohawk Warriors and the Canadian army over plans to develop a golf course on lands claimed by Aboriginal people. These events and others laid to rest once and for all any illusions that First Nations issues could continue to be ignored or relegated to a bullet point in the agenda of multiculturalism.

## Fallout

By the end of November 1989 the Board had agreed to initiate immediate steps to establish goals and timetables for the employment and promotion of racial/visible and ethnic minorities at all levels in the Board. It asked the Personnel Division and the Personnel and Organization Committee to come up with a plan of action.

Alok was eager to push ahead before the issue lost momentum. A few weeks later, at the first of his scheduled meetings with Joan Green, he explained that his job description needed to be reshaped to allow him to take on the job of implementing employment equity full-time. Joan Green agreed. But when Bev Brophy, the new head of the Personnel Division, called him into her office just before Christmas, she told him that the plan was to create another Employment Equity Committee. Alok would be a staff member. He wasn't pleased. "To be a member of yet another committee, without any authority, was just nonsense," he said later. He submitted a letter of resignation on the following day and left the Board soon after. "The others could be forgiven by the system because the conference was not their event," he said later. "I had warned the Board, and I had been upfront about it in writing, and I had been quite visibly informing people and egging them on. That's one of the contradictions of that job. The institution expects you to be an advocate and an activist and suspects you for the same reason."

With Alok's sudden departure, Claire Chen See, who held an administrative position in the Staff Development Department, was appointed acting race relations advisor. Given the temporary basis of her position the question now, according to Domenic Bellissimo, was: "Which way was the Board going to go? Was it going to hire someone to continue to challenge the system, or was much of the work going to move backwards?"

To resolve that question, in March 1990 the Board contracted Arnold Minors, a local consultant, to do a review of the Equal Opportunity Office. His review and consultations turned into a complex power struggle among factions of the Board's administrative structure. To ensure that nothing like the November 1989 Anti-Racist Educators' Conference could ever be repeated, the upper bureaucracy wanted to tame the Equal Opportunity Office and strip away its last connections to training and running programs. They wanted a pared-down Equal Opportunity Office controlled by the Human Resources Division – the new name given to the former Personnel Division – to focus on developing policy and to handle harassment complaints. The Staff Development Department had its eye on the Equal Opportunity Office's training programs. Some trustees wanted a more compliant Equal Opportunity Office that would focus on personnel issues; others still saw it as an instrument for systemic change. The new Consultative Committee on the Education of Native Students wanted a First Nations advisor with the same broad responsibilities as the existing race relations and affirmative action advisors. The Curriculum Division wanted to secure its hold on the expanding student camp programs and pushed for the transfer of the student program workers out of the Equal Opportunity Office and into its own domain. Domenic and I lobbied against a move to Curriculum. We believed that our ability to advocate and organize for systematic change would be much more tightly controlled there.

## Destreaming

While the shape of the Equal Opportunity Office was a major concern for those of us working there, larger issues – in the long run probably much more relevant to the lives of students – were also being tackled. The Board was seriously taking on the issue of streaming.

Trustee Olivia Chow, for one, was convinced that streaming was a structural problem and that unless the structure was changed, no number of workshops or trainings for guidance counsellors was going to make a difference. She continued to push the Board, the NDP caucus, and the provincial government to destream schools. In the meantime she, Pam McConnell, and other trustees worked to transform Castle Frank Secondary School, a basic-level school suffering from declining enrolment, into what would become Rosedale Heights Secondary School, a model destreamed school. The structure of Rosedale Heights ensured the involvement not just of administrators and teachers, but also of parents and students. "We worked to make sure students felt empowered and we recognized how important it was that the teachers actually believed in what they were doing," Olivia Chow said. "We looked at how curriculum should be written, policy developed and embedded, and how hiring should be done." Rosedale Heights opened in September 1990.

## Ruby Lam

In 1990 Ruby Lam joined the Equal Opportunity Office as a third student program worker, hired specifically to focus on ESL issues – a position that became necessary especially after the ESL camp was established as a permanent program. At first Ruby worked only half-time, spending the rest of her workweek as a student worker for the newly destreamed Rosedale Heights.

Ruby was a valuable addition to the Office's student work. She came from a Chinese immigrant family of eleven children and had personal experience of being ignored in the education system and of harassment on the street – of being called "chink" and worse. "It was frustrating being a kid, growing up and being completely powerless," she said, "having people assume that you were stupid and ignorant and a burden to society, despite the fact that you knew your parents were working so hard."

When she joined the Equal Opportunity Office Ruby was just twenty-four, but drawing on her own experience, and facilitating the ESL camps, she quickly developed a unique vision of work with new immigrant kids. "In those days most new immigrants were not white. In addition to facing the issues that other teenagers were facing, many of them came here poor. Many came through the trauma of the refugee experience. Others were here alone with no parents, supporting themselves and people back home. They had a disproportionate amount of responsibility that Canadian youth culture couldn't possibly begin to understand."

Even the culture of equity work was often inhospitable to these students, she found. The work "required people to be articulate, extroverted, demanding, and clear about what they wanted." Many students coming from other countries found it difficult to assert themselves that way. "They're dealing with a language barrier and are not familiar with the way the system works. In many cultures people don't challenge their teachers or authorities. Imagine asking these kids to stand up in front of the principal and say, 'I'm not happy with what's going on in this school.' "

ESL work, she believed, had to stress affirmation and confidence-building, and for many of the students the program offered a life-changing experience. "It was the first time they were able to talk about what had happened to themselves and really understand that the way society sees them is not the way they really are." She recalled, for example, a Vietnamese student from the west-end Parkdale Collegiate Institute. He was "the kind you wouldn't want to meet in a dark alley. He was a self-professed gang member, the sort of kid that the rest of society saw as a danger." The camp program was able to establish "a safe place for kids like that," able to provide a sense of alternatives, a way of making "sense of some of the chaos in their lives and their experiences in Canada."

For Ruby, though, the focus of the ESL program remained on building an understanding of racism. Putting together a facilitators' handbook for the ESL camp, she insisted on including the introductory chapters on the history of racism from my original handbook – something I thought wasn't really necessary. My experience was that students at the ESL camps were mostly concerned about fitting in and were often unaware of the nuances of racism. For Ruby the desperate need of the ESL kids to fit in made a discussion of racism even more important. The key issue wasn't their ability to fit in; it was the willingness of the other side to accept them.

## The Controversies Continue

In the Equal Opportunity Office, the ongoing skirmishes around anti-racist issues did not abate. Late in 1989, for example, a teacher complained to the Race Relations Committee about the use of the term "Redmen" and a feathered Indian-head logo on team uniforms at Danforth Collegiate and Technical Institute. The committee recommended that the logo be changed. The school's staff maintained not only that the logo "honoured" Aboriginal people, but also that Danforth was being singled out when other schools also had logos that could be considered offensive.

Before his departure Alok had taken the Danforth argument to heart and had the Board call for a system-wide review of all school symbols for racial and ethnic stereotypes. A few months later, in the context of that more general review, the school was ordered to change its logo. In May 1990 nearly one hundred Danforth students walked out of their classes to demand that the decision be reversed, and the issue became a *cause célèbre* for right-wing commentators who railed against the destruction of hallowed school traditions in the name of "political correctness." As the new race relations advisor, Claire Chen See found herself taking most of the flack.

That same spring the South African government began sending Toronto schools a publication called *INDABA* – essentially pro-apartheid propaganda. Some of the material made its way into classrooms, which immediately sent the anti-apartheid movement up in arms. The Equal Opportunity Office was deluged with calls, and the Board complained to the Department of External Affairs. The right-wing press howled censorship.

Next came a controversy over the Royal Ontario Museum's "Into the Heart of Africa" exhibition, which purportedly recounted the ideas and perceptions of nineteenth-century Canadian missionaries in Africa. The display was organized around photographs and artifacts that the missionaries had sent home, and, as usual, school groups were organized to tour the exhibit. Elizabeth Parchment of the Committee of Anti-Racist Educators had been appalled by the promotional materials for the exhibition. She believed the advertising portrayed Africans as stereotypical savages, and complained to the Board. In response the ROM organized several focus groups of African Canadians and defended itself by pointing out that offensive terms such as "Darkest Africa," "the unknown continent," and "barbarous people" – which sprinkled the exhibition text – were couched in quotation marks and therefore meant to be read ironically. For critics the depictions of Africans clearly reinforced traditional nineteenth-century racial stereotypes. Those depictions were the most powerful images of the exhibit, especially for younger children who were unable to read the finely printed text or understand the significance of quotation marks. A newly formed Coalition for the Truth about Africa began to picket the museum on weekends. There were scuffles with the police, and arrests.

As more people saw the exhibition, community outrage grew. Toronto teacher Clem Marshall complained in a letter to *The Globe and Mail* that the exhibition "infantilized the African peoples." Other teachers recounted racist comments from the guides who were leading school groups through the exhibit. While some trustees defended the museum, Olivia Chow was excoriated in the *Sun* for her support of those picketing, especially after a Board megaphone lent to the demonstrators was allegedly used to assault a policeman. Parchment, who had originally brought her concerns to the Race Relations Committee, became increasingly vocal and angry with what she described as "the endless discussions about appropriateness" and demanded that the Board take a stand.

Hari Lalla was ordered to prepare a report, which turned out to be critical of the exhibition. The Board declared that field trips to see the exhibition were "inappropriate for students in the Primary and Junior Divisions" and only permissible for students in the Intermediate and Senior Divisions – so long as there were structured lead-up and follow-up activities. It suggested that teachers seek the assistance of the Coalition for the Truth about Africa in their planning.

Around the same time I was approached by a group of women who were putting together an anthology of writing by young women of colour. It seemed like a valuable project, and I sent out a flier to all the high-school English departments asking them to bring it to the attention of interested students. In several schools the heads of English, deciding that the book project was racist and discriminatory against white males, demanded that the flyer and any Board co-operation be withdrawn. When Claire Chen See and I met with their representatives, two white English heads, they made the standard "reverse racism" arguments and wrung their hands at the prospect of teachers having to identify people of colour in their classes. As a temporary advisor Claire had little authority to face them down. Still, she also had little to lose and refused to withdraw the flyer.

The issue of sexual orientation was also heating up again. A draft resource guide on homophobia prepared by the Physical Education Department as a result of Olivia Chow's pressure finally began to make the rounds of committees. The guide was an ungainly document produced by a consultant terrified of controversy, uncomfortable and unfamiliar with the issues, and advised by a divided committee made up of physical education teachers, several of them closeted gay people, and one notoriously homophobic psychiatrist. Those of us who had been doing anti-homophobia work in the schools for years were left out of the process. The draft guide satisfied neither the lesbian and gay community, represented by the Board's newly formed Lesbian and Gay Employees Group, nor the homophobic right.

In the midst of this I was invited, along with Olivia Chow, to speak to the gay and lesbian group at the University of Toronto about the Board's efforts to combat homophobia. I had recently been working to evaluate the Board's anti-homophobia efforts, extrapolating from the main principals of anti-racist institutional change. On almost every count, whether it was encouraging community involvement, changes to ensure visibility across the curriculum, or harassment policy, the Board came up short.

Someone higher up the ladder must have complained, because Claire called me into her office to dress me down for criticizing the Board in public. It was a tense meeting. Obviously uncomfortable, she said that as an employee I had to be careful about what I said about the Board, but she wouldn't tell me who had complained. I argued that it was my job to criticize the Board around issues of prejudice and discrimination, and that furthermore it was no one's business what I said on my own time.

The proposed book on anti-racist education, which Barb Thomas had been commissioned to put together, also became an issue. The project had been creeping forward for more than a year, partly because everyone's attention had been focused on organizing the Anti-Racist Educators' Conference. Money had been paid out to the Doris Marshall Institute (DMI), where Barb was working, but there was no book to be seen. Rumours began to circulate that Alok had siphoned off money to be paid after he had left the Board. The book had to be pulled together quickly. Much of the weight of the work had fallen on Barb. The project was originally envisaged as a collaborative effort involving Barb, Alok, and Fran Endicott, but Alok had been focused on the conference and Fran was undergoing treatment for cancer. Barb was caught up in the time-consuming process of soliciting articles and arranging interviews from people who had been involved in different aspects of the work over the years.

The draft finally arrived on Claire's desk in December 1990. Barb, as an outsider, was in no position to shepherd the manuscript through the system, and it soon became a political football. The Consultative Committee on the Education of Native Students was unhappy with the draft's inadequate treatment of First Nations educational issues. Others were disappointed in the absence of an institutional history to connect the push for anti-racist education to the earlier struggles around heritage languages. The exclusively anti-racist focus of the book ran against the grain of Myra Novogrodsky's new push to connect the range of equity issues. The draft was also far from a celebration of the Board's accomplishments. Barb had implicitly criticized white employees for using anti-racism as a means of career advancement. Her contextualization of anti-racism issues within a critique of Canadian immigration and economic policy and controversies around racist policing practices was seen as being too political for an institutional product.

"Office politics" were added to the mix. Some noses were out of joint because the book was seen as an exclusively Equal Opportunity Office project and the Curriculum Division had not been consulted. Alok was listed as a coauthor, and he was not a popular figure in some circles after the blow-up at the anti-racist conference. The publication of the book was put on ice.

The Employment Equity Committee, which was to develop goals and timetables for the hiring of visible minorities, also had its share of difficulties. The conference proposal, which had been accepted under duress, had called for employment equity for visible and racial minorities. According to Susan McGrath, who attended the committee meetings with Claire Chen See, Board chair Silipo insisted that any employment equity policy also include white ethnic and cultural groups, such as Italians and Portuguese. "That was a very divisive issue," Sue said. In addition to going outside the original commitment, such a broad range would be difficult to monitor. "We spent a lot of time trying to figure out how we were going to deal with that and making lists about how we were going to break people down."

## Young Women's Retreat

In the spring of 1990 Marg Wells, now replacing Myra Novogrodsky, who had gone back to the classroom for two years, took the initiative to run the first retreat for young women on gender issues. She was determined that the camp would meet student needs, and female students were surveyed to find out what issues they thought were important to talk about. The results were surprising. Most work on gender had focused on issues like challenging notions of appropriate careers, encouraging young women in maths and science, and problems of self-esteem. According to Myra, "What they told us in overwhelming numbers in that survey was that they were afraid. The issues of gender-based violence in their lives were the most important things that they wanted to talk about." As if to underscore the survey results, the "Montreal Massacre" took place on December 6, 1989, at the École Polytechnique, the University of Montreal School of Engineering. A young man who was convinced that "feminists" were destroying his life gunned down fourteen female students. Clearly, issues of violence against women had to be a pivotal piece of the program.

The organizers of the new women's retreat took a deliberately low-key approach. They were especially sensitive about not being seen as attempting to recruit young women to feminism. But at the retreat increasingly acrimonious discussions about the profile of feminists in the program became hopelessly embroiled with questions of identity around race and sexual orientation. Three of the five community facilitators, all women of colour with experience at Kandalore, and two of them lesbian, left on the third day of the five-day retreat, stating that they felt disrespected. The remaining adults had to scramble to reconfigure the program and explain what had happened to the students.

Despite the difficulties, the retreat laid the foundation for future programs with young women and men around sexism. But lingering bitterness about the facilitators' actions leaked into relations between the Race Relations Office and Women's Studies in the Curriculum Division. In retrospect the incident was yet another indication of the increasingly volatile nature of identity politics.

## Pay Equity

In 1990 the provincial government finally passed legislation requiring major employers to re-evaluate jobs to ensure that women were receiving equal pay for work of equal value. As affirmative action advisor, Sue McGrath found herself in the centre of a vast bureaucratic undertaking. The Metropolitan Toronto school boards began meeting to develop a joint plan and choose a consultant who could be paid through the Metro budget. In the end the other Metro boards chose a large U.S. firm, but the Toronto Board itself broke ranks and hired a smaller company that seemed more in sympathy with the values of pay equity. "That was a tense moment," Sue recalled. "We felt that the consultant that Metro hired was there to make sure it cost as little as possible – not in terms of the consultant's fees but in terms of upgrading women's salaries. We were openly in favour of the legislation. In that regard, we were probably out of step with the rest of the personnel people from the other school boards."

After the consultants were selected, each board had to start doing job evaluations. Under pay equity, aspects of women's work that had previously been ignored began to be weighed. A standard example was that mechanics got paid more for working with grease and dirt, but nurses were not compensated for working with blood and vomit. Sue realized that employees' future salaries depended on how they filled out the evaluation forms, and took it upon herself to organize workshops for employees and union reps to ensure that everyone knew how to describe their jobs properly. Some members of the executive office were upset that staff should receive workshops to help increase their pay. Somehow the Employment Philosophy Statement's commitment to fair compensation had still not managed to permeate the institution.

## The Minors Report

A different way of operating an education system – or, at least, the ideal system – came to the fore in September 1990, when Arnold Minors delivered the discussion paper that was to be the first stage of his review of the Equal Opportunity Office. Minors' report began with "Vision, 2001," a description of a "desired and possible" Toronto secondary school in the future year 2001, done as a scenario. A group of international visitors are taken on a tour of the school by the principal (a woman). The first thing they see is an interdisciplinary display combining art, history, and sociology and showing what Canada would look like if First Nations principles of ecology and development had governed social policy in the twentieth century. The drama room has been redesigned to accommodate a teacher who uses a wheelchair. An English course focuses on literature and sexual identities, and students are discussing homophobia. Thanks to clear goals for hiring of designated groups and a peer-mentoring project, the teaching staff is made up of over twenty-five different racial groups, and the support staff is equally diverse.

In the middle of the tour the director of education (who is Chinese) arrives to show his commitment to resolving a racial incident. The incident, which grew out of a conflict over dating and involved racial epithets and punches, is being mediated by a group of students trained at the Board's race relations camp. The principal is relaxed and not at all embarrassed to talk about the school's response.

As the visitors pass the office, they see a large group of parents who serve as volunteers and work as language and cultural interpreters for frequent parent-teacher meetings. Many parents are also active in the classroom and have enrolled in night-school courses concurrent with subjects that their own children are studying; that way they can offer better support. When a girls-only science class passes the visitors in the hall, we learn that this experiment at junior levels has produced a better balance of men and women in senior science classes and a reduction in sexual harassment.

The vice-principal explains that equity has become the work of the school and that the vast majority of the staff is onside because of the school's supportive, non-threatening process around the issues. Although subtle ideas and practices that perpetuate inequity are still being uncovered by different groups of staff, parents, and students, the school is proud of its response, and satisfied that careful monitoring has shown a consistent improvement in the achievement levels of all students.

In retrospect, "Vision 2001" appears to have been both bravely utopian and touchingly naive, but it did reflect the spirit of optimism permeating equity work at the time. If apartheid could be brought down in South Africa, anything was possible. The paper also reflected the increasing use of the term "equity" to describe the work we were doing.

The notion of equity brought together the parallel struggles of different marginalized groups, and reiterated the need for affirmative action. Equity was not the same as equality. It was not just about treating everyone the same. It was about giving different groups what they needed to level the playing field. Equity would be measured by results – when factors such as race, gender, and cultural background were no longer correlated with differences in success.

Minors' report made clear that if this vision of equity was both desirable and possible, it was still far from being achieved. Recent research report findings revealed that teaching and non-teaching staff still did not reflect the racial composition of the city; racial minority staff were underrepresented in positions of responsibility, even though they tended to be more highly qualified for their positions; racial minority candidates for hiring and promotion were not being accepted at a rate proportionate to their applications; women staff members were still underrepresented both in positions of responsibility and in non-traditional jobs; Black students were still overrepresented in basic-level programs.

Minors identified major strategic choices for reshaping the Board's approach to equity and the role of the Equal Opportunity office. The first issue was the question of centralization. In a centralized model, equal opportunity functions would be assigned to a central unit mandated to monitor and resolve issues of discrimination and harassment, and with the "clout" to enforce sanctions against inappropriate behaviour. In a decentralized model, such functions would be assigned to local school principals or administrative departments.

The Equal Opportunity Office was operating under a target-group delivery model, with one advisor for women's issues and one for race. If this structure was to continue, the Office would have to decide whether its focus should remain restricted to women and racial minorities, or expanded to include Aboriginal peoples, people with disabilities, and gay and lesbian people. The other option was to hire personnel for competence in specialized functions such as research and complaints resolution, and to expect everyone to work with all designated groups.

The Board needed to clarify reporting lines. The Office could report to the chair of the Board, the director, an associate director, or to a designated superintendent. Decisions needed to be made about whether it should continue to work with students and teachers and be involved with curriculum issues, or whether responsibilities should be restricted to personnel and employment.

## Social Democracy in One Province

In September 1990 the New Democratic Party unexpectedly won the provincial elections. Suddenly a party with at least a rhetorical commitment to anti-racism was in power. Expectations were high: for the first time there would be concrete government support around the issues that the left on the Board had been pushing for a decade.

Despite a series of reports calling for change,[3] Ontario's traditional Conservative governments had consistently failed to implement suggested reforms around racism in the education system. After the Tories were finally defeated in 1985, the new Liberal government of David Peterson set up a Provincial Advisory Committee on Race and Ethnic Relations, promising to look at racism in the education system. Conferences with educators were held, and more recommendations were duly produced, but the Liberals were never willing to require the province's boards of education to develop anti-racism policies. When Karen R. Mock and Vanara Masemann surveyed Ontario's 124 Boards for the Ministry of Education in 1989, they found that only 39 had such policies.[4] There was therefore immediate public pressure on the new NDP government to deliver on promises for change.

The election of the new government raised the stakes around equity programs, and the debates at the Board moved beyond the role of the Equal Opportunity Office to look at the institution's equity efforts in general. By this point, Myra Novogrodsky and Hari Lalla were jockeying to increase the importance of women's and race relations issues within the Curriculum Division and proposed the creation of a new Equity Studies Centre (ESC) that would combine their two portfolios. As Myra pointed out, "All the important scholarly work was on the links between gender, race and class. We worked together anyway so it seemed to make a lot more sense to merge." A pivotal issue convinced Hari of the importance of integrating the work. A Vietnamese girl at a downtown school was attacked by five boys, some of whom were Black. "Some of the anti-racist teachers at the school took the position that because there were so many Black kids in the gang, their priority had to be to support the boys, because the police would be especially hard on them. Myra was appalled, as was I, because it was a complete misunderstanding of who the victim was, and who had to have priority."

A joint meeting of Labour Studies, Status of Women, Race Relations, and the Native Advisory Committee was called to discuss the proposal for establishing an Equity Studies Centre, and from Myra's point of view things got off to a discouraging start. She had believed that "the experience of identifying with one kind of oppression" would leave the participants "open enough to hear about someone else's." Instead, she found a notable lack of empathy. The Status of Women representatives, all white women, "didn't want to be tainted by dealing with issues of racism. Some of the union people didn't understand why gay and lesbian issues should be their concern. The Native Studies Committee didn't show up at all because they felt they had a different experience completely. People were worried that there wouldn't be enough money left for them if we started divvying it up to all these other groups who hardly had a toe in the door. There was no common ground." Despite the atmosphere at that first meeting, the Equity Studies Centre proposal went ahead, and the Centre was duly established within the Curriculum Division.

The election of the NDP government did more than encourage hopes for change. Two NDP trustees, including the chair, Tony Silipo, had won seats in the legislature, and the Board required by-elections. One of the newly elected trustees, Luz Bascunan, was the first trustee from a Latin American background. For me, her election represented an important opportunity to further expand the Board's student work.

The success of women-only activities, the ESL camps, and the Black student conferences had convinced me of the importance of homogeneous group work. When they no longer found themselves having to explain and justify themselves to others, youth could draw enormous strength and inspiration from talking with peers who shared their experience. The left at the Board, however, had always been suspicious of such "segregated activities."

I had been approached by a young Salvadorean activist who was alarmed by high dropout rates and social problems facing newcomer Latin American youth in the city. Most recent Latin American immigrants were from Central America and northern South American countries. Many were of working-class or peasant background. Their children were often still struggling with English, and many were experiencing serious difficulties in school. They were in marked contrast to the earlier wave of Chileans, Argentinians, and Uruguayans who had come to escape political persecution after the right-wing military coups in the early 1970s. That population tended to be white, professional, and well educated, and in the intervening years had put down roots in the city. Many of their children were now in high school, and having grown up in Canada they were often estranged from their parents' cultures and language.

I crafted an argument about the unique nature of the Latin American community, and how a camp could bring the newer and older populations together. The camp would be conducted in Spanish and English. Newcomers would meet peers who could serve as models for successful integration into Canadian life. Second-generation youth would get in touch with Latin American culture and language. The groups could discuss how racism and national rivalries divided and undermined their communities. The goal would be to establish a Board-wide Latin American students' group. Luz Bascunan was immediately interested in the community development potential of such a venture.

We brought together a group of Spanish-speaking teachers and school community advisors to plan a program and identify potential facilitators. Luz steered the proposal through the appropriate Board committees and by April 1991 we had approval. Now, if we could make the Latin American camp a success, the Board would be hard-pressed to ignore the needs of other "at risk" communities. I had visions of developing similar programs for Vietnamese, Somali, and Caribbean youth to help them identify their issues and cultivate a voice for their communities within the schools. It was an ambitious and optimistic vision, but with the new Board and the new provincial government, everything seemed possible.

## New Structure

After months of meetings, lobbying and manoeuvring, the Board approved a new equity structure in May 1991. Like the results of most institutional processes, it was a compromise between competing interests. The office wasn't as large and powerful as some of us wanted, but it did substantially strengthen the "equity establishment." The mandate of the new Equal Opportunity Office would focus on ensuring that the Board achieved equity "with specific reference to advocacy and employment of women, visible/racial minorities, aboriginal First nations people, and persons with disabilities." These four categories had been identified by both the federal and provincial governments as groups most likely to face employment discrimination and to be significantly underrepresented in positions of responsibility. Effectively, that meant that the Equal Opportunity Office would concentrate on dealing with complaints and personnel issues. The term "advocacy" in the mandate was open-ended enough that room remained for some political work aimed at promoting institutional change. The Equal Opportunity Office also still retained an important aspect of its traditional independence, reporting directly to the Director's Office and thus avoiding potentially stifling control by the Human Resources Division.

In addition to the existing positions for women and visible/racial minorities, the Equal Opportunity Office would expand to include an advisor on Aboriginal First Nations peoples. The recommendation to hire an advisor on disabilities was lost – probably a combination of budget concerns and the absence of a strong disabilities lobby. Responsibility for disability issues would be shared by the other three advisors. Each advisor would have a support staff, and an administrative assistant would manage joint projects.

The new Equity Studies Centre in the Curriculum Division was mandated the responsibility "for curriculum development and implementation activities related to anti-racist education, women's issues, sexual orientation, the education of Native Canadian students, the education of Black students and the disabled." Hari Lalla and Myra Novogrodsky retained their co-ordinator positions, and they would co-ordinate the work of two new consultants, one focused on race relations and multiculturalism and the other on women's and labour studies.

The student program workers were beefed up to four. We would remain in the Equal Opportunity Office and continue to be advocates for students. But we were also cross-appointed to the Equity Studies Centre and would report to Hari and Myra around "curriculum issues." The borderline between student advocacy and curriculum was left deliciously vague, leaving us lots of room to manoeuvre.

The Staff Development Department was not forgotten. It would hire two trainer/facilitators to assist the Equal Opportunity Office and the Equity

Studies Centre in staff training around equity. The model also foresaw a "representative co-ordinating team for joint projects," between Equal Opportunity, Staff Development, and Equity Studies.

Not everyone was completely happy with the new arrangements. Pat Case worried about the continuing division between the Curriculum and Personnel components. Although she saw advantages to a "unified approach," Keren Brathwaite expressed reservations with what she perceived as lack of clarity by the Board, worrying that Black students might be shortchanged in the broader equity focus. Still, it was a significant expansion in staff dedicated to equity issues. Including support staff, nineteen people were to be spread across three departments.

The expansion in the equity staff was not the only positive sign. In April 1991 the fragmented school community advisors managed to pull together the Board's first major parents' conference since 1982. A thousand parents attended and approved 120 recommendations calling for the strengthening of the Board's work around anti-racist education, sexism, multiculturalism, heritage languages, parental involvement, and Native and environmental issues. Soon after that Tony Silipo, former chair of the Board, was appointed minister of education for the province. After a dangerous storm and a long calm, the winds finally seemed to be blowing in our favour.

Chapter 9

# Equity and Identity

IN FALL 1991 PAT CASE BECAME the Board's third race relations advisor with the formal title "Equity Advisor, Visible and Racial Minorities." The motion from the November anti-racism conference had finally put employment equity on the agenda, and an "Employment Systems Review" was underway. Pat found himself caught up with a number of issues. He was still concerned about what kids were being taught in schools – he admitted later that he "tended to focus on that way too much." He was also under pressure to restart the "Challenging Racism" training for teachers and principals, which had been so crucial in producing change agents throughout the system, but which hadn't taken place since Alok's departure. The Race Relations Committee itself needed urgent attention. According to Pat, the meetings did not seem to be going anywhere, and committee members were becoming disgruntled. They were still largely excluded from the inner workings of the system and lacked the detailed information they needed to make informed interventions. Indeed, Pat soon found out that senior administration was actually trying to find ways of getting rid of the committee.

Some items inevitably slipped off the table. One was a plan for an annual community conference that would discuss the implementation of the race relations report recommendations. Alok had managed to hold one such conference, but after a couple of attempts to get things started Pat concluded that it was "too much work for too little return." Another item was the publication of Barb and Alok's "Anti-Racist Education in Practice" manuscript.

## The Lost Book

When he arrived on the job as race relations advisor, Pat Case found the "Anti-Racist Education in Practice" manuscript sitting on his desk like an unwanted orphan. Aware of other pressing issues, the convoluted opposition to much of the project's content throughout the system, and that much of the material was by this point almost five years old and would require a huge amount of work to get into shape, he decided to focus on the future rather than the past, and he put the project aside, never to be completed. The decision was understandable but unfortunate because the manuscript, for all its faults, was a remarkable snapshot of the state of anti-racist education at the end of the 1980s.

The first part of the text defined racism, discussed broad social, economic, and political considerations, and looked at barriers to progress within the education system. It defined the purpose of anti-racist work as equipping people, individually and collectively, to recognize and challenge racism in all its forms. This work was to be measured not only by shifts in individual behaviours and attitudes, but primarily by more equitable results for people of colour in all aspects of school life. In its content, anti-racist work needed to distinguish between and connect systemic practices, individual expressions of racism, and racist ideas, and it needed to build strategies to address all three areas. In terms of method, anti-racist education needed to build on existing knowledge and critical thinking, draw on differences, and help people locate and use their own voices, even when that was uncomfortable. Anti-racist education welcomed pressures for change from both inside and outside. Seeking support from the top, it attempted to build common cause with staff, students, and the community. The section concluded with three basic assumptions: anti-racist education is not neutral; in a racist society, inaction is complicity; people can change unjust, inequitable systems, and they feel more empowered to do so as they attempt action together.

That first section of the manuscript revealed that the theoretical description of anti-racist education was becoming more refined. In the following section the ten authors of twelve chapters displayed that, in practice, the field still encompassed a wide range of approaches. The articles included calls "to raise awareness of staff without seeming critical of them as professionals" and to build "self-esteem" of minority children through community speakers and multicultural concerts. But they also included assertions that anti-racists needed to be "confrontational," "outspoken," and "unequivocal." There were attacks on those who used anti-racism for career advancement.

A recurrent theme in many of the chapters, and a major preoccupation of anti-racist educators at the time, was the impact of personal racial identity. Some writers struggled with the challenges of being seen as white liberal do-gooders; others struggled with the anger of being discounted because, as people of colour, they were perceived as having a chip on their shoulder. Writer Barb Thomas asked, "How can I as a white educator work effectively with Black students? How can I act against racism from something more solid than guilt?"[1] Alok recounted the dilemma he faced when he was called to testify at a human rights hearing after the Board had been accused of racism. He was torn between the desire to appear to be supporting a fellow community member, and his professional opinion that the specifics of the complaint were unjustified. "The pull between my responsibility to the organization that employs me, and to myself in my own skin, in my own community, can drag me in totally different directions."[2]

Facilitators in mixed-race teams also had to deal with tricky dynamics:

the "slippery line" between a white person using whiteness strategically and catering to the discomfort of whites, or people of colour finding themselves representing their "race."

The attention to the importance of interpersonal dynamics in anti-racist education was characteristic of a world in which the slogan "the personal is the political" had become a fundamental axiom of progressive work. But the preoccupation with such dynamics also ran the risk of unwittingly contributing to a climate in which any disagreement could be reduced to a racial power play, sending discussions into a downward spiral of self-righteous imputations of blame and claims of victimhood.

The manuscript left many questions unanswered. Was the goal of anti-racist education primarily to build racial minority children's self-esteem or to end white dominance and redistribute power? Was it about challenging and holding white people accountable for racist behaviour, or winning everyone over? Was it about making the existing curriculum more inclusive, or fundamentally changing the relationship between teachers and students and the way that schools worked? Was it about gradual transformation in people's understanding and action, or taking advantage of institutional crises to provoke immediate change? Was it a strategy aimed at laying the basis for fundamental social transformation, or an attempt to make the system work better for everyone? Around many of these questions, there was clearly still no consensus.

The document's real strength was that it drew together many of the different strands and strategies for change in a large education system, and it identified organizational and individual difficulties faced by change agents. Although "Anti-Racist Education in Practice" turned out to be a kind of swan song for anti-racist education as an independent strategy, its insights were enormously relevant to the other equity issues with which anti-racism was soon inextricably bound up. In its absence, the wheel would have to be invented many times over.

## Equity Studies

The new Equity Studies Centre, established in the Curriculum Division in September 1991, included Hari Lalla and Myra Novogrodsky as co-co-ordinators, two consultants, and the cross-appointed student program workers: myself, Domenic Bellissimo, Ruby Lam, and a new addition, Vanessa Russell. The student program workers were still officially in the Equal Opportunity Office, although we reported to Myra and Hari around curriculum issues. Marg Wells, who had done both Myra's and Hari's jobs in the past, became the women's and labour studies consultant, and Carmen Marshall, an elementary school teacher, was race relations consultant. As a school race relations rep Carmen had written several articles in "Anti-Racist Education in Practice" and was involved in the organization of the Board's annual Black student conference. The idea was that everyone on this team would work together. It was perhaps a utopian hope in an era characterized by identity politics.

The new, fourth, student program worker, Vanessa Russell, was an out lesbian who came from a family decimated by the Holocaust. Vanessa remembered learning powerful, contradictory lessons from her father. "The world is evil. Don't trust anybody. They're going to come and get you. You've got to keep fighting to make it better." After working at a battered women's shelter, she decided to enter medical school. Completely "aghast" at the inequities she found there, she went into teaching. Since the three other student program workers were largely focused on race and language, Vanessa was to work primarily around gender issues.

The integration of the student program workers in the Equity Studies Centre was not completely smooth. Earlier, before the cross-appointment, Myra, Domenic, and I had already had a major set-to in the midst of the first Gulf War in spring 1991. The war had produced a predicable wave of anti-Arab and anti-Muslim sentiment. Some schools reported that a sizable number of their Muslim students were simply not attending classes. There was another side to it as well: the controversial U.S. activist Angela Davis had just spoken in Toronto, and her mention of the Iraqi missile attacks on Israel had drawn applause from some sectors of the audience. Even those normally critical of Israel were concerned by the heightened anti-Semitism stirred up by the passions of war.

Domenic and I decided to hold an after-school camp reunion on racism and the war and invited speakers from the Canadian Arab Federation and a Jewish women's anti-war group. At the meeting, when the Jewish speaker criticized Israel as part of her talk, teacher Marsha Melnik complained that the speaker's comments were unsubstantiated and promoted anti-Semitism among the attending students. Myra wanted to know why she had not been consulted on the choice of speakers. Dom and I insisted that criticism of the Israeli government could not be equated with anti-Semitism, and that we never consulted her for Equal Opportunity events. Now, given our cross-appointment, both Domenic and I were more than a little anxious about the prospect of having to report and clear all our future activities with Myra.

As usual, the institutional culture of the Curriculum Division also led to difficulties. As student program workers we were action-oriented. We would meet when we had to plan something, or bounce ideas off each other on the fly, but we generally spent most of our time working on programs with students. We saw ourselves as gadflies, stinging the system into action. Personally I was also increasingly involved in AIDS Action Now! and the culture of AIDS activism tended to have a low tolerance for long meetings and slow bureaucratic processes. We wanted immediate results. In even the slightly longer term, we were all likely to be dead.

When Myra and Hari instituted regular half-day staff meetings full of seemingly endless reports and discussions about how to better meet the needs of the system, we were not particularly pleased. To the extent that the meetings were aimed at building group cohesion, they were helpful, even necessary. With such a diverse group of people with different politics and histories of focus on different issues, the Centre would never have functioned unless we spent time learning to work together and to trust one another, and we could all be more effective if we shared our contacts in the system. Still, the half-day staff meetings seemed tedious and unproductive with so much work to be done in the schools. We also had a nagging feeling that at least part of the goal of the meetings was to prevent the student program workers from doing anything that would rock the boat. Dom worried that the increasing integration of equity was "homogenizing" our work and making us less critical of the system.

## Homophobia

A major bone of contention was homophobia. In May 1990, well before the establishment of Equity Studies, I had come up with a proposal for a student conference on the topic. The new Sexual Harassment Policy was going to include homophobic harassment, and the Board was even investigating the feasibility of extending benefits to same-sex partners. It seemed an ideal time for a conference to raise the profile of the issue among students and in the system.

Claire Chen See, who at that time was still acting advisor and my direct supervisor, was not up to launching any new student conference on such a controversial issue. She suggested it would need to be organized through the Curriculum Division. When I raised the idea with Myra, she said she would have to consult with curriculum superintendent Ted Gordon. After a long delay Gordon finally told her that he could not permit such a conference unless the Board instructed him to do so – which was complete nonsense. We had initiated student conferences all along without going to the Board for clearance.

Olivia Chow, Myra, and I had already been meeting to try to figure out how to break the deadlock that was developing around different aspects of the issue. Even though his caseload of lesbian and gay students had increased exponentially, a recommendation to make Tony Gambini's job in the Human Sexuality Program full-time had been turned down, and he was increasingly being burdened with other general responsibilities. The physical education document on homophobia was lost in limbo. Now the Curriculum Division was blocking the conference proposal. When I raised the issue, Olivia was reluctant to intervene. Trustees were not supposed to interfere in program decisions. Besides, an election was coming up in the fall, and we all knew that NDP trustees tended to become a little skittish with the issue of homosexuality around elections. It was just not the right time. To me it seemed very much a repeat of the scenario that had occurred around the Equality Rights Conference in 1987. The upper bureaucracy would do everything it could to suppress discussion of homophobia, and no one was willing to buck them.

I expressed my frustrations about the continued invisibility of gay issues and the slow pace of change. It seemed it was never a good time to take a clear stand. In the meantime, lesbian and gay kids were being harassed. They were dropping out, turning to substance abuse, and committing suicide. I finally said that maybe it was time for the gay community to run its own candidate for trustee downtown. Both Myra and Olivia looked alarmed. That would split the progressive vote, and a right-wing candidate might win. I said that from the point of view of the gay community, if the left wasn't willing to take a stand and deliver change, it hardly mattered. At least we could raise the issues. It was an idle threat, but I think the realization that gay people were no longer willing to wait patiently at the back of the bus did catch their attention.

Lynda Lemberg of Oakwood Collegiate finally suggested a strategy. Why not organize the conference under the auspices of an alternative school? That school could invite other alternative schools, and because it would be a school-initiated activity, it wouldn't need central approval. Since I still wasn't formally connected to the Curriculum Division, I wouldn't even need to tell them it was happening. I immediately approached the co-ordinator and staff of West End Alternative School. They thought it was a great idea. Tony Gambini and I worked out the program, and the school took on the logistics of inviting the other alternative schools to send students. By this time we were already well into the spring of 1991, and the event would not be able to take place until the fall, which would put it right in the middle of the election campaign. That would make it all the more difficult for the NDP to downplay gay issues.

At it turned out, one hundred and forty students from six alternative schools attended the conference, held on October 9. The opening speaker, Anthony Mohamed, a young gay man, recounted his experiences as a student at Western Technical-Commercial School in the aftermath of the Zeller murder six years before. Workshops emphasized the importance of challenging the stereotype that the community consisted only of affluent white gay men, and highlighted First Nations, Asian, and Caribbean lesbian and gay experience. Other topics included lesbian and gay youth, lesbian invisibility, and religious perspectives on homosexuality. The day closed with a panel of resource people who addressed ways of challenging homophobia in the education system.

Participating students gave glowing evaluations. Not surprisingly, one parent complained and we were in the papers again. Trustee Alex Chumak tried to turn the event into an election issue and demanded that the director prepare a report to reveal who had authorized the conference, whether alternative programs had been provided for students, how workshop leaders had been selected, and whether parents had been consulted. Since I was now part of the Equity Studies Centre, the Centre found itself on the spot, and Myra Novogrodsky was not exactly pleased. But given the new equity mandate, both the Centre and the superintendents found themselves having to defend the conference. When the dust settled I got a call from John Davies, the superintendent in charge of West End Alternative. He assured me that he supported anti-homophobia work among students, but asked that the next time I organized such an event in one of his schools, he would appreciate it if I could let him know in advance. We had gambled and won, but the whole experience did not exactly enhance my reputation as a team player in the Equity Studies Centre.

In the November election, a progressive majority was returned to the Board, including ten members of the NDP caucus, among them long-time caucus assistant John Campey, an openly gay man. Despite the system's efforts to downplay the issue, homophobia was once again front and centre for the Board. Campey's election changed the equation around homophobia. He would make it a priority to rally the other trustees and the community to take on the issues that were fast coming to a head.

Although homophobia was one of the Equity Studies Centre's five mandated issues, in practice, other than Vanessa Russell and myself, no one else seemed really comfortable taking it on. The others in the Centre tended to have their own areas of concern, from women and labour to Holocaust issues, multiculturalism, and racism. Ruby Lam was immersed in ESL issues, and Domenic Bellissimo worked with younger students, where questions of sexuality were still generally considered taboo. But with other people now concentrating on race and gender – with those issues generally recognized as being legitimate – Vanessa and I decided we could focus more of our energies on homophobia.

In an era of identity politics, when the right to speak was grounded in authentic personal experience, as the two queer employees of the Equity Studies Centre, Vanessa and I were also legitimately expected to take that leadership. Just as whites tended to defer to people of colour around questions of race, or as a male I expected women to take leadership around sexism, gay issues belonged to gay people. Personal identity was perhaps even more important around queer issues, because the presence of real live homosexuals was seen as crucial to confronting homophobia in a world in which gay people were still largely invisible.

One of the jobs that I took on in the fall of 1991 was helping Tony Gambini facilitate his new lesbian and gay students' support group. Every

Wednesday after school, a dozen or so young people from across the system would gather at the Board to talk and share their stories. Most of them had been referred to Tony for counselling. The group was intimate and safe for these kids. Most of them came from immigrant families and many were people of colour. Some were living on student welfare because of family difficulties. Most of those who were still at home were devoting huge amounts of energy keeping their sexual orientations secret. The sessions revealed that they faced enormous harassment and lived in fear in their everyday lives in our schools.

By this time a Lesbian and Gay Employees group had also become established as more gay and lesbian teachers tentatively started coming out of the woodwork. The group had been initiated by John Campey when he was still a trustee assistant, and although it could never really make up its mind whether it was an advocacy group pushing for recognition and change or a support group in which members could commiserate with one another, it did further raise the profile of the issue at the Board.

A day-long Lesbian and Gay Employees meeting in January 1992 came up with an ambitious agenda for institutional change. It asked Campey to work to repeal the 1981 Board policy prohibiting the proselytization of homosexuality. He was also to press for the immediate extension of spousal benefits to same-sex partners, a standard policy to deal with incidents of homophobic harassment and discrimination, the preparation of a booklet to guide teachers in dealing with homophobia in their classrooms, and mandatory staff development for teachers on gay and lesbian issues.

On the political level, the meeting recommended the establishment of a "constituent assembly" made up of lesbian and gay parents, students, staff, and community agencies to liaise with the Board. Given that questions of sexuality were confined to the physical education curriculum, discussions about lesbians and gay men had to escape from the phys ed straitjacket and be integrated across the curriculum if homophobia was going to be challenged. The group called for the development of a bank of books and materials, with lesson plans and study guides appropriate to different age levels and subject areas, that would be distributed to all schools. It called for the inclusion of resources in school libraries, and the establishment of a resource centre that could lend such material to interested teachers and students across the system.

The meeting also demanded an expansion of counselling and support services for lesbian and gay students, and it raised for the first time the notion of a special program for gay and lesbian kids who couldn't fit into the regular school system. It suggested encouraging schools to set up clubs for gay students. Tony Gambini also agreed to work on building a network of staff contacts in all schools to help distribute information.

In general the meeting's recommendations closely mirrored the strategies that had been painstakingly developed by multicultural, anti-racism, and women's rights advocates at the Board during the preceding fifteen years. The expectations on Campey to broker a game of catch-up for the gay and lesbian community were tremendous.

## Working Together

The new cross-appointment of the four student program workers served as a bridge for developing common strategies and strengthening the relationship between the Equal Opportunity Office and the Equity Studies Centre. By January 1992 we were in a position to do a joint evaluation of the range of activities that had been initiated over the past ten years. Compared with the previous lack of programming, the list of student work was impressive. There were now five camp programs: the original race relations programs at Kandalore; the Grade 7/8 camp; regular ESL camps; the Latin American camps; and the retreat on gender issues. Regular student conferences were being held on apartheid and on non-traditional employment aimed at senior elementary students (Horizons). Other ongoing events were the Black Students' conference and "Patterns of Racism," which was pitched towards Grade 10 history classes and examined examples of racism in Canadian history. Classroom material about the Montreal Massacre and the five-hundredth anniversary of Columbus's landing in America, as well as support materials for the schools, were being prepared. The Drama Department had initiated a co-op program with a focus on race relations.

Questions were raised, though, about the predominantly anti-racist focus of Kandalore – should the camps continue to have an issue-based focus? The student program workers directly involved in organizing the camps argued for the importance of that approach. We did not want the edge taken off our programs. A consensus was reached that the main weakness of the camps was the resistance to follow-up work in the schools, but there was less agreement on the nature of that problem. Was it a matter of conservative schools opposing anti-racist work, or were camp programs not sufficiently integrated into existing school activities? The first analysis led to developing strategies to press schools for deeper changes in the way they operated; the latter raised the spectre of modifying the camp programs to make them more acceptable to the existing school power structure.

An inventory of schools' participation in our programs showed uneven results. Some schools had a track record around multiculturalism and race relations, while others were stronger around sexism and gender. Other than a few alternative schools, few were doing anything around homophobia or class. Disability issues were hardly addressed anywhere, even in schools with large numbers of disabled students. Other schools were doing nothing about anything. Some were actively hostile to our programs – which led to another debate. Should we concentrate on deepening the work in schools that seemed favourably inclined, and that had a history with one or more issues? Or should we be trying to ensure that some sort of equity work was happening in every school in the system?

Our division of labour was somewhat clearer than in the past, but tensions remained around overlapping roles. The Equal Opportunity Office was responsible for the new Sexual Harassment Policy, and Sue McGrath was starting a system-wide training program for senior staff and sexual harassment resource people. Pat was preparing a new "Challenging Racism" course. Should the Equal Opportunity Office be responsible for training? Or should that work be the responsibility of Curriculum or Staff Development?

Differences over appropriate roles and strategies were sometimes amplified by personal conflicts. A range of strong personalities, identity politics, ideology – or philosophies around challenging the system – and the protection of established terrain all led to clashes. The tactics taken up could also create harsh differences. "Some people would want to approach things in a very safe way, and others would want to be right in your face," Domenic recalled. "As student program workers we could take a bit more of the heat because we had less to lose. It didn't seem to be as dangerous to our careers. We knew we weren't going to rise very far in the organization. People saw us as troublemakers."

Despite these questions and differences in approach, there was a sense of excitement to be part of a group of people who collectively might wield some clout in the push for systemic change.

One weakness in the discussions around our programs was that they were limited to the Equity Studies Centre and the Equal Opportunity Office, when the Staff Development Department should also have been involved. The final equity plan had called for two "equity trainers" in Staff Development, but only one trainer had been hired, and nobody could get a straight answer out of anyone about when, or if, the other position was to be filled. When we asked the one new trainer to attend a Kandalore camp, he said he had been told that it wasn't his job to work with students. We were puzzled as to why Staff Development had received the two training positions in the first place, because the Equal Opportunity Office had always done its own training. The lack of communication and co-operation from Staff Development underscored the importance of establishing an Equity Council, a "representative co-ordinating team for joint projects" to hammer out strategy and build a common understanding of the issues, but the senior bureaucracy proved very reluctant to establish such a body.

## Vern Douglas

Vern Douglas, the new First Nations advisor in the Equal Opportunity Office, had years of experience as a teacher and an activist in First Nations communities when he came to the Board. He was a seasoned teacher, with a degree in Native Studies. After university he had moved to Parry Sound to teach at a school that had a mixture of Native and non-Native students. He soon immersed himself in curriculum development because at the time he believed that the reason Native kids weren't doing well was not only because teachers didn't know anything about them but also because of the insensitivity of the curriculum.

By his late twenties Vern had begun to develop a deeper understanding of the colonial relationship imposed on Native people by the Canadian settler state, and the importance of traditional Aboriginal teachings in healing its effects. As a member of the executive of the Ontario Federation of Friendship Centres, he applied that knowledge in helping design the group's first training manual. After five years in Alberta as program director of the Sacred Circle Project with the Edmonton School Board, he returned to Toronto and became active with parents involved in the Wandering Spirit Survival School, an elementary program with a focus on Native children. He ended up teaching at the school for a year. In 1987 he was appointed vice-chair of the Social Assistance Review Board, but continued with his consulting, training, and organizational development work in Toronto's Aboriginal communities.

From the beginning Vern was ambivalent about his location in the Equal Opportunity Office – in his job interview he had expressed his concerns about lumping Aboriginal issues together with multiculturalism and anti-racism. Although he saw those as legitimate social and political issues, he did not believe that the Aboriginal agenda belonged in the same grouping. It seemed to him that Native issues would never get addressed there because First Nations peoples were so marginalized. Although his interviewers assured him that they would work to separate the issues, Vern soon learned that despite the Board's progressive reputation the Aboriginal agenda "was all but non-existent." Like the other advisors in the Equal Opportunity Office, he found himself "outside the pyramid" – with no one above him, and no one below him. "I had almost no authority," he said. "It was very token. I always felt like an outsider. Everybody around me had come up through the system and people were often surprised to hear that I had that much teaching experience and that I'd been an administrator in Edmonton. They thought they'd plucked some token Native guy out of the job pile somewhere."

## Identity Politics

By the beginning of the 1990s, the concept of identity politics still had very fluid meanings. In a positive sense, it referred to the struggles of different marginalized groups to articulate and challenge their oppression in their own voices. On the negative side, it was also beginning to mean reducing everything to questions of personal identity.

Barb Thomas, for instance, experienced the impact of the phenomenon on her work – and as a white person found herself being ambivalent about the concept. When she was hired to do training of the graduates of the anti-racism facilitator course, helping to prepare them to teach the course themselves, she heard someone say, "Why the hell is a white person being hired to do this?" She did not see the question as attacking her personally. "It was more around being tired of white people being in on it all the time." She saw the validity of the question, and quietly bowed out of the project.

She had, she said, "always been hired by people of colour and worked under their supervision. I felt that it was up to them to use me well, and not use me for things that other people should do." It was "irritating" when white people would listen to another white person more than they'd listen to a person of colour. She added: "Always having to work your identity strategically affects the relationship between people. It could be very tiring."

Myra Novogrodsky also felt the impact of identity politics on her work. At the time, she said, "Identity politics were being played out in very ugly ways in the city and in the province. There were a lot of excesses. There were a lot of experiences where people were shouted down or felt uncomfortable saying anything about another group's strategies or even their own group's strategies." Now that the NDP government was finally giving people a better chance of getting their issues on the table, things were going a little crazy. Myra said: "I guess in the long run I would hold a Marxist view that it was a necessary stage. One of the unfortunate things was that it depoliticized a lot of people who didn't want to get involved anymore. Was there racism? Probably. Isn't there everywhere? But there must be a way of talking about it and moving through it that doesn't leave people running for cover and humiliated and not wanting to touch anything political again. I think one thing about the Centre was that we eventually became able to talk from our starting points and to listen better in terms of other people's starting points."

Vanessa Russell was concerned about what she perceived as the limits that identity politics were placing on the work. "We always knew how important it was to start with kids' own lived realities when doing anti-oppression work, but I think we didn't work hard enough on moving them out of their own autobiographies and into building allies and working together to end all kinds of oppression."

Still, the formative days of the Equity Studies Centre were by no means primarily negative. Even Ruby Lam, who was probably among the most critical staffers, looked back on the period with a certain amount of fondness. It was a "fertile time of thinking," she said. "On a personal level I felt that I really grew and my politics became really clear." Part of that politics was working for social justice, "not just for one group but for everybody."

## Sexual Harassment Policy

Although the student program workers were worried that our cross-appointment to Curriculum might give us less margin to manoeuvre, the approval of the new Sexual Harassment Policy strengthened our ties to the affirmative action side of the Equal Opportunity Office. The Board's 1981 Sexual Harassment Policy had become seriously out of date, and in the new, more comprehensive policy, which took effect on January 1, 1992, sexual harassment was no longer simply a matter of using a personal position to extract sexual favours. The new policy included a wide range of sexist behaviours, including teasing and innuendo, inappropriate language and comments, anti-gay slurs, and sexually explicit photos or cartoons that might make someone feel uncomfortable, degraded, or unsafe – in short, any sexually oriented behaviour that might interfere with work or school performance. The policy covered everyone on Board property or in a Board-sponsored program – students, employees, volunteers, and visitors.

Since most of those experiencing sexual harassment were vulnerable students and employees, it was clear they would need support in laying complaints. The policy called for a network of sexual harassment resource persons to assist complainants with the process. Most of the SHRPs, as they became known, were drawn from employee bargaining units and associations, but Vanessa and I were designated as SHRPs for students.

It seemed like a simple assignment, but on closer inspection the policy and procedures were complicated and legalistic. Everyone's rights needed to be protected, and because a finding of fault could result in discipline, the actions taken had to be transparent and fair. We had to master the ins and outs of the procedure and policy and consider elements such as personal privacy and the nature of evidence. We had to know the boundaries between sexual harassment, an administrative matter, and sexual assault, which fell under the Criminal Code. Dealing with minors involved further complicated questions of age of consent and parental rights. In certain cases there were obligations to inform the Children's Aid Society, and in others there were ethical questions of confidentiality.

The large group that began the several days of training as SHRPs slowly whittled itself down. As participants poured through the policy and attempted to apply it to scenarios it became clear that there were very different levels of sophistication in understanding and ability to act as advocates. Some participants still seemed to think that the whole thing was much ado about nothing. Others were filled with righteous anger and ready to hang anyone accused of sexism from the proverbial lampposts. Over time, with training, selection, and supervision, most of the inappropriate candidates were eliminated. The remaining core group was not large, but played an important role, both as advocates for complainants and resource people for ongoing training of administrators and other Board staff.

The workshops introducing the new policy to the education system as a whole were also not an easy ride. Teachers raised the spectre of false accusations. Administrators resented the cumbersome investigation procedures. Union members were suspicious of a policy that might supplant grievance procedures. Men complained that they could be punished for giving someone a "compliment." Those with religious or moral concerns about homosexuality grumbled that the policy undermined freedom of speech. Potential complainants feared retaliation.

According to Sue McGrath, many of the sessions turned into a kind of awareness training. The first step was to get people to understand the issues. "The majority were on board, but there were always a few very resistant people, especially around sexist language." Sue spent considerable time talking, for instance, about why calling a woman a "cow" was a problem, or why supervisors should deal with pin-ups in lunchrooms – when what she really wanted to do was talk about the mechanics of the procedures to be followed in sexual harassment cases.

Although most complaints were resolved at the local level with the assistance of the SHRPs, occasionally complainants would not be satisfied with the outcome and would exercise their right to refer matters to the Board's executive office. Many of the senior officials were uncomfortable taking on cases, Sue found, and they disliked the new reality: that complaints never went away. "They would handle a couple at the beginning and then they'd realize that there was going to be another one and another one. I think too that complaints sometimes unsettled their view of a benign and ordered school system."

Despite such difficulties, the first complaint I ever facilitated illustrated the impact of the policy on an individual level. A Vietnamese youth started coming to the lesbian and gay students support group, although calling him a participant would be a bit of a stretch. He was quiet, made little eye contact, and in the group go-around would hardly say more than his name. One afternoon he arrived visibly upset. When it came his turn in the check-in, he blurted out, "He did it again." It took us a few minutes to pry the story out of him. For quite some time another boy in his class had been harassing him, leaving copies of *Playgirl* on his desk, calling him names, telling everyone he was a fag, bumping into him in the hall, generally making his life a living hell.

I told him that the Sexual Harassment Policy covered that kind of behaviour, but to do anything about it he would have to make a complaint. He was reluctant. It might just make things worse. Would all the teachers know? Would they tell his parents? The procedure was supposed to be confidential, I told him, and since he was over sixteen there was no obligation to contact his parents. The administrator who would handle the complaint would know what was going on, however, and it was impossible to predict the reaction of the harasser. He went away to think about it. The next week he said he was ready.

I took down the details, filled out the forms, and let the school principal know that a sexual harassment complaint was about to arrive. A few days later the student phoned me to say he had been called into the vice-principal's office and grilled about what he had done to "provoke" the harassment. That kind of questioning was clearly out of line. The policy also said that, as the young man's advocate, I was to be present at any meetings. Still, the student was satisfied with how he had handled himself. He told me the harasser had also been called in. I considered calling the school to complain but decided to wait and see what happened. When the student showed up at the support group the following week, he was animated and eager to tell his story. The harasser had been raked over the coals and threatened with suspension if he got so much as within ten yards of the complainant again. If there was one thing that administrators knew, it was how to discipline kids.

Later I made sure to point out to the principal that in the future he should ensure that complainants were properly represented in any meeting with the administration. But as it was, for me the experience offered a couple of lessons: how policy could be used to make the system take harassment more seriously, and how the policy could make a difference in the life of a vulnerable kid. As I dealt with complaints over the next five years, those same lessons would be reinforced time and time again.

A larger problem was that, after the original training of key administrators, most Board employees, students, and community members still received no training at all on the new policy. Workshops were typically offered only in locations where some sort of problem had been identified. Vanessa and I began to offer student workshops on the new policy wherever we could.

We adapted a simple exercise in which small groups would come to a consensus on whether a list of behaviours – comments about someone's body, sexual jokes, asking someone on a date, staring, hugging – were "always, sometimes, or never" sexual harassment. The exercise soon made it clear that depending on the context, and the people involved, almost all these behaviours fell into the "sometimes" category. Sexual harassment was not like a speed limit. Sometimes a particular behaviour could be harassment, and in other contexts the same behaviour could be inoffensive.

The group then looked at underlying principles and recognized that what made a behaviour harassment was that it was unwelcome, unwanted, or intimidating, and that it had to do with power.

That work set the stage for a discussion about when someone should be expected to know that a particular behaviour was inappropriate without being told, and when there was a responsibility to communicate discomfort. What were the barriers to such communication? The group finished by talking about the possible impact of harassment on an individual's ability to study or work. They analyzed scenarios and brainstormed around what they could do to make their schools free of sexual harassment. Over the years we ran hundreds of such workshops in elementary and secondary schools.

## Parallel Retreats

The "parallel retreats" program grew out of the young women's retreat on gender issues. Myra had become convinced that work against sexism had to include young men. "What's the point of talking about sexism without talking to the people who were most likely to be perpetrators? That just reinforces the rage of the victims without changing anything." To work with boys she called in Michael Kaufman, a founding member of the White Ribbon Campaign, a project that used the December 6 anniversary of the Montreal Massacre to draw attention to violence against women.

The resulting retreats recognized two principles: the importance of educating young men on questions of sexism, and the importance of young women having the space to discuss issues among themselves. For the first three days, boys and girls were housed at different campsites, going through parallel programs. On the last morning the boys were bussed to the women's site, and together the young men and women shared their insights from the previous three days and came up with action plans to take back to their schools.

For the first few years the boys' program had its rough edges, but it evolved through experience. According to Domenic Bellissimo, a regular facilitator at the boys' retreat, the program successfully got young men to look at their behaviour and language – "how misogynist it was, or how sexist some of their ideas were." They would typically sit around in groups of ten or twelve and discuss issues "they had never been allowed to discuss before." Domenic was "struck by how few positive male role models they actually had in their lives." He also saw a surprisingly consistent level of homophobia in the boys' groups. Even though they might be sensitive to women's issues, they tended to share a basic discomfort around issues of homophobia and homosexuality.

Vanessa worked to have that issue addressed. She pointed out that the two facilitators – one man and one woman – who led the retreat's sexuality section only talked about heterosexual sex, and she pushed to have that section become more inclusive, and to broaden out the discussions in the other sessions as well. Facilitators worked to figure out how to talk about sexual orientation attached to body image, violence, or harassment.

## Non-Traditional Employment

While the promotion of women teachers to positions of responsibility was on target, a much more difficult task facing Sue McGrath was changing the gender makeup of the Board's non-teaching staff. Even getting the effort approved was a struggle. The right-wing trustees on the Personnel and Organization Committee responded with snickers and laughter to the idea that a woman might want a non-traditional job and that the Board should work to integrate more women into male-dominated job areas. Nevertheless, a "non-trad" committee was established. It began by discussing high-skill jobs such as computer programming but ended up focusing on "easier areas" such as caretaking, the trades, and transportation. But many of those "easier areas" did not turn out to be so easy after all. Often the system itself was not ready for a mixed-gender workforce – at least one school had no female washroom for the caretakers, for example.

The only success in the trades was with a woman who had originally been a caretaker and who, after "herculean efforts," was trained and placed as a carpenter. Other women faced enormous resistance. The Board's one woman delivery driver was sexually harassed in the workplace and ended up leaving and suing the institution. The male drivers had peed on her truck and her car, and, as if that weren't enough, according to Sue they had finally got her to quit the job when "they propped up a female mannequin with its legs spread and a picture of a piece of fish or steak or something stuck between its legs." The theory was that these men had low-status jobs and the entry of women into those jobs lowered their status even more. "We really needed a different strategy," Sue said. "It wasn't right to hire one woman and put her in the middle of a workforce where a few of the other drivers would just make her life hell."

The Equal Opportunity Office helped organize regular meetings for women in non-traditional jobs to identify problems, and Sue went into the workplaces to try to resolve the issues. These could be difficult situations. One time she did a workshop with the caretaking staff in a high school and one of the male SHRPs escorted her to the parking lot because he thought she might need protection.

## Racist Jokes

At the same time the demand for our services in the schools was increasing – helped along by the Board's expanded equity structure and the profile of the new provincial government. In 1987 Alok, Hari, and I had produced a booklet on racist jokes, and a workshop related to that work was in considerable demand.[3]

One of the standard responses used to downplay the importance of racist comments and name-calling was that they were all just jokes and that people shouldn't take them so seriously – "Sticks and stones will break my bones but names will never hurt me." The workshop addressed that assertion.

The standard workshop approach would have been to have participants analyze a number of real jokes, but our experience with the booklet warned us against taking that direction. When it was first released we got complaints about the jokes that we had included as examples. Before the booklets could be distributed in schools we had even been compelled to affix a sticker in each copy, warning of the content. It seemed ironic that part of the system would be completely apoplectic about seeing such material in writing, while another part was intent on dismissing the issue as insignificant. But such was the culture of the Board.

In the workshops, to overcome these objections I adopted the names of imaginary countries from another game we sometimes used and inserted them into the standard racist jokes. What do you call a Lanivian with an IQ of 200? A village. How do you keep five Zhaboris from raping a girl? Throw them a basketball. Did you hear the one about the queer Valdestan? He preferred women over whiskey. Why do Syralis have big noses? Air is free. Why wasn't Jesus Christ born in Montzia? God couldn't find three wise men or a virgin there. We handed out a sheet with these "jokes" to small groups and then asked them to describe everything they knew about Lanivians, Zhaboris, and the others. The groups would generate a cornucopia of stereotypes. Since nobody had ever heard of these "countries" before, we would ask participants to tell us how they had come up with the ideas for these characteristics. They would end up relating a mental process of inference motivated by their desire to "get" the joke. It became very clear that these simple jokes conveyed a great deal of information. That made it much more difficult to sustain the idea of the innocence of the jokes.

Next the participants would think through possible interventions. Students could also make recommendations on how they thought teachers and administrators should respond. Like many of the one-shot workshops we were increasingly being asked to deliver, this one did not result in much of an action plan, but it raised issues and challenged hegemonic ideas. Little by little, it seemed, we were making a difference.

# Chapter 10

# A Single Spark

THE SPRING OF 1992 PROVIDED EVIDENCE, if any was needed, that racism was certainly more than just jokes. The Rodney King verdict, clearing a group of police in the brutal beating of a Black man, despite video images of the incident being broadcast across the continent, had left Los Angeles in flames. In Toronto the dramatic events south of the border resonated with continuing police abuse and shootings of young Black men. When a demonstration linking the issues marched up Yonge Street on May 4, years of frustration with the police erupted into mayhem. Compared to what was going on in Los Angeles, the "Yonge Street Riot" was a low-key affair: no deaths, a few arrests, several broken windows, an overturned hot-dog stand. Still, in Toronto terms it was a major event, shattering illusions that racism was not a Canadian problem.

The Board's regular anti-apartheid conference was held a few days after the Yonge Street march. At the final plenary, Faith Holder, a student who had attended the anti-racism camp and was a member of the Oakwood Afro-Canadian Club, called on the Board to immediately organize a student conference on local issues. The motion received resounding support.

When the upper administration proved reluctant to move ahead with that conference, Pat Case resorted to subterfuge. He created a poster calling for a meeting, and his son Ben put the poster up in several schools. Pat then took a copy to the office of the associate director of Human Resources and warned the staff that unless the Board did something, students were going to take things into their own hands. It seemed likely that Harold Brathwaite – who had finally been promoted to the position of associate director of Human Resources in September 1991 – would catch on to the ploy. Harold, Pat said, "smelled something. He kept looking at me out of the corner of his eye. But that's what forced them into doing it."

Several hundred students showed up at the conference. Small groups managed by student facilitators aired issues and developed recommendations. At the final plenary, director Joan Green and Board chair Pam McConnell faced a crowd of angry and impatient young people. The administration could talk about the Board's wonderful policies all they liked, but the students were seeing little difference in the everyday life of the schools.

The students at the conference adopted a series of demands. They called on the director to take concrete steps to ensure that all policies dealing with racism were communicated to staff and students and implemented in all schools. There should be mandatory anti-racist courses for all students and training for all teachers. Black history should be incorporated in the regular history curriculum. There should be a review of all textbooks to ensure that they reflected a multiracial and multicultural perspective. The Board should increase the representation of racial and visible minority teachers and administrators.

Student empowerment was also a major theme. The conference called on student councils to take steps to ensure that they were representative of the racial and cultural mixture of their schools, and demanded that they be given a stronger role and voice in school decision-making. More opportunities should be provided for students from different schools to work co-operatively on issues. If complaints were not being addressed in school, students should be encouraged to report racist incidents directly to the Equal Opportunity Office. ESL students should be better integrated into the schools' regular social and cultural life.

Participants did not restrict themselves to school-based issues. They also called on the province to investigate the extent of racism in the media and to set up a "totally independent authority" to hear complaints from young people about their treatment by the police. All levels of government should co-operate to come up with a plan to create jobs for young people, including jobs in the field of race relations.

Finally, the conference founded STAR, Students of Toronto Against Racism, the first system-wide anti-racist student organization, and demanded that it be officially recognized by the Board. I became staff liaison. The final goal of the job description that Tony Souza had drawn up for me ten years before was at last being implemented.

## The Lewis Report

The "riot" also caught the attention of the provincial government. Premier Bob Rae asked elder statesman Stephen Lewis to conduct an inquiry. After a whirlwind series of consultations, Lewis delivered his report on June 9, prefacing it with four observations. The fundamental problem, he stated, was anti-Black racism.

> While it is obviously true that every visible minority community experiences the indignities and wounds of systemic discrimination throughout Southern Ontario, it is the Black community which is the focus. It is Blacks who are being shot, it is Black youth that is unemployed in excessive numbers, it is Black students who are being inappropriately streamed in schools, it is Black kids who are disproportionately dropping out, it is housing communities with large concentrations of Black residents where the sense of vulnerability and disadvan-

> tage is most acute, it is Black employees, professional and non-professional, on whom the doors of upward equity slam shut.[1]

Lewis noted the extent of the "anger, anxiety, frustration and impatience" among visible minority communities and the "weary and bitter sense" that he was engaged in yet another reporting charade. Then there was fear, especially from the Black community and in particular from mothers. "The eight shootings over the last four years, and the sense, real or imagined, of unpredictable police encounters with Black youth have many families very frightened."[2] Finally, Lewis reported that everyone he had spoken to was tired of talk and wanted to see speedy action.

After a series of recommendations on the criminal justice system,[3] Lewis attacked the government's "disappointing" record on employment equity and recommended the passage of legislation without delay. He called for the upgrading of the Ontario Anti-Racism Secretariat, the establishment of a cabinet committee on race relations to meet with representatives of visible minority communities at least four times a year, and funding for community development projects to deal with health, social service, and employment problems faced by minority communities.

In the section of the report focusing on education, Lewis remarked on the recommendations that had come from the STAR conference.

> The long and the short of it is that when you read those recommendations, it's as if virtually nothing has changed for visible minority kids in the school system over the last ten years. . . . The lack of real progress is shocking. . . . Where are the courses in Black history? Where are the visible minority teachers? Why are there so few role models? Why do our white guidance counsellors know so little of different cultural backgrounds. Why are racist incidents and epithets tolerated? Why are there double standards of discipline? Why are minority students streamed? Why do they discourage us from university? Where are we going to find jobs? . . . How long does it take to change the curriculum so that we're a part of it?[4]

While Lewis's recommendations seemed eminently reasonable to those of us who had been dealing with the issues for years, opposition Tory spokesman Bob Runciman had a different perspective. In a joint press conference with Metro Police Association president Art Lymer, Runciman accused the government of capitulating to "vocal interest groups."

> Stephen Lewis' report on Race Relations virtually ignored the views of police. Art Lymer had to request a meeting with Mr. Lewis to voice his concerns but you won't find those concerns anywhere in Mr. Lewis' report. Instead, Mr. Lewis focused exclusively on equality of opportunity and treatment of visible minorities while ignoring issues of public safety, police morale and individual responsibility. It is shameful.[5]

Three years later Runciman would become solicitor general, the provincial cabinet minister in charge of the police.

The report moved the NDP government into action. Summer jobs for youth programs were expanded, employment equity legislation was introduced, and the solicitor general tabled legislation requiring police to report the use of force and receive training in the use of alternatives. The Special Investigations Unit was given new resources and independence.

The report also awoke the Ministry of Education out of its lethargy. A new bill was passed giving the minister authority to require school boards to develop and implement ethnocultural equity and anti-racism policies. As well, a new assistant deputy minister position responsible for anti-racism and ethnocultural equity was established to provide leadership in the development of anti-racist curriculum and to monitor school boards' implementation of their new policies. The NDP was finally making good on its long-time promises.

## Black Heritage

The crisis around the "Yonge Street riot" and the recommendations of the Lewis report gave special urgency to the Board's continuing implementation of the *Report on the Education of Black Students in Toronto Schools*. One of those recommendations had been to establish teacher-training courses in African heritage.

The first course, delivered by Akwatu Kenti and Imam Abdullah Hakim Quick during the 1992-93 school year, was too general to satisfy the teachers taking part – most of them were interested in a recipe for teaching African heritage courses. The following year, Hari Lalla called on Bernard Moitt, co-ordinator of African Studies at the University of Toronto. Moitt delivered university-level lectures that he justifiably believed were necessary background information for anyone taking on the responsibility of teaching about African history and civilization. Most of the teachers were frustrated that they were still not being given "practical" material that could be used in the classroom. Moitt described the experience as "largely negative."[6]

The problems were symptomatic of the difficulties of organizing courses for teachers struggling with the demands of large classes and enormous course loads. Hari reluctantly came to accept the necessity of "hand-holding" in teacher-training. "You've got to write the notes for them, write the questions for them, and then provide the answers to the questions. If you give it to them like that they'll teach it. It's a sad commentary on teaching, but that's what they say – "Don't give me theory. Just show me what to do and how to do it."

For subsequent Black heritage courses and others about Vietnamese, South Asian, and Native studies, Hari resorted to the time-honoured strategy of organizing the courses himself with the aid of a reference group and then bringing in different speakers for different sessions. At least with that approach, if there was a bad fit between a particular instructor and participants, the next session would be different.

## A Homophobia Blow-Up

In spring 1992 I was trying to write a short flyer on homophobia – it would work in tandem with a flyer on the new sexual harassment policy. It had occurred to me that if people didn't know what sexual harassment was, they would certainly know even less about homophobic harassment, or even that it was covered in the policy. Together the flyers would be distributed widely to teachers, parents, and students. Or at least that was the plan. Even though I took as a model a similar flyer that had been available for years, in a number of languages, on the race relations policy, the flyer I was preparing soon came up against heavy opposition from my co-workers at the Board. That April, even though the policy and support documents were the business of the Equal Opportunity Office, the subject of my flyer inexplicably appeared on an Equity Studies Centre agenda. There was going to be enough trouble trying to get the system to accept dealing with sexual harassment, someone said. Just because a gay trustee had been elected didn't mean that things were going to change overnight. Shouldn't senior administrators be involved? When I called the response what I saw it as being – homophobia – that sparked another round of meta-recriminations. How were we ever going to be able to work together if we didn't trust each other? How could we trust each other when we accused each other of bigotry at the first disagreement? How, I replied, could we trust each other when certain issues were always pushed off the table? When it was never the right time to take a stand? The flyer went on the back burner.

In the meantime, since his election in November 1991 John Campey had been quietly laying the groundwork for implementing the recommendations from the Lesbian and Gay Employees Group and building support for a major leap forward around the Board's approach to dealing with homophobia. The showdown came in May and June when lesbian and gay parents, students, and staff and their allies once again faced off against the homophobic right.

In a meeting in May Campey gave notice of a motion that Tony Gambini's job as counsellor for gay and lesbian students be made a full-time permanent position and that an openly lesbian counsellor be appointed to work part-time with lesbian students, recommendations that had been stalled in the bureaucracy for more than a year. He asked the Board to immediately approve the sexual orientation curriculum document that had been in the works for six years, to repeal the clause that prohibited the "proselytization" of homosexuality that had been on the books since the debacle of 1981, and, finally, to establish a Consultative Committee on the Education of Gay and Lesbian Students.

Campey had to ensure that the NDP caucus and the one or two swing votes were on side, and that anti-gay voices led by trustee Alex Chumak were isolated. He framed homophobia as one more piece of the equity agenda both for the caucus and the Board. The proposals all fit within the Board's existing framework and structures. The Consultative Committee on the Education of Gay and Lesbian Students was modelled on similar committees for Native and Black students. There had been social work and counselling focused on different communities since the 1970s. Curriculum documents on different issues were common. It was hard for anyone to argue that the proposals were asking for special treatment.

Campey had also worked hard to build good relationships with both sides of the Board, and found that his presence was educating even the right-wing trustees. "They got to know me and saw what got directed at me. If anybody didn't have a face to see how homophobia played out, I was right there."

Campey also saw to it that the community was mobilized – students, parents (gay or lesbian parents or members of Parents and Friends of Lesbians and Gays [PFLAG]), and Board employees groups came out to meetings to put pressure on the Board to deal with the issues. The students in particular, Campey said, "played an incredibly important role," making a huge impact on the trustees and undercutting the right-wing. Local residents were identified in each ward and encouraged to call their trustees to urge their support. Campey also built bridges to other constituencies. He had labour support through his NDP connections and his involvement with the Labour Education Committee. The Status of Women Committee already had an analysis that extended to issues of sexual orientation, and with his work in support of international languages Campey had connections with the leadership in a range of immigrant communities.

The opposition that did emerge included *The Toronto Sun,* which railed against the "lunatics" on the Toronto Board who were "brainwashing our kids" and "promoting homosexuality," the standard Christian fundamentalists, and a new "secular" group calling itself Citizens United for Responsible Education, or CURE. As an opponent, CURE was far more sophisticated than the fundamentalist religious groups. It took its cue from a new wave of homophobic organizing taking place in the United States at the time. The group's handbook specifically advised members not to make religious arguments or quote scripture in public. It also instructed them not to sit together in parent meetings but to spread themselves throughout the audience to appear more numerous. The handbook was filled with distorted "scientific" information about gay men and lesbians. It attacked the new curriculum document on sexual orientation because it "glossed over the health dangers of homosexuality" and did not advocate therapy to "cure" homosexuals or feature testimony from "ex-gays."

Despite the opposition, Campey had the votes lined up, and all his motions passed by the end of June. A few weeks later, Fran Endicott, who had just been appointed the new chief commissioner of the Ontario Human Rights Commission, congratulated the Board on the achievement.

Homophobia had now become a burning issue within the Board, and the need for intensive internal education had become obvious. In June the Equity Studies Centre brought in Suzanne Pharr, author of *Homophobia: A Weapon of Sexism*,[7] to conduct a workshop with the equity staff from both the Centre and the Equal Opportunity Office. Pharr was a feminist, founder of the Little Rock, Arkansas Women's Project, and a long-time social justice and anti-racist organizer in the Southern States. She was also an open lesbian. Grey-haired, grandmotherly, and speaking with a soft Southern drawl, Pharr was the antithesis of the stereotype of the strident lesbian activist. While the workshop did not produce a complete consensus on the issues or heal all the suspicions of identity politics, it seemed to me that it marked the beginning of the long process of sharing and trust-building among the equity personnel.

The Pharr workshop also helped pave the way for an expansion of the annual spring equity conference at York University. Begun in the early 1980s as an affirmative action/women's studies event for Board staff, the conference had been co-sponsored over the years with the North York and York boards. When she took over Women and Labour Studies, Myra Novogrodsky approached Meg Luxton, the director of York University's Centre for Feminist Research, about setting up a partnership modelled on the Boston "Facing History and Ourselves" example of interaction between academics and front-line teachers. Soon all the other boards in the Greater Toronto Area became involved. The focus on gender issues was expanded to include anti-racism, but the inclusion of homophobia had remained a stumbling block because the organizing committee feared alienating participating Catholic boards. With Pharr's workshop putting the issue forward as part of the Equity Studies Centre mandate, that position had become less and less tenable. After a little strong-arming of Myra by Vanessa Russell and myself, the conference planning committee included homophobia in the following year. From there it was an inevitable progression to incorporate all equity issues, including disabilities and class.

## Marsha Melnik

In September 1992 Sue McGrath went on leave and was replaced by Marsha Melnik. Like many others attracted to social change, Marsha had worked overseas before taking up teaching in Toronto. As a teacher she had been an affirmative action rep, had set up a women's group in her school, and was a member of the Status of Women Committee. She had been "blown away" by her experiences as a teacher and facilitator at the Kandalore Camp. Still, despite her strong experience, it seemed to Marsha that she was dropped into Sue's job without adequate training or orientation. There were no introductions and no overlap time with Sue. She walked into the office to find a pile of files on her desk.

One of those files contained my draft homophobia flyer. Marsha also had objections, but hers I could not attribute to homophobia. She pointed out that my draft was confusing major differences between the race relations and sexual harassment policies. The flyer needed to reflect the new policy properly, and should mirror the still-to-be-produced general flyer on sexual harassment. If it met those requirements, she would do everything she could to get it published.

Vanessa Russell and I reshaped the draft to Marsha's satisfaction, but it soon became clear that objections were coming from higher up. Marsha found herself requiring permission from the Director's Office to put out a simple information pamphlet, and we found ourselves in a meeting with Superintendent Grant Bowers, who represented the "Second Floor" (the offices of the senior administration). Bowers spun out one argument after another against the flyer. Why should one group be singled out? People might get confused and think that the Board had two policies. The race relations flyer didn't specify particular groups. People might not understand what the word "homophobia" meant. Why were we so insistent on calling it "*homophobic* harassment"?

Marsha, Vanessa, and I refused to back down. Vanessa and I knew how to play the identity card. We were a lesbian and a gay man. Our community called it "homophobic harassment." Was he saying that our community didn't have the right to define and name our own oppression? Did he think he was more of an expert on our oppression than we were? Marsha backed us up, saying that calling it homophobia delivered an important message to gay students and staff, and if people didn't know what that was, it was important to educate them. After asking, "Couldn't we just call it something like harassment on the basis of sexual orientation?" Bowers scuttled off for more consultations with the Second Floor.

The meetings went on and on, and Marsha became more and more discouraged. Finally, one day when she was leaving the office late in the evening, Marsha chanced upon Harold Brathwaite in the subway. Harold told her, "Oh, by the way, go ahead with that pamphlet." Marsha had no idea where the decision came from, or when it had been made. "I had no connections. That was the problem – if you have connections you know what is happening before the fact."

## Learning Curve

As the Equity Studies Centre and expanded Equal Opportunity Office struggled through their first year, we tried to sort through the pressing issues of our new equity mandate in a series of internal workshops. One of the first focused on "cultural appropriation." A report by the Canada Council's Advisory Committee for Racial Equality and the Arts in the spring of 1992 had the press buzzing with issues of authenticity, the right to self-definition, and accusations of "political correctness" and censorship. The report's allusion to concerns about members of one cultural group writing in the voices of others had sparked an angry reaction from several prominent authors. Timothy Findley, for example, intoned, "If I want to write in the voice of the tea cozy sitting in front of me, believe me I'm not going to ask for its permission."

My partner Richard Fung had been a member of the Canada Council committee throughout its deliberations and met with our team to discuss the controversy. He pointed out that such issues were not new. Documentarians, for instance, had struggled with ethical concerns around representation and appropriation for years.[8] While asserting the importance of recognizing that there were no essentially pure cultures and admitting that concerns could sometimes be phrased in ways that overlooked cultural hybridity and seemed to promote essentialist notions of authentic voice, Richard argued that there was a "special urgency" to the preservation and autonomy of Aboriginal cultural resources in particular. Once Aboriginal culture was lost, it was gone for ever.

As the discussion around cultural appropriation indicated, Aboriginal questions were much in the public eye, and our understanding of the issues was admittedly superficial. Vern Douglas took on the responsibility for a session on that question. His presentation was based on the traditional First Nations medicine wheel with its four directions and four colours. While we all knew we had a lot of learning to do about treaty history, land claims, First Nations positions on multiculturalism, and the demographics of Toronto's Aboriginal population, we were a very secular crowd, and therefore had some uneasiness about Vern's traditional approach to First Nations spirituality.

I had no problem with the philosophical system itself, which seemed elegant, insightful, and flexible as a tool of analysis, psychology, and pedagogy. But my eyebrows raised when the four colours were applied to race. Vern explained that traditional teachings said the four colours also represented the four races: white, black, red, and yellow. The Creator had given each of these races different gifts, which they were to share on Turtle Island. When he described the "gifts" or qualities that each race supposedly specialized in, they sounded to me like a rehashing of common racial stereotypes. Hari wanted to know where brown people like himself were supposed to fit in, and was not very happy when Vern told him that South Asians were white.

For Vern, however, the teachings were a fundamental belief, handed down over generations. He was more concerned with healing the spiritual, psychological, and social effects of centuries of colonialism, violation and marginalization experienced by Aboriginal communities in North America than he was with theories of the social construction of race. For him the return to traditional teachings was fundamental if this healing was to be accomplished.

The issue continued to be a source of unease, and I finally asked to meet with Rodney Bobiwash, then director of Aboriginal Programs and Aboriginal Student Services at the University of Toronto. Rodney was Anishnabe from the Mississagi Nation, a member of the Bear Clan, and held degrees in Native studies and history from Trent University and Oxford. He was a major intellectual force in anti-racist activism in the city at the time, a founder of Klanbusters and a central figure in ultimately successful human rights cases and subsequent criminal proceedings against the neo-Nazi hate group, the Heritage Front.

After taking the tobacco I offered him, Rodney asked me what he could do for me. I explained that I wanted to know his opinion on the notion that the four colours could be used to describe racial characteristics. I told him I wondered if it wasn't likely that the application of traditional Aboriginal philosophy to race was a relatively recent innovation under the influence of dominant nineteenth-century European ideas. He looked at me thoughtfully for a while and finally said that what I was suggesting was an "interesting theory" but I would get into a great deal of trouble if I proposed it in public. He was, as usual, completely right. I kept my speculations to myself. There were some things that simply couldn't be reconciled.

At our workshop on anti-Semitism Marsha Melnik recalled the discomfort of many Jewish students and teachers in "outing themselves" as Jews in the exercise at the camps where people grouped themselves according to their racial identification.

"Why were we afraid to say we were Jewish? Sometimes comments would be made. I remember one time when we spoke and some Black kids said, 'What are you complaining about, you all have maids.' That's very hard because that's the reason so many people were killed in the Holocaust, because we were all supposed to be rich and running the world."

Marsha subsequently established a focus group for Jewish students which met for six months before making a presentation to the Race Relations Committee. The experience underscored the work that needed to be done. When two girls from the group made the presentation it was met by "silence," Marsha said. "Then at least two people from the committee accused them of making the issue bigger than it was. How dare they want to take attention and money and resources away from the groups that really needed it?" The only support the group got was from a Jewish woman on the committee. "What happened?" the girls said to Marsha. "We don't get it. Why are they mad?" Marsha "was shocked" by the experience: "It was my naïveté about connecting the isms. If you are anti-racist you must be for women, you must be anti-homophobic, you must be against anti-Semitism, you must be because you believe in equity. Bullshit."

For the in-service workshop on homophobia everyone was given a gift certificate for Glad Day Books, Toronto's lesbian and gay bookstore. Participants were expected to buy a book of their choice and prepare a book report. During the lunch break, as an experiential exercise, we asked everyone to put on some gay liberation buttons and walk a block to a local restaurant holding hands with a member of the same sex. Vanessa remembered, "They didn't even want to go into the bookstore, that seemed too much." After lunch, when we asked people why they didn't do it, one response was that they wouldn't necessarily feel comfortable doing it with an opposite-sex person either. Even one of them who did it said, "Oh my god, I was so embarrassed that people might actually think I was a lesbian." For Vanessa, "What was really significant was realizing what they really felt about us. It was so hard."

## Losses

The rawness of some of the discussions we had in meetings and workshops was no doubt exacerbated by emotions generated by three serious personal and political losses that we suffered in the fall of 1992. First, in July, Joan McGrath died after a year-long struggle with cancer. Joan had been a regular contributor to *Focus on Equality*, writing reviews of children's books. As a library consultant, she had been a major ally, helping school librarians analyze materials for bias, training them to carry out reviews of their collections, and encouraging them to make their libraries more inclusive.

At the end of September Doug Wilson died of AIDS. Doug had worked until the end, editing and publishing *Focus on Equality*. Speaking at his memorial service, Pat Case noted that Doug had become so associated with the Equal Opportunity Office that several published obituaries credited him with holding Pat's job as the equity advisor on race relations.

In November Fran Endicott died of cancer at age forty-nine. During her eight years as trustee she had been instrumental in developing Board policies and programs on anti-racism, affirmative action, literacy, destreaming, and early childhood education. She had been appointed chief commissioner of the Ontario Human Rights Commission only months before her death. She had "driven the equity agenda," John Campey said. "She really named racism and institutional racism as something the Board needed to challenge." Because of her background in education, Campey said, she could deal with the Board administrators "as peers, and could really move them along. She is one of the underrecognized heroes in all of this."

## Hate Rears Its Head

In 1992 a new far-right coalition, the Heritage Front, burst onto the scene. The Front, which had been quietly organizing since 1989, was more than just another incarnation of the sporadic neo-fascist presence that had plagued Toronto since the 1930s. It brought together seasoned neo-Nazis with the violent racist skinhead subculture to form a far more aggressive and dangerous movement, specifically targeting youth for recruitment.

The Front, perhaps most notably, had set up a telephone hate line – recorded messages full of racist and anti-Semitic invective, encouraging callers to get in touch if they liked what they heard. Legal challenges to the line were in the courts. In the fall of 1992 the Front was actively leafleting at least six secondary schools in the east end. At Riverdale Collegiate Institute on Gerrard Street East, students arrived one morning to find material slipped into their lockers and business cards left in school library books. Terezia Zoric, a teacher at Riverdale at the time, remembered the incident. "I was walking down the history hallway seeing these things on the floor as the kids were opening their lockers. The focus of the pamphlet was about stopping Third World immigration. I knew we were going to have to do something about this."

In response, an ad hoc neighbourhood group, Citizens Against Racism, joined with school staff and Riverdale Against Discrimination (RAD), a group organized by the school's Kandalore graduates, to mount an anti-hate group rally at the school. Students from surrounding schools marched to Riverdale on a bright but freezing afternoon in January 1993. Also on hand were local trustees, MP Dennis Mills, and city councillor Peter Tabuns. In the school auditorium Riverdale drama students performed a series of skits illustrating racial conflict and sexual stereotyping, and the crowd was entertained by student rap artists. Speaker Martin Theriault from the Canadian Centre on Racism and Prejudice reminded the audience how east-end residents had mobilized to oust the Klan from the neighbourhood in the early 1980s. "Simon," a charismatic high-school student and spokesperson for Anti-Racist Action (ARA), delivered the message that students themselves had the responsibility to make sure that "white supremacy" did not gain a foothold in their schools. Meanwhile a gang of neo-Nazis led by Heritage Front leader Wolfgang Droege had arrived near the front of the school. Members of the ARA quickly formed a line, shoulder to shoulder, and physically prevented them from getting close to the building. The police eventually intervened and escorted the Nazis away.

Back at the Board offices, Director Joan Green sent out a letter to staff drawing attention to the Heritage Front problem, but offered no suggestions for action. Students of Toronto Against Racism fired off a reply, expressing concern that Green's letter "disregarded possible solutions." Calling for "immediate action," STAR suggested that assemblies be held in all schools to inform students that the Board would not tolerate racist activity, and to encourage them to report incidents. STAR also recommended establishing "a central gathering place for information" so the Board could understand the magnitude of the problem.

Pat Case called a meeting of senior officials and quickly set up such a system for schools to report hate-group activity to the Office. Reports of leafleting and graffiti began to trickle in from across the city. A series of training sessions were organized for administrators, featuring several young ARA militants. The Anti-Racist Action members were our major support throughout the next few months. The group had superb intelligence on the different neo-fascist organizations and their leaders, symbols, tactics, and recruiting methods.

ARA drew from a wide range of people, but unlike other groups concerned about the rise of the neo-Nazi right, such as the Jewish human rights organization B'nai B'rith or the Urban Alliance Against Racism, it was based in anarchopunk youth culture and had first-hand knowledge of neo-Nazi street activity. Its mandate was to "expose, oppose and confront organized racism and the far-right agenda, through education, mass action and support of broader anti-racist struggles." In practice that meant confronting the Heritage Front *en masse*, making it impossible for them to operate in public. The group had first made headlines in November 1992, when it exposed a Heritage Front meeting and white power music concert welcoming British Holocaust denier David Irving to Canada. Members pelted the venue with eggs.

Most ARA members had a deep distrust of mainstream institutions. "We never operated with the idea that you should just go to the authorities and get them to fix the problem," one young organizer said. "We felt people had to take care of things in their own ways using their own resources. You can't go crying to the principal all the time." ARA also had a tense relationship with the police – especially given the members' growing conviction that the institutional culture of the police didn't take racism seriously. Members regularly appeared at rallies in hoods and bandanas to protect their identities. Most spokespeople used pseudonyms in public. Marsha could never remember the different names that "Simon," our prime contact, was using at any given time, and finally began referring to him as "Sally." The ARA's militancy and determination led to more than one clash with the Heritage Front, and the police – and to a wave of negative media coverage. I was able to do damage control at the Board, and our co-operation with the ARA continued, though the calm was short-lived. In June ARA conducted one of its most spectacular actions when group members led several hundred people into an east-end neighbourhood and trashed the front of a residence that housed the Heritage Front hate line.

The controversy over the group's tactics disrupted the close relationship that had been forged between the Equal Opportunity Office and the ARA in the early months of 1993. I continued to maintain contact with the group – as far as I was concerned, they were still the best source of street-level information available on neo-fascist groups. They had also been remarkably successful in focusing attention on neo-Nazi activities in the city and chasing them out of the schools and off the streets of downtown Toronto. After the closing down of the hate line, for example, the Front abandoned attempts to raise money to establish a "white community centre."

## From Hate Groups to White Supremacy

By 1994 the Heritage Front was in decline, especially after one of its key organizers, Grant Bristow, was exposed as a police agent. The immediate crisis around fascist recruiting in Toronto schools had abated. Nevertheless, Ruby began the process of finding, evaluating and getting permission to reprint material for a resource kit on "hate groups" that could be distributed to the schools. My contribution to the kit was a short piece that contextualized the groups within the history and logic of white supremacy.

The term "hate groups" had emerged as official Board terminology for the resurgent neo-fascist right. It was a term that resonated with the Criminal Code and the Board's institutional culture. Who could be in favour of hate? Even those who had for years opposed our initiatives against racism, sexism, or homophobia could be on the right side of this one. But the term was also slippery. It avoided coming to grips with the history or political agenda of the Heritage Front and its fellow travellers. Our experience with the police had shown that the term could be expanded to include any anti-social or unpopular individuals. One time, for instance, a police "expert" had put together a package of "hate group symbols" for schools that included Black power, Satanist, Wicca, and heavy-metal rock-band emblems. The groups that did truly qualify for the term were often in a state of flux, with new formations and new names and symbols constantly emerging. What was important were the common themes that connected this movement, no matter what manifestation the groups might take.

The major connecting thread was, of course, a belief in race and racism. Although "race" was no longer considered a valid scientific term, "hate groups" shared the belief that it was possible to divide the human population into distinct races whose different physical appearance indicate differences in character, abilities, or morality. They asserted that there was a struggle for survival between these races. The hate groups that were recruiting, encouraging, and committing acts of violence in Toronto all came out of the tradition of "white supremacy" that claimed the biological, intellectual, cultural, and moral superiority of whites. As a result, they opposed non-white immigration and interracial marriages, on the grounds that "mixing" would dilute the potential of the "white race."

A second major commonality was anti-Semitism – hostile attitudes and behaviour directed at Jews. Although most Canadian Jews are physically indistinguishable from the "white" population, white supremacist groups insisted that Jews represented a separate race and accused them of conspiring to take over the world. They either denied that the Holocaust happened or applauded the Nazi genocide, wishing that Hitler had been able to "finish the job."

Sexism, homophobia, and a contempt for people with disabilities were also part of the mix. The groups tended to be male-dominated and patriarchal. Women's role was to biologically reproduce the race. White lesbians and gay men were denounced as "race traitors" because our sexuality was not reproductive. People with disabilities were biologically inferior and consequently a detriment to the strength of the race.

In workshops I gave on the topic, I drew on my roots in rural Ontario to fashion an analogy with the relationship between white supremacist groups and other more mainstream expressions of racism. When I was growing up in Beaverton, my father would sometimes take me to the town dump to hunt rats with his .22. It was a common pastime for many people in the town. One day I asked him how come, if so many people went out to shoot the rats, there always seemed to be so many rats running around. You'd think that sooner or later there wouldn't be any left. There were hunting seasons for other wild animals; otherwise they would go extinct.

My dad just said, "Tim, no matter what you do, as long as there's garbage lying around, there's going to be rats."

I argued that it was the same with hate groups. As long as there was no real equality in society, as long as institutions and individuals got away with discrimination, as long as school curriculum and media ignored the contributions of particular groups of people, that kind of garbage was going to be a fertile breeding ground for white supremacy. Unless we were successful in cleaning up those kinds of situations, we would never be successful in getting rid of groups that took those common racist, sexist, and homophobic ideas to their violent extremes.

Chapter 11

# Re-Evaluations

BY THE EARLY 1990s, THE NOTION of the imminent possibility of a better socialist world had collapsed, along with the old bureaucratic socialist regimes. In most cases too, rather than ushering in a golden era of democracy, the result was nationalist chauvinism, fratricidal ethnic cleansing, religious fundamentalism, and a rise in neo-Nazi racism.

Still, public commitments by the NDP government in Ontario – including the introduction of the Employment Equity Act and mandatory anti-racism policies for school boards – and a growing body of legal decisions under the Charter of Rights and Freedoms signalled an increasing interest in overcoming racism and other forms of discrimination. This situation raised the previously heretical notion that while socialism had not resolved the "national question," significant changes to racial and other forms of inequality might be possible within capitalism.

While economic forces and interests still obviously benefited from marginalized labour and a segregated labour force, there also seemed to be strong tendencies to do away with irrational historical divisions based on skin colour or culture or gender. Faced with the huge social costs of excluding large numbers of people from the benefits of society, capital was, it seemed, beginning to recognize the advantages of more fully integrating all people into the economy and tapping their productive potential regardless of race or gender. I consoled myself that if it didn't seem like we were going to change the world, at least we might be able to make the present system less oppressive.

Another problem in all of this was that the anti-racist movement was experiencing a theoretical and practical crisis characterized by the rise of identity politics. Accusations and counteraccusations of racism were tearing apart long-standing progressive organizations. Important issues were awash in waves of hyperbole, with disagreements often reduced to contests to determine who was most oppressed and therefore most in need of attention. The tendency to establish a hierarchy of oppressions infected all progressive groups, including the women's and gay movements. Cynical jokes circulated about how only poor Black disabled lesbians could be true revolutionaries. Important discussions between potential allies spiralled into antagonism and were shut down. Our concern with the authenticity of experience and people not speaking for others was transformed into "You wouldn't understand it. It's a black/female/gay/etc. thing" and "you have no right to criticize me."

While the deployment of accusations of racism, sexism, or homophobia could sometimes be transparently self-serving, there was also something vital about the politics and insights that developed around different identities – something key about the principle that groups should define their own issues and speak for themselves on the basis of their own experiences. How could we affirm that principle without being pulled down into the destructive infighting that was tearing apart so many social movements?

## Back to Freire

I began to wonder if something was fundamentally wrong with how we had been approaching the issues. To try to sort some of this out (and still working on my Masters degree), I enrolled in a course on Paulo Freire and began rereading his work, the inspiration for much of the anti-racist pedagogy of the 1970s and 1980s. The first thing that struck me was the sense of duality that pervaded the work. According to Freire, the world is divided into two groups: the oppressors and the oppressed. There are two models of education: the "banking" model of the oppressors, in which teachers treat students as objects to be filled with information; and the "problem-conscious" model of education, in which teachers and students "educate one another through the medium of the world." While banking education encouraged passivity and domination, problem-conscious education nurtured critical consciousness and called for action.[1]

Freire's worldview was basically black and white, which was probably reasonable considering he was working in rural Brazil with impoverished, illiterate peasants in a state politically dominated by huge landowners. Differences in power were stark. Perhaps for that reason, there was not much direct discussion of power in Freire's writing. Power was something that oppressors had and the oppressed didn't have, at least until they became "empowered" by problem-conscious education. Perhaps because power was so naked and obvious, Freire didn't feel an need to analyze or define its nuances. Still, with "empowerment" so central to his writing, the absence of a discussion of power was striking, especially because he always asserted that it was the naming of the world that enabled people to transform it. The absence of a discussion of power made it exceedingly difficult to talk about relations *among* the oppressed.

I began to see a common thread in Freire and other recent left theories of social change. The problem was that a world of complex issues was continually being reduced to an underlying polarity. For the Maoists, everything was a manifestation of one class struggling against another. For anti-racists, everything was a manifestation of racism and the power of whites over others. For many feminists, everything was a manifestation of sexism and patriarchal male power over women. Then anyone who cared about these questions would have to decide what was the most important fundamental duality.

Mao had warned against this kind of dogmatic and stereotypical thinking as far back as 1937 in his essay "On Contradiction."[2] He insisted that the real world was incredibly complex and could not be reduced to simple polarities. He reminded his readers of Lenin's statement – that the most essential thing in Marxism, the living soul of Marxism, was the concrete analysis of concrete conditions. He continued, "Our dogmatists have violated Lenin's teachings; they never use their brains to analyse anything concretely, and in their writings and speeches they always use stereotypes devoid of content, thereby creating a very bad style of work in our Party."[3]

Freire's simple polarities reflected the reductionist notion of power that Mao (unsuccessfully) tried to escape. For Freire, if the oppressed were seen to engage in activities that oppressed others, it wasn't because a web of power relations could render people *simultaneously* oppressors and oppressed – for example, the poor peasant fighting for a better deal from the landlord could still be sexist to his wife, who in turn could be racist to her dark-skinned neighbour, and everybody could beat their children – but because they had internalized false consciousness. The oppressor had somehow sneaked inside their heads.

Before his death in 1984 the French philosopher Michel Foucault had put forward a much more complex notion of power.

> The omnipresence of power [is] not because it has the privilege of consolidating everything under its invincible unity, but because it is produced from one moment to the next, at every point, or rather in every relation from one point to another. Power is everywhere, not because it embraces everything, but because it comes from everywhere.[4]

Foucault was far too abstract and theoretical to have much impact on the nitty-gritty of anti-racist education in the early 1990s. As in Freire, anti-racist education tended to classify people as being either oppressor or oppressed. Even disagreements between members of the same oppressed group would often result in one (or both) sides being accused of *internalized* racism, sexism, or homophobia. Jews who opposed Israeli policy, for example, were regularly denigrated as "self-hating Jews."

## Resistance

Around this same time I was invited to write a chapter in a book being compiled by Lorna Weir, an old friend from *The Body Politic* days who was now a professor at York University. The book, *Beyond Political Correctness: Toward the Inclusive University*, looked at struggles in post-secondary educational institutions around the demands of "subordinated social groups."[5] Lorna wanted me to write about resistance to change in the public school system. As a result, in thinking about my decade or so of experience at the Toronto Board – and with the identity wars in mind – I began to wonder if we too had been guilty of "stereotypical thinking" by assuming that the resistance we regularly faced in our efforts at the Board was simply motivated by racism. I found myself trying to define what was essential to anti-racist education to see what exactly seemed to be sticking in the system's craw. After rereading the work of a number of key anti-racist educators, I ended up distilling six basic principles and considering the shape of resistance in each area.

1. **Anti-racist education** started from the assumption that observable differences in behaviour between human groups were historical and cultural in origin, not biological. Given that assumption, anti-racist education had to deal with the concept of "the social construction of race."

The notion of the social construction of race challenged traditional racist ideas that biology equalled destiny, but it also conflicted with the neutral, "colour-blind" approach adopted by many liberal educators. As a social construction, race was real and important and did need to be taken into account. Anti-racist education unsettled racists and liberals alike.

2. The motor force in **anti-racist education** was the struggle for justice of oppressed groups. Institutional change resulted from political pressure.

A clear example of resistance here was the dismantling of the School Community Relations Department in 1986 – a backlash based on the notion that the department was "too political." Community activism came into conflict with an institutional culture that understood the education system as neutral, professional, and above politics. Anyone facilitating community struggles to transform the way in which schools worked was encroaching on the prerogatives of professionals who knew what was best.

3. **Anti-racist education** could not be an add-on. Changes were required across the curriculum, and they would necessarily alter the content of all subject areas.

Depending on the subject, there were various arguments against curriculum change. In English, teachers evoked the importance of the "classics," which were "great" because they rose above specific ethnic, racial, or cultural specificity to deal with "universal human values." With all this universal greatness filling up the school day, not enough time was left over to introduce material because of its ethnic, racial, or cultural specificity. Similarly, history departments argued against the inclusion of "other people's history" when there was barely time to cover "our own." Particular subject areas, specifically the "hard" sciences, often maintained that their content was neutral.

The very idea that material from outside of the European sphere of influence could not equally communicate universal values was in itself potentially racist; and the notion that Western history was somehow unique and unconnected with the rest of the world was clearly Eurocentric. Still, we had to recognize that the school curriculum was indeed crammed, and that resistance also had to do with the material that teachers had been trained to deliver and what they felt confident about teaching. Teachers often resisted the introduction of new material because they were already overburdened. While the argument that science was above all this anti-racism stuff was belied by many concerned science and math teachers who provided an anti-racist classroom experience – through different kinds of group work, culturally based metaphors, examples, and problem content, the notion of the neutrality of science was a hegemonic idea shared by many people who were clearly not racist.

Another common argument was that talking about examples of historical injustice or discrimination would "open up old wounds," making white students defensive and guilty and students of colour angry, uncomfortable, or embarrassed. All of this would disrupt the fragile harmony of the classroom. Was this racism, or real anxiety on the part of teachers who, alone in their classrooms and without support, often felt they were sitting on a powder keg?

4. **Anti-racist education** needed to be system-wide, reaching into all parts of the institution's functioning. Students learned from the global school environment, which meant that non-curriculum-related areas such as personnel policies, assessment and placement, discipline, community relations, social work, counselling, and a recognition of cultural symbols were all implicated in reproducing institutional racism.

All of these areas had seen resistance to change. Affirmative action supposedly undermined the merit principle. Those in charge of assessment and placement responded to evidence of systemic racial and cultural streaming of students with indignation, assuming that they were being accused of intentional bias and of failing to meet the neutral and objective standards of their profession. Social workers used arguments about generic professionalism to resist calls for the hiring of personnel from particular communities and for the service of those communities. Those opposed to playing down or making Christmas and Easter celebrations more inclusive argued that such moves were censorship, "banning Christmas," destroying time-honoured childhood traditions, or that such celebrations were already secular and universal anyway. Could these arguments be attributed to racism, or to fears that hard work would not be rewarded, to professional insecurities, and to simple nostalgia?

The instructive case was discipline. As time went on discipline was the area that seemed to generate the least opposition. Discipline against particular forms of speech and behaviour, especially by students, was already a common practice in school culture. Teachers' expression of bias was seen as undermining the supposed neutrality that was part of their professional responsibilities. Elementary teachers could see racist comments as corrosive of their efforts to teach students to "play and work well with others." Administrators were also aware of how a failure to control racist speech could escalate personal conflict into group confrontations.

A handful of educators might still quote "sticks and stones" or paraphrase Nietzche's "what doesn't kill you makes you strong" in an attempt to downplay the seriousness of racist speech, but generally this ran against the patronizing instincts of the majority of them – people who believed that their role was to guide their charges and keep them from harm. For all these reasons, even conservative voices resisting other kinds of educational changes could hardly oppose policies and practices that amounted to stiffer discipline, at least for students. Schools already knew how to discipline bad behaviour. This was the area in which anti-racism was most congruent with traditional institutional power relations and existing school culture.

5. **Anti-racist education** had its own particular pedagogy. The goal of anti-racist pedagogy was to equip students and staff to understand and challenge unjust power relations. It needed to be based on learners' social experience and be pertinent to their lives. Teachers and students needed to be partners in exploring their social realities and developing critical thinking.

Issues of pedagogy generated resistance around issues of control. Encouraging students to challenge power relations raised fears of a breakdown in lines of authority. If students' experiences were an important part of classroom content, teachers might lose their position as experts. Critical thinking might also lead to other challenges to authority. School culture still saw students as empty vessels to be filled with approved knowledge, not as partners in creating knowledge and pushing for social change. Programs such as the bias contest raised a storm of controversy because they put students in the driver's seat, and because teachers and administrators were sure that they were all going to crash – and not because schools were necessarily interested in defending racist material.

6. **Anti-racist education** had to be willing to engage learners concerning other forms of oppression, such as sexism, homophobia, or class prejudice, as they arose in the educational process. All these areas involved questions of power, and understanding them would make the understanding of racism more acute.

The resistance in this regard depended on the particular issue. Bringing up questions of class ran against the grain of the common consensus that we lived in a classless society, or at least that someone's class was the result of individual merit. The suggestion that the education system might somehow be complicit in the reproduction of class difference was met with hostility because it challenged the notions of neutrality and objectivity of the system.

Even some anti-racist educators saw the introduction of other issues as corrosive of the solidarity necessary to combat racism. Wouldn't talking about sexism divide people of colour on gender lines? Wouldn't talking about class divide people into the more and less successful? Homophobia was highly charged because it raised questions of religion and sexuality, issues that fit uncomfortably into a secular school system traditionally squeamish towards talk about sex.

Recognizing that the motivation for resistance was complex and that a conflict existed between the principles of anti-racist education and the institutional culture of the education system was very different from simply characterizing resistance as a manifestation of racism. But from the point of view of outcomes, such resistance, no matter what its motivation, was certainly a barrier to anti-racist change. If we were to be successful, the complexity of resistance would have to be taken into account.

## Natural Selection

The growing recognition that resistance to change might come as much from institutional culture as from individual racism was a double-edged sword. As anti-racist educators became more successful in avoiding the pitfalls of disrupting traditional educational practices, how much of our radical potential were we losing?

This latest formulation of anti-racist principles showed a striking shift in emphasis from the work that Barb Thomas had done in *Currents* almost a decade before. The newer principles were much less concerned with questions of pedagogy and the relationship between teachers and learners than with institutional and structural change. On the one hand, this approach reflected a recognition that education is embedded in a broad institutional context. On the other, that shift in emphasis could also represent a retreat from the focus on a pedagogy of liberation that was such a central part of earlier anti-racist thinking. Was the consistent resistance to an anti-racist pedagogy – as compared to the acceptance of more inclusive content and sharper discipline – producing a subtle but profound effect on our work?

The goal of reaching teachers led to a constant pressure to conform to school culture and accepted practices rather than to challenge them. For the student program workers, such pressures were intensified by our association with the Equity Studies Centre, which placed a greater emphasis on packaging anti-racist, anti-sexist, or anti-homophobia content in forms that were teacher-friendly and classroom-friendly. For example, what was originally a "World History of Racism" game played by groups of fifty or more students over a half-day, followed by a freewheeling discussion about the experience, ended in my delivering thirty-minute lectures on the same topic to high-school history classes.

A kind of natural selection was going on. Programs congruent with education culture were more successful. Those that aroused torrents of opposition or that just couldn't easily be fit into a normal school day tended to fall into disuse or were modified. Over the years anti-racist education had moved away from its goal of preparing and mobilizing people to change their daily relationships and challenge and confront an unjust social system. It had become largely an attempt to make the system, as it was, more "inclusive" of a range of identities and backgrounds. All this dovetailed quite nicely with the idea that overcoming racism might be possible within capitalism and would not require fundamental social change.

## Identity Crisis

If anti-racist educators needed to begin to recognize the complexity of resistance and deal with anxieties about gradual co-optation, a more visible crisis was being generated by the infighting and distrust generated by the reduction of all conflicts to fundamental issues of identity. My foregrounding that anti-racism needed to include other kinds of oppression was a significant change in emphasis from formulations in the 1980s. It was a response to identity politics. It was not that Barb Thomas and other writers would have disagreed with the idea, but that they would more likely have considered it a detail of pedagogy rather than a stand-alone principle.

Identity politics of whatever mould turned on the insistence that essential differences existed between groups, and that in the end those differences were unbridgeable. The writings of Kwame Anthony Appiah, a Ghanaian philosopher, came into this environment like a breath of fresh air. In his best-known work, *In My Father's House: Africa in the Philosophy of Culture*, Appiah presented a historical analysis of Pan-Africanism, which he accused of simply reversing the biological determinism and other aspects of nineteenth-century European racism.[6] Classical racism was a system that tried to explain differences in culture and the social position of individuals and groups by reducing them to an effect of biology and colour. So dominant were these ideas that even much of the reaction against racism did not challenge the fundamental assumptions, but simply reversed the value placed on so-called racial qualities, asserting that those oppressed by racism were intrinsically more noble and better than their oppressors.

In a 1994 article, "Beyond Race: Fallacies of Reactive Afrocentrism," Appiah turned his critical sights on the "Afrocentric Paradigm."

> This negative thesis is argued as the prolegomenon to an alternative, positive, "Afrocentric" view, in which African cultural creativity is discovered to have

> been at the origin of Western civilization, while Western civilization, especially modern Western civilization, is either asserted or implied to be morally depraved; incapable, in particular, of living peacefully with others. The most extreme version of this is the "sun people" – "ice people" pseudohistory, presented by Leonard Jeffries at New York's City College and others, of the black sun people being cooperative, collective and peaceful, and the non-black ice people as competitive, individualist, and exploitative.[7]

Appiah and others attempted to shift the discussion from reductionist and essentialist notions of inherent racial qualities to an understanding of what was coming to be known as "the social construction of race." This approach looked at the complex ways in which different groups were "racialized," turned into the racial other. It saw "racial" differences as socially and historically produced rather than grounded in any essential, biological differences. The approach also opened up considerable room to consider the importance of and interaction with other socially produced contradictions around sex or sexuality or language or class.

The Equity Studies Centre began to consider how this approach might shape our anti-racist work and how it could be communicated in an age-appropriate manner to students who did not have a great deal of historical or philosophical background. How could we get across the idea that racial differences were not "natural" and that people were essentially the same without leaving the impression that we were endorsing the old "let's all just be colour-blind" positions of those who wanted to ignore the real impact of racism? How could we communicate the idea that race was invented – that race did not exist as a biological category – while still stressing that racism did exist – that the colour categories into which people's lives were organized did matter, that they produced profoundly different experiences and shaped cultural differences?

## Where to Start?

To bring people towards thinking about race in a different way, we would need to deal with the history of ideas of race and racism. Marg Wells and Myra Novogrodsky's work with "Facing History and Ourselves," which examined the process of racialization experienced by European Jews, was a good foundation. Here was an example of people who were racialized despite their colour. We also needed to look at different experiences of groups who were racialized because of their colour. In practice, launching immediately into a history lesson was not necessarily the best approach for most audiences. Giving people the answers before they asked the questions was not a good way to go. If we were going to get people to be interested, we somehow had to start by making them question – if they hadn't already – common-sense notions of race as a biological category.

Our strategy, then, was to ask participants to list the physical characteristics that determined someone's "race." They easily produced a list: skin colour, hair texture, eye shape, body shape, noses, lips, and so on. Sometimes the participants would get into an interesting discussion about clothing or accent, which would not only help to clarify the difference between race and culture but also illustrate how non-biological clues were often used to categorize people racially. One fair-skinned South Asian student, a Muslim, explained that when she put on a hijab – the veil used to cover the hair or forehead – people saw her as "brown," but when she took it off and dressed in "Canadian" clothes, they assumed she was "white." Effectively, a person's race might depend on the clothes they were wearing.

We would list the physical features in a vertical column on a blackboard or flip chart and then ask about the main colour names of "racial groups." That was easy too: black, white, red, yellow, brown. We wrote these names horizontally across the top of the board. There might be a debate on where Jews or Latinos fit in. From there it was easy to draw horizontal and vertical lines to make a table. Then we'd work at filling in the squares, connecting physical features with the colour names. What kind of skin colour, noses, hair, was a particular group supposed to have? Which features were more important? Why did some people classified as brown have lighter skin than others classified as white, or darker skin than others classified as black? Why should someone with almond eyes and dark skin be classified as black while another person with the same eyes and fair skin was classified as yellow, even if their skin was lighter than someone else with blond hair who was classified as white?

Participants would begin to see race as a complex classification system, with the inconsistencies and drawbacks of all classification systems. Race was no longer something "natural." We could then pose the question of how this classification system came to be – and that got us to history.

Many groups we worked with had only limited historical knowledge, so using a blackboard or a large flip chart we would enter the year 3000 BCE at one end and the present at the other and add a few other centuries in between and ask people to locate events they knew about. We could usually establish Egyptian pyramid construction at one end, maybe add the Greek and Roman eras, the birth of Christ, Columbus's arrival in the New World, and a jumble of more recent events. I would ask participants to guess where on the chart we should place the invention of the racial categorization system. They would usually disagree about when this happened. Most people thought there had been racism from the beginning, which led to more talk about history.

What I knew, in outline, about the invention of race was that in the classical world skin colour was seen as an irrelevant by-product of climate.[8] In the early Christian and Muslim civilizations, all humanity was assumed to be of "one blood," and religious differences were paramount. It was not until the rise of the colonial slave economy of the seventeenth century that skin colour began to be legally and socially associated with inferior status. Then eighteenth-century naturalists, such as Carolus Linnaeus, began categorizing human populations into colour groups and attributing different characters to these so-called "races." A hundred years later Charles Darwin's notion of evolution was used to assert that different racial groups were on different levels of the evolutionary ladder. The need of the "lesser races" for governance by superior "white Europeans" became a major justification for European imperialism and colonialism. Ideas that character, morality, intelligence, and civilization were racial characteristics were further amplified by the eugenics movement, which swept North America and Europe at the beginning of the twentieth century and culminated in Nazi policies of extermination of "inferior groups." Biological determinism also reinforced ideas of women as baby machines, non-reproductive sexuality as akin to treason, and the disabled as expendable.

It wasn't until after the Second World War – not that long ago – that colonized peoples were able to begin working to regain their countries' independence and reassert their full humanity, and that ideas about racial hierarchies became officially condemned. Now we were still dealing with the results of that history – from bitter poverty in many parts of the world to economic inequality and the advantages of racial discrimination for dominant groups.

Before the workshops, at best most participants had conceptualized a history of racism as a list of bad things that happened to particular groups in less enlightened times. They had never before thought of ideas of race and racism as a relatively modern historical phenomenon connected to economic and political conditions and scientific knowledge. They came out of the workshop with a different grounding. For me our ability to teach about the social construction of race – the connections it made, the windows it opened up to an understanding of sexism and heterosexism, and its implicit challenge to the narrow essentialist versions of identity politics – was one of the most important achievements of the Equity Studies Centre. It was not a cure for identity politics, but it provided a common social vision that could, if all went well, breach some of the solitudes.

Chapter 12

# War of Attrition

THE COMING CRISIS SLOWLY CREPT UPON US. With the end of the Cold War there was talk about a peace dividend, but the new resources that were in theory supposed to be freed up by the dismantling of the nuclear balance of terror failed to materialize. On the contrary, Western governments were now being told in no uncertain terms by certain influential sectors of the business community that the welfare state was too expensive to maintain. Corporations and their media mouthpieces began complaining that taxes were too high.

To make matters worse, in the spring of 1990, in the midst of the corporate chorus crying out for cutbacks, lower taxes, and less government regulation, the economy slipped into recession. In November 1991 the Toronto Board of Education received a report on the impact of the economic downturn on the budget, and the director was instructed to prepare a report on potential lost revenue. Two months later, in January 1992, the Board was discussing tax appeals. Toronto's domed stadium, occupying some of the city's most prime real estate, had challenged its tax assessment, arguing that as a Crown corporation it should be exempt from education taxes. Lawyers for the Eaton Centre mall filed an appeal to its assessment based on equally creative reasons. Soon the banks were following suit. At first the Board planned to challenge these appeals, but by the end of January trustees decided to withdraw from all of the cases except that of the Sky Dome, "given the recession, the uncertainty of success, and the high costs involved."[1]

Cutbacks began. By the end of the year several heritage-language weekend classes had been suspended for lack of money. In January 1993 the Board moved to extend a hiring freeze for support staff with the goal of reducing 15 per cent of that staff by attrition. In February the director was instructed to identify areas for further cuts. At a time when the struggle for equity was preparing for a major expansion, resources had begun to shrink.

The impact on the Equity Studies Centre and the Equal Opportunity Office was slight at first. In May trustee Alex Chumak lost a motion that would have let to a significant reduction of the Equity Studies Centre's budget. Instead we faced only the same 15 per cent reduction experienced by other departments. Budgets for activities were trimmed, but our major programs remained intact. The immediate changes did not seem unbearable.

The most serious loss was the erosion of administrative support. We had always prided ourselves on a teamwork approach – on trying to overcome the traditional distinction between educators and support workers in the office. Many of the administrative assistants in both the Equal Opportunity Office and Equity Studies Centre took an interest in the work and made initiatives well beyond the call of their designated duties. But these positions were slowly whittled away and the workloads for the remaining staff increased, creating constant pressure for a more traditional division of labour.

The political climate was changing along with the economy. Parent-organizing, traditionally the backbone of pressure on the Board for change, was shifting. The Quality Education Movement, a reaction to the reforms of the previous decade, proclaimed that schools were in crisis and standards were falling. Discipline was lax. The bureaucracy was bloated. Teachers' unions were too powerful and spending was out of control. In a swipe at heritage languages and equity initiatives, the Quality Education Movement complained that the curriculum was "too crowded." Spokespeople demanded a return to traditional teaching methods and attacked child-centred pedagogy and whole-language approaches to reading. Now a trustee, Tam Goossen saw the new right-wing parent movement as a barometer of wider transformations and of increased business pressures on public education.

The system was also facing new demands from the provincial NDP government. Boards across the province were gearing up to implement employment equity legislation introduced by the province, and the Ministry of Education released a new common curriculum requiring the destreaming of the first year of high school. At the Toronto Board, a steering committee, advisory council, and goals and timetables for employment equity were already in place. But the new employment equity legislation set out additional requirements. It would be necessary to inform employees about the legislation, conduct a new survey of designated groups, review policies and practices to identify barriers to employment, and develop a plan to remove those barriers and measure progress. The tasks required the establishment of a new Employment Equity Office in the Board to co-ordinate the work.

All of this effort raised nagging questions. What kind of progress on changing staff composition was realistic in the midst of a hiring freeze and potential layoffs? Where were the resources for these tasks to come from? Destreaming had been a long-time goal of many trustees and parents, and the model destreamed school, Rosedale Heights, was up and running. But many secondary school teachers had always opposed destreaming, at least in part because of the perceived difficulty of dealing with heterogeneous classes. Even teachers who supported the idea were uncertain as to how, without training, preparation, or support, they were supposed to teach and evaluate students in the new multi-level classes. In essence, the Board was being asked to implement a fundamental retooling of its workforce practices and curriculum delivery with fewer and fewer resources.

By that time the provincial NDP government was itself in trouble. Elected on a platform of "Agenda for the People," which included equity and a minimum corporate tax to finance social spending, the NDP had immediately found itself under attack from corporate interests. Due to high interest rates, a reduction in transfer payments from the federal government, and declining tax income and increased social spending due to the recession, the deficit that the NDP government had inherited from the previous Liberal regime ballooned. In summer 1993, against the advice of its key supporters, the Rae government legislated a "Social Contract" requiring public employees to take time off without pay and introducing a wage freeze and restrictions on the right to strike. The government soon found itself under attack from its traditional allies in the labour movement and municipal governments, as well as from its corporate enemies.

## Culture Wars

Ironically, as the political and economic storm was building, much of our attention was focused on two theatre productions.

Early in 1991 Garth Drabinsky, head of Livent Productions, announced plans to open North York's new Ford Centre for the Performing Arts with a production of the musical *Show Boat*. The play, first performed in 1927, had a history of productions both on stage and screen portraying common stereotypes of Afro-Americans as passive, lazy boozers, happily singing and dancing their lives away.

Drabinsky was aware of the play's racist associations. In October 1992 he met with a number of prominent Black community members, including lieutenant-governor Lincoln Alexander, to talk about possible community reactions to the production. The group expressed reservations, and at the end of the meeting, when Drabinsky asked them to approve a prepared statement endorsing the show, none of this relatively mainstream and conservative group agreed to sign.

Drabinsky was undeterred.[2] That same fall Livent asked permission to construct a box office on North York School Board property adjacent to the theatre. That brought the production to the attention of Stephnie Payne, North York's only Black school trustee. After reading the play, Payne objected to such a production opening the new publicly funded theatre, and asked her Board not to allow students to attend the musical on field trips. Drabinsky asked the trustee for a meeting, and she brought a number of African Canadian community leaders and a representative of B'nai B'rith. This group again raised concerns about the show and the stereotypical images of Blacks that were already appearing in its pre-publicity advertising.

Drabinsky defended the production, arguing that, as a Jew, he could not be considered racist.

Later, when Drabinsky denounced the opposition in the media, CTV televison interviewed Stephnie Payne. Unfortunately, the only part of the interview aired was her statement that "What really hurts is to see that musicals, plays, and movies that portray people of African ancestry in a negative way are always done by a white male and usually a Jewish person." The news media had their frame. Suddenly the issue was no longer the racist depictions in *Show Boat*, but Black-Jewish relations. Payne's apology two days later could not dampen the whirlwind of accusations and counteraccusations of Black anti-Semitism and Jewish racism. Even relations within the Equity Studies Centre were strained. The Centre's Carmen Marshall was convinced that the show needed to be stopped, while Myra Novogrodsky believed that such action was unrealistic. She was concerned about the anti-Semitism that the controversy was stirring up.

The Coalition to Stop Show Boat began a regular vigil outside the theatre every weekend and asked local school boards not to expose students to the racist representations in the production. As the October opening drew nearer, lines hardened. When the United Way of Metropolitan Toronto decided to proceed with a fundraiser using *Show Boat*, nineteen of the twenty-two members of its Black and Caribbean Fundraising Committee resigned in protest. When the Ontario Anti-Racism Secretariat failed to become involved, rumours began to circulate in the Black community that Premier Rae had instructed it to keep out of the debate. Ironically, Livent subsequently announced its intention to sue the Ontario government for $20 million in damages, alleging that the Secretariat had funded the anti-*Show Boat* coalition.

Although it was outside the epicentre of the debate, the Toronto Board requested an investigation be carried out, and a report produced, on the question of student trips to see the musical. It recommended that no student trips be scheduled until the report was received.

The furor about Black-Jewish relations that erupted from *Show Boat* caught Marsha Melnik's attention. She was involved in a Jewish feminist group which decided to bring together Jewish and Black women for dialogue about the controversy. The meetings revealed that both communities were steeped in stereotypes about each other, and the Jewish Women's Committee decided to offer workshops on the issue to their community through Hadassah, a Jewish women's organization. Marsha volunteered to help run the workshops.

She started the workshops by asking the Jewish participants what they knew about Shakespeare's *The Merchant of Venice*. One of them said, "Well, I was the only Jew in my class and so I had to play Shylock. I didn't like that." That started the conversational ball rolling. She quoted from passages towards the end of the play that were clearly anti-Semitic, and asked the participants how they would feel if a brand-new entertainment centre was being opened and a musical version of *The Merchant of Venice* was chosen to open it. The response was, uniformly, that they "wouldn't like that." After going through some of the *Show Boat* content, Marsha said, "More or less 70 per cent of the people I talked to were convinced that *Show Boat* wasn't appropriate."

As the *Show Boat* debate heated up in the fall of 1993, a delegation from Asian Revisions, a group of Asian feminist activists, came to the Race Relations Committee to express concerns about student trips to see a second play, *Miss Saigon*, which had opened at the new Princess of Wales Theatre in downtown Toronto in May. A modernized version of Puccini's *Madame Butterfly*, the play had a storyline featuring an innocent Vietnamese orphan who becomes a bar girl servicing U.S. soldiers before the liberation of Saigon. She bears a son with a white American soldier, patiently waits for his return, endures the schemes of an unscrupulous Eurasian pimp and a despotic Vietnamese communist soldier, and ultimately kills herself so that her son can go back to America with his father.

Asian Revisions brought forward issues similar to those raised around *Show Boat*, except that, in this case, sexual stereotyping and U.S. imperialism were added on. When *Miss Saigon* opened, patrons were greeted by demonstrators distributing flyers objecting to the musical's misrepresentation of Asian cultures, distortions of the history of colonialism in Vietnam, and its racially and sexually stereotyped images of the Vietnamese characters. The Vietnam War, which had played so large a part in the radicalization of the 1970s, was once again a burning issue, only this time fought on the stage of representation.

By that time the Board had already struck an advisory committee to recommend policy around *Show Boat*. The committee was under pressure from all sides. The Organization of Parents of Black Children and others insisted that no students should attend the production on school-sponsored trips. But many drama teachers wanted to take classes to see the year's biggest theatrical production. Livent, eager to sell tickets, and the right-wing press both demanded that the Board not cave in to "censorship." When the advisory committee presented its report in November 1993, it began with a long list of issues that had provoked intense discussion, including racism, anti-Semitism, censorship, artistic integrity, curricular relevance, depiction vs. propagation of racism, community reactions, parental and school responsibilities, controversial issues in literature, and the adequacy of teacher training.

The final recommendations tried to strike a compromise among the conflicting interests and positions. Although only eight of the advisory committee's eleven members endorsed the report, the Board approved their recommendations. Participation in organized school trips was limited to students registered in Grade 11 or above. No students could be required to attend

*Show Boat*, and all students under eighteen needed to have signed parental authorization. Teachers needed to personally preview the show before ordering tickets. They were required to contact the Equity Studies Centre to arrange for adequate resource support, and had to present their principal with written lesson plans after this consultation, prior to students viewing the production.

Three months later, in February 1994, a similarly constructed advisory group on *Miss Saigon* was unanimous that the musical contained both racist and sexist depictions, many of them decidedly offensive, and brought forward an almost identical set of recommendations on school trips to that production. The Equity Studies Centre produced curriculum packages for both productions.

Whether all this attention was completely merited became a subject of great debate among my colleagues at the Board. For Myra Novogrodsky, "attacking cultural productions that only a tiny number of kids went to see anyway" was not necessarily the best way of confronting the continuing experience of racism. Pat Case more or less agreed with that sentiment: "If you looked at TV any night of the week, the images of Black people were every bit as bad, or even worse. Moreover they were images that were seen by young people. *Show Boat* wasn't. I was frankly much more concerned about *Pulp Fiction* putting the use of the word 'nigger' back into constant public usage."

## PPM 119

In July 1993 the Ministry of Education finally released its Policy/Program Memorandum 119 requiring all boards of education in the province to introduce policies on anti-racism and ethnocultural equity. The policies were expected to address ten major areas of focus: harmonization of board policies, guidelines and practices, leadership, school community partnerships, curriculum, student languages, student evaluation, assessment and placement, guidance and counselling, racial and ethnocultural harassment, employment practices, and staff development. The boards were to draw up five-year implementation plans, with action plans that would identify and eliminate racial and ethnocultural biases and barriers, and they were to establish partnerships with local communities. The policies and implementation plans would have to be submitted to the Ministry for approval before March 31, 1995.

The job of monitoring compliance fell to the new Ministry of Education Anti-Racism and Ethnocultural Equity Branch, one of four branches within the Anti-Racism and Equity Division, which had an extensive mandate on almost everything to do with equity – from Native education and violence prevention to early childhood and special education. The creation of the division had been the result of the recommendations of the Lewis Report and of skilful lobbying by the recently formed Anti-Racist Multicultural Educators' Network of Ontario (AMENO), a support and advocacy group for people in multiculturalism and race relations positions in educational institutions.

Both the Anti-Racism and Equity Division and the Anti-Racism and Ethnocultural Equity Branch had strong representation from the Toronto Board. The Division was headed by Ouida Wright, who had been appointed assistant deputy minister shortly after she retired from the Board. Nora Allingham, with years of anti-racist experience behind her, was appointed head of the Anti-Racism and Ethnocultural Equity Branch.

Nora Allingham tried to ensure that the policies established under PPM 119 were real, and that Boards had the capacity to implement them. Training sessions were held across the province to convince senior administrators that the policy was necessary and could meet their local needs. The most difficult part of the task was reviewing policies sent in for approval. "Every time we sent one back with something that needed to be rewritten," Nora said, "I would get a call from some director of education cursing me out for wasting his time. They didn't want to do it. Why would they? Why would Orillia feel that they had to do anything? Apart from the fact that there were all those kids in the reserve across the lake."

Nevertheless, every Board in the province eventually put a policy into place – every board, except, that is, except Toronto. That was because, as Pat Case found out when he went over the requirements of PPM 119, the Toronto Board was already in compliance. Although the Board did not have a unitary policy, based on its race relations report, Report on the Education of Black Children, and the work already being done around complaints, curriculum, and employment equity, it was already doing what PPM 119 was telling it to do. Not just that, but even in the areas where the least was being done, such as guidance assessment and placement, the Toronto Board had surpassed the official requirements.

## Class Bias

In June 1993 the Toronto Board went a little further on the equity path by passing a policy on class bias.[3] The policy statement came to the Board through the Labour Education Committee chaired by trustee John Campey. In the early 1970s the Board's concerns about the education of working-class students had led it to an investigation of questions of race and ethnicity. Now it had come full circle.

The statement opened by asserting that educators were becoming increasingly aware that socio-economic class bias, like bias based on gender and race, should be a significant concern. It defined class bias as an attitude that led to discrimination based on educational background, occupation, social status, and/or economic means, and it listed several examples:

> The assumption that intellectual work is inherently superior to physical labour; the omission within the curriculum of the contribution of working-class people, including the efforts of such groups as the labour movement to create a more equitable society; the attachment of stereotypes to socioeconomic class; the assumption that academically successful students should pursue professional careers rather than skilled trades; and, the undue emphasis on competition, as opposed to collective and cooperative efforts in student activities, and in evaluation procedures.

The statement committed the Board to the promotion of equity of outcome for all students. Echoing the 1979 race relations policy, it condemned the expression of socio-economic class bias in any form. It revisited examples of efforts such as inner-city programs and the work of the Labour Education Committee.

All education experiences should respect "the fundamental human dignity and worth of working-class and socioeconomically marginalized people." Students' educational experiences should enable them to understand the economic system from various perspectives, and the efforts of working people to address inequities. It should encourage students to think critically with respect to the contemporary world of work and workers, "and to act both collectively and cooperatively, as well as individually, to influence decisions that would result in a more equitable society." The understanding of class, though, should acknowledge "the interrelations among various inequities based upon race, ethnicity, creed, colour, nationality, ancestry, place of origin, gender, sexual orientation, marital status, disability and age."

Compared to the detailed provincial requirements for building a policy on race, the class bias policy statement was strong on fine sentiments and weak as a blueprint for institutional change. It had no concrete goals or timetables and no implementation plan to alter specific practices. It was also more than a little ironic that only a few months later, as part of its cost-cutting, the Board would reduce by a further 15 per cent the budget for inner-city programs specifically aimed at combatting the effects of socio-economic inequality. Still, the class bias policy statement drew on the Board's experience around issues of race and gender and provided a foundation that could have been built on had the world developed differently. Unfortunately, it was to be the last major initiative supported by the Board's progressive majority.

The reaffirmation of socio-economic class as an equity issue raised interesting and convoluted questions in the equity staff's discussions. Was class simply another equity issue that could be added to the list? The traditional left position was that class divisions were inherently unjust, and class itself needed to be abolished. This was quite different from our approach to other equity categories. No one suggested that the solution to racism was to make everyone the same colour. The fight against sexism did not require hermaphroditism, nor did overcoming homophobia or heterosexism mean that everyone needed to return to a state of bisexual polymorphous perversity. Those struggles only meant that the stereotyping, prejudice, and discrimination against non-white people, women, and gay people needed to be done away with – or as Martin Luther King had succinctly put it, that a person be judged by the content of her or his character rather than by colour of skin or, by extension, gender or sexual orientation.

The discussions made clearer the limits of our notion of equity. When we talked about the measure of success being equity of outcome, we meant that there would be roughly the same dropout rates among gay and straight kids, that roughly the same percentage of Black, Asian, Aboriginal, or white kids would be found in the university-bound or technical streams, and that the enrolment and success rates in different subjects would be more or less the same for boys and girls. Equity did not imply that there would be no inequality, only that there would be no correlation between inequalities and incidental characteristics such as race, culture, gender, or sexual orientation.

When we talked about classism, then, did we just mean overcoming the stereotyping, prejudice, and discrimination against working class and poor people? Were we arguing for measures to ensure individual class mobility so that someone born into a poor family would not be disadvantaged by that poverty? Or, conversely, that someone born into a rich family would not be privileged by that accident of birth? If so, contrary to the Board's policy on class bias, we were calling for an even playing field on which competitive individualism could run its course and where everyone could scramble up the class ladder as high as they were able. That argument implied that theoretically at least we could have a relatively "equitable" society in terms of race and gender, but one still polarized in terms of class. The only difference would be that the same proportion of rich and poor would be found in each racial (and by analogy, gender, sexual orientation, cultural) group. But what did that mean for people with disabilities? Were we fighting for equity or for social justice? (See Diagrams A, B, and C on the next page.)

Those questions led to arguments about social justice. Could differences in character ever be so great as to correspond to or justify differences in class privilege? Could we argue that Microsoft founder Bill Gates was really billions of times smarter or more industrious than someone else on the planet and that therefore he deserved to be billions of times richer? The fallback social justice position argued for the redistribution of wealth and resources, maintaining that there was a level that no one should fall below. It argued that access to education, health care, or housing was a fundamental human right. That, coincidentally, was the rationale behind inner-city programs that justified allocating more resources to communities with greater needs. Sometimes social justice and equity seemed to be the same thing. Sometimes they didn't.

These were very anxious questions for equity workers. In practice, a

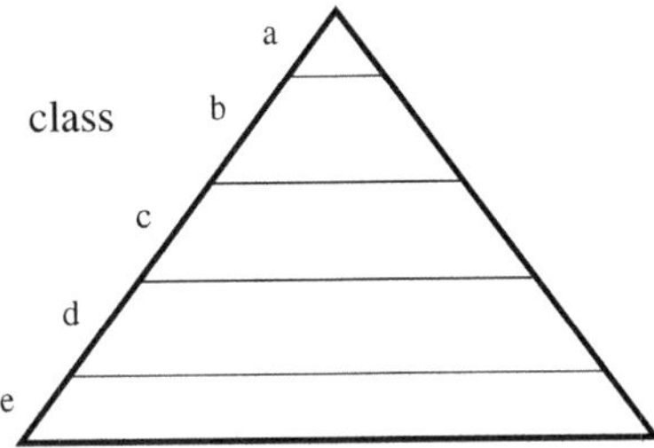


Diagram A: *Class society*. A triangle with horizontal lines is a simplified representation of the different classes in society: marginalized, working class, middle class, and upper class.

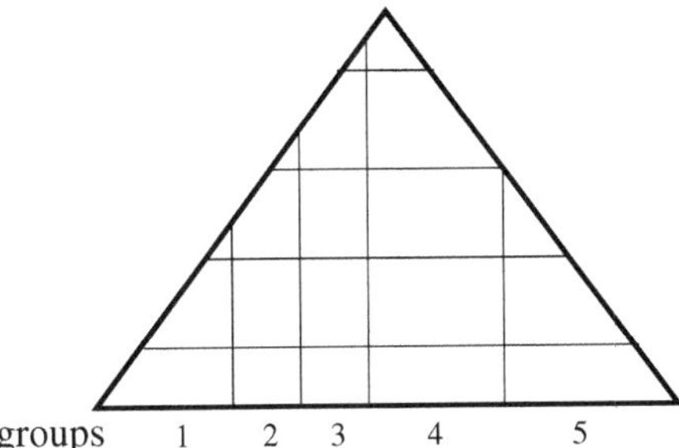


Diagram B: *Race in class society*. The same horizontally divided triangle now has vertical lines representing different racial groups added. Some vertical columns (in the centre) will reach the apex of the triangle, therefore including upper class members. Some vertical columns ( more towards the outside) will reach the edge of the triangle well before the apex. Their highest class component will be middle class. The most peripheral will only reach the lower lines and therefore will contain only the marginalized and working classes.

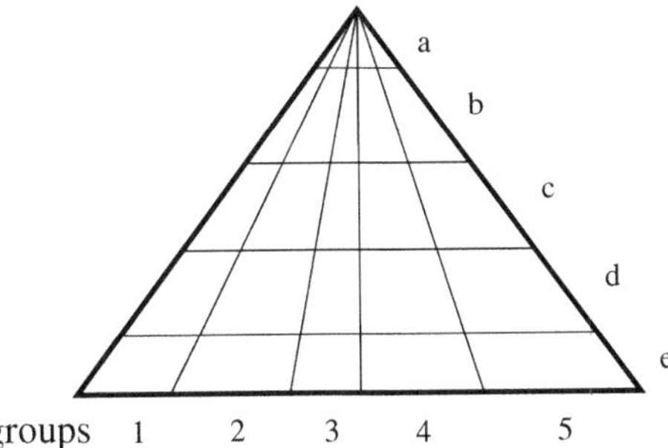


Diagram C: *Racial equity and class society*. This time the formerly vertical lines all radiate down from the apex of the triangle to the base; thus each race column shares proportionally the same class composition.

murky consensus emerged around two points: the importance of challenging the stereotypes and prejudices that limited the opportunities of working-class and poor people; and the promotion of a more egalitarian society by redistributing resources and reducing the range of inequality. Some of us who held out hope for a fundamentally different, more egalitarian society consoled ourselves with the notion that any work that exposed class differences and inequalities could eventually contribute to a more fundamental movement for change.

We were reaching a point, however, when even the most reformist notions of social and economic justice would be under devastating attack.

In February 1994 the Board announced a target for cuts of a further $20 million, and by March $13 million had been slashed from the budget. These new cuts were applied to a system that was already short of resources and in which there was an increasing demand for programs and increasing numbers of students. For the first time my colleagues and I began to become seriously concerned about the sustainability of our current programs and the impact on the Board's ability to follow through on its equity agenda.

## Pepsi and Other Wars

In December 1993 trustees John Campey and Dorothy Ottoway moved that Pepsi-Cola be given exclusive rights to all soda and juice vending services in secondary and senior public schools. The deal would bring substantial additional financial benefits for the Board, they argued. Revenue would be credited to the cash-strapped School Food Services Department and allocated to secondary and senior elementary schools on a per student basis. Primary and junior schools were also offered the opportunity to strike a similar deal. The motion passed, and all existing competitor soda and juice vending units were to be withdrawn and replaced with Pepsi-Cola units effective February 1, 1994.

The motion slipped through the Board without much notice, but as the new year opened, opposition to the deal was building. The Toronto Association of Student Councils complained that insufficient notice had been provided to students, and that the deal set a precedent for increased commercial interests in schools. The students decried the loss of autonomous decision-making, and that control over the funds went to school administrators. Previously many student councils had financed their activities by negotiating their own deals with different vendors. The students also questioned Pepsi's environmental, labour, and human rights record.

By March the Toronto Board of Health waded in on the issue, calling on the Board to establish a committee of stakeholders to develop a comprehensive policy on food and beverage availability and urging a review of the three-year Pepsi-Cola contract to ensure that it provided incentives for the purchase of nutritious foods and beverages. The Board refused to reopen the question. The coalition of progressive and NDP trustees that had dominated the Board for most of the previous two decades was split. Some, such as Campey, supported the deal, arguing that it was necessary to save jobs in Food Services. Others focused on the dangers of corporate intrusion in the schools and marketing to a captive student audience.

Marx's famous dictum that history repeats itself, first as tragedy and second as farce, was confirmed several months later when members of the Status of Women Committee found themselves debating whether the ice cubes pictured on the new Pepsi vending machines actually contained "subliminal sexual content" in violation of Board sexual harassment policy. Someone had complained that one of the ice cubes looked like a breast.

The left had lost its unity and momentum, but the response to the Pepsi issue was only a symptom of a deeper malaise. A political movement that had emerged in a world in which public institutions were seen as having a strong role in promoting social change had been thrown into disarray by a new world order in which public institutions themselves were under attack by aggressive corporate and right-wing political interests. For some of the old progressive bloc, compromise was necessary to prevent the further erosion of services. For others such compromises undermined the fundamental principals of institutional integrity.

Still, initiatives from the left had by no means ground to a halt – though by 1994 there was no doubt that the work seemed scattered and often symbolic rather than system-wide in scope. The Consultative Committee on the Education of Lesbian and Gay Students, for instance, continued to pick away at the symbols of homophobia. The group lobbied the Board to see that the updated 1986 version of the Ontario Human Rights Code including sexual orientation was posted in all schools. It successfully pushed to have field trip permission forms changed from "mother/father" to "parent/guardian," and it complained that material distributed concerning the United Nations Year of the Family made no mention of gay and lesbian families. When an omnibus bill to recognize same-sex relationships was under debate at Queen's Park, Campey convinced the Board to support the legislation. After a "Whose Children Awareness Rally" in spring 1993 at Board offices – where a crowd largely bussed in from suburban churches heard speakers condemn Board policy, the curriculum document, and gay people in general, complaints by lesbian and gay observers convinced the Board to strengthen its supervision of permitted activities to ensure that they did not contravene Board policy. Also in response to the rally, activist members of the Lesbian and Gay Employees Group joined with youth and parents to create a new organization that came to be called Education Against Homophobia. In the following autumn the group organized a massive rally and conference in support of anti-homophobia initiatives at the Board office.

The Status of Women Committee expressed its concerns about the disproportionate impact that the continuing cuts were having on women. The committee also raised a fuss about the Board's submission to the Royal Commission on Learning, which had been developed for Director Joan Green without input from the Equal Opportunity Office or Equity Studies Centre, and which omitted any mention of issues such as class bias, homophobia, and sexism from its discussion of equity. The Equity Studies Centre was given the green light to participate in the organization of student focus groups around a proposed video on the rights of youth employed in the fast food industry – over the objections of the Ontario and Canadian Restaurant Associations. Campey, who believed that student involvement was a key issue, succeeded in establishing student trustee positions to give students a voice at the Board level. There were struggles to make the institution more environmentally responsible. Critics pointed out, for example the inequity of some people getting free parking while others had to pay for public transit.

## A New Policy on Racial and Ethnocultural Mistreatment

As a former trustee, Pat Case was acutely aware of the malaise affecting the left-wing bloc at the Board level and the loss of community pressure on the system. As lawyer, he seized upon the tools of his trade, the law, as a new major potential lever for institutional change.

Board procedures to deal with racist incidents were seriously out of date. Incidents were addressed under Standard Procedure 45, which dealt with both physical and racial mistreatment of students by staff. The definition of racial mistreatment was not as comprehensive as the definition of sexual harassment in the Board's Sexual Harassment Policy, and also fell short of the definition in the Ontario Human Rights Code. The standard procedure also only applied to incidents between teachers and students, and was therefore ineffective in addressing issues involving other staff, parents, volunteers, and school permit holders (people who get a permit to use school facilities for various activities in off-hours). Pat argued that this situation left the Board vulnerable to legal action. He was also eager to establish procedures that could bring closure to complaints that had been lingering in the system for years.

When he took his first draft of a new policy to a meeting of senior officials, they were concerned that he was suggesting moving from "a Volkswagen to a Cadillac in one step." Indeed, it took more than a year of consultation, but eventually, in October 1994, the Board approved the new Interim Policy on Racial and Ethnocultural Mistreatment for a year's field testing.

The Interim Policy emulated the 1992 policy on sexual harassment, including both formal and informal processes for resolution of complaints and allowing third-party complaints. The policy set out procedural protections such as the right of representation and the required steps for investigations, but with one key difference from the sexual harassment policy. That earlier policy was complainant-driven, and if a complainant got cold feet she or he could end the process. The Interim Policy on Racial and Ethnocultural Mistreatment included the principle of mandatory response, which meant that all Board personnel had a duty to report observed racial mistreatment, and administrators had a duty to investigate all such reports. The issue was complicated. To be more empowering for young women, the sexual harassment policy had opted for an approach that gave complainants a certain control of the process. It had been argued that those being harassed might be less likely to disclose the case if they believed that they would be caught up in an inflexible administrative machinery with unforseen consequences. With this policy Pat was more concerned with the Board's legal responsibility to protect its employees and students from racism, and with the liability that might arise from not exercising due diligence.

In a major innovation, the new Interim Policy also addressed the concept of "poisoned environments." That is, the policy could serve to channel complaints not just about individual actions but also about more general conditions that perpetuated stereotyping or prejudice. It could therefore theoretically enable individuals to push for systemic change by laying complaints against systemic practices themselves – textbooks, courses of study, even hiring practices. Pat also believed that enforcement of human rights belonged in the field, and that managers had to take on much of the implementation. The Equal Opportunity Office would only become involved in formal complaints that could not be handled locally.

The new complaints policy was one more tool that could be used to achieve institutional change. The policy allowed enough central control to gather statistics and ensure accountability, and the complaints, in aggregate, would reveal areas in which systematic work was necessary. For example, it was when Pat Case found himself investigating the complaints of three Black teachers who had been passed over for department headships in schools that he began to become more intensely aware of how discrimination was accomplished within the system. As part of the investigation he spoke to the principals involved and reviewed the selection committee notes, but couldn't find anything wrong. Puzzled, he asked staff in the Human Resources Department to do research on the qualifications for everyone who had received a headship during the previous three years.

When he looked at that data, a pattern just "jumped out" at him: "In all but three cases, every single person who had been promoted to a headship had been either an *acting head* or an *assistant head* before they became head of the department." The job ads did not require an applicant to be an acting or assistant head. As for how people became assistant or acting heads, it was the principal's decision, the principal's choice – there was no selection or hiring committee. In a couple of cases people were made acting heads in May – which was the time when the principal knew who was retiring and wouldn't be back for the next school year. The person made acting head of the department in May became acting head for the following year – and would then, based on that position and experience, get the full headship when it finally came up. "That's where the discrimination was," Pat said. "There was no discrimination in the interview. It had all happened before."

The processes of the Employment Systems Review opened Pat's eyes to the realities of the institutional culture. In the meetings, it became "as clear as a bell where the systemic problems lay," he said. "They were everywhere – from the hiring kit that was filled with all kinds of racist and sexist assumptions, to the imagery of who an interview team was, right down to the kinds of discretion that principals had in hiring. It unfolded in front of my eyes. You could read the collective agreement provisions and they didn't say that seniority was the sole factor. It said that seniority was one of four factors. What are the other three? Why not start beefing those up to start hiring people?"

The system, he found, wasn't nearly "as mysterious and mystical" as it had seemed from outside. These experiences began to change his understanding of institutional change. Policies such as goals and timetables of hiring could not be implemented from the ground up. They had to come from the apex on down. "This stuff operates by power. This is the organization at its most powerful, its ability to hire and fire. Certain expectations have to be set, but the fundamental thing is that the people at the top have to genuinely buy into it. They have to know what they're doing and want to do it. You convince others as it cascades down through the organization that it's the right thing to do, or at least that it's the right thing for them to do if they ever aspire to go up."

By the mid-1990s the community and parent movements of the previous decades had largely melted away – or, as Pat Case pointed out, had proved ineffective in their attempts to intervene in the Board's complex institutional processes. The absence of such popular pressure was both reflected in and amplified by the equity activists' increasing resort to legal arguments, including the Charter of Rights and Freedoms, as a strategy to advance change. "People had become demobilized by the law in some respects," Pat observed. "Those who could use the law and its provisions were now in the know, and people who couldn't were left behind. The masses didn't matter any more. They were technically disenfranchised."

Equity initiatives had, as a result, become enormously vulnerable to political change at the top – and at the top the balance was about to shift.

# The Good Fight

## Chapter 13

STUDENTS OF TORONTO AGAINST RACISM (STAR) had kept a low profile since the group's founding in 1992. In fact a Toronto *Star* article had contrasted STAR's "boardrooms" strategy with ARA's tactics of "confrontation."[1] Members participated on panels aimed at training teachers on policy, organized student conferences, sent representatives to the Race Relations and Student Affairs committees, and helped plan the Anti-Apartheid Conference and Asian Heritage Month.

But by the fall of 1994 most of the original STAR members had graduated, and a new generation was taking over. They were a multiracial group who had come of age during the turbulence around the fight against the Heritage Front, and many of them had a much more in-your-face approach. Several also belonged to ARA. In a recruiting flyer distributed in September 1994, STAR described itself as a Board-wide group of students dealing with equity issues who "push the suits to listen to our needs as students."

The revitalized STAR first created ripples when they distributed a poster protesting "European Heritage Week." The week was a propaganda vehicle for Don Andrews's Nationalist Party, another neo-Nazi formation attempting to fill the vacuum left by the declining Heritage Front. Under the guise of promoting multiculturalism the NP encouraged city councils to proclaim the week, and it had succeeded with a number of municipalities unaware of the group's background. In Toronto, glossy NP posters urging students to celebrate the glories of Euro-heritage began appearing on hoardings and telephone polls around schools at the end of September. Careful scrutiny of the poster revealed images of Hitler, slave boats, and witch burnings.

STAR's response was a poster of its own headlined, "If you celebrate Euro-heritage week you are celebrating 500 years of oppression." It exposed Andrews as founder of the neo-Nazi Western Guard, criticized the "Eurocentric" school curriculum, and urged students to tear down the NP posters whenever they saw them.

The Toronto Mayor's Committee on Race Relations commended STAR on its poster, but many teachers and administrators objected, both to the characterization of school curriculum as Eurocentric and to STAR's advice to students to tear down racist posters instead of going through the proper channels. I received a number of letters of complaint from teachers. To some extent, as the group's staff liaison I took the administration's heat for their activities. Personally I was delighted that the students were shaking things up, and saw my role as facilitating what they decided to do, not directing it. I figured that if some superintendent wasn't calling for my head at least once a year, I probably wasn't doing my job.

One of the reasons for STAR's success was that the group managed to negotiate the dangerous shoals of identity politics. "With identity politics, people's discussions so often became such a big fight about whose politics was right, that they forgot about the bigger picture," group member Fatema Mullen said. "With STAR and Camp Kandalore there were discussions around race, class and sexuality and people were developing political analysis, but there was actual activism too. We were trying to see the bigger picture without being bogged down in constant discussions that would turn into bickering sessions about who was a racist and who was a classist and all that." Another member, Claire (Yaya) Yao, said that, for her, STAR was an important opportunity for "interacting with white people who were taking responsibility for racism and fighting it, and getting out of the paradigm of white people as enemy. Being able to actually talk to white people about racism was a real step."

The new STAR members gravitated to an anti-oppression approach, taking it for granted that the group should be involved in anti-sexism and anti-homophobia work as well as fighting racism. In October 1994 they decided that a major focus for the year would be inclusive curriculum.

## Targeting Curriculum

With the destruction of the British anti-racist education movement by the Thatcher government in the early 1980s, Canadians had increasingly turned to U.S. thinkers for inspiration. Myra Novogrodsky had introduced the work of Peggy McIntosh to the Equity Studies Centre. McIntosh, associate director of the Wellesley College Center for Research on Women, had first garnered attention in 1988 when she published a seminal essay on issues of white and male privilege.[2] By the early 1990s McIntosh was focusing her attention on the inclusion of women and people of colour in school curriculum, and had developed a five-phase typology of inclusion.[3] In phase one, women and people of colour were simply absent. In phase two, famous or especially successful representatives might be mentioned. In phase three, the difficulties faced by women or people of colour would be covered, with the subjects portrayed as problems or victims. In phase four the experiences of marginalized groups would be central to the curriculum, with the work going beyond studies of oppression to take in the wholeness and intricacies of their experiences. Phase five, yet to be attained, would require "a vocabulary for perceiving, feeling and analyzing which is both plural and coherent, and will put us in a new relation to ourselves and the world."[4] In our discussions in the Equity Studies Centre, we recognized that Toronto Board curriculum tended to be a mix of McIntosh's first three phases, depending on the school, the subject, and the teacher.

While the Centre discussed how to move teachers further along this continuum, the students in STAR decided to take a more activist approach. The plan, hatched at STAR's October 1994 meeting, was to ask schools for copies of course outlines for all history, social sciences, and English classes. The group would evaluate the courses for inclusivity and prepare a report for the Board. If, as the students strongly suspected from their personal experience, they found that actual curriculum was not nearly as inclusive as Board bureaucrats liked to brag, they considered the possibility of laying formal complaints under the poisoned environment provision of the new Interim Policy on Racial and Ethnocultural Mistreatment.

I knew the project would ruffle feathers, but I was still surprised at how quickly it ran into trouble. When STAR members began trying to collect course outlines from their own schools – even though each school office was required to make the outlines publicly available – administrators wanted to know why the students wanted them and what they intended to do with them. When the students mentioned STAR's project, the material suddenly became unavailable.

At STAR's next meeting, in November, with no success whatsoever in getting the course outlines, the group decided to send a letter to Director Joan Green asking for assistance. Two weeks later Don Irwin, the chief superintendent of Curriculum, acknowledged STAR's letter and communicated that he had asked the secondary school superintendents to facilitate the collection of the appropriate course outlines.

By the new year no outlines had been received. STAR reps on the Race Relations Committee raised the issue and received the committee's endorsement. A superintendent at the meeting once again promised to facilitate collection. A month later no outlines had yet arrived, and STAR reps brought up the issue again. Now more than a little embarrassed in front of the committee, the superintendent promised to look into the matter immediately.

## Hate Again

In the meantime the issue of hate-group activity once again bubbled to the surface. At Humberside Collegiate Institute, the largely white-majority school in the west end where years before Nora Allingham had done her pioneering work to transform the English curriculum, a South Asian teacher was found unconscious at the foot of a stairwell. When he came to in the hospital hours later, he recounted being pushed down the stairs by two unidentified white males. The same teacher had received a threatening racist letter from within the school when he had begun work in September. A second letter, this time delivered to four teachers of colour, the principal, and the vice-principal, announced that a group called "Fight for White Rights" was active in the school and would use physical force to eliminate teachers of colour. Although the administration had called the police at the time, the issue had been kept quiet.

After the alleged assault the school held an emergency meeting and the Equal Opportunity Office trained a core group of students to facilitate classroom workshops focusing on the new Racial and Ethnocultural Mistreatment Policy. A community-parent meeting drew over three hundred people. Several speakers criticized both the school's failure to confront the flaunting of white supremacist attitudes and symbols and its still-Eurocentric curriculum, which they argued contributed to violent racist activity. In response the school scrambled to announce a new dress code, banning displays of racist symbols and red and white laces on Doc Martin boots, popular codes for white supremacy and fascism. In time-honoured fashion, the system's first move was to discipline students rather than look at its own practices.

Superintendent Rick Kollins quickly got involved with the issue. Kollins had grown up as Jew in downtown Toronto, when the city was still very much a preserve of the Loyal Orange Lodge, so he had an appreciation of what it meant to be a minority. He certainly had no fondness for neo-Nazis. But he was also very much a member of the old-boys' club that dominated the world of secondary school principals and superintendents – men who were used to giving orders and being obeyed.

Kollins decided to hold another series of forums on hate groups for school administrators and senior officials. STAR was asked to send two representatives to the planning committee, and Geoff MacDonald and Fatema Mullen agreed to attend for the group. Both were also involved in ARA and were keenly aware of the important role of community organizations in previous Board work. After two months of often frustrating meetings, the young people succeeded in convincing the planning committee to adopt a community-based approach.

Kollins had not attended the planning committee meetings, leaving an assistant in charge. When he learned of the committee's decision, he was not pleased. He had already arranged that the centrepiece of the forums would be a keynote address by Dino Doria of the Metro Police Hate Crimes Unit. In January he came to a meeting to advise the planning committee of his decision. Faced with objections, he refused to back down.

At its next meeting STAR voted to withdraw from the planning committee unless Kollins agreed to compromise and include community speakers. When they went back to the planning committee they suggested Ellen Murray, a teacher who had been instrumental in the anti-Heritage Front event at

Riverdale Collegiate, or a student from HARM, the Humberside anti-racist student group, organized by Kandalore graduates, as possible speakers. Kollins was not interested in compromises, and STAR withdrew from the committee.

The superintendent apparently underestimated the wrath of student activists scorned. At the first of the two forums, in February 1995, Fatema Mullen arrived and distributed a photocopied letter to all participants. It recounted the superintendent's overturning of the decision to feature community speakers, denounced the planning process as window-dressing, and accused Kollins of organizing the forum only to promote himself as a candidate for the director's job. It finished by savaging the dismal record of the police force on fighting racism. This was beyond the bounds of propriety expected by school board culture.

The second forum a few days later closed with a similar commotion. Detective Doria, with characteristic aplomb, described Malcolm X T-shirts and the raised-fist image of Black power as hate-group symbols, and Pat Case exploded. The subsequent screaming match between the Board's advisor on race relations and the representative of the Police Hate Crimes Unit quickly spread to include other participants. Kollins later accused Pat of masterminding the STAR letter to sabotage the forums, and another shouting match ensued.

STAR got its last dig in on the issue with a newsletter distributed to all secondary schools through the Board mail system later that spring. The newsletter had articles on the impact of budget cuts, Native land-claims struggles, the Zapatista rebellion in Mexico, "reverse discrimination," a report on STAR's forum critiquing racist socio-biology in *The Bell Curve*,[5] and the ongoing fight to obtain the course outlines. But it also had a piece outlining Kollins's role in the organization of the forums, and another detailing the Metro police's "notorious reputation" for racist violence.

## Freedom of Information

When Joan Green left her post as director at the end of April, Kollins did not get the nod. Instead the top job went to John Davies. According to Pat Case, it was a good choice. Davies, he thought, had a genuine interest in supporting equity. "As with any senior administrator in that organization, he was constantly trying to balance interests, and that meant making compromises, but overall he was somebody I could trust. He facilitated the work around Employment Equity. For me it really cleared the way. Nobody doubted that I would go straight back to him if they gave me trouble."

By spring 1995, despite repeated visits to the Race Relations Committee and personal promises from four different superintendents and the director that the material would be provided, STAR had received course outlines from only eight of the system's thirty-six secondary schools. One superintendent I phoned screamed at me about who the hell was I working for. The increasingly frustrated students concluded that the system was stalling in the hope that they would lose interest, but by now they had invested too much in the project to back down. In May 1995 they filed an official Freedom of Information request and sent copies to all trustees, superintendents, and the minister of education.

The reply from the Freedom of Information co-ordinator was the epitome of a bureaucratic Catch-22: she was unable to assist in obtaining the material because it was already public. The group returned to the Race Relations Committee with a copy of the letter. By this point even the trustees were becoming embarrassed in the face of the students' tenacity, and they began to lean heavily on the school administrations to deliver.

For the students, the struggle to get materials they had every right to see was teaching them as much as the evaluation itself promised to do. The issue "became way more than just about the curriculum," Carolyn Goossen said. "It became a matter of battling the system and that's what I learned about most. I remember feeling pretty empowered." Yaya Yao said the students "learned a lot of lessons about bureaucracy." They were able to figure out "the ins and outs of the system and how to deal with it," and that "was important learning."

STAR's tenacity contributed to the pressure on the system to take issues of inclusion more seriously as the Board continued to develop its new Common Curriculum under Ministry guidelines. The Equity Studies Centre arranged for Peggy McIntosh to meet with curriculum co-ordinators and superintendents to discuss how to make the new curriculum truly inclusive, and she also delivered the keynote speech at that spring's York Equity Conference. In October 1995, when Davies issued his five-year plan for system improvement, "Taking Responsibility for Improving Schools," he listed equity as the second of three priorities for the Board. It was the first time that a director had given such clear direction about his expectations for the system. Course outlines from the remaining schools finally began to trickle in.

## Cutbacks in the Equal Opportunity Office

A new director and a clearer commitment to equity did not mean that the financial outlook had improved. By April 1995 a further $19 million in cuts were forecast. Education assistants, student support services and assistance programs, school hall monitors, and curriculum consultant positions were all on the chopping block. Continuing education programs were to be scaled back and fees increased. An additional 25 per cent of management positions would be lost. By now anyone paying attention was becoming alarmed: more than three hundred deputations opposing cutbacks were delivered to the Education Finance Committee, and hundreds more written submissions were sent in. But with the continuing erosion of the tax base and the provincial government's lack of financial commitment to education, the question was not if, but where, to cut.

For the first time equity programs were in jeopardy. Hardest hit was the Equal Opportunity Office. Chimbo Poe Mutuma, who had been parachuted into the office after his original position as Superintendent of Information Services had been eliminated, was finally let go that spring. The rest of us had never believed that the office needed a manager to co-ordinate activities but now, with the manager gone, the administration concluded that the staff of the Equal Opportunity Office needed to be reduced. Despite our protests, the student program workers were transferred into the Equity Studies Centre in the Curriculum Division. We speculated about how much of this was "optics" to demonstrate that the Equal Opportunity Office was taking its share of the cuts, and how much had to do with a desire for closer control on student program worker activities, especially given all the fuss that STAR was causing.

Vern Douglas was also transferred to the Curriculum Division, but he welcomed the move. His heart was in developing more Aboriginal programming, and Curriculum was the logical location for that kind of work. By September 1995, the Equal Opportunity Office was reduced to the same two advisors' positions that it had held when Tony Souza and Myrna Mather were first hired in 1981.

My worst fears about the camps were soon realized. The budget for these programs, which had been a safe line-item in the Equal Opportunity Office for so many years, now overshadowed everything else in the equity studies budget. The logic was inexorable. To maintain the range of other programs that directly serviced hundreds of students and teachers, the camps, which only involved fifty or sixty students at a time, had to go. By insensible gradations, selected by the logic of the system, the rationale of service had so overcome that of mobilizing for change that we had become our own executioners. Although I didn't know it at the time, the anti-racism retreat held in April 1995 was to be the last.

The camps, which had run in an unbroken sequence since Tony had first established them in 1981, had been the core and the heart of student anti-oppression efforts at the Toronto Board. They had spun off parallel programs such as the ESL, Grade 7 and 8, Latin American, and gender issues retreats. They had inspired and provided basic training for several thousand budding student activists over almost fifteen years. They had been a window for equity staff into the functioning of racism and other forms of oppression in schools. It was truly the end of an era.

Still, a bright light at the time was the establishment of the Fran Endicott Resource Centre in 1995. Myra Novogrodsky, increasingly concerned with the deepening crisis and the reduction in the Equity Studies Centre's ability to provide services, saw the only long-term solution as embedding the work in the day-to-day practices of teachers. She began lobbying for the development of a new, expanded resource library that would hold materials on all the equity issues and be accessible to teachers and students across the system. A site was found in an unused library at the newly founded Ursula Franklin Academy, named after a renowned Canadian woman scientist. Equity was to be a major component of the new academy's philosophy. It was central, close to the subway, and had adequate parking.

Although there was never enough money to make it the high-tech centre for teachers and students that Myra envisaged, the resource centre, named in honour of trustee Fran Endicott, soon became not only a library resource for equity materials, but also a gallery for equity-based student art, a training area for workshops, and a meeting place for groups and committees struggling to maintain the Board's equity initiatives.

## Disabilities

By spring 1995 the Equity Studies Centre had a track record of programs and work around all its mandated issues, save one: disabilities. Our failure to deal with disabilities was a constant source of concern and guilt, but none of us had any first-hand experience in the area, and the demands of other programs always seemed to mean that, despite best intentions, nothing ever got off the ground.

Our first attempt had come in the spring of 1992, when Carmen Marshall had arranged an Equity Studies Centre tour of Sunny View Public School, a school for children with severe physical disabilities. In retrospect it was not a good place to start. The children at Sunny View were so dependent on care that it was difficult for us to get our heads around how a rights-based equity paradigm might apply. The issue languished for almost two years, until March 1994, when Vanessa Russell arranged for the student program workers to meet with the staff and some of the board of the DisAbled Women's Network of Ontario (DAWN), an activist organization of disabled women working to achieve access, equity, and full participation. The women of DAWN were smart and articulate and approached their work from a feminist anti-oppression and anti-discrimination framework. For me, anyway, it became clear how much of my discomfort and confusion about how to approach disabilities as an equity issue was the result of my own stereotypes about who people with disabilities were, and what they were capable of doing.

Vanessa and I worked out a strategy. We had learned most of what we knew about other issues from listening to students talk about their experiences. What we needed was a similar process to bring together students with disabilities, to give them an opportunity to share their stories, identify the issues they were facing, and brainstorm around what needed to be done. A number of secondary schools had programs for students with disabilities. We could organize disabled students to demand change in the same way that we had organized other groups of students. For a brief moment everything seemed simple and clear.

In practice, however, things proved far more difficult. Vanessa started by contacting the Special Education Department to see how we could go about organizing focus groups. Special Education seemed quite uninterested in the project, and Vanessa came up against one barrier after another. Phone calls were not returned. Then it was always someone else she needed to talk to. Technical problems were raised. Since many of the students we wanted to work with had caregivers, we wouldn't be able to meet with them privately. Transport was an issue. After school students needed to be returned to their homes, and it would be difficult to organize sessions during school time – students shouldn't miss class. There was always one reason or another as to why the project couldn't go forward. In the end Vanessa did succeed in meeting with a group of disabled students at the City Adult Learning Centre, but our visions of bringing together disabled secondary school students from across the system went nowhere.

At the time neither of us understood where this resistance was coming from. We were both unaware of the Special Education Department's conflicted relationship with the Board's left-wing. We tended to think of disabilities as the last issue that the Board had come to; in reality it had been one of the first. As far back as the 1950s, Special Education had taken ownership of education for differently-abled students. But that was well before the emergence of the human rights and anti-discrimination paradigms that had shaped the response to issues of race and gender in the 1970s. Special Ed provided services, usually in a segregated environment.

The activism of the 1970s had been a serious challenge to the "Special Education Empire," as Myra Novogrodsky called it. "The left position, led by trustee George Martell," Myra said, "was that one of the ways that poor students were discriminated against was by being identified as learning disabled and put into Special Education classes. The education they received there was dead-end and deadening. For Martell, Special Education was one of the worst examples of streaming."

The Special Ed lobby argued that special-needs students were not being adequately serviced, and demanded more resources. As Myra put it, there was an "ideological war between the people who said that there was no such thing as a learning disability and that it was all just class bias, and those who were saying there were tons of learning disabilities, although they could never quite explain why there seemed to be so many more of them in [the poor area of] Regent Park than in the wealthy north end of the city."

Marg Evans concurred. "In terms of curriculum, disabilities lived in Special Ed. They felt they knew about wheelchairs and elevators and all that. They were the experts. They had the resources. It was a very strong empire. It was very much an establishment view of things. There was a real political antipathy between Special Education and the reformers who were always criticizing Special Ed as a dumping ground for kids. I guess that antipathy endured forever."

Through the 1980s, Myra noted, the pendulum had swung "from parents being ashamed of their kids and wanting to take them out and hide them in segregated settings, towards ideas that there was no disability that was great enough that a kid shouldn't have the right to a fully integrated education." The Special Education Empire was under attack. It was understandable that the department would be suspicious of attempts by Equity, long associated with the left, to get access to their students for a fishing expedition to look for complaints about their education and treatment.

A second realization for us was that although disability was a handy umbrella notion, in reality the "disabilities community" was exceptionally complex. Disability was a term that encompassed very different kinds of challenges around vision, hearing, mobility, development, and learning. In each area there were different degrees of ability. Struggling and living with these challenges generated different experiences and notions of community.

The complex internal challenges of developing a significant equity-based approach to students with disabilities merged with the increasing external constraints of shrinking resources. We were already cutting back on some of our most treasured and valuable programs. How could we plan for a major expansion into an area in which we had no experience, and that seemed so difficult to penetrate? We didn't completely abandon the notion of trying to hold focus groups in the following school year, but by then the world would be fundamentally changed. Provincial government cuts deprived DAWN of both its staff and its office, and attacks on public education sent the Toronto Board's equity efforts into turmoil. The project was never realized.

For me, the failure of the disability project reinforced the idea that the motor force of equity issues had to be the political organization of communities of people who were directly connected to those issues. In the absence of strong community pressure from the outside, we were unable to overcome barriers within the institution.

Unbeknownst to us, just such a movement was starting to organize. Late in 1994, inspired by the passage of the U.S. Americans with Disabilities Act, a small group of disabled people and their supporters founded the Ontarians with Disabilities Act (ODA) Committee to push for comprehensive legislation to remove barriers across the province. In 1999, when I was finally able to return to the issue and develop curriculum for the senior elementary level on human rights and disabilities, the ODA Committee had become a force across the province, and its work to raise the profile of disabilities as a human rights issue was a major support for our efforts.

## Body Image

A second area in which Vanessa Russell took the initiative was the development of programs on body image. She had received a call from an alternative senior elementary school, where a student had been diagnosed as anorexic. When the student came back to school, the class was working on a holocaust unit. "The boys chased her up and down the hall with pictures of survivors from concentration camps telling her that was what she looked like. Talk about equity gone awry."

In her work with the girls in the school, the first challenge Vanessa faced was the popular conception of body image. Questions about body image usually called up ideas about fat and thin, eating disorders, dieting. People would think, "Oh, she's going to try to stop them from throwing up." There might be jokes. "God, if you can't make fun of the way people look, what's left?" Then there were the stereotypes about who struggles with these kinds of issues. "People generally think that it's only an issue for white middle-class girls who don't have anything better to do with their time," Vanessa said. "This was certainly not our experience. Body image struggles and body-based discrimination cut across race, class, sexual orientation, and ability among the students we met and worked with."

To broaden the idea of body image, Vanessa and Carla Rice from the Women and Body Image Project at Women's College Hospital came up with an eight-week support group program called "Embodying Equity."[6] The goal was to look at how race, gender, sexual orientation, class, and disabilities shaped young women's identities and how they felt about their bodies. The issue then became much more than a matter of size and shape. "It was an organic way to link equity issues through the body," Vanessa said. With age-appropriate modifications, the program was run in over a dozen secondary and elementary schools, and then developed into a retreat program that ran twice before funds disappeared.

## New Schools: Triangle and Nighana

By spring 1995 John Campey had been working quietly for over a year to negotiate a new school program. Tony Gambini's experience as the human sexuality counsellor had given him ample experience of the devastation that was occurring in the lives of many gay and lesbian students as they struggled to get an education in homophobic secondary school settings. In response Tony came up with the idea of a school for gay and lesbian youth modelled on New York's Harvey Milk program. Openly gay and lesbian staff would deliver curriculum stressing gay and lesbian history and culture. The school would be an oasis for queer kids at high risk of failure or dropping out. The proposal became known as the Triangle Program.

Campey described his role in setting up the program as one of a "marriage broker." Aware that the atmosphere at the Board would hardly be congenial to such a politically charged idea as a gay school, he proposed establishing Triangle as a satellite program to the downtown Oasis Alternative School, which already had several off-site programs. Establishing one more such program would be an administrative rather than a political matter. The school's staff was enthusiastic and began meeting with Gambini to flesh out the idea, and Campey sold the project to the Director's Office.

If there was evidence that schools were failing in the education of gay and lesbian students, the evidence for Black students was even stronger, and the creation of Black-focused schools had been a long-standing goal of activists within the Black community. The election of the NDP had reinvigorated those aspirations. In 1992 a multi-level government task force, the African-Canadian Community Working Group, proposed that a predominantly Black junior high school be set up in each of the Metro Toronto boards. The Organization of Parents of Black Children supported the concept in its submission to Ontario's Royal Commission on Learning in 1993. When it released its report in 1994, the Commission itself recommended that Boards collaborate with representatives of the Black communities "to establish demonstration schools in jurisdictions where there were large numbers of Black students."[7]

Despite that recommendation and the community pressure, administrators and trustees in Toronto remained leery of any program that might be seen as segregating Black students. Finally the Davenport Perth Community Centre in Toronto's west end conducted a study on Black youth who had dropped out, and approached OPBC about the possibilities of a project that would help to educate such students in a holistic way and keep them connected to the education system. OPBC asked two prominent Black academics, George Dei and Carl James, to represent the case to the Toronto Board. By that time, the 1994 approval of full school status for the First Nations School had set an important precedent. If a special school focused on Native culture and traditions, and primarily serving Aboriginal youth could be justified, why couldn't similar programs be established for other groups?

So it was that Triangle made its way through the administrative approval process, in tandem with a proposal for a similar Black student program, to be called Nighana. While both programs were ground-breaking, they were small in scope. Neither was classified as a "school." Both were established as programs of already existing alternative schools. Neither of them would involve more than twenty-five students, and they would be students considered most at risk. Neither would fundamentally change what was happening to gay or Black students in mainstream schools.

When it opened in September 1995, the Triangle Program was fortunate to have John Terpstra as its first full-time teacher. Terpstra had held the prestigious position of head of English at Jarvis Collegiate, but heading into his last years at the Board he decided to give up that job to take on the challenge of teaching a group of marginalized kids in a one-room school house. The gay and lesbian community also rallied to support the fledgling program, establishing volunteer nutrition and tutoring programs. The largely gay Metropolitan Community Church provided free space for the classroom.

Although it also survived, the Nighana program did not fare so well. It suffered from staffing problems and lack of resources. When Pat Case gave the director the name of somebody he though might be good to teach in the program, the answer he got was, "But Pat, why would she want to do that?" The idea was that the teacher was "on a trajectory to get promoted" and the Nighana program would not be a good career fit. For Pat, "the 'victory' of Nighana was muted" because the Board put so little into it. "That in itself is a manifestation of racism." The school was left to struggle along on its own.

Triangle and Nighana had squeaked in just under the wire. By the time they opened in fall 1995, the political complexion of the whole province had changed.

## The Onslaught

In June 1995 the Conservatives under Mike Harris crushed the NDP in the provincial election. NDP Premier Bob Rae was a tragic figure. He had tried to be "Premier of All the People" and ended up being despised by almost everyone. Part of it was just bad luck – he presided over the worst economic recession in years. But the Rae government had also alienated its traditional allies. The government had bowed to corporate interests in failing to introduce promised tax reform and no-fault auto insurance. The union movement was up in arms over Rae's introduction of the Social Contract. Many in the Black community were let down in the struggle over *Show Boat*. Members of the gay community were upset by the decision to put Bill 167 – the gay rights bill – to a free vote, which led to the defeat of the effort to amend the definition of spouse to recognize lesbian and gay partnerships.

As the NDP sunk in the polls, the Harris Tories consolidated the support of big business on Bay Street and small business on main street with promises of major tax cuts and less government. Harris appealed to reactionary and racist circles with coded promises to end preferential treatment for "special interest groups" – meaning people of colour, immigrants, women, and the gay community. To rural voters he represented traditional values against the supposed depravity of big-city Toronto. The victorious Conservative Party did not offer an old-style, patrician Tory leadership like the one led by former premier Bill Davis. Harris's Tories were hard-right-wing ideologues. Unlike the NDP before them, they wasted no time in consultations to win people over or develop consensus. They simply launched into the business of hacking the province into their own image. In July, just six weeks after the election, the new minister of finance, Ernie Eves, announced $2 billion in cuts. Long-term health care, workplace health and safety, and the provincial wage protection fund were the first targets. NDP labour law reforms and incentives to employers to hire low-income earners were also dismantled. The Ministry of Labour staff was cut in half. A third of employment standards inspectors were laid off.

By September minorities and the poor were in their sights, as well as labour. An unarmed Aboriginal activist, Dudley George, was murdered by police sent to end the occupation of Ipperwash Provincial Park by Natives demanding recognition of a Chippewa burial ground on the site. In October the government announced the closure of Ontario Welcome House, an internationally recognized centre that for decades had provided language classes and settlement and support programs to new immigrants in Toronto. It also closed down similar institutions across the province. The Ontario Anti-Racism Secretariat was soon eliminated. Welfare rates were slashed by 21.6 per cent, and youth welfare was restricted. Nearly four hundred co-op and non-profit housing projects were cancelled. Most ominous for the Board was Minister of Education John Snobelen's candid admission of plans to "create a crisis in education" and to "bankrupt" the system to justify dramatic changes.

The Tories attacked on a staggering number of fronts. In November the government announced a further $3.5 billion in cuts, slashing health care and grants to school boards, colleges, and universities. Child-care subsidies were eliminated. Grants to municipal governments were reduced by almost 50 per cent. Transit grants were cut by 21 per cent. Libraries lost $12 million. Funding for recycling programs was eliminated. Conservation authorities were cut by 70 per cent. Some $220 million in support was gutted from art galleries, museums, and public broadcasting. A number of environmental laws were scrapped. Freedom of information laws were changed to make government information more difficult to get. In December the NDP's Employment Equity Act was repealed and pay equity was eliminated. The government tabled legislation to amalgamate the six municipalities of Metropolitan Toronto into one giant megacity, and as part of this process the Toronto Board of Education would be submerged into one huge Metro board.[8]

"We tried to alert the community to what kind of threat we were looking at, especially for inner-city schools," trustee Tam Goossen said. "We had a press conference at Queen's Park warning about cuts to heritage language programs, and later, when the Anti-Racism Unit was cut, we protested that as well, but it was totally reactive. There was nothing we could do, except to make sure the communities knew."

"When the Tories came in," John Campey said, "any kind of progress was stopped. There was no point in trying to initiate new stuff. It became a matter of what could get tucked away." Board staff worked to make sure that as much as possible of the program work survived. They also now had to turn their attention to the possible shape of the post-amalgamation board – who would be the new director, how many trustees there would be, what money would be left in the system and what they could do with it.

## New Blood, and Triage

The fall of 1995 saw major changes in the composition of the Equity Studies Centre. Ruby Lam had left to go to graduate school, and because of the Board's financial crisis she was not replaced. The terms of both Carmen Marshall and Marg Wells were also finished. Despite our worries that we might lose those positions as well, they were soon filled by Alice Te and Terezia Zoric, both of them relatively young teachers. Alice had been teaching senior public school for six years, and Terezia had been a secondary school teacher for five.

Alice, whose family came from the Philippines, considered herself a latecomer to social activism. She had attended Pat Case's "Challenging Racism" courses and had begun her own exploration of her identity as an Asian woman through involvement with International Women's Day and the Chinese Canadian National Council. In her new job at the Board Alice would spend most of her time in the schools on projects requested by teachers and administrators.

Terezia had started her political work early on in life – by Grade 3 she was arguing about sexism with teachers and her "patriarchal" Croatian immigrant parents. In Grade 5 she organized the girls to commandeer the baseball diamond. She considered herself a "social justice crusader" in high school, and as "a nerdy bookish kid who had a big mouth" she became a radical student activist at university. Teaching at Riverdale Collegiate, she was involved in Riverdale Against Discrimination at the time the school was being targeted by the Heritage Front, and she had worked against the effects of the NDP Social Contract as a member of the executive of the teachers' union. In her new job at the Board Terezia saw the Harris election as creating "an emergency" and immediately began organizing against the attacks on the poor and the education system. She soon found her focus in the Equity Studies Centre around questions of class, which she saw as being absent in the curriculum. From her background in the teachers' federation she realized that "labour folk" often "didn't speak the same language as equity people." The two sides were not particularly strong allies, or even important contacts. She proposed pulling together material on class, anti-poverty, and labour for a curriculum document.

What started as a ten-day summer project wouldn't stop growing. She saw my *Resources for Anti-Racist Education* as being too learner-centred a model to apply to issues of class.[9] In her experience, she said, "Kids don't have the language of class to talk about it. It seems invisible to them." She wanted something that would serve as a curriculum document rather than an activity package. Terezia continued to work on the document during her time at the Centre, adding materials she developed for schools and labour education courses for teachers.

There was continuing resistance to the Tory "new world order." An inner-city forum to shape creative responses to help children and families hurt by the social assistance cuts called on the Board to take into account the increased need for support, and to document the cuts' impact on the academic, social, and personal growth of students. It asked schools to hold discussions of the cuts as a critical issue. A Board resolution at the end of October opposed the closure of Ontario Welcome House and the loss of valuable services to new immigrants. In December a Board meeting moved that consultations be held to determine the impact on programs of the defunding of many community organizations that had established partnerships with the Board.

In September the Board and the Ontario Secondary School Teachers' Federation presented their joint anti-racism awards, and several STAR members were among those honoured. They included Fatema Mullen, who received one of two city-wide awards for senior students. But within days I found myself reporting to STAR that the Equity Studies Centre had decided to cancel that fall's anti-racism student camp. The students were ready to go to the barricades, but the problem was that the decision had been made by Equity Studies itself, not some racist politician or bureaucrat.

The loss of the camps suddenly made the issue of tax rebates concrete for the students activists. The stark contrast of a Board unable to afford $15 thousand to run an anti-racist student retreat while being forced to return $3.5 million to the TD Bank as a result of its successful tax appeal could not be ignored. Later that fall, STAR produced material about the extent and impact of corporate tax appeals and began to distribute it throughout the schools. The material generated interest from a whole new group of student activists. But by this point, STAR members were pouring through boxes of course outlines that had finally arrived for the much delayed inclusive curriculum project. In December, the group called a meeting to found a second organization, Students Against Corporate Tax Appeals (SACTA), to concentrate on the tax appeal issue.

In the Ministry of Education, Nora Allingham was involved in salvage operations. The Tories eliminated the umbrella Anti-Racism and Equity Division, leaving only the rump of Nora Allingham's small Anti-Racism and Ethnocultural Equity Branch to wind down programs. As the government began systematically repealing equity legislation, the one thing Nora managed to save was PPM 119, the Policy/Program Memorandum 119 of July 1993 – the memo that required boards of education to set in place policies on anti-racism and ethnocultural equity. In fact, her office hid the memorandum in "a masterpiece of obfuscation," she said, by inundating the premier's office "with so much other stuff that they didn't notice what we left out. I spent hours crafting information sheets and briefing them without mentioning it. And when they finally realized that they had missed it, all the other repeals had taken place and it would have looked very cheesy of them to go back and do an entire new set of regulations to repeal that one memorandum, so they just left it alone."

She also began to farm out Ministry projects to community organizations. "After the election, everything that we submitted was shot down by the new boys in the minister's office. We couldn't get anything approved referring to race or equity. They were bad words. So I started ferrying money out of my budget to other organizations to get them to do it. I could have been fired on the spot, but that was the only way of getting the money used." Under that strategy, for instance, a video, *Reflections*, on anti-racist education was released by the Metro Toronto Board, and a document on hate groups in the schools, which had been blocked by the Premier's office, was published in part by the OSSTF.

Opposition to the Harris government was growing across the province. London and Hamilton were shut down as the labour movement organized its "Days of Action." Students protesting education cuts disrupted the legislature. Public service employees walked out to protect job security. But it was all to little effect. The Harris juggernaut rolled on.

## A Report Card

By early February 1996, after weeks of evening and weekend meetings sifting through boxes and boxes of course outlines, STAR had finally completed its work on the curriculum project. The results were published in a pamphlet, "Toronto Board Secondary Schools' Report Card: Is Our Curriculum Inclusive?" The introduction explained the process.

> English course outlines were marked in terms of their inclusion of authors who are: women, people of colour or out lesbian and gay men and whether materials dealt with social justice issues.
>
> History and Social Sciences were examined in terms of their inclusion of the contributions of major world civilizations, women, people of colour, a range ethnic groups, and discussion of a range of incidents of historical injustices.

The criteria were given numerical grades and the average for each department was calculated. The values were then translated to letter grades: "A – excellent (keep up the good work), B – good (it's getting there), C – fair (needs work), D – poor (improvements are necessary), F – fail (great strides are needed)." The students were judicious but critical markers. Only one school, Central Commerce Collegiate, scored as high as an A- in English, along with a B in history. Evaluators' comments read, "Canadian Women's Course is a step in the right direction but could be improved by dealing more with women of a variety of cultures, races and backgrounds."

Good intentions were clearly not enough. Although the philosophy statement of one alternative program, at the School of Life Experience (SOLE), stressed "the inclusion of women and minorities, actual course outlines in history are still very male-focussed and eurocentric," noted another comment.

Several schools submitted outlines only for courses they thought would receive good marks, but to no avail. They received an "incomplete." The report also noted the ghettoization of inclusive courses. "Although the grade 9 and grade 11 English courses are very eurocentric and male, Northern [Secondary] has two excellent English courses they should be proud of." At Harbord Collegiate, "Several English courses are doing well around topics of gender and multiculturalism but this needs to be distributed throughout all courses."

A common problem noted was the failure of schools to deal with lesbian and gay authors and issues. Inglenook Community School, a small alternative school, received a B in English and a B+ in history. The students commented, "Inglenook is making good progress. With work on lesbian/gay issues it will merit an A." Rosedale Heights, the Board's pilot unstreamed school, earned the comment, "Rosedale's courses were strong on social justice issues. With a bit more work, especially on gay/lesbian issues, this school could be getting straight A's."

The students noted that it was often the high-ranking academic schools that did most poorly. Malvern Collegiate, a predominantly white middle-class school in the east of the city, received a D in English and was told, "In general, English courses provided very little or no mention of women, people of colour, out lesbian/gay authors or social justice issues." Lawrence Park Collegiate was scolded. "No work was handed in despite requests. Very poor showing for Lawrence."

In general, the report card was peppered with F's, C's, and D's – not a good evaluation for a system that had supposedly been working to make its curriculum more inclusive for almost twenty years.

The report slowly filtered through the Board. Pat Case showed it to director John Davies, who, he said, "just grinned from ear to ear. He said you wouldn't use it as a scientific report but it sure makes the point." It made its way in February to the Race Relations Committee, where the students were commended on the report and their perseverance, and in March copies were sent to all secondary school principals. The response was subdued. It seemed that the system had decided on a strategy of indifference. In late March STAR invited the news media to a press conference at Inglenook Community School to release the results to the public.

On the afternoon of the press conference I received an urgent call from Don Irwin, chief superintendent of Curriculum. He asked me to speak on behalf of the Board at the event – and particularly to stress all the efforts that the Board had made towards a more inclusive curriculum. I told him, sorry, but it was not a Board press conference: the students had organized it. I had not been invited to speak. I suggested that if the Board wanted to contact the press about its efforts in the area he should speak to the Public Information Department.

*The Toronto Star* did contact Board officials before publishing an article under the headline "Courses Ignore Cultural Diversity, Student Group Says."[10] The *Star* quoted STAR spokesperson Claire (Yaya) Yao. "We call on the board of education to take immediate action on this issue. This is something that affects the self-image and identity of every person who sits in a classroom. What's taught tells you whose history and culture is important and whose is not."

Superintendent Rick Kollins found himself defending the "extraordinary lengths" that the Board had gone to in ensuring that courses reflected the experiences of non-Europeans. "I'm the first to admit what's on the written page is out of date," he told the *Star*. "Many textbooks still don't have the inclusivity we'd like, so it means the teachers have to supplement what they do." Kollins promised that STAR would be invited to discuss its concerns as the Board redrew its high-school courses.

By now the schools, especially those that had received bad marks, were also abuzz. The minutes of STAR's April 16 meeting noted, "Teachers are upset, taking it personally. But we caught their attention. Superintendent Kollins requests a meeting May 1. What will we ask for?"

The students drew up a series of six recommendations for the meeting. They called for student input in the ongoing process of curriculum evaluation and change. Superintendents should immediately request a detailed report from each school about efforts to make its curriculum more inclusive. English and history consultants should prepare lists of grade-appropriate inclusive materials in consultation with teachers from schools that had scored well on the report card. A committee should be set up to establish criteria for inclusive curriculum in order to assist schools in identifying goals and evaluating their programs. Schools should report regularly on their efforts to the Race Relations and Status of Women committees. Finally, the Board should establish a timetable for the implementation of these recommendations.

The atmosphere at the May 1 meeting was tense. Few principals and vice-principals attended, and most of those who did were there to complain that their schools had been unfairly treated. They criticized STAR's methodology and argued that course outlines did not tell the whole story about what was happening in classes. The students argued that if the system did not find that their methodology was adequate, why hadn't it used its enormously greater resources to conduct its own study? Why was this the first time that students had been invited to such a discussion? What was important was not the shortcomings of the report card, but how to achieve the changes that everyone claimed to be interested in. The meeting broke up without an implementation timeline being established, but there was an agreement to have regular student representation at future committee meetings.

Certainly not everyone was happy about the STAR report card. Myra Novogrodsky had her reservations. As someone who worked in Curriculum and as a teacher she said she had "a different feeling about how you should treat teachers if you wanted them to do equity work." She thought that better results would be more likely to come from "educating people" than from "humiliating them or embarrassing them. Although I found many teachers maddening, I didn't feel that was the way to get them on board."

The OSSTF Anti-Racism Committee expressed its appreciation for the students' work the following October. Whether the kick in the pants that STAR had given the system would have speeded up curriculum reform is a moot question. There were certainly advances. Later that spring, for example, Kollins agreed to fund a project through his Inclusive Curriculum Committee to encourage more schools to offer African civilization courses.

But without the regular camp programs to develop new generations of activists, STAR was beginning to shrink as key members graduated. Student participation in the Inclusive Curriculum Committee waned. By the following year STAR had been reduced to a handful of members. They organized one last conference to try to attract new recruits, but by that point the system was filled with so much turmoil that the group had lost any hope of maintaining a critical mass. STAR ceased to function.

Although Pat Case sometimes had his conflicts with STAR's tactics, he believed the group showed how students could be central to the process of change in equity education. Despite the group's small size, he said, it did have a noticeable influence on affairs at the Board. "More importantly, I think it was an example of some of the best pedagogy that can take place. At the end of the day, people come into a school system and they leave. The effect of an organization like STAR is not so much to be measured as what it does in the school system, but as what it does for people who are members while they are there and afterwards." Pat pointed out to me that both of us knew young people who had been in STAR and who continued afterward to be active and believe that they could play a role in making change. "It's all about people feeling their own agency and getting a sense of that, and then you're on your way. There isn't any other pedagogy like that. It's activism but it's also pedagogy." STAR, by that measurement, was a highly successful project.

## Chapter 14

# Under Siege

BY EARLY 1996 THE PROVINCIAL GOVERNMENT was making good on its promise to create a crisis in the education system. In February the School Board Reduction Task Force recommended province-wide pooling of commercial and industrial assessment, the reduction of 168 school boards to 87, the dissolution of the Metro Toronto School Board, and the capping of trustee remuneration. In March the province reduced transfer payments to school boards by $400 million and provided a "tool kit" to Boards to assist them in making cuts. The Education Amendments Act made junior kindergarten an optional program, reduced funding for adult education, and declared a moratorium on capital projects.

Faced with an unprecedented attack on the public school system, the left and the right in Toronto largely forgot their differences and denounced the provincial "tax grab," but more reports that signalled government intentions were in the wings. In November 1996 a report on school board/teacher bargaining (the Paroian Report) recommended that the province dismantle bargaining, legislate teacher workload and class size, remove teachers' right to strike, and take principals and vice-principals out of the teachers' unions. David Crombie's "Who Does What Report," released the same month, called on the province to restrict board decision-making and to remove local taxation powers, and recommended the outsourcing of all board business functions.

The Harris onslaught had a profound effect on equity work. Now, as Terezia Zoric put it, "Everything became about defending what existed. There weren't any rich conversations about what the future should look like."

In the Equity Studies Centre, after more than eleven years as curriculum advisor on race relations, Hari Lalla retired in the summer of 1996. The continued stresses of the job and the Harris attacks on public education had clearly been wearing on him. Because of the financial crisis, he was not replaced. Myra Novogrodsky became the sole co-ordinator of the Equity Studies Centre. Hari's departure left Alice Te as the only person of colour in the Centre. In a world in which people of colour were seeing their concerns being pushed off the table with the repeal of employment equity legislation and the defunding of immigrant services, the absence of any Black or South Asian presence in the Centre was a serious problem. The perception that the Toronto Board and Equity Studies Centre had lost interest in issues of race would emerge as a worrisome liability in the struggles to come.

## Corporate Partnerships and Class Bias

In June 1996 the Labour Education Committee released its proposed policy on "corporate partnerships." The document began with a concise description of the issue:

> Public education is a major victim of provincial budget cuts and underfunding. Successful corporate tax appeals have worsened the situation in Metro Toronto. This underfunding of education has provided a greater opportunity to business interests to fill a financial void. Business-education partnerships are increasingly being promoted across Canada. Business is seeking a convergence of the functions and goals of both. The business world has become increasingly attracted to the classroom as a venue for its commercial interests.[1]

Corporate involvement took many forms: assistance to schools in the form of equipment, expertise, or company-developed curriculum materials; sponsorship of school teams, clubs, and field trips in return for publicity; the purchase of advertising space on school buses; monopoly contracts to food and beverage companies; and even, in some cases, fast-food venders taking over school cafeterias.

The document noted that while some educators welcomed such partnerships as a solution to the deepening financial crisis, others expressed serious reservations. Students were a captive audience, and partnerships could give the impression that schools endorsed particular products. In a corporate partnership curriculum might end up being used for marketing and ideological purposes, undermining the democratic intent of publicly funded schools. Corporate donations also took the politicians responsible for maintaining the public school systems off the hook. In terms of equity, the trend to corporate involvement increased disparities and discriminated against students in poorer areas that did not attract corporations, which usually sought out more affluent customers. Critics noted the dangers of censorship and self-censorship that resulted when schools became financially captive to corporate funding.

The document stated that corporate partnerships needed to be beneficial to all students and could not become a substitute for the Board's responsibility to address equity of student opportunity. It called for clear guidelines to evaluate proposed business contributions to education and suggested that businesses that wanted to contribute resources should donate to a publicly administered foundation to ensure the equitable use of funds. Partnerships should only be considered with companies whose labour, human rights, equity, workplace safety, and environmental policies were consistent with those of the Board. It called for the banning of corporate logos and advertising in schools, and the evaluation of business-proposed curriculum for accuracy, objectivity, and completeness.

Meanwhile the changes in the political atmosphere had not stopped Terezia Zoric's work on her class bias document, and a draft, already 150 pages long, had begun circulating throughout the system. "Challenging Class Bias" went far beyond looking at attitudes. Its collection of exercises and activities gave teachers material they could use as a starting point for working with students to build an analysis of class stratification and inequality in Canada.

The first section tested students' knowledge of the extent of poverty in Canada, with an emphasis on the relationship between poverty and gender. It asked students to record their food consumption and compare the cost with the amount that the official government policy suggested as being adequate for families on social assistance. Other exercises helped students broaden their conception of human rights to include such social rights as access to food, housing, health care, education, and a clean environment.

Section two looked at media messages about class and how advertising shaped students' ideas of "the good life." A third section investigated why people were poor, contrasting the stereotypes that the poor were lazy or stupid with the material realities that generated poverty – lack of jobs, low minimum wages, racial and other forms of discrimination, lack of access to education, natural disasters, and the breakdown of family support systems. It included case studies on individuals and families struggling with poverty in Canada and around the world.

The draft also looked at wage discrepancies for different kinds of work in schools, the causes of unemployment, and examples of struggles for social justice in different sectors of the workforce. Its final two sections explored the international division of labour and wealth distribution, asking students to think about practical ways in which they could use the privileges of living in a relatively wealthy country to fight for change. Appendices included the Board's statement on class bias to give teachers a rationale for dealing with such issues in their classrooms.

## Fighting Back, Going Down

In autumn 1996 public opposition to the Conservative government reached its peak when the fourth of the union-led Days of Action took place in Toronto. On Friday, October 25, the city was closed down by a general strike. A million people stayed away from work. Public transit, the post office, municipal services, construction sites and most factories, and all levels of education from pre-school to universities ground to a halt. Pickets were set up at over three hundred locations across the city. Students surrounded the Ministry of Education, and demonstrators disrupted the stock exchange.

The following day nearly 300,000 people marched on the provincial legislature at Queen's Park in the largest demonstration in Canadian history. But in the face of the Tory government's intransigence, the momentum could not be maintained. The unions began to bicker among themselves and with their community allies on strategy. What was the point of holding demonstration after demonstration that appeared to have no effect on government policy? Wouldn't it make more sense to focus energy on defeating the Conservatives in the next election? Calls for a general strike as a means of striking back were considered by most of the union movement to be unrealistic and inflammatory. After the Toronto protest, the "Days of Action" quickly petered out.

At the end of the year the Tories introduced Bill 103, The City of Toronto Act, and close on its heels, Bill 104, The Fewer School Boards Act. Bill 103 legislated the amalgamation of the six cities that made up Metropolitan Toronto: Toronto, Scarborough, York, North York, East York, and Etobicoke. The supposed rationale was cost-savings and the elimination of duplication in government, although studies of other such megacities had revealed that amalgamation not only increased costs and bureaucracy but also eroded democratic community decision-making. For some critics in Toronto, the first item on the Tory agenda was just that: to wipe out a whole layer of government that had been the breeding ground for progressive politicians; to silence the most vocal critics of provincial downloading of costs onto municipal governments. In response a new grassroots group, Citizens for Local Democracy, sprang up and organized a huge demonstration that snaked down Yonge Street on February 15. On March 3, in a municipally conducted referendum across Metro, 75 per cent of voters opposed amalgamation.

The fight against municipal amalgamation – against the backdrop of hospital closures, defunding of libraries, and increasing poverty and homelessness – generally eclipsed opposition to Bill 104, which amalgamated school boards, limited the number of trustees, and capped trustee salaries at $5,000 per year. Most critics believed that if the creation of the megacity could be stopped, the amalgamation of Metro school boards would not be able to proceed. Nonetheless, the Toronto Board organized parent information meetings and public hearings on the impact of amalgamation on education and participated in legal challenges to the Bill, even appealing to the federal government to intervene. In a referendum conducted by Young Citizens for Local Democracy and the Toronto Association of Student Councils, 81 per cent of Toronto secondary students expressed opposition to municipal amalgamation, 85 per cent opposed the amalgamation of the school boards, and 86 per cent opposed the proposed tax restructuring.

Despite the spirited opposition, the Tory majority in the legislature passed both bills in April. Amalgamation of the cities and the boards would be effective on January 1, 1998. At that point my colleagues and I would be working for the expanded Toronto District School Board (TDSB).

## As Night Falls

For those of us who had been involved in the Board's equity efforts, the passage of the amalgamation legislation at the end of April 1997 meant that in eight months the organization we had been working to change for twenty years would cease to exist. A few weeks later, if we needed any more indication that we were in serious trouble, the province finally dissolved the Ministry of Education's Anti-Racism and Ethnocultural Equity Branch. It seemed all too possible that the inclusive approach developed in Toronto would be lost with amalgamation. Personally, I was especially worried about anti-homophobia work, which was still anathema to most of the suburban boards.

Between the six of us left in the Equity Studies Centre and the two advisors in the Equal Opportunity Office, Toronto had by far the largest staff commitment to equity. North York had two anti-racism consultants, and Scarborough had a co-ordinator of anti-racism and ethnocultural equity in its Student and Community Services Department. The York Board had a project leader for fair employment practices. Etobicoke had an equity program advisor and a couple of other related positions. East York had a person in its Program and Educational Resources Department with a focus on ESL. Myra Novogrodsky took the initiative to invite our counterparts in the other boards to a meeting in order to try to develop a unified voice to position equity work in the amalgamation process.

The formation of the Metro Equity Workers Network (MEWN) was a delicate operation. While many of us knew each other from our participation in the Anti-Racist Multicultural Educators' Network of Ontario or work around the York Equity conferences, we were coming from very different locations in our organizations and reflected different institutional cultures and approaches with different priorities. Toronto was the only one of the six boards that had developed an inclusive approach embracing race, gender, sexual orientation, disability, and class. The other boards had tended to focus primarily on race and culture, with some attention to gender. Those of us from Toronto tended to see the efforts of the other boards as underdeveloped and narrow. While several members from the suburban Boards saw amalgamation as an opportunity to broaden their equity work, it was also the case that people from those boards often found the larger, Toronto group, with its more plentiful resources, to be domineering and arrogant.

These differences were exacerbated by the uncertainty we all faced. Nobody knew what stand the new board might take on equity, or what kind of resources and positions were going to be available in the new formation.

There was a general fear that the programs and issues we cared most about might lose out in the shuffle of reorganization. To be effective advocates for equity issues in the formative period of the new organization, we would need to build trust and take a common approach to issues.

After several exploratory meetings, Myra asked me to draft a proposed basis of unity for the group. If we could come to an agreement on a set of common principles, the group members could then take those items to their home boards for ratification. If all the boards signed on to a common position on equity and what was necessary to achieve it, we would be in a stronger position to establish a clear framework for the new, amalgamated Toronto District School Board.

I based my draft on the principles of anti-racist education, which had begun to apply to other areas of equity work. After a lot of back and forth and revisions, a manifesto called "Equity in Education: Basic Principles" emerged, which the MEWN members then took to their respective boards.

At the Toronto Board, "Principles" was endorsed by a joint meeting of Race Relations, Labour Education, Status of Women, and the Committee on Education of Gay and Lesbian Students in early June 1997, and approved by the Board shortly afterwards. The manifesto stated:

> Educational systems in Canada have often not served individuals associated with certain groups. There is consequently a need for change to overcome institutional and individual racism, sexism, homophobia, class bias, ableism and other forms of discrimination.
>
> The goal of equity in education is to overcome these barriers to educational success, so that the range of educational achievements will be the same for all groups whatever their "race," ancestry, place of origin, nationality, colour, ethnic origin, creed, sex, sexual orientation, family/marital status or socio-economic class. All individuals can learn, and must be encouraged to achieve to the maximum of their abilities.

It went on to argue that to achieve equity in education the people who had faced barriers to an equitable education had to be recognized as the "driving force" that would produce changes in educational institutions. "The school system therefore has a responsibility to work with them and encourage their participation." As well, equity in education could not be "an add-on" – it required changes across the curriculum. "Equity must be reflected in all program areas and at all educational levels in an appropriate way." It also had to be system-wide – to ensure equal opportunity for all students, staff, parents and communities, it had to be reflected in personnel hiring and promotion practices, assessment, discipline, school community relations, social work, and counselling. Moreover:

> Equity in education requires *pedagogy* which encourages and equips students and staff to understand power relations and challenge unjust systems. It must

> be based on learners' experience and must be relevant to their lives. Teachers, students, families and communities are therefore partners in an exploration that encourages responsibility and critical thinking.
>
> Equity in education must help learners understand the *connections, similarities and differences* between different forms of oppression and discrimination. Only with such understanding is it possible to work together to build a more just society.

Given their key position in the struggle for equity on a day-to-day basis, front-line educators had to "have the *support and resources* necessary to successfully meet the many challenges of providing an equitable and inclusive education to all students."

## Attempts to Hold On

The impending amalgamation made urgent the elaboration of a new human rights policy that would supercede the Racial and Ethnocultural Harassment and Sexual Harassment policies already in place – pulling together all the protected rights in the Ontario Human Rights Code. Having two harassment policies with different parallel procedures had led to serious complications. If, for example, an incident of harassment involved both race and sex, half the complaint might sail off down the racial and ethnocultural stream on the basis of mandatory response, while the aspects of the same complaint that involved sex would follow the complainant-driven sexual harassment path. Some groups were not covered at all. Oddly enough, the initiative for the new policy came from the Second Floor – an indication of the extent that concern with equity issues had begun to permeate the upper bureaucracy after years of struggle.

Pat Case and Sue McGrath frantically began work on the new policy. If it was not in place in Toronto by the time the Toronto District School Board was formed, it was anybody's guess as to how long it might take for the new board to find the political will to consider such an innovation in the midst of the confusion and upheaval of amalgamation. As well, the policies of existing "legacy" boards were to remain in effect in their local areas until the new Board developed system-wide policies to replace them. Not only would the existence of a human rights policy in Toronto be a strong argument for such an inclusive policy approach in the new TDSB, but it might also be operational in Toronto schools for the foreseeable future.

Toronto made a less successful attempt to establish a commitment to employment equity. The Tories demanded that statistics gathered under the previous legislation be destroyed. According to Sue McGrath, although the Board did find a loophole and preserved its statistics, ultimately the effort was doomed. She and others tried to set up meetings to work on an employment equity strategy for the whole system, "but all the other boards had dropped employment equity as soon as the legislation was gone. All their programs had been disbanded or had just totally petered out. Toronto was the only one interested in continuing."

The silver lining to the failure of the employment equity initiative was that Sharon Snider, the Board's employment equity co-ordinator, found herself free to concentrate on disabilities issues for the first time. According to Marg Evans, the Board's response to disabilities had become a public embarrassment. "It was very late in the game. We didn't even get around to painting the disabled spots in the parking lot until God knows how late in the process. We hadn't done the most basic of things. We were even beginning to get complaints from the province."

Working closely with Michael Gamble, a disabled gay man in her department, Snider put out a disability newsletter, compiled a manual on disabilities for managers, and produced a workplace accommodation policy that was approved by the Board. She also managed a budget for workplace accommodation requests and organized a focus group that eventually produced a Disabled Employees Network. Although Snider co-ordinated the effort, Sue McGrath funded the Network through the Equal Opportunity Office until it was "finally overwhelmed" by amalgamation.

## Homophobia Redux

In the midst of all the turmoil, we were still trying to provide programs to schools and students. If there was any indication of how much the Board and the world had moved at least on one issue, it came in May 1997 with our first day-long conference on homophobia for senior elementary school students.

Some six years before, when I had proposed such a conference for secondary school students, I had been stonewalled and had to go behind the back of the system to organize the event with a sympathetic cabal of alternative schools. This time nobody raised an eyebrow. The Equity Studies Centre planned the event and advertised it to schools throughout the system. Elementary schools quickly signed up, and we were soon at maximum registration. The students attended a series of workshops discussing a range of issues with openly gay and lesbian resource people. Unlike 1991, when the secondary school conference had sparked an uproar in the press and the creation of the vocal anti-gay group CURE, this time we received not a single complaint.

The conference reflected an increased demand for anti-homophobia work with younger students. Vanessa Russell found that elementary school students were "less homophobic than their high-school counterparts," but noted that it was still "absolutely important for them to see 'out' lesbian and gay role models." One time she ran a workshop with Grade 3 and 4 kids who had created a committee at their school to challenge racism, sexism, and homophobia. She started by asking, "So how many of you have ever met a gay or lesbian person?" None of them put up their hands. "Well, guess what," she said, "you're meeting one now." The pupils "started laughing and whispering, they were so uncomfortable," but later on "they were fine." She was convinced that if she hadn't been out-front about her own sexuality, they would not have been able to do the work required.

Another contrast was the profile of homophobia at the ESL camps. In the early 1990s, Ruby Lam and Hari Lalla had found themselves having to defend the participation of gay facilitators. At one camp, after a facilitator came out, a student "freaked out." A teacher complained that the students felt unsafe because the facilitators' sleeping quarters were attached to their own, questioned whether a gay person should have been put "in a moral leadership role," and argued that parents should have been informed that a gay person would be leading a group. Now, a few years later, the atmosphere had noticeably changed. "The kids brought up the issue of homophobia and students were coming out all over that camp," Vanessa said. "Everybody wanted to talk about sexual orientation."

Vanessa and I started working with a group of high-school youth called Teens Educating and Challenging Homophobia. Eventually most of the TEACH members identified themselves as lesbian, gay, or bisexual. They led classes on an exploration of the stereotypes and prejudices faced by lesbian and gay youth and talked about their own experiences with homophobia. Western Tech, where most of the students involved in the murder of Ken Zeller had studied a decade before, now held annual anti-homophobia workshops with all Grade 9 students at the end of the first term. Vanessa also developed and put together "Safely Out," Canada's first curriculum document to address issues of homophobia for senior elementary and secondary levels.

We had also become much better at integrating the issues. In the early days I often went into classrooms alone to deliver anti-homophobia workshops, and no matter how much I talked about the diversity of the community, I embodied the stereotype that "homosexual" meant middle-aged white gay men. By the time I was organizing the workshops at Western Tech I was insisting on pulling together a racially and culturally diverse panel consisting of both males and females. Our annual "Patterns of Racism" conferences regularly had workshops on interracial relationships, which opened with students attempting to identify who was partners with whom in a diverse panel. The panel included a lesbian couple – one Black, the other white – mixed in with the heterosexuals. We had also organized several multi-session lesbian and gay studies courses for teachers.

Occasionally it seemed to us that we had indeed succeeded in changing the world – though my trips to schools often reminded me that we were still a long way from the day when anti-homophobia work would permeate educational practice. One time at a school, for instance, I was leading a workshop on the Sexual Harassment Policy and noticed a number of interesting posters on the wall. Among them I recognized at a glance James Baldwin, Gertrude Stein, Tennessee Williams, and Audre Lorde – well-known gay and lesbian authors. This is a breakthrough, I thought to myself, and in the next break I went over to investigate more closely. Sure enough, the posters portrayed a pantheon of famous queers, but when I looked more closely I saw the series was entitled "Modern American Authors." None of the little bios under each picture mentioned that their subject was gay, even though questions of queer sexuality had been prominent in all their work. It was a strong example of the continuing institutional erasure of gay and lesbian identity.

## Towards the Final Curtain

In June 1997 Vanessa Russell left the Equity Studies Centre to take up a teaching position at Oasis and the Triangle Program. Myra Novogrodsky replaced her with Nora Allingham, who had recently lost her position at the Ministry with the liquidation of the Anti-Racism and Ethnocultural Equity Branch. With years of experience in equity issues and as an English teacher, Nora could spend her last year before retirement editing and polishing our draft documents so that they would be in more publishable shape to be distributed across the new Toronto-area Board – and not lost forever. Domenic Bellissimo had left in January 1997 to become a provincial organizer for the OSSTF, but Myra somehow also got permission for a replacement, and in September Sandy Wong took a secondment from his position as a school community advisor to take the job. Sandy, a regular facilitator at the camps, had a background in community organizing and Third World solidarity work and was glad to get the opportunity to work on equity issues in a more straightforward way.

Over the summer of 1997 the Equal Opportunity Office had taken on the task of organizing a city-wide equity forum to be held on Sunday, September 28, 1997, and bringing together parents, students, and teachers from all the equity-seeking groups to establish a strong voice in the new Board and the upcoming trustee elections. The event itself, held at the North York Board of Education building on Yonge Street North, was not all that successful. The keynote speech by Joan Grant Cummings, the president of the National Action Committee on the Status of Women, was solid but not particularly focused on education issues and the workshops were too brief to be effective. But one positive item did emerge: the forum endorsed the "Equity in Education: Basic Principles" statement. That was at least one more step in laying the groundwork for an inclusive approach by the new Board, even if the meeting did not result in any coherent community organization to put muscle behind the words.

In October, at what was to be its second-last meeting, the Toronto Board passed the new Policy on Human Rights in Schools and Workplaces and Standard Procedure Dealing with Complaints of Discrimination and Harassment, which would replace the racial and ethnocultural harassment and sexual harassment policies. For the first time, Board policy listed all the grounds protected under the Ontario Human Rights Code plus gender identity and social class. It established a uniform procedure for dealing with complaints – informally, through mediation, or through formal procedure. The policy included the concept of poisoned environment, which opened the door for complaints around biased and non-inclusive curriculum. Human rights resource people would be established to act as advisors, advocates, and mediators. The policy was up-to-date, comprehensive, and well positioned to be the basis of a new human rights policy for the Toronto District School Board.

Four days after the October Board meeting, and almost exactly one year after the Toronto Days of Action, teachers in Ontario began a work stoppage to protest the introduction of Bill 160. Across the province schools closed down in what amounted to the largest labour action in Ontario history.

Bill 160 completed the government's attack on public education and dealt a harsh blow to local democracy in the education system in Ontario. The bill removed school board control of taxation and educational spending. Henceforth the province would set property taxes and funding levels as it saw fit through a new education funding formula. Boards were stripped of their powers of financial management. Teachers lost their basic collective bargaining rights. The bill enabled the government to control teachers' terms and conditions of employment, which had traditionally been negotiated locally. The length of the school day, preparation time, class size, and the resulting number of teachers would be set by provincial fiat. The government could expand the use of non-qualified instructors. It could sell schools, toss out collective agreements, and dissolve boards for non-compliance. If there had been any hopes about the new Toronto District School Board having the flexibility to continue in the path towards equity, those hopes were finally dashed by this legislation.

The October work stoppage was officially illegal, and Board administration made a half-hearted effort to keep the schools and the Education Centre open, ordering everyone to report to work. The Equity Studies Centre and the Equal Opportunity Office unanimously decided to defy orders and honour the strike. Day after day we trudged the picket lines in one of the coldest Novembers in years. Huge demonstrations convened on Queen's Park. A week before the strike began, government plans to use the legislation to cut a further $667 million from the education budget were leaked. The teachers managed to carry the message that they were defending the public education system against draconian cuts that the Tories were using to finance their $5 billion tax break going to the wealthiest citizens of the province. An unexpected groundswell of support occurred as parents attended picket lines to show their backing for the strike.

When it failed to win an injunction ordering the teachers back to work, the government decided to wait the strikers out. The leadership of the teachers' unions, not particularly militant at the best of times, found themselves facing an implacable foe. They had no plan. Although chants calling for a general strike regularly swept through the many demonstrations at Queen's Park, and there was lots of supportive rhetoric from other unions, there was no concrete strategy for a united effort. After two weeks the solidarity and stamina of the five participating teachers' unions unravelled. On November 7, three of the five unions announced that they were going back to work. Although Toronto elementary teachers accused their provincial leadership of betrayal, and the OSSTF and the English Catholic Teachers waited a few more days before capitulating, the strike was broken. Across the province, teachers returned to their classrooms with a few brave words about having made their point and continuing the struggle by other means. Bill 160 passed into law a few weeks later.

On December 18, 1997, the Toronto Board of Education held its last meeting, which endorsed three resolutions adopted at a "Joining Together to Save Our Schools" community convention held at Central Tech earlier in the month. The first called on the Toronto District School Board to adopt a statement of commitment that it would

> do everything within its power to ensure that every student in our school system has access to the best quality programs and services, especially those which serve the special and diverse needs of all our students and to ensure the provision of adequate resources and supports to help teachers, support staff, administrators and parents build caring, healthy and successful school environments for all learners.

The second resolution asked the TDSB to endorse a list of twenty-four programs and services, including ESL, international languages, environmental education, inclusive curriculum, and community involvement as "*essential components* of our publicly-funded educational system." The third called on the TDSB to "demand that the government of Ontario place the interests of students and parents first, by guaranteeing adequate funding to serve the needs of all our students and schools."

The unanimously carried motion was a fine, brave closing salvo for the Board. In truth most if not all of us understood that the TDSB would have neither the resources nor the political will to meet those commitments.

## The Accomplishments

Through years of community struggle for an equitable education system the Toronto Board of Education had managed to weave a complex web of important programs. In the year leading up to its destruction the Board generated a cornucopia of reports to document its successes and to try to protect them in the impending amalgamation. The areas listed went far beyond the immediate responsibilities of the Equity Studies Centre and the Equal Opportunity Office and described a closely knit ecology of programs and services that together began to approach the goals of equity for all students.

The Board was by no means a paradise of equity. There were still considerable problems. Those last reports were an indication both of how far we had come and what remained to be done.

In the hiring and promotion of women teachers, the Board's goals had been regularly met or exceeded since the adoption of goals and timetables in 1988. That had not been the case for visible minorities, however, even after the Board was finally forced to adopt a policy in 1990. The failure to meet those goals had produced a great deal of frustration over the years, but in March 1996 and again in April 1997 the Board heard reports on the "Hiring for Diversity" program, which seemed to be finally turning a corner by reshaping hiring practices to address the systemic barriers faced by visible minorities.[2]

Under the new system adopted in 1995, an application form with a voluntary equity questionnaire was introduced for the use of all applicants. Ads were produced outlining the subjects, levels, and teacher-characteristics that the Board required, and these were placed in both mainstream media and twenty-five ethnic papers. Under Pat Case's guidance, the Board had adopted "behaviour description interviewing," which was based on the assumption that an individual's past performance was the best predictor of future performance. Rather than posing hypothetical questions about how candidates might act in the future, interviewers were trained to ask them how they had dealt with concrete issues in the past. Interviews were conducted by a number of trained teams, and applicants were shortlisted based on a range of criteria: subject qualification (10 points), multi-qualification (10 points), and membership in designated group (10 points). Asset points of three each were awarded for a number of other characteristics. The new procedure ensured that all candidates were asked the same questions and judged on a single rating scale.

The first round of interviews established an "Eligible for Hire" pool with a large number of candidates from designated groups. Principals would interview candidates from that pool as need arose. The effects of the new system were immediately evident. In the 1994-95 school year, 5.5 per cent of elementary teaching positions had been filled by people of racial minority background, with no positions filled by Aboriginal people or persons with disabilities; in the 1995-96 school year, under the new system, 21.5 per cent of positions were filled by racial minority candidates, 2.8 per cent by Aboriginal people, and 1.9 per cent by persons with disabilities. In secondary schools the hirings of racial minority or disabled candidates rose to 17 per cent. Principals were generally pleased with the new system and the calibre of applicants available. While the achieved levels still did not attain the Board's target for racial minority hiring of 29 per cent, they were a huge advance. It seemed reasonable to believe that with further fine-tuning the system could soon meet its goals.

Underachievement and high dropout rates among Black students had been a long-time concern. In response the Board had established a wide range of programs and services, often in co-operation with community organizations – everything from orientation programs for Caribbean immigrant youth, mentoring for prospective Black teachers, career planning, and stay-in-school programs for youth at risk to partnerships with universities to encourage Black youth to consider post-secondary education. The Board had also set up an annual African Canadian Students Conference and Black cultural heritage programs.[3]

In April 1997 the research department published "Meeting the Special Needs of Students," a booklet that began with a profile of the Toronto school population.[4] Half of the students were from non-English-speaking families representing over seventy-six language groups. A third were recent immigrants coming from over 170 countries. Many were of refugee background. A quarter of all the Board's students required ESL assistance and support. Visible minority students accounted for half the secondary-school student population.

A significant number of students came from families of a low socio-economic status, and one out of every three students was living on social assistance. One in four students was from a single-parent family. The City of Toronto also had a higher mobility rate than did the rest of Metro and the province. Fully two-thirds of the Board's secondary-school students were from other countries or other school systems. One in ten students did not enrol at the beginning of the school year – they came in at other points, making it difficult to integrate them in the course content.

The Board had developed a wide range of programs to meet the resulting special needs, including breakfast and lunch programs, bursaries, public transit tickets, subsidies for supplies and gym equipment, clothing exchanges, additional staff allocations and funding for local school initiatives, and honoraria for inner-city secondary school students to provide tutorial sessions to younger peers. A range of early childhood education, junior kindergarten, and child-care programs, parenting centres, and family literacy programs were in place. The Special Education Services Department funded learning centres, speech and language programs, and behavioural, gifted, learning disabilities, and reading classes, and offered intensive support for seriously disabled students. Almost sixteen thousand Toronto Board students received special ESL programs. Intensive ESL and English skills programs for newly arrived students with little or no knowledge of English were offered at Greenwood Secondary School, and the Board maintained two reception welcoming centres for new immigrant and refugee students. More than fourteen thousand elementary students were enrolled in international language and Black cultural programs, and twenty-four hundred secondary students were involved in credit courses offered on fourteen different languages.

The School Community Services Office provided translation and interpretation services and co-ordinated parent and community conferences. School community advisors were attached to families of schools to facilitate parental and community involvement. Some fifteen hundred families were involved in parenting courses offered in three different languages. More than three hundred adult students were receiving secondary school credits, and nearly six hundred adults, mostly immigrants and refugees, were involved in literacy skills upgrading. Nearly thirty thousand adult students were enrolled in non-credit ESL courses.

The Board also provided a range of "expanded opportunities" programs that provided enrichment opportunities, such as summer assistance for those needing literacy and numeracy support. The Board's Boyne River and Toronto Island Natural Science schools provided free residential outdoor education and natural science programs as well as arts and music activities. Visiting artists worked with teachers and students on a variety of projects in their classrooms. Several different drama, dance, and theatre programs were in place, and over thirteen thousand students a year participated in activities sponsored by the Toronto Urban Studies Centre to learn about urban ecology and environment. A number of schools offered innovative credit courses in Native studies, women's studies, and African civilization.

The Human Sexuality Program provided individual counselling and group support on issues of sexual orientation to gay, lesbian, bisexual, and transgender students and their families, and the Triangle Program offered a gay-focused curriculum for students who couldn't function in the mainstream system. Alternative school programs provided environments tailored to different student needs. Social work, psychological, and guidance services were provided in a number of languages. The Board's Conflict Resolution Team provided programs in most schools, and the Youth Alienation Committee funded local school programs and projects to improve school climate and address student alienation.

The Equal Opportunity Office continued to provide training and information on human rights issues for teachers, administrators, and students. It administered the new Human Rights in Schools and Workplaces Policy and kept statistics on complaints' resolution. The Equity Studies Centre had a stable of nearly forty workshops on a range of equity issues – it could deliver them to teachers and students on request – and had developed an impressive list of curriculum documents and resource kits. The Centre also regularly co-ordinated a number of student conferences. There were women's self-defence courses, and a "Boys for Babies" program to give Grade 5 and 6 boys a hands-on experience of nurturing and caring for infants and toddlers. For staff, there was the annual, two-day Equity in the Classroom, Equity in the Curriculum Conference held in co-operation with the Women's Studies Program at York University and other Metro boards of education. Regular sessions on teaching about the Holocaust as well as Vietnamese, South Asian, lesbian and gay, labour, and Black studies courses were available; summer institutes were offered for those interested in more intensive investigation.

At the apex of the organization, the director listed the Board's fundamental priorities as "High levels of achievement through a commitment to: Excellent curriculum, Equity and Accountability."[5] It was the only board in the country that listed equity as a fundamental priority.

The obvious question was whether all of this activity made any difference. The work of the Research Department was enormously important in evaluating the results of the Board's approach to equity and identifying problem areas that still needed to be addressed. For example, an analysis of the last "Every Secondary Student Survey" in 1997 pointed out how the public school system had helped to equalize opportunities for students in a number of areas.[6] The chance for students from low-income families to participate in music and arts activities on a frequent basis was much higher in school than outside of school. Over 80 per cent of secondary school students, regardless of their socio-economic status, did not believe that cost was a barrier to their participation in various school activities. The data showed that the disparity in awards received between high and low socio-economic status students was much smaller in school than outside. The majority of students reported that they had the opportunity to learn about the contributions of different cultural, racial, and religious groups and women in their classrooms. More students from low-income families reported frequent use of school computers than did their peers from well-to-do families.

But the report also pointed out the areas of "significant disparity" that needed further attention from the system. Despite the gradual improvement over time, students of low socio-economic status and from Portuguese, Black, Aboriginal, and Latin American backgrounds were noticeably underrepresented in the university-bound and gifted programs. While the majority of students reported that they had been taught about gender and racial issues, they said that they had much less opportunity to learn about poverty, disabilities, and sexual orientation. Most students did not believe that there were barriers to their full participation in school activities, but those who did were more likely to be female, of racial minority status, associated with a religion other than Christianity or Judaism, and/or disabled. Female students were found to use computers mainly for word processing; male students were more likely to use computers for a wider range of functions, including on-line communication, information search, and computer games.

The survey found that students of low socio-economic status were significantly less confident than their counterparts from more affluent backgrounds in many areas, including problem-solving, oral communication, leadership, and writing. English as a second language students, in particular those of East and Southeast Asian descent, evaluated themselves much lower than did other students, and evidence indicated that Asian students who lacked confidence in communication skills tended to limit their career aspirations to the math and science/technology fields.

The participation rates of high-income parents in school activities were two to three times higher than those of low-income parents. Likewise, white English-speaking parents were more likely to be active than were parents of East and Southeast Asian origins. In terms of homework, compared to high-income and/or white English-speaking parents, fewer low-income and/or non-English-speaking parents were able to provide support for their children.

Much had been accomplished, and much remained to be done. But for the Toronto Board of Education itself, time had run out.

Chapter 15

# Blueprints for an Invisible Future

DURING THE LAST FIVE WEEKS of the Toronto Board's existence the Equity Studies Centre managed to scrape money together to conduct its last two student camps. Like almost everything else we did during 1997, the camps were seen as an attempt to establish prototypes for future work in the amalgamated board.

The first to take place was a multi-issue equity camp. Although we realized there would never be funding to provide the kinds of retreats we had done in the past, we hoped there might be resources to support one program involving a range of issues. The new program attempted to give the range of equity issues equal treatment and time, drawing together elements from the anti-racism and ESL camps, the parallel retreats, and Terezia Zoric's "Challenging Class Bias" document. Originally planned for October, the camp was delayed by the work stoppage until the end of November – an even more formidable time of year to be up on the Shield. The weather was dreary, dark, and damp. Students and teachers were still shell-shocked from the disruption and trauma of the two-week work stoppage. It was a miracle we managed to go at all.

The experience raised more questions than it answered. The program was packed with introductory exercises to all the different issues, which I found made it rushed, superficial, and not quite as student-centred as usual. We had much less time for trust-building. Although the program touched on all the relevant issues, it did so in a far more intellectual way and for the campers, I thought, did not result in a deep identification with the experiences of others. The action plans produced by the participating schools turned out to be almost indistinguishable from those of the anti-racist retreats. If so much had been lost in terms of bonding and depth of investigation, and the range of issues visible in the outcomes seemed so similar, we found ourselves asking what had been gained by the new format.

While two of the schools dutifully mentioned "classism" in their lists of concerns, none produced any action plan items to deal with that issue. The students' reluctance to speak about class was striking. The participants seemed to have had no problem identifying themselves in terms of race or gender, but whether they came from affluent families or were receiving social assistance, whether they were sixth-generation Canadians or new immigrants, they all claimed middle-class status.

Was this reluctance "false consciousness" or simply a matter of shame? Students could come to the conclusion that characteristics such as skin colour, gender, or sexual orientation should not matter when it came to life opportunities. They could therefore understand discrimination in those areas as being unfair, perhaps even build pride in their resilience in overcoming such barriers. But in a society that obsessively promoted itself as a meritocracy, did talk about class make poorer students feel guilty because they believed that they and their families were somehow responsible for their poverty? Did wealthy students, born into privilege, feel guilty because they knew they couldn't claim to have earned the advantages they experienced in life?

Some facilitators believed that class was simply off the radar – so suppressed as a category of identity in a supposedly classless society that students were unclear and uncomfortable with the concept. Others wondered if class was just too big a problem. The essence of class differences was inequity in access to resources and opportunities. The inequity could only be challenged in schools that had sufficient financial wherewithal to provide resources and opportunities for everyone, in addition to the assistance that students' families might be able to offer. This was much more than a matter of changing curriculum or challenging stereotypes or prejudices.

First attempts at new programs are always fraught with difficulty, and it was hard to distinguish what parts of the retreat required fine-tuning and what problems were more fundamental in nature. The camp also raised general questions. Was the problem simply one of depth? Could a more in-depth exploration of *any* one of the key issues have led to an appreciation of other areas of oppression, or did different issues have different potentials as windows? My experience with the anti-racism camps was that they inevitably opened into other issues. Were students simply taking advantage of the open-ended format to talk about what was on their mind, or was there something special about the centrality of racism in our society that, given appropriate pedagogy and time, opened doors to a discussion of a range of different kinds of oppression?

We concluded that the success of the multi-issue approach was at best ambiguous. We had hoped that what we would lose in depth we would make up in breadth of approach. In retrospect it appeared that we underestimated the importance of the personal growth and mutual bonding that was intrinsic to an in-depth approach. We reached people's minds but not their hearts. Finally, digging into the reality of class differences required a great deal more time for trust-building and more thought about the nature of class and its connections to other aspects of social identity in Canadian society.

## Inclusive Curriculum

A few weeks later our second student retreat was held on quite a different model. An outgrowth of the work that the Equity Studies Centre had been doing around inclusive curriculum, it was funded by the Inclusive Curriculum Committee.

When the first school-wide pilot aimed at generating more inclusive curriculum had taken place at Northern Secondary the year before, it had largely been restricted to workshops with staff. But the STAR report card had placed student involvement front and centre. The 1997 program at Western Tech attempted to mount a whole-school effort to transform the curriculum involving administration, staff, and students.

The original Kandalore model had attempted to mobilize students to "bombard the headquarters" in order to achieve on-the-ground implementation of the Race Relations Policy against the resistance of the system. That focus on students had been both its strength and its weakness. Students understood the reality of racism in their own lives, and had no vested interest in preserving the institutional structures and practices that supported it. They could be counted on to speak their minds. Yet they were also inexperienced and far from the levers of power when it came to institutional change. The program for Western Tech, held almost two decades after the original Kanadalore experiment, took a much more integrative approach. Students would be part of an intensive school-wide effort, working together with administrators and teachers. We hoped that what was lost in autonomy would be regained by the power of this new alliance.

With support from the school administration, Myra Novogrodsky, Terezia Zoric, and Alice Te worked three full days with twenty-five of the school's staff, including at least one representative from each department to ensure that all subject areas were involved. The teachers became acquainted with McIntosh's theories about phases of inclusivity in curriculum. They used an equity assessment grid to evaluate the state of equity in the school and spent time looking at the connections between racism, sexism, homophobia, and class bias. Nora Allingham led a workshop on changing the English curriculum; Kathy Bellamo, the Board's science consultant, talked about transforming the science classroom to make technology more female-friendly.

The student camp itself was short, only three days, but it was predicated on this work with staff. One of the most innovative exercises was the student investigation of "isms" at different sites in the school. Before they left for the camp, all participating students had analyzed one of five school sites: a classroom, the gymnasium, the school library, a hallway, and the school cafeteria. They had been asked to observe these sites during a normal school day and make notes on a series of questions specific to each site, including who was contributing most, who was taking up more space, who received attention or reprimands, the diversity of learning materials, accommodation for ESL students or those with physical disabilities, and the dynamics between males and females. At the camp the student participants reported on their observations, enabling all of us to draw up a comprehensive map of how factors such as racism, sexism, homophobia, class bias, and bias against students with disabilities were playing out in the school. The studenst then produced an action plan for each site.

Although the Western Tech camp had some of the same problems as the multi-issue camp – trying to cover too much material in too short a period of time, and the loss of important components of the issue-specific camps – it did seem to be more grounded in student reality. Given time, the experience might have been the basis of an important model for building new programs uniting teachers and students to transform their schools. As it was, given the dissolution of the Toronto Board only a few days later, that potential was never realized. After amalgamation, the resources necessary for that kind of student program would not be available, at least for the foreseeable future.

## Triangles and Icebergs

With the end of the camps, I found myself doing more in-school workshops with students. These situations did not provide the opportunity or time for the kind of trust-building, intimacy, and exchange of personal experience that had characterized the camp experience. They often took place at lunchtime or after school. At best I might have a couple of half-days to work with a group, usually to prepare them to deliver some sort of peer education program.

I recognized that I needed to come up with an approach to learning about different oppressions that would work in a shorter space of time. But I was determined not to slip back into what Freire had called the "banking approach to education" – otherwise no matter how radical-sounding the content, the work would be no more than another theory, another intellectual exercise to be memorized, and irrelevant to the hearts of the young people I was working with.

I found myself playing around with and adapting an exercise that we had used as part of both the multi-issue and inclusive curriculum camps. In the exercise, we placed what students knew about experiences of racism into three categories: institutional/systemic, individual expressions, and common ideas. In turn we arranged these three categories onto a triangle.

When the group had finished listing the experiences we asked them to think about where, in all of this, racism started. That would usually produce a lively debate, but the most common response was that racism starts with ideas. Individuals act in a certain way because of the ideas they hold. Institu-

### Mapping Experiences of Racism

INDIVIDUAL EXPRESSIONS
- Name-calling
- People tell racist jokes
- Won't sit beside minority person on bus
- "Mixed" couples get hassled
- ESL kids made fun of
- Got beat up

COMMON IDEAS
- Blacks good at basketball
- "Chinese" good at math
- Latin Americans = drugs
- East Indians smell funny
- ESL kids are stupid
- Indians are drunks

INSTITUTIONAL/SYSTEMIC
- School courses ignore many cultures
- Police hassle Black youth
- Basic-level schools in poor areas
- Employers want "Canadian experience"
- Media stereotypes
- Schools ignore racist behaviour

tions act in a certain way because of the ideas of the people who run them. We would then draw an arrow from COMMON IDEAS to INDIVIDUAL EXPRESSIONS, and another from COMMON IDEAS to INSTITUTIONAL/SYSTEMIC.

But where do these ideas come from? The typical response: people learn them in school, come across them in the media, watch how authorities like the police treat particular groups and draw the logical inferences. We would draw an arrow from INSTITUTIONAL/SYSTEMIC to COMMON IDEAS. The connection runs both ways.

Do ideas just come from institutions? Don't people draw inferences from how they see particular groups being treated by others? Don't we learn stereotypes from racist jokes? If you realize that nobody wants to sit down beside a particular person, would you think there was something wrong with that person? Individual actions, then, also communicate ideas. Now we had arrows running back and forth between INDIVIDUAL EXPRESSION and COMMON IDEAS.

Are there any direct connections between how individuals behave and how institutions behave? If the individuals who run institutions act in a certain way, institutional power would amplify their actions and their actions would become part of the way in which the institution functions. That meant an arrow from INDIVIDUAL EXPRESSION to INSTITUTIONAL/SYSTEMIC.

Does it work the other way as well? Can institutions directly shape individual action, other than through promoting certain ideas? This question was often the most difficult for participants. I would ask, "What does your school take more seriously, sexism or smoking? If someone lights up a cigarette in the hallway or a classroom, what happens?" Everyone agreed that there would be an immediate reaction. Students would be sent out of class, taken to the office. They would be immediately and unambiguously disciplined.

Here I have to note that I usually used sexism as an example instead of racism not just because of the alliteration but because the potential for violent escalation around issues of racism meant that many schools did take racist comments almost as seriously as smoking – which in the case of this exercise would make the point more difficult to see.

"If somebody makes a sexist comment, what happens?" Well, it depends. It depends on the comment. It depends on the teacher. It depends on whether anybody got upset. Clearly the institution had greater tolerance for sexist comments than for smoking. "So what do you see more of in the school – sexism or smoking?" The answer would always be sexism.

People, then, often behaved in ways that the institution let them get away with. Now we had double arrows connecting all three groups of experiences. The exercise revealed that racism worked as an unbroken cycle. So what did we have to do to break down this cycle? For example, how do we change people's ideas? That one was obvious: *education*. But what would happen if we educated people but didn't change how institutions or individuals were acting? People would tend to forget the new ideas we taught them, and relearn attitudes and ideas from the world around them. We needed to change institutions and individual actions too.

How do we change individual behaviour? The first response would be: through education and changing their ideas. I would go back to smoking. Do schools just count on education about the evils of smoking to stop people smoking in class? No. There are *rules and consequences* that are enforced. But how do you get an institution to develop rules and consequences and enforce them? How do you make an institution change the kinds of things they are teaching? Talk to them. Lobby them. Elect a new leadership. Protest. Petitions. What do you call all those kinds of things? *Political action*.

Any strategy that is going to be effective has to include all of these: political action, education, and rules and consequences. If you concentrate on just one area, the influences from the other corners of the triangle will probably undo your efforts.

When asked about their experiences with racism, sexism, etc., most participants would focus their responses on individual actions. Institutional processes tend to be more hidden and less obvious. Ideas are equally invisible until they are expressed in actions such as comments, jokes, or derogatory names. I was able to get students to think about this relationship by comparing the triangle to an iceberg with individual actions on top and institutional practices and ideas hidden under the waterline. Although they aren't immediately visible, the underwater aspects support the individual actions that appear above the surface.

The iceberg metaphor also gave new energy to the image of the necessity of dealing with all three areas to bring about change. What happens if you simply try to suppress individual actions (like many schools do) through rules and discipline? It's like pressing down on the top of an ice cube in a bowl of water. When you let go it just pops back up. If we really want to move that iceberg, we need to grasp all three corners at once. Otherwise it will always just slide away and the cycle will remain intact.

If participants were to become effective agents of institutional and social change they also had to be prepared for and understand the kinds of feelings and behaviours they would encounter during their work. I would ask groups what feelings and emotions would be expected from people who found themselves frozen in the centre of the triangle, subject to the ideas and stereotypes about themselves, the actions of individuals, and the practices of institutions. The list usually included confusion, depression, despair, self-hate, anger, determination to break out – a pretty powerful mix of emotions. What kinds of behaviours do we expect to see in individuals who are living their lives in the swirl of such feelings? The participants would come up with a list of self-destructive behaviours: withdrawal, dropping out, drug abuse, different kinds of acting out and striking back, plus overcompensation, resistance, and individual determination to overcome the obstacles or collective action to work for change. Sometimes the feelings and emotions can fuel positive work; sometimes they can get in the way. Self-destructive behaviours might produce patterns that further reinforce and generate stereotypes among those who are on the outside of the triangle.

What feelings and emotions can we expect to see in those who are on the outside looking in? Indifference, superiority, fear, and guilt usually topped the list. What are some associated behaviours? Refusing to recognize the problem, blaming the victim, self-segregation, demands for more law and order, posing, or deciding to work for change would all be mentioned.

The exercise gave participants a way of recognizing and evaluating their own feelings and motivations and those of others. With a little luck it might help them, in the end, to choose and encourage the more constructive kinds of responses.

## Similarities, Differences, and Identity Politics

We could also adapt that exercise to facilitate a broader discussion of equity. In that case we would begin by getting the students to define stereotypes, prejudice, and discrimination and then ask them to list experiences around these open-ended terms. This time the content of the triangle would include examples of racism, sexism, homophobia, classism, or ableism. All the other steps of the exercise worked the same way but with more varied raw material.

That approach assumed a similarity between these forms of oppression.

I often found it useful to be more explicit about these similarities, not only to validate all the different forms of oppression but also to lay a foundation for an honest discussion of the differences. Focused talk about similarities and differences was the best antidote to the ever-present tendency of identity politics to rank oppressions.

For starters, all oppressions involve stereotypes, prejudice, and discrimination. All involve a targeted group with less social power. All produce feelings of anger, pain, frustration, fear, and sometimes self-hatred. If we wanted to go more deeply, Suzanne Pharr had detailed the common elements of oppression in her *Homophobia: A Weapon of Sexism*: all oppressions assumed a defined norm; involved institutional and economic power; were maintained by violence or the threat of violence; made people invisible; distorted history; blamed the victim; and undermined group solidarity by promoting hostility within the group, assimilation, tokenism, and individual solutions.[1] That part of the exercise usually succeeded in getting across the idea that nobody's oppression was something to be sniffed at.

When participants saw their own experiences being validated, we could more easily look at the differences in how oppressions worked themselves out; and we would avoid the defensiveness and one-upmanship that could often come into play. We would look at the impact of visibility – at the different range of visibilities experienced by different groups – and the patterns: how those differences influenced each group's experiences and coping strategies. We would look at the different opportunities for social interactions and at the patterns of segregation and integration in social and family life. Those patterns could be quite different for different groups. For instance, most women (including lesbians) are born into families that include men and heterosexuals; most gay men are born into families that include straight men. They may therefore experience their domination in the home. Most visible minorities and Jews are born into families that are made up of other visible minorities and Jews. They therefore have the opportunity to develop and transmit cultures and strategies for coping and resisting from a very young age. Women in our society tend to have opportunities for social interaction that are both same-sex and opposite-sex, and it is in the same-sex environments especially that they often develop cultures and strategies for dealing with their oppression. Visible minorities have historically found themselves excluded from social interaction with dominant groups and are therefore more likely to develop parallel social institutions in which they are in the majority.

All of these factors influence how the results of oppression accumulate over generations for some groups more than others. For example, particular visible minority groups have been excluded from better-paying jobs and education for generations, and therefore early in life members are more likely to experience an environment shaped by the results of that past discrimination.

Their opportunities are shaped by their present class position, which is in turn the result of discrimination both in the past and in the present. Women and lesbians and gay men, though, are born into all families and social situations. Those who find themselves growing up in wealthier families will experience more of the privileges and advantages that accrue to that class position.

How does the experience of young people in these groups differ in terms of reacting to and learning how to deal with the oppression they face? Young women can always go to their mothers or sisters or identify other young women with similar experiences when they are seeking advice on dealing with sexism. Most visible minority youth can also easily identify communities of peers or talk to family members when they need to share strategies or anger. Often such youth will band together for mutual protection and a sense of power. Young lesbians and gay men, though, often feel isolated when they cannot identify peers or adults who have experienced the same difficulties. They are therefore more likely to become depressed, withdrawn, or suicidal.

In this work I found it also important to point out that while for the purposes of discussion we may treat the various groups as discrete entities, in the real world it usually doesn't work that way. After all, we all have a race, a gender, a sexual orientation, a class background, a level of education, and different abilities. A particular person can simultaneously be a woman, lesbian, and person of colour. None of us are just one-dimensional. I would ask participants to describe which aspects of their identity has led to discrimination and which has given them privilege and power. It was fascinating to see how much more comfortable people were talking about the discrimination they faced rather than the power they had. When they talked about their privilege they would tend to attribute it to a personal quality, something they could take responsibility for. They were hard-working. They were smart. They were persevering and disciplined, for example. Few people wanted to relate privilege or advantages to conditions created by their particular gender or race or sexual orientation or class background.

## Deeper into Structures

Under the direction of Lynda Lemberg, Oakwood Collegiate had a long history of peer education programs around equity issues. I would come in each year and train groups of students to deliver workshops with their peers on a topic the group had chosen. Racism or sexism was usually the focus. I regularly used the triangle format in the training.

In the spring of 1999 the Oakwood group decided that they wanted to turn the year's focus onto poverty and class. Increased poverty and homelessness – the results of almost four years of the Tory attacks on social programs – had become an increasingly obvious and burning issue to students in downtown Toronto. That time, using the familiar triangle, but with a focus on class, we began to consider the stereotypes and prejudices that poor people faced. What kinds of discrimination had an impact on their lives? What kind of individual and institutional manifestations of this discrimination did students see? What feelings and behaviours could we expect to see among people in the centre of this triangle? What kinds of feelings and behaviours might we expect from those on the outside?

Everything went smoothly until we reached the point at which the group needed to talk about solutions – what could be done? Suddenly the students were putting forward very different and contradictory proposals. Some of them, including many students of colour, suggested actions such as the arrest of panhandlers or sending welfare recipients off to work camps; some wanted harsher penalties for drug and alcohol abuse. Others, led by several of the white kids, talked about reversing the welfare cuts, building more public housing, and introducing progressive taxation to lower the cost of education. The group was at loggerheads. I realized that I was facing a fundamental difference in outlook among students.

Luckily it was the end of the day and I had some time to mull over an approach. The next time we met I began by explaining that there were very different explanations as to why people ended up being homeless or poor. Some people looked at factors *internal* to the individual – factors for which an individual was ultimately responsible: that they were lazy, stupid, immoral, criminal, weak, had no self discipline. Others looked at *external* factors, outside an individual's control: government economic policy, business cycles, lack of educational opportunities, lack of affordable housing, lack of medical or disability insurance.

Until we came to a consensus as a group on the causes of poverty, I said, we were never going to agree on the solutions. I asked them to form a line across the room. I wanted those who believed that the main causes of poverty were internal factors to go to the right side of the room. Those who believed in external factors should go to the left. Those who believed that poverty was caused by a combination of these factors should position themselves across the room depending on what they thought about the relative importance of the factors.

We did a rough scale based on the importance of the factors. The internal side of the line was zero, the external side was ten. Each person would give a numerical value to the position they had chosen. I asked them all to justify their choice of location on the line.

Without exception, the young people of colour tended to place themselves at the internal end of the scale. Given that they had come to the workshop as part of a leadership program, they were, of course, "high achievers" – perhaps taught from birth that they had to work harder to overcome the barriers of racism if they wanted to get ahead. If they and their families could overcome the challenges of discrimination through effort and hard work, they reasoned, why couldn't everybody?

Towards the other side of the line were the white working-class kids who had never had to face visible barriers such as racism and had therefore not been so imbued by their families with the ideas of competitive individualism as a means of overcoming such challenges. But they were very aware of their families' sometimes precarious situations, and how easily external factors outside of their control, like a recession or a layoff or a major illness, might propel them into a cycle of poverty.

I told the group that we couldn't continue until they arrived at a consensus about the mix of internal and external factors that were responsible for poverty. The discussion was heated as both groups drew from their own experiences. Ultimately the arguments about the importance of external factors proved stronger. The young people of colour, for all their competitive individualism, had to admit that external factors such as racial discrimination could deprive people of opportunity and could explain their poverty. To do otherwise would have led them too dangerously close to positing some sort of inherent or even biological inferiority to explain the undeniable statistics that showed a correlation between racial minority status and lower income in Canada. Once they had recognized the importance of external factors for their own communities, they could scarcely deny its importance for others.

They didn't relinquish their position easily, however. The numerical value of the group consensus was 6.3, closer to the external side but still allowing significant influence of internal factors. But with that established, their brainstorming of solutions started off in a constructive direction.

## Two Approaches: Idealism and Materialism

When I began to think back over the strategies we had used in the camps for so many years, it was clear to me that we had always struggled towards a recognition of the social as an external force shaping the lives and reactions of individuals. We opposed dominant ideas about how what happened to individual lives was primarily the result of internal qualities. The exercise around stereotypes, for example, had noted the association of Black men with basketball and crime. The racist explanation was a biological form of an internalist argument that proposed a direct connection between a "racial" group and particular behaviours. I began to recognize that the problem was deeper than just racism. According to the dominant ideology of our society, the outcome of an individual's life is fundamentally determined by the qualities invested in that individual: good individuals produce good outcomes; bad individuals produce bad outcomes.

The argument for creating a better world therefore becomes centred around creating better individuals. Within that general framework there are many currents. The conservative religious approach calls for strict religious instruction, a return to traditional morality, and sharp discipline for those who stray from the straight and narrow. Eugenics calls for better breeding. Traditional racism, moving up one level from that of the individual to the "race," calls for the elimination of inferior races or at least their strict segregation to prevent contamination. Even liberal notions of individualism, characterized by the civil rights movement or reformist social democracy, seek to remove the barriers to individuals achieving their fullest potential by providing "equal access" to education or employment opportunities. These are what I thought of as the idealist position: that people's ideas or consciousness lead to their actions and shape the world they live in. From an idealist point of view, the "subjective" factor is the most important force in society; and it is what needs to be understood.

A materialist approach, on the other hand, focuses on the conditions of life that people face. People's consciousness is a reflection of the material conditions they live in. A materialist approach asserts that good outcomes are produced by good environments. Bad outcomes are produced by bad environments. The key, therefore, is to change the conditions of life. That logic was the basis of the alliance with civil rights approaches and reformist strategies of liberal individualism that had characterized our work in the Board. Removing barriers to individual access in one respect can be seen as changing the conditions of life. But the materialist approach tends to go further and deeper than just removing barriers to equal opportunity. It calls for strategies that produce *equity*, equality of outcome.

That framework also contains several different currents of thought. Some people see capitalism itself as the fundamental source of inequality; if we are to produce good outcomes for the whole human population, we need to abolish the capitalist class structure. Others see equity for all as a possibility within a reformed capitalism. Capitalism is, after all, rational. Racism, sexism, and homophobia are irrational vestiges of the past. Affirmative action, equalizing the participation of all groups at all levels of a capitalist society, is a means of producing a system truly based on merit and made fair for everyone.

The political debates and struggles that take place between the different individual expressions of these two fundamental approaches – radicals vs. conservatives, fundamentalists vs. secularists, welfare vs. law-and-order – produce a complex pattern of different political positions that twist and turn and grow and form alliances depending on their perceived immediate interests. In the shifting terrain between these "species" of political positions, the fundamental division between the two different approaches, materialist and idealist, has often been lost.

A progressive pedagogy – and by that I mean a pedagogy that builds on a materialist understanding of the world and recognizes the necessity to transform the social to produce better outcomes for both the individual and the group – had to address and clarify these fundamental assumptions of both the materialist or idealist outlooks.

Although some people resolutely close their eyes to evidence of misery, many more will not deny what is in front of their faces. Homelessness, for example, has become an increasingly visible problem in Canada. For people who share the underlying assumption that the root of the problem rests with the individual, it is the homeless themselves who are the problem. The solutions offered therefore include such measures as stricter laws against panhandling, incarceration of the mentally ill, work camps, stricter prohibition of drugs and alcohol, and mandatory treatment programs. Until the underlying assumptions are re-evaluated, the people who believe in these solutions will never be able to understand the approaches proposed by those who see homelessness as a result of social conditions and therefore call for action such as changes in housing policy, full employment opportunities, better social services, welfare and education programs, graduated taxation policies, or indeed the construction of an entirely different socialist society.

If educators are to help learners understand any of these alternative solutions as possibilities, we must work at ensuring that the learners understand the validity of an approach affirming that people are the products of the conditions of their lives. Only from that point can we begin to debate how and which conditions need to be changed in order to produce a better world. As the students in my group preparing a workshop on homelessness at Oakwood discovered, there is room for compromise. In the end, though, a materialist position that does not recognize any role for individual consciousness and responsibility as a force for change can lead only to an inevitably impotent politics of command, manipulation, or coercion. Consciousness, the internal, must also be recognized as a material force. If it is not, there is no point to education at all.

Chapter 16

# Thermopylae

THE IRONICALLY NAMED Local Education Improvement Committees (LEIC) was a body set up in each board by the provincial government to oversee the forced amalgamations across the province. Just before the Toronto amalgamation took effect at the end of 1997, Toronto's LEIC chose Marguerite Jackson, former director of the North York Board, as the new director for the impending Toronto District School Board (TDSB). In retrospect the choice was an obvious one.

Jackson had never ruffled any Tory feathers, and best of all for the other suburban boards whose representatives dominated the LEIC in the Metro Toronto area, she was not from downtown. Jackson immediately began stacking the commanding heights of the new organization with her confidants. Her coronation was the beginning of what Toronto people soon began to describe as a "hostile takeover" by North York.

It quickly became obvious that the amalgamated Board's twenty-two trustees would not be taking the kind of hands-on role that had been customary in the old Toronto. Trustees now represented huge wards containing more than two dozen schools each. In all the new Board had over six hundred schools. The days when trustees personally knew school administrators and local parent and community leaders were gone. With a maximum remuneration of $5,000 per year for their work at the Board, most of the trustees held other full-time jobs. We had been thrown back to the 1960s, when trustee was a part-time, almost honorific position.

The complexities of trying to oversee and negotiate the harmonization and amalgamation of six large organizations in an accountable manner would have been a daunting task even for experienced, full-time representatives. Most of the new trustees were stretched far too thin to take any effective management role of the massive new organization. They could scarcely keep up with skimming through the documents prepared for them by administration for decision-making at each Board meeting.

As the Tories had planned, the locus of power was now firmly in the hands of senior bureaucrats, well out of reach of befuddled elected representatives.

## Harmonizing Policies: Basic Principles

Although the boards were not officially amalgamated until January 1, 1998, the work of preparing for integration had begun as soon as the legislation was passed in spring 1997. As part of this work, the Toronto-area LEIC set up a number of subcommittees to recommend ways of "harmonizing" particular policy areas. The equity subcommittee included senior superintendents, trustees, and staff as well as parent and community representatives. Several members of the Metro Equity Workers Network participated as "Work Team Representatives." In all there were about thirty people in the subcommittee. According to Myra Novogrodsky, from the beginning a "tremendous struggle" occurred over the meaning of equity. One of the two co-chairs, left-wing Toronto trustee Tam Goossen, supported a broad definition that included race, gender, sexual orientation, disabilities, and class. The other co-chair, right-wing Etobicoke trustee Suzan Hall, was adamantly opposed to dealing with anything other than race. North York trustee Stephnie Payne, who was also on the committee, was an outspoken advocate for the position that equity efforts be restricted to visible minorities. She regularly locked horns with Pat Case over the issue. Myra, Susan McGrath, and parent representative Jackie Latter also tried to make the case for a broad approach in the face of resistance and incomprehension on the part of many of the participants from the other boards.

The equity subcommittee's final report, issued in December 1997, reflected an ambiguous compromise. The first recommendation was that the TDSB endorse "Equity in Education: Basic Principles" (the document I had written for the Metro Equity Workers Network) "as the basis for the development of board policies, procedures, programs and resources." The subcommittee also called for a unitary complaints policy on human rights and harassment. A section on inclusive curriculum proposed that "criteria be developed with which to select materials and write curriculum validating the experiences of all students including their gender, place of origin, religion, ethnicity and race, cultural and linguistic background, social and economic status, sexual orientation, age and ability/disability." These recommendations indicated the endorsement of a broad approach to equity by the subcommittee.

Then came the fuzzy part. Recommendation 1(a) under "Anti-racism and Ethnocultural Equity Policy" recommended "a six month process to establish a harmonized policy following the template of Memorandum 119" and that the harmonized policy be implemented beginning in September 1998. Recommendation 3 proposed "that equity policies on other human rights grounds, including gender, sexual orientation, disability and socio-economic status be developed using the structure which is contained in the Anti-racism and Ethnocultural Equity Policy (Memorandum 119)," but established no timelines.

Nonetheless, Myra Novogrodsky, Pat Case, and Nora Allingham left the subcommittee believing that they had been successful in ensuring that new Board policies would take all issues into account. It would soon become clear that others had a very different interpretation.

Although we were now officially all part of the same organization, the different departments of the hastily legislated TDSB would not actually become integrated for some time. In the meantime, parallel "legacy board" administrations and departments continued to operate as before. The Metro Equity Workers Network continued to meet to try to work towards a common front to lobby the new administration on equity issues.

But amalgamation and the impending reorganization made matters more, rather than less, difficult. Despite the apparent agreement on the "Basic Principals," tensions remained around establishing priorities. A meeting in February 1998 with Marguerite Jackson went badly when a carefully planned agenda was, according to Myra Novogrodsky, "hijacked" and sent off in a different direction. The trust level in MEWN began to unravel. The group limped along for the next few months, exchanging materials and attempting to ensure that equity-minded people were available to sit on the whirlwind of committees meeting to discuss curriculum changes in different subject areas, and participate in any organizational restructuring that might have an effect on equity.

By May things came to a head, beginning with the first meeting of a task group that had been set up to draft the new Antiracism and Ethnocultural Equity Policy. In that meeting, held on May 5, 1998, Myra proposed that, in the spirit of the LEIC recommendations, the policy include the full range of equity issues. Sharon Bate, chair of the task group and a superintendent from the former Scarborough Board, now executive officer for Student and Community Services, stated that the task group's mandate was to deal with a policy on race and colour only. Marcela Duran, an equity worker and member of MEWN from the North York Board, backed up that interpretation. Together they maintained that the mandate of the task group was to draft a policy to comply with the requirements of PPM 119 and nothing more. Other issues could be dealt with sometime later, if and when the Board decided to mandate another committee to do so. Ironically, the task group had no problem in accepting Marcela Duran's suggestion of adding "faith groups" to its mandate – a category that was novel to the wording of PPM 119. Meanwhile, a second task group working on the complaints policy interpreted its mandate broadly and began drafting a document that included all the groups protected under the Ontario Human Rights Code.

Myra realized that in the turmoil of amalgamation if the committee proceeded with a race-only policy it might take years for the Board to return to the question of setting up other committees to address other equity issues. Without policy support to mandate work on gender, sexual orientation, class, and disabilities, Myra recognized that "in a few years everything else was going to be dead on the vine." Back at the Equity Studies Centre we began to try to figure out a strategy to salvage an inclusive approach.

Part of the difficulty was that it was unclear where the impetus for a narrow policy was coming from. Were there orders from the top, or was this an idiosyncratic interpretation of the task group mandate coming from Sharon Bate? Was Marcela Duran just trying to better position herself as the head of the new Equity Department, which would eventually be set up to implement the policy, or was she too following orders? Was this just a knee-jerk bureaucratic response in the absence of proper consideration of the LEIC's recommendation to use the "Basic Principles" to orient the work, or was it part of an established plan?

Homophobia was obviously a big part of the equation. There had never been an organized voting block of gay voters to push the issue outside of the downtown core, and none of the boards other than Toronto had developed policy dealing with sexual orientation. Conservative trustees in Scarborough and Etobicoke had actively blocked proposals aimed at meeting the needs of gay students, and most suburban schools were hostile places for lesbian and gay students and staff. Indeed, Toronto's programs had become a magnet for queer kids and staff fleeing the homophobia of the outlying areas.

My analysis was that the new Board's administration, now almost completely dominated by bureaucrats from the suburbs, had calculated that if they stuck to the letter of the law requiring them to have a race and ethnocultural equity policy, they would probably not face great opposition from their constituencies. But if they went on to include the other issues, the volatile issue of homophobia might blow up in their faces. In retrospect I think I underestimated the potential for opposition to other equity issues as well. At first glance, for example, disabilities seemed to be a relatively non-controversial area. Who could object to trying to ensure that disabled kids had an opportunity to get a good education? The disabled might have been ignored and patronized, but certainly they were not hated and feared in the way that gay people were. It didn't occur to us that the bureaucrats might not want to frame disabilities as an equity issue because they did not want to commit themselves to high-cost architectural accommodations. Class bias was also a factor. For many of the new TDSB trustees and administrators from the suburbs, any talk about class was akin to communism. If people were poor, it was because they didn't work hard enough. Anybody who really wanted to make things better could pull themselves up by their bootstraps: end of story.

In the Equity Studies Centre we decided on a three-part strategy. Myra would continue to attend the task group meetings and raise demands for inclusion of all groups. We would begin to lobby key trustees to make them understand the significance of an inclusive policy. I agreed to draft a petition that we would circulate in the community as a means of identifying supporters there and rallying the troops.

## Setbacks and Mobilization

I was in a polemical mood the evening I drafted the petition. My prime concern was building arguments for community activists to use, rather than crafting something that might eventually be received by the committee. I set the document in the form of an open letter addressed to task group chair Sharon Bate. It characterized the decision to ignore other equity-seeking groups as sexist, homophobic, classist, ableist, and, ironically, racist as well because it abandoned the interests of the majority of people of colour who were not middle-class, able-bodied, straight males, and cut off their natural allies in other equity-seeking groups.

The letter pointed out that education was a service under the Ontario Human Rights Code and that by not dealing with the full range of issues, the Board would open itself up to legal liability. I called on the committee "to immediately reverse this embarrassing and destructive decision before it causes any more damage to the already difficult struggle for equity education at the TDSB." The bottom of the single page had a space where those in agreement could affix their names, signatures, organizational affiliations, and phone numbers.

The problem with letters is that once they begin to circulate they take on a life of their own. On the same day that the letter began to be distributed, May 20, 1998, the Toronto Schools Equity Advocacy Committee, a community group spearheaded by a North York parent, was holding its first meeting. Someone took a copy of the letter to the meeting, and the group endorsed it. The next day the parent publicly presented the letter to Sharon Bate at a task group meeting. Bate found herself being accused of racism, sexism, homophobia, class bias, and bias against people with disabilities in front of her colleagues on the committee. This was not the kind of polite communication she had become accustomed to in Scarborough. Bate, obviously unnerved, went off to consult with higher-ups in the Policies and Procedures Project Team, a body established to oversee the work of all teams created to develop policies for the new Board. She received clear instructions in a letter from the team's manager, Gary Parkinson, who thanked her for the update about the recent meeting and instructed the task group to "confine itself to its original mandate" – the development of a policy on anti-racist education and ethnocultural equity.

Parkinson went on:

> The Policies and Procedures Project Team is compiling a list of outstanding policy issues which will need early attention by the executive officers. These items are coming to our attention through the work of the various task groups

> and from other projects taking place during the transition. If it becomes apparent that issues outside the mandate of your task group should be dealt with, these concerns will be carried forward by the project team in this manner.

The letter was copied to one person, Marguerite Jackson, Director of Education. Apparently, the decision to bypass the other equity issues had approval at the top.

The task group also asked for a legal opinion on the question of liability, which the petition had raised. Ignoring Myra's suggestion that a legal firm with a background in human rights be consulted, the members went to Board lawyers. The confused, if not unsurprising reply – that it would not be illegal for the Board to comply with the requirements of PPM 119 – was then employed as a cover for the administrative decision to deal only with race and culture.

It was a depressing time. Terezia Zoric saw the writing on the wall and resigned from the Equity Studies Centre to take a history headship at Central Tech. With the existence of the Centre increasingly uncertain, and the Board now apparently interested only in questions of race, she concluded that someone like herself, who had focused on class issues, would not have much of a future there as a consultant. In a large multi-racial, working-class school like Central Tech, she would have a rare opportunity to focus on curriculum leadership.

Myra saw her life's work around equity being dismantled. There was almost no support for our program outside of the minority of former Toronto people still on the task group. Like a voice crying in the wilderness, she continued to try to run interference as best she could and remembered being "very disruptive" and often feeling "she was going to explode" in the meetings. After a complaint that she "was in cahoots with some of the trustees," she was called into the director's office and told she was "no longer permitted to speak to trustees." What was clear was that if anything was going to be done around broader equity issues, she and her co-conspirators would have to mobilize the communities.

Ironically, it was Marcela Duran, one of the major proponents of the race-only approach, who provided an opportunity to begin that mobilization. Shortly after we came back to work after the summer layoff in September 1998, I received an invitation from Marcela and a Scarborough curriculum co-ordinator, Stephanie Wade, inviting me to bring "one or two representatives (teachers) of the gay community" to the inaugural meeting of the "Toronto District School Board Sexual Orientation Committee." Marcela signed the invitation as "Chair of the Sexual Orientation Committee – former North York," and Wade described herself as "Chair of the Scarborough Board of Education Working Group on Sexual Orientation." I was surprised, because as far as I knew neither of the Boards had dedicated staff or policy to the issue, but I attributed my ignorance of the existence of the two committees to my Toronto chauvinism. I was delighted at any opportunity to establish a vehicle to deal with homophobia in the amalgamated board.

The meeting took place on October 5 at the old Scarborough Board offices. Fewer than ten of us were there, representing Toronto, North York, and Scarborough. Everyone was extraordinarily polite as we tried to feel each other out. We shared information about the positive things that the different boards had been doing. It turned out that both Scarborough and North York had support-group meetings for gay and lesbian students, although the Scarborough group was not allowed to meet on Board property. Scarborough, East York, and North York had electronic conferences on lesbian and gay issues for teachers. Scarborough had also established what I saw as a very interesting moderated electronic conference for lesbian and gay students. I had been wrong: things were happening outside Toronto.

After some discussion the group decided on a name, the TDSB Anti-Homophobia Equity Committee (AHEC). Stephanie Wade was a bit nervous that anything with "anti" in it sounded too negative, but was persuaded otherwise. Next we dealt with the group's mandate. During the discussion I suggested three points:

- to build a TDSB network of educators interested in anti-homophobia work;
- to lobby for the inclusion of sexual orientation issues in the full range of equity initiatives at the TDSB;
- to challenge, through curriculum and program development, the poisoned environments that exist in our schools for lesbian, gay, bisexual, and transsexual youth.

Stephanie Wade said she found the term "poisoned environment" a little strong. We didn't want to alienate anyone. She was quickly challenged by several participants who asked her how she would describe the harassment that gay and lesbian kids faced on a daily basis. The participants finally decided that we would all take time to think about the mandate and talk about it again at the next meeting. We also decided to return with the details about our various support groups so that the information could be combined on a single flyer to be distributed to the schools.

## Policy Showdown

By the fall, despite Myra's continuing protests, the task group was finishing its deliberations, and by the beginning of October a draft policy was ready to go to the Board. We saw this as our last opportunity to convince the TDSB to adopt a broad equity policy.

Although weakened by the Harris educational reforms, which had led to the disappearance of anti-racism and equity positions in boards across the province, the Anti-Racist Multicultural Educators' Network of Ontario was still functioning. After retiring from the Equity Studies Centre, Hari Lalla had taken over the co-ordination of the group. AMENO still had the credentials and stature to make a credible intervention at the Board.

The AMENO executive was very much in favour of a broad equity approach, and on their behalf I took on the task of reshaping the task group's proposed policy to make it inclusive. It was not difficult. Other than its failure to address issues beyond race, culture, and faith, the proposed policy was a generally sound document. It followed PPM 119 in committing the Board to reflecting anti-racism in all aspects of its policies, practices, and leadership, stressed the importance of effective school-community partnerships, and had specific sections on curriculum, student languages, assessment and placement, guidance, employment practices, staff development, and harassment. All I really had to do was replace references to race, culture, and faith with a longer list of equity issues. After some wordsmithing by AMENO members, we agreed on a parallel document, "Antiracism and Equity for All."

Nora Allingham had been responsible for the implementation of PPM 119 when she was at the Ministry, and so we decided that she was the best person to argue that the memorandum should be considered a minimum requirement, not a restriction to developing broader policies. She presented AMENO's document to the Board when it met on October 21 and called on the committee to recommend that the document be made the basis for a planned public consultation scheduled to take place before the final policy was approved.

We made sure that each trustee had a copy of "Antiracism and Equity for All" and a package of support letters we had gathered from education professors, city councillors, community groups, and staff from several schools. But most of the beleaguered politicians were by that point too overwhelmed to read much more than the agenda, and they simply moved to receive the task group's version of the proposed policy. Nora only managed to get assurance that Hari would be allowed to speak to the Board on behalf of AMENO when the final decision on the consultation was made a week later, October 28.

Meanwhile Jackson and her team must have realized that they were facing serious opposition. On the day before the meeting, Hari received a phone call informing him that his name had been removed from the list of speakers. Apparently the only people who would be allowed to address the Board were a handful of supporters of the race-only policy. The administration was taking no chances that the trustees might be swayed.

The October 28 meeting dispelled any remaining doubt about the Board's intention regarding other equity issues. When the motion was made to receive the task group's report and to proceed with the public consultation, trustees Brian Blakeley and Irene Atkinson moved an amendment: "That a draft policy to address issues of bias, harassment, homophobia and gender identity be presented to the Board in December 1998." The amendment was defeated. There was to be no timeline for dealing with any other equity issues.

The Board began sending out copies of its proposed policy for response and comments from individuals, school councils, students, and parent-teacher associations. Four community forums – in Scarborough, North York, Toronto, and Etobicoke – were announced for late January, 1999. In an attempt to placate opposition to the Board's single-issue approach, the director proposed the establishment of a broad Equity in Education Advisory Committee at some future date.

## Controversy in AHEC

The next meeting of the Anti-Homophobia Equity Committee took place a few days after the October 28 decision to proceed with the race-only policy and had quite a different character from the careful politeness of a month earlier. Marcela Duran and Stephanie Wade had been called away at the last minute and were unable to attend. In their absence the conversation of the eight or so people in attendance was much more frank. The two teacher representatives from Scarborough talked about their frustration in trying to advance gay and lesbian issues in that board. It had taken years to get permission to set up the electronic conferences. Their analysis was that the Scarborough Working Group on Sexual Orientation had been organized to derail initiatives around lesbian and gay issues rather than to promote them. It turned out that the teacher from North York was in the process of laying a human rights complaint against her board because she had been refused permission to advertise North York's electronic conference on lesbian and gay issues within the system. Things were not quite as rosy as they had first appeared.

I described what had been going on around the new Board's equity policies and the recent decision to proceed on a policy restricted to race and culture. The others present were quite appalled. If I and my colleagues from Toronto had been anxious that sexual orientation might get lost in amalgamation, those who had been working on the issue in the other boards had hoped that amalgamation would be an opportunity to finally make progress in their parts of the new city. There was immediate talk of finding a parent to lay a human rights complaint against the Board on the grounds of being excluded from the equity policy, and discussion of a possible class-action suit on behalf of students who had been driven out of the school system by homophobic harassment. The group agreed that AHEC should join with other groups that had been left out to demand an inclusive approach in the upcoming consultation process.

Marcela Duran and Stephanie Wade saw the minutes of that meeting, and both of them made sure to be there the next time the group met. After some shadow boxing around the mandate, Scarborough teacher Susan Clifton and Toronto's Greg Pavelich moved that AHEC support the "Antiracism and Equity for All" document in the upcoming consultations. After a heated discussion the question was called. Marcela and Stephanie demanded a recorded vote. A narrow majority voted to support the motion, with a number of participants abstaining. The meeting decided that because several people had still not had a chance to read either of the documents, more information would be collected and the issue would be revisited at the next meeting.

The December 7 AHEC meeting was the largest so far, as both sides rallied the troops for the final showdown. After perfunctory discussion of the ongoing problems in extending the existing North York and Scarborough electronic communications networks, and approval of the joint flyer advertising student support groups and the revised mandate, we got down to the real bone of contention, AHEC's position on the proposed equity policy. I distributed copies of both policy documents and the list of endorsers of "Antiracism and Equity for All." By then the list read like a who's who of lesbian and gay organizations and supporters.

The debate was spirited. As it was drawing to a close, Marcela Duran tried to assure the group that sexual orientation would be the very next issue to be tackled after the anti-racism policy passed. Susan Clifton pointedly asked why sexual orientation should be the next priority – what about women? As a woman she was concerned about gender equity. How long would it be before women's issues were addressed? Was sexual orientation more important than gender? When and why had the board established this order of priorities? Of course the Board had established no such list of priorities, nor could such a list be justified. The question was called again. AHEC voted to support "Antiracism and Equity for All."

Stephanie Wade and Marcela Duran left the meeting, announcing that they could no longer be associated with the committee. The two other reps from North York silently followed in tow.

Three days later, Myra and I were called into the office of the Board's executive officer, Rod Thompson, the former director of the East York Board of Education. It was one of the most surreal scenes of my career and a vivid demonstration of how much the institutional culture of the Board had shifted. When we entered the reception area we were greeted by a secretary wearing reindeer antlers. The room was festooned with Christmas ornaments and Christmas carols blared from a tape recorder decorated with a red Christmas bow. In the corner a three-foot mechanical Santa Claus with flashing eyes and a revolving head maniacally wished us "Merry Christmas! Merry Christmas! Merry Christmas!" Myra had spent her career fighting the traditional Christmas deluge of Christian hegemony in our supposedly secular school system; now I thought she was going to have an aneurism. We staggered through the holiday house of horrors and into Rod Thompson's office.

Thompson, a normally mild-mannered man, started off trying to be gruff but ended up confiding in us about his worries about the "excessively personal" turn the debate on the policy was taking. He encouraged us to try to make sure the discussions about the policy remained civil.

Later we found out that following the AHEC meeting Marcela Duran and Stephanie Wade had sent Thompson letters disassociating themselves from the committee and accusing AHEC of being "oriented to political lobbying against the policy making decisions of the Toronto District School Board." The letters were accompanied by a copy of the AHEC minutes, which listed the names of the teachers who had supported the AMENO document. When the letters finally came to our attention, several of the teachers in AHEC believed that they constituted an "adverse report" to a supervisory official and considered filing a grievance. Eventually it was decided that there was more than enough work on the group's plate without getting involved in internecine legal wrangling.

## The Consultations Heat Up

AMENO realized that with only the anti-racism policy in circulation, there would be little opportunity for the others involved to consider the option of a more inclusive approach. The group reasoned that for a real discussion to take place, people needed to consider both policies. AMENO members had always used the internal mailing systems of the different boards to communicate with members and supporters. We therefore decided to distribute copies of "Antiracism and Equity for All" to the system. Within a few days, using the Board's mailroom, Hari Lalla and Pat Case were distributing the document, along with an explanatory cover letter under AMENO letterhead, to parent councils in every school in the system. Soon the document was circulating throughout the schools. Marguerite Jackson, obviously upset at this "unauthorized" use of Board facilities, immediately decreed new security precautions for the use of Board mail. But the cat was out of the bag. All over the system people began discussing the relative merits of the two approaches. The groundwork was laid for a discussion of the substantive issues at the forthcoming public consultations in January 1999.

Supporters of the inclusive approach continued to organize. AMENO and the Toronto Schools Equity Advocacy Committee called a meeting for the afternoon of Sunday, December 13. Community groups such as the Chinese Canadian National Council, Education Wife Assault, Culturelink, the Coalition for Lesbian and Gay Rights in Ontario, and the Urban Alliance on Race Relations sent representatives. Ana Larsen came from the District Labour

Council, and lawyer Hugh Scher brought an activist perspective from the disabilities movement. Professors involved in education work from all three local universities attended, as well as teachers from across the newly amalgamated Board. After a general background discussion, the meeting broke into work groups that focused on legal and media issues, general outreach, lobbying of trustees, and preparing for the public consultations.

The coalition was remarkably successful. Over the next two months *The Toronto Star* published three major articles supporting a broad equity approach. Hundreds of copies of the AMENO policy were distributed, along with background information and a two-page flyer rebutting many of the arguments being raised against a broad approach. The Law Union of Ontario produced a legal opinion urging the Board to adopt "Antiracism and Equity for All" as the basis for its policy. By the new year nearly forty prominent individuals and community organizations had endorsed the AMENO position. Some school community advisors defied orders and shared the AMENO document with their parent communities.

The most vocal group opposing the AMENO policy was the Toronto District Muslim Educational Assembly (TDMEA), an ultraconservative Muslim group led by an Etobicoke couple, Ibrahim and Ihsan El Sayed. The El Sayeds were unabashedly homophobic. Indeed, a Toronto teacher eventually laid a complaint with the Human Rights Office over what she considered hate literature on the TDMEA website. But the TDMEA went beyond homophobia. In a submission to the Board's consultation on Islamic accommodation, the group expressed its opposition to music, dancing, sex education, and any social activities that involved the "intermingling" of sexes. The El Sayeds' acerbic style soon alienated even those in the Board administration who were opposed to the AMENO position.

A far more serious opponent was Jasmin Zine, a doctoral student at the Ontario Institute for Studies in Education. Zine, who published an article about her take on the battle in the *Cambridge Journal of Education*, was much more sophisticated in her arguments and able to negotiate the nuances of equity discourse.[1] Also a devout Muslim, she appeared at the public consultations to argue that the inclusive policy displaced race, ethnicity, and religion and centred sexual orientation by attempting to include gay and lesbian issues in the curriculum. She argued that "Antiracism and Equity for All" tried to equate all forms of difference, which was unacceptable to religious and ethnic communities.

The support of long-standing anti-racist groups like the Chinese Canadian National Council and the Urban Alliance on Race Relations helped defuse arguments that a broad policy would displace the focus on racism. Keren Brathwaite of the Organization of Parents of Black Children described that group's position:

> There are many places where anti-racism is left out of equity, so we wanted it to be there. We didn't want any form of discrimination against any group. We believe that faith, sexual orientation, gender, class, and disability all should be part of the equity policy. Class is very much underserved. Poor kids continue to do so badly. The Board does not do a good job around disability. It's the same for Aboriginal people.

For Brathwaite and others, the equity agenda needed to be not only broad but also deep. People needed to work together and support each other, but resources still needed to be targeted to students "who have not been performing and who have been sidelined by the system."

At the public consultations the battle lines were drawn. AMENO and the Advocacy Committee succeeded in shifting the focus of the forums to the debate around whether the policy should be inclusive of all equity-seeking groups or not. But despite our attempts to ensure that those supporting the broad policy represented the full range of issues and the ethnic and racial diversity of the city, the forums polarized around attitudes towards homosexuality. According to Myra, who attended the meetings, the anti-gay, mainly Muslim fundamentalist parents tended to be on one side and the lesbian and gay community on the other.

> There were a few people from the Jewish community who were worried about anti-Semitism. Black parents were hardly at those meetings in any numbers, nor were ethnic groups like the Portuguese. There certainly weren't many kids left, although there were a few who made good presentations. Mostly other communities just didn't show up. So it turned into a showdown between the fundamentalist Muslim parents and the gay and lesbian community.

For many people in the Muslim communities, the question of including sexual orientation in the equity policy became a lightning rod for all their concerns and anxieties about maintaining cultural values in an often hostile society. A form letter circulated among parents by the TDMEA requested exemptions for students from anti-homophobia activities. It described the TDSB's "Human Sexuality Agenda" as promoting "an unsafe environment that puts our/my children at risk and undermines their morals and values . . . We/I understand the so-called human sexuality agenda as a convenient guise and institutional tool for the deliberate and conscious promotion of homosexual, bisexual and morally corrupt lifestyles on our children in the public schools."

In the end the strategy of using homophobia as an organizing tool to oppose the broad approach to equity was unsuccessful. Worse, it probably contributed to common stereotypes of Muslims as hysterical fanatics. The rhetoric employed was often so extreme and hateful that it shocked the trustees and task group members receiving the deputations. After he spoke in support of an inclusive approach, Mohammed Khan, spokesperson for El

Fatiha, the Muslim gay and lesbian group, received death threats. In contrast, the pleas for tolerance and inclusion mounted by the supporters of "Antiracism and Equity for All," who outlined experiences of prejudice and discrimination that they or family members had faced in the schools, were moving, persuasive, and congruent with a dominant liberal human rights discourse.[2]

## Victory

In the face of city-wide political pressure, the message finally began to get across to the task group members. According to Myra, "a very hard nosed Etobicoke principal" in the task group said the process "had been one of the best learning experiences of his professional career, and that he finally understood what I had been talking about."

Trustee Stephnie Payne continued to stir the pot into the spring of 1999. In March *NOW* magazine reported her comments that including other groups in the equity policy "would put us 100 years backwards." She told the magazine, "If you're a white lesbian, I'm going to see you first as a white woman of privilege." Payne was running for the NDP in the upcoming provincial elections, and *NOW* writer Leah Rumack acidly commented, "And doesn't she find it odd that an NDP candidate thinks gender, ability and (hello?) class aren't important enough areas to be covered under the baseline equity policy of the largest school board in Ontario?"[3]

Payne was now very much in a minority. In its final recommendations in May 1999 the task group reported, "The expressions of concern received throughout the consultation process clearly indicated that this draft policy was not deemed to be a sufficient response to the broader issues of equity as outlined in the Ontario Human Rights Code."

While a "compromise" solution was designed to save face for Jackson and the Board, it was basically a capitulation to the public protest. The task group called for the development of a "foundation statement" based on "Equity in Education: Basic Principles," to be approved by the Board by June 1999. While it would not adopt "Antiracism and Equity for All," it recommended the development of parallel documents on "Gender, Sexual Orientation, and Socio-economic Status," all of which would come before the Board for final approval at the same time as the anti-racism and ethnocultural equity document in December. The only outstanding matter was the inclusion of disabilities. The committee called for a review of the Special Education Plan "to determine if any gaps exist with regard to discrimination against persons with disabilities."

All of us involved in this fight were elated, but I was still worried. Lloyd McKell, head of Community Services, was appointed to chair a committee to draft the foundation statement, and I dropped by his office to discuss the process he was going to use and to suggest that the "Basic Principles" document be adopted as it stood. It already had a history of approval from several legacy boards and community groups. I feared that any major redrafting might result in it being watered down or open up a whole new can of worms. Lloyd insisted that the format of a foundation statement had to be quite different and tried to reassure me that nothing would be lost. The most I could achieve was his agreement that I could sit on the committee.

Although the El Sayeds appeared at the subsequent meetings held to draft the document, by now the tide had turned and they were isolated. Even other Muslim groups opposed to the inclusive policy were trying to distance themselves from the TDMEA. In the end, my fears about the document being watered down were unfounded. All the major points of the "Basic Principles" were translated into the "Foundation Statement." The only formulation that was weakened was a change in wording from the recognition of communities as the "driving force" producing institutional changes to a commitment to "value and encourage" the contributions of diverse communities. The "Foundation Statement" even went beyond the "Basic Principles" to place special stress on the need for an effective complaints process and evaluation procedures to review the Board's progress. The document passed the Board on schedule in June 1999.

## Denouement

Although the parallel task group drafting the new TDSB human rights policy dealing with complaints procedure agreed that the full range of groups should be protected by the policy, its deliberations had not been without political fireworks. Although by this time he had drafted two human rights policies for the Toronto Board, Pat Case had originally been "frozen out" of the Human Rights Task Group, which was managed by his old nemesis Rick Kollins. It wasn't until Kollins retired that Pat and Sue McGrath were given the task of producing a draft. Then it was a matter of facing down the rest of the bureaucracy. Pat would hear about "a sense of discomfort" among the administrators. He would be told that the Scarborough board, for instance, was not ready for this. He would say, "I'm sorry, but this is the law, what are you going to do about it?" He also regularly butted heads with Stephnie Payne. "She would cause huge arguments," he said, "and then she would storm out of the meeting accusing everybody of being racist towards her." One time after she left the superintendent made a remark about feeling "very uncomfortable" with what had just happened. Pat told her, "I don't. Black people have the right to be as stupid as anybody else, you know."

But for Pat, "The net was closing in." He saw less and less responsibility being delegated to the Equal Opportunity Office by the new administration, and he couldn't keep quiet about what was happening. "By that time I had written three five-page diatribes to the new director. I realized that a whole lot of us had spent a whole lot of time over the years educating the senior administration of the Toronto Board, and to some extent we had been reasonably successful at raising people's consciousness. Did I now want to spend the rest of my life, because that's what it would be, educating a new group of ignorant white people? The answer came back loud and clear. No! I just didn't want to do it." Pat was offered a job at Ontario Hydro, and he left the Board in February 1999.

Myra Novogrodsky was exhausted as well. "I didn't have the heart for it anymore. I was feeling very worn down. I was not sleeping. I was already fifty-one and I just felt that I couldn't have the same fights that I'd had twenty years before. I didn't think I was able to give particularly good leadership any longer. I don't think I was very easy to live with those last two or three years. I needed to take a different direction."

She had to make a decision quickly. As the "Foundation Statement" passed, the Board was finally ready to amalgamate equity work into a new Equity Department. After those scheduled to retire were gone, a district-wide co-ordinator (DWC), three instructional leaders (consultants), and two student program workers would be left. Given the size of the new Board, the complement was a far cry from the staffing and resources that equity had commanded before amalgamation. Myra pondered applying for the new DWC position, but she was sceptical of her chances of getting the job given her battles with administration. She was offered a secondment to the York University Faculty of Education and left the Board at the end of the school year in June 1999.

## The Equity Department

Terezia Zoric had been at Central Tech during the battle around the equity policy, so she had not developed a reputation with upper administration. She successfully applied for the position of district-wide co-ordinator of equity for the TDSB and took up the job in September 1999. Marcela Duran, who had also been an applicant, was compensated with a secondment to prepare a religious accommodation policy. That task released her from the day-to-day workings of the Equity Department until she was ready to take a retirement package.

Terezia's job would not be an easy one. The department staff members were drawn from different organizational cultures with different notions of equity. They were of different levels of political sophistication and skills, and had been on different sides of the fight around the policy. Several of them were waiting for retirement.

Terezia operated like a general preparing for the final assault. There was a December deadline to write the parallel policies on gender, sexual orientation, and class, and within weeks she had task groups set up to prepare drafts. She also decided that she would not wait around for approval to proceed on the question of disabilities, and simply designated a task group to draft a policy. There were particular modifications to be made around different issues – it was important to maintain confidentiality for lesbian and gay students, for example – but in general it was understood that the more the policies resembled one another, the more difficult it would be for the Board to accept some and reject others. With Terezia putting in especially long hours – consulting with different committees, even typing the different policy sections herself – the result was five nearly identical parallel policy documents.

One last battle royal occurred when the draft policies went to the Board in December. This time the fundamental issue could not be obscured by bureaucratic subterfuge. The issue was homophobia. On one side were those opposed to the passage of a policy that legitimized anti-homophobia work, mostly right-wing Muslims: the TDMEA, Islamic Society, Islamic Council of Imams, and Concerned Muslim Parents Group. On the other side were the gay and lesbian communities and their supporters: Parents and Friends of Lesbians and Gays (PFLAG), Coalition for Lesbian and Gay Rights of Ontario (CLGRO), Family Service Association, Asian Community AIDS Services, and Chinese Canadian National Council. The Board was once again deluged with written deputations: forty-four were in favour of adopting the package of five policies; and thirty-five, plus fifty-six form letters, were opposed to the sexual orientation policy.

By this time, though, the trustees had no choice in the matter. They could not hide behind vague promises that certain other issues would be dealt with later; they could not offer excuses about administrative process. They could scarcely be seen as rejecting policies promoting equity for women, the disabled, and the economically disadvantaged. If they accepted these policies but rejected the one on sexual orientation, it would be a clear case of discrimination against lesbian and gay students, parents, and staff. With sexual orientation a protected category under the Ontario Human Rights Code, such a move would put the Board in an indefensible legal position.

On December 15, trustee Christine Ferreira, seconded by Shelley Laskin, moved that the five "Commitments to Policy Implementation" be endorsed. The motion carried and the "Commitments to Equity Policy Implementation: Anti-Racism and Ethnocultural Equity, Anti-Sexism and Gender Equity, Anti-Homophobia, Sexual Orientation and Equity, Anti-Classism and Socio-Economic Equity and Equity for Persons with Disabilities" together with the "Equity Foundation Statement" finally became the new equity policy for the Toronto District School Board.

Terezia Zoric saw the passage of the policies as a victory on several levels. Just to get all those policies passed by the end of the year made a contribution "to the building of the department as a unified, proud and self-conscious entity," she said. "Getting something like that accomplished was huge." Still, she was less than sanguine about the overall effect of setting a policy in place. Just because they now had the multiple policy did not mean that "things would automatically happen."

The Toronto District School Board's adoption of a broad equity policy was the climax of almost thirty years of struggle that had begun in the Toronto Board in the 1970s. It was a dramatic example of how popular mobilization in conjunction with progressive forces inside an institution – in combination with legal imperatives – could force a conservative bureaucracy to bend to community demands. Unfortunately, it would also once again demonstrate the limits of such factors in bringing about true institutional transformation in a hostile climate.

Chapter 17

# Aboard the Titanic

THE WINNING OF THE FIGHT for an inclusive equity policy in the country's largest school board, finally achieved with the passing of the five policies in December 1999, was the last great popular victory of the twentieth century in Toronto education politics. The policy umbrella provided cover for a number of initiatives around different issues.

Over the following year the new Equity Department organized two board-wide student conferences on issues of socio-economic justice and prepared a manual for senior public schools on human rights education based on the UN Declaration of the Rights of the Child. Anti-homophobia work blossomed across the former suburban boards as teachers and students began using the new policy to legitimize workshops that would have previously been frowned upon by conservative administrators. To meet this increased demand the department organized "Speakout," a panel of over thirty culturally and racially disparate lesbian and gay youth, trained to tell their stories of coming out and dealing with homophobia. The Anti-Homophobia Equity Committee organized two successful conferences for lesbian and gay parents, transforming itself from a group of Board staff into a body that represented the voice of an emerging parent community. Trustee Irene Atkinson, who had led the charge to have Tony Souza fired in 1981 after he had booked a school for a gay community meeting following the bath raids, now proudly rode on the Board's school-bus float in Toronto's Gay Pride parade. We produced a binder on disabilities and human rights, and held training sessions on disability issues for teachers across the system.

Nor did anti-racism work fall off the table. The student conferences for Asian Heritage Month continued, and although the Black student conferences were never revived in the Toronto District School Board, the Equity Department distributed curriculum materials for Black History Month and subsidized artists and speakers to make presentations in the schools. After September 11, 2001, the department also organized a large public forum on "Islamophobia."

The Equity Advisory Committee was transformed into the Community Equity Reference Group, and despite efforts by the upper administration to sideline and marginalize them, group members managed to hold together and continue to ask uncomfortable questions about issues such as the state of policy implementation, the effects of continued cuts on vulnerable groups, and the failure of the Board to implement employment equity goals and timetables.

Still, clearly all was not well in the new Toronto District School Board. The institution now had no employment equity plan. Huge fee increases for the community use of schools put the buildings out of reach for most groups. ESL programs were reduced. Natural science centres were mothballed. Waiting lists for special education assessment lengthened. Schools began to physically deteriorate because there was no money for repairs. For a year after he left the Board Pat Case continued to sit on the Community Equity Reference Group as a representative for the Urban Alliance on Race Relations. Nobody at the top of the organization paid attention to the group's recommendations, he said.

After amalgamation the Equal Opportunity Office found itself doing almost nothing but handling harassment complaints. According to Sue McGrath, "It was impossible to do proactive work. There was no funding. Employment equity, the conferences, workshops, meetings with the reps, the non-trad stuff, all evaporated. Education generally seemed to be under attack, and within that system, there was the feeling that nobody had time for equity because there were all these other issues to deal with."

When the long-awaited human rights policy and procedures were finally adopted in spring 2000, the new Human Rights Office that was to administer it turned out to be a shadow of the original plan. Originally proposed as an office of eight staff persons, it was first cut down to one position and only restored to three after a public outcry led by the Community Equity Reference Group. The office was also part of the Human Resources Department, a location that undermined its independence. Sue McGrath, discouraged by the new Board's lacklustre commitment to equity and "really sick of complaints," took an early retirement package.

The first years of the new century also marked a period of continuing labour strife as the new Board tried to live within the meagre resources of the provincial funding formula. Programs were disrupted as education workers attempting to preserve their jobs and working conditions went on strike and work to rule. In the face of protests and turmoil the administration became increasingly paranoid. There was no money for textbooks, but apparently enough for a video surveillance system to be installed at the Board offices. All employees were soon required to carry and display photo identification badges. Large men in black military-style uniforms guarded the entrances to 155 College Street.

As Sandy Wong put it, "In the former Toronto Board of Education the administration had to be cautious. They at least recognized that there were limits." After amalgamation, he said, community and unions became afterthoughts, and "the powers that be" more or less had licence to do their will. "An example is the system's application of the Safe Schools Act. There are thousands of kids from as young as kindergarten being suspended these days, and no one calls it into question."

As the cuts continued, the Ministry of Education tightened its grip on curriculum, eliminating wherever it could the windows we had used to introduce issues of equity. Things began to feel more and more hopeless. My metaphor for the year 2000 was "lower decks of the Titanic, small bucket." The only good piece of news that year was the September return to the Equity Department of Vanessa Russell as a consultant or (as the position was now called) instructional leader. Vanessa had been excited by the passage of the broad policy and eager to continue the work. But with only three consultants and two student workers, and a budget a fifth of what it had been in the old Toronto Board for a system now five times larger, she soon realized that things would never be the same.

There were increasing internal stresses as the Equity Department struggled with its effectiveness. Terezia Zoric's proposed model – "a mile wide, an inch deep" – reflected her commitment as district-wide co-ordinator of equity to ensuring that our efforts were distributed across the system's more than six hundred schools. She reasoned that we needed "to plant the seeds of equity work in places where something would grow after we were gone." She took aim at the many "places that had never done anything at all that needed to get something started." She argued later, "It didn't make a lot of sense for us to keep going back to our old friends in Toronto, delivering what was essentially service provision when we had six hundred schools and a policy that needed implementing."

Vanessa and I argued that the opposite strategy – "a mile deep, an inch wide" – would ultimately be more effective. It was better to do meaningful work in the places that were eager to work with us than try to spread ourselves thinly across the system. We wanted to avoid reducing our work to the lowest common denominator – which meant, from our point of view, basically doing nothing, with the "cutting edge progressive stuff" getting lost. As Vanessa put it, if we spread ourselves thinly, the schools that really wanted our work would "get pissed off. You're not meeting their needs. They call and say 'we need this.' Too bad. We can't do that." She added: "It's really not surprising that often the number of people showing up to central events was dismal. The less we went into schools, the less people knew about us, and the less they cared if we existed as a department or not."

It was not a new debate. Myra Novogrodsky said the Equity Studies Centre had struggled with similar questions. "One approach was to support the people in the system who had the best ideas and who were having the most success with them. Another was to try to get something going at every single school. I always preferred being engaged in the deeper work. I got a lot more out of it personally. I also think the people who were involved in that kind of work had the potential for more and longer-lasting leadership. In our heyday within our smallish system, we were able to do both broad and deep work. It wasn't as hard a choice for us as it became after amalgamation, when there were five times the number of schools and fewer resources to go around."

A second interconnected area of debate was around our emphasis on the five mandated equity areas. Traditionally, consultants and student program workers had allowed schools to define their own needs and to request our help on problem areas that they identified. For Terezia such a laissez-faire approach meant that some issues were not being confronted. "Race and anti-homophobia education tended to be covered, but nobody called us around class issues. We did little of any substance on gender, and disabilities worst of all," she said. " I didn't think our department's work was particularly inclusive. I had this notion that equity meant equality of emphasis."

The department's focus increasingly shifted to curriculum-writing. We produced documents on African and Asian heritage and the Roma. "Rainbows and Triangles" focused on lesbian and gay issues. The work became far more technical – now all curriculum had to fit into templates, themes, and expectations designed by the Ministry – and we lacked the resources to train teachers to use the new material. The shift to curriculum-writing also tended to leave the student program workers increasingly out of the loop. We were not teachers, and our expertise was not producing curriculum to meet the ever more rigid Ministry requirements. We were skilled at working with people.

Vern Douglas, who was not a part of the Equity Department but continued to work in Curriculum, also felt the pressure. He had gathered a group of interested teachers together to produce "practical achievable" documents to challenge common stereotypes about Indians. "Native People in Contemporary Urban Society: A Native Studies Unit for the Junior Division" featured pictures of a dozen Aboriginal people who lived in the city, the communities they were from, and their jobs. "Contemporary Life in a First Nations' Community" looked at modern reservation life. A third package listed audiovisual material that could be used to teach Native studies, and lastly the group produced a Grade 6 curriculum aid, "Origins, Relationships and Contributions: A Grade Six Aboriginal Studies Unit." Vern's unit did training for about three hundred teachers, at a time, he said, "when none of that was supposed to happen any more." The Grade 6 curriculum aid went to every elementary school in Toronto, "but then there was no one around to do the ongoing training and the resources weren't available to buy the materials that were needed to do it," he said.

"My last year in the job I was told not to work with teachers because we didn't have the resources to do that any more. That's when I thought it was about time to leave. If you work for a school board and you're trying to implement changes, and you're not allowed to work with teachers, something is wrong. I was only supposed to work with groups of teachers after school. I wasn't permitted to go to classrooms. I just kept doing it anyway because, quite frankly, no one knew."

Vern's position was finally eliminated. He was offered a lesser post in another area with a substantial pay cut. He left and took a package. "No one said good-bye to me. I gave my secretary Kitty a hug, and I walked out the door. After ten years. Everybody was getting screwed in those days."

The increasingly toxic environment and an overwhelming administrative workload exacerbated Terezia's growing frustrations. The debates within the Equity Department on strategy, priorities, and regional loyalties became more intense. By that point I had changed my metaphor to "lower decks of the Titanic, violin."

Complaints had come in from administrators who said they didn't know how to implement the new equity policies. Despite protests from the Community Equity Reference Group, the Board director stalled for eighteen months before Terezia was finally given the go-ahead to make a system-wide effort to introduce the material. For Terezia, the stonewalling came down to a matter of trust. "The new Board was a hierarchical place that still depended intensely on personal relationships," she said. "There was just so much schmoozing to be done." The turnaround came after she finally managed to gain the trust of a number of senior staff and in particular one executive who had the ear of the director. "She was able to advocate on my behalf and on behalf of the department." Delivering session after session of training on the policies to groups of administrators became the primary labour of the department for the 2001-2002 school year.

Vanessa Russell was cynical about the effects. "It was a train-the-trainer model. People who went for the day liked it. They got food and it was pretty flashy. But out of the six hundred schools you could count the number on one hand where administrators actually took it back and did a workshop for their staff. That just didn't happen." The administrators who did become excited by the new policy and interested in follow-up work in their schools had to be told that the department's resources were being completely absorbed by the in-house training sessions.

For Alice Te the training sessions at least had a concrete goal, and she found them to be among the more rewarding work she did. "At least there were groups of people we had to train and once we met the quota we knew they knew something as opposed to nothing." Still, it was frustrating presenting the policies with limited prospects of follow-up. "Even if they were committed, they weren't going to do too much about it. They couldn't. There just wasn't enough backing."

In the fall of 2001 Marguerite Jackson resigned as director and got a $360,000 golden handshake for her troubles. She was replaced by David

Reid, whose claim to fame was a record of budget-slashing at the Halifax Board of Education. In February 2002 a narrow majority of suburban trustees pushed through the sale of the Board's headquarters at 155 College Street, relocating themselves high on Yonge Street in North York and scattering what remained of the administration to various inaccessible sites well outside the unruly downtown.

By fall 2001 I too was gone. My doctors finally convinced me that living with AIDS for two decades had taken its toll and that I needed to stop work and concentrate on taking care of what was left of my immune system. I went on disability leave.

It was a year before our office finally received permission to fill my position, and by that point Terezia Zoric had left to take a teaching position at the Ontario Institute for Studies in Education. "I left because I didn't want to be a workaholic anymore," she said. "There was too much anger. I wanted to land in a place where I could be somewhat less driven, healthier, and be able to maintain more perspective."

Vanessa Russell reluctantly applied for the position of district-wide co-ordinator and found out later she was the only applicant. "How's that for systemic issues?" she mused. "In three short years the job went from a highly attractive position, for which many qualified and long-time equity educators competed and applied, to a job that nobody wanted." She was offered the position but turned it down when she realized the boundaries that were being set. As co-ordinator, she was told, she would no longer be working with the city's communities and would not be able to meet with or speak to trustees. Her current position would not be replaced, which meant that her staff would be cut by one position. "Human rights complaints were to be none of our concern," she said. She was also told that it had been decided to move equity from the Instruction Division (which had become the new name of the Curriculum Division) to Staff Development.

"When I think about dismantling any system of oppression, I think of a number of essential tools," she said. "We need trustees and community to apply political pressure to challenge institutional barriers. We need 'curriculum' in its broadest sense to challenge the stereotypes, ideas, bias, and prejudice that live in the heads and hearts of individuals. And finally we need a strong implementation of the rules (a Human Rights Department) to challenge oppressive behaviours that exist within the system. The department was being completely disabled. After speaking with all my colleagues, we decided I should reject the district-wide co-ordinator position and leave a gaping hole in the department to bear witness to the community."

In the absence of a co-ordinator, the training on the policy ground to a halt. For Terezia Zoric it was a major disappointment. "A policy is something that a small number of people wrote to try to somehow make sure that everyone is going to have to change their practices. Our little implementation team actually did get to tons of people, and if we'd had even one or two follow-up sessions it would have been more effective. The failure to continue was a huge loss."

Alice Te also wearied of battling the bureaucracy and returned to teaching. She had gone into education to work with kids, and the consultant's job had become far removed from that. "I felt that it was time to go back to my own classroom to work with some kids and to actually practice some of the theory that I'd learned."

That same fall of 2002, when Terezia and Alice left, the Board trustees belatedly drew a line in the sand and refused to make any more cuts to meet the demands of the province's ridiculously insufficient funding formula. The Tories replied by suspending the Board and appointing a "supervisor." With the trustees out of the way, the new supervisor, Paul Christie, in collusion with the upper bureaucracy, continued slashing at the foundations of public education to comply with the funding formula. By the spring of 2003, in another wave of cuts, despite protests, the remaining school community advisors were laid off. They were the last major legacy of the wave of educational reform that had swept the Toronto Board in the 1970s.

The process had been anything but straightforward. We fought to get non-hegemonic identities recognized and found ourselves entangled in the worst excesses of identity politics. We aligned ourselves with the people who knew most about the Nazis on the street and it blew up in our face because they were fighting Nazis on the street. We were on the outside fighting to get in and when we got inside we found ourselves co-opted by the logic of the organization that we were now part of. We started out pushing from the bottom, found out the limitations of that approach, and switched to pushing from the top, only to find out how completely vulnerable that made us.

When the NDP was in power the bureaucracy at least wanted to look like it was interested in equity, but when the Tories got elected and amalgamated the boards, the educational establishment was more than compliant in rolling everything back. We had a strong enough public movement to win the broad equity policy in 1999, but weren't strong enough to ensure that it was implemented. A generation started with high hopes, but although we had accomplished real change, twenty years later we were just about all burned out.

## Looking Back: Pondering the Nature of Change

In his magisterial final opus, *The Structure of Evolutionary Theory*, Stephen J. Gould describes a continuing tension between two approaches within evolutionary thought: the externalist, which understands change and development as the result of outside, environmental pressures on essentially plastic organisms; and the internalist, which proposes that the inherent characteristics of organisms are largely responsible for the direction of evolutionary movement. Gould also contrasts understandings of evolution as a slow, almost imperceptible process to ideas of evolution as a periods of relatively rapid change that punctuate long periods of stability. Although Gould's book deals with questions of natural development and change, it raises sharp questions about institutional and cultural transformation.

At the Toronto Board of Education, concerns about class, which were central to the educational activists of the early 1970s, increasingly became embroiled in issues of culture, language, race, and gender, and finally evolved into a broader struggle against a range of different forms of oppression under the umbrella of the notion of equity. Why did this evolution take place? Did the external decline of traditional socialist class politics lead to a fragmentation into different identity groups, each organizing around its own oppressions and clamouring for a place at the table? Was the equity approach an attempt to reimpose unity on these increasingly fractious constituencies? Or was it that the internal logic of the questions raised around class led inexorably to issues of race and gender, and the resulting insights into the nature of social power illuminated the situations of other oppressed groups? Are oppressions fundamentally so linked and similar that their vocabularies and struggles necessarily must flow together? Or did the contingency of common enemies and an appropriation of conceptual tools, at least for a period, bring these different struggles into a kind of alliance?

These are more than just academic questions. On one hand, the notion of a deep correspondence between racism, sexism, heterosexism, and the oppression faced by working-class people and the disabled legitimizes the strategy of taking up these issues and dealing with them together, as a unit. On the other hand, if they are seen as separate struggles with different impacts, histories, social functions, and interests, other strategies become necessary. At best the different oppressions might borrow from one another. At worst, some of them could be seen as opportunistically hitching a ride on the coattails of others that have more serious grievances.

Based on my experience at the Toronto Board, I would argue that despite significant differences in the histories and impacts of racism, sexism, homophobia, and in the issues of class and disability, the importance of cross-fertilization among different ideas and strategies, the similarities in the kind of institutional remedies necessary to achieve change, and the importance of combined political muscle to successfully implement those remedies justify a unified equity approach. We should never forget, however, that such an approach can only be effective when it attends to the specific problems faced by different groups and when the voices of all those who have been marginalized are clearly heard. Nobody can fall off the table.

The history of the struggles at the Toronto Board also raises questions about institutional change. Is that change uniform, gradual, and regular? Or does an institution leap forward in response to crises to take on qualitatively new characteristics? Do institutions slowly respond to the pressures from their environment in the classic Darwinian sense, or is their evolution constrained and channelled by their own internal processes? Here again the answers lead to different strategies. If change is uniform and gradual, people in search of that change might take the long view and focus on the incremental education of stakeholders and on slow reform, avoiding unproductive conflict at all cost. If change comes in leaps and bounds in response to crises, the strategists might favour the politics of confrontation. If institutions primarily respond to outside pressures, activists would need to organize that pressure. If change is channelled by internal processes, they would find it most productive to work on the inside. Then again, given that institutions are profoundly hierarchical structures, is it more effective to educate or put pressure on the top or the bottom? Do advocates for change seek promotion into positions of influence and power, or do they concentrate their efforts on mobilizing at the grassroots?

Like Gould, I believe that change involves both internal and external processes and our strategies as change agents must reflect that reality.

When the Young Turk trustees won control of the Board at the beginning of the 1970s, they saw themselves as part of a broad socialist tradition. Their primary concern was the streaming of working-class kids into dead-end vocational schools. The reformers and their community constituencies believed that streaming and even special education were attempts to legitimize the segregation of poor and working-class kids in inferior education settings, and they demanded fundamental changes.

The reformers' concerns with the inequities of class propelled them to consider other issues. Questions of culture came to the fore. Because of postwar immigration patterns, the working class in Toronto was largely made up of new immigrants. Questions of class and ethnic discrimination were compounded. The focus on multiculturalism inevitably raised issues of race. New immigrants were also increasingly people of colour. Civil rights struggles and the Black power movement in the United States and anti-colonial struggles in the Third World framed the issue as one of racism and racial discrimination. People organized around colour and culture demanded changes in the education system.

The neighbourhood and community organizations were the motor force in all these struggles for change. They organized themselves, elected local trustees, and demanded that their kids have a fair access to a good education as a key component of upward mobility. To achieve those goals there was a huge push to democratize the system. Dozens of committees providing community input were set up with the assistance of the newly formed School Community Relations Department. Education bureaucrats could no longer make decisions without at least going through the motions of consultation. It was a classic moment of external pressures enabling a group to seize positions of power in an institution in order to change it.

Early in the 1970s, with the second wave of women's liberation, the role of women in the institution also became a concern. Although predicated on a broad social movement, here the motor force came from within the institution, from the majority of women staff who were regularly smashing up against the glass ceiling that protected male access to positions of power and privilege. The primary issue then became employment equity, which ultimately raised questions around the curriculum and the streaming of young women. Although there was certainly resistance, the large pool of female staff already within teaching meant that the goals of promotion and employment equity were generally successfully met.

In contrast to the struggles around the employment and promotion of women, the communities organized around culture or colour were primarily concerned about what was happening to their children in the classroom. Questions of employment equity took a back seat, and when those questions were raised they were usually justified in terms of providing role models for youth. Employment equity for "visible minorities" was also a far more difficult problem. Because of systemic barriers, these groups were not as present in the institution as women were. Solutions required far deeper structural and institutional changes.

Employment equity for visible minorities moved slowly compared to the successes of mostly white women in achieving positions of responsibility. On the other hand, anti-racism work among students met with early success, while work around women's issues was relatively weak. By the beginning of the 1980s this unevenness had led to the adoption of different strategies. The race relations effort relied more heavily on sources of power outside the traditional organizational structure, which meant, for instance, that I could get a job organizing students to "bombard the headquarters." The School Community Relations Department could play the same role in organizing ethnic communities. There was no comparable student program worker position around women's issues, and no gender retreats for students until the early 1990s. The SCR Department did not contemplate organizing on the basis of gender. The push for change around gender primarily still came from female-dominated areas in the teachers' unions.

Still, the affirmative action and race relations efforts did undergo an important cross-fertilization, even in this early period. Despite the focus of the women's movement on employment and affirmative action, a women's studies consultant was appointed in the Curriculum Division in 1975. In the Equal Opportunity Office the two advisors worked together and often faced resistance from the same quarters. Their co-operation in setting up the Visible Minority Women Employees' Group was an example of early integration of the issues. Ultimately, the position of curriculum advisor on race relations was set up to parallel women's studies in the Curriculum Division. Women's success around employment strengthened the race relations focus on employment equity, and the example of anti-racism work among students strengthened the hand of those who wanted to deal with gender in the curriculum.

The dismantling of the School Community Relations Department in 1986 undermined much of the community pressure that had been pushing the Board around issues of culture, language, and race. After that the work relied much more on individuals whose positions within the system had been created during the previous period. Only by seizing the opportunity of the tenth anniversary conference in 1989 was it possible to apply enough public pressure to force the Board to establish goals and timetables for the hiring and promotion of visible minorities. The push for affirmative action for women, because it was primarily driven by employee groups within the Board, was not dramatically altered by the loss of the SCR Department, and women continued to make gains throughout this period.

A product of the unevenness was a bitterness that fed into the negative aspects of identity politics. Some critics argued that employment equity for visible minorities lagged behind that for women because the system was more racist than sexist. Others said that if programming for students around race often seemed to eclipse that around gender, it was because the system was more interested in appeasing racial groups and less committed to the fight against sexism.

The gay community's first attempt to assert its presence in the education system in 1980 was another example of the system responding to pressure from the outside. The initial demand was for the establishment of a community liaison committee modelled on the ones set up to connect with a variety of ethnic communities. A shift in the political winds that strengthened the right-wing and the absence of strong advocates within the system resulted in the failure of that push for change. It would not be until the second half of the decade, when pro-gay voices in the system were much stronger, and the profile of the community had been raised (ironically, by the AIDS epidemic), that the issue would once again come to the fore. The importance of co-operation between outside and inside forces in the struggle for institutional change was, again, obvious.

The election of the first provincial NDP government in 1990 sped up events. After the "Yonge Street riot," boards across the province were required to develop race relations policies and employment equity legislation was passed. But this time of great opportunities was also marked by the effects of an insular identity politics. The collapse of a socialist alternative undermined common understandings that all these movements were participating in a project for the general reshaping of society on a more egalitarian model. In the midst of the jockeying and infighting among groups in the communities, activists involved in various issues at the Board tried to overcome differences and suspicions and build a more inclusive equity approach. There was an internal logic to the extension of the concepts developed around anti-racism and feminism to include other oppressed groups; but as important as that logic was, it is doubtful that it would have been recognized and selected in the absence of demands by those groups themselves, organized on the basis of identity. The issue of disability continued to be avoided until the emergence of a more vocal disabled people's movement. Class was eclipsed until the provincial NDP government amplified the voices of the labour movement. Once their issues were addressed, different groups borrowed and copied concepts and strategies that worked. The very practicality of those approaches across issues reflected the concrete similarities in the challenges faced by different oppressed groups.

With community pressures now much weaker than they had been in the 1970s, the cadre of equity workers and activists within the system became an important force, working with trustees to push the institution forward. Their efforts could find support in the more inclusive orientation of the NDP government, the legal implications of the Charter of Rights and Freedoms, and the levers of power available to those within the system. They could also find at least a modicum of support at the top of the administrative hierarchy, and that support helped to overcome resistance throughout the institution. The Equity Studies Centre was set up in the Curriculum Division, and a First Nations advisor was added to the Equal Opportunity Office. Equity became a system priority.

These changes made a difference in the level of confrontation and conflict with the Board's institutional culture. Equity workers became more integrated into the system and learned to play by the rules of the game. But the successes brought with them a subtle transformation in the radical goals of the original push for anti-racist education. The ideas of a pedagogy of liberation were displaced by a focus on institutional changes to "include" previously marginalized groups in the status quo of the standard curriculum and staff of the institution. Women and people of colour who were willing to fit into the institutional culture were promoted to carry out functions that had previously been carried out only by white men. Even when the curriculum was successfully broadened to include previously ignored groups, it was most often delivered in a conventional way – a way that privileged particular kinds of learners. Programs and services were developed to try to meet the needs of the most disadvantaged, but the idea that education had a role in challenging the social roots of those disadvantages was slowly eclipsed. For those who believed that "change takes time," these developments signalled a maturation of the work, and at least the beginning of progress. For others they were evidence of retreat, evidence that little in the way of fundamental change seemed to be occurring.

The election of the Harris Conservatives in 1995 was a catastrophe in the evolution of equity. The province amalgamated boards and defunded the public education system, severely altering the environment that had allowed for integration of the concerns of marginalized groups. Only a last-ditch public campaign managed to preserve an inclusive approach to equity in Toronto, but this proved to be only an ephemeral success in a protracted and often discouraging series of battles to preserve the best of the public education system.

Still, the evolution of equity has never been gradual or uniform. Every significant advance came in response to some internal or external crisis. The struggle for equitable education evolved from the idealism and political mobilizing of the 1970s, adapted itself to the insights of the new social movements of the 1980s, and struggled for a vision to overcome the narrow identity politics of the 1990s. The defeat of the provincial Tories in October 2003 and the new Liberal government's dismissal of the Toronto Board's supervisor rekindled some hope of a return to democratic control. The policy framework passed in 1999 remains in place and can provide the foundation for new initiatives.

Soon enough, we hope, out of this recent deep crisis new configurations and social forces will come together and once again begin the push towards the goals of equity in education.

# Notes

## 1 Back Story

1 In 1969, for example, a group of working-class women who had banded together to oppose the redevelopment of their neighbourhood formed the Trefann Court Mothers to challenge the systematic class-based streaming faced by their children in Toronto schools. See Kari Dehli, John Restakis, and Errol Sharpe, "The Rise and Demise of the Parent Movement in Toronto," in *Social Movements/Social Change: The Politics and Practice of Organizing*, ed. Frank Cunningham et al. (Toronto: Between the Lines and the Society for Socialist Studies, 1988), pp.209-27.

2 In 1968 New York City set up several local community school boards to increase local involvement in school governance and improve the quality of schools in largely Black and Puerto Rican low-income neighbourhoods. When the board in the Oceanhill-Brownsville section of Brooklyn attempted to transfer out eighteen white teachers accused of trying to undermine the goals of community control, the move resulted in a racially polarized city-wide teachers strike that pitted community control against union rights.

## 2 Beginnings

1 Liaison committees were informal committees promoted by the reform trustees and made up of community members, usually from a specific ethnic community, working to bring community concerns to the Board.

2 Toronto Board of Education, "Draft Report of the Subcommittee on Race Relations," May 1978, p.18.

3 Ibid., p.8; emphasis added.

4 Ibid., p.16.

5 Interview with Tony Souza, who was involved in organizing some of the meetings held to discuss the draft report's findings.

6 Toronto Board of Education, *Final Report of the Subcommittee on Race Relations*, May 1979, p.1.

7 Toronto Board of Education, minutes, May 4, 1972, quoted in Janet Louise Sheffield, "From Barriers to Bridges: Selected Aspects of an Affirmative Action Policy of One Board of Education, 1970-1990," D.Ed. thesis, University of Toronto, 1992, p.79.

8 Ibid., p.83.

## 4 Beachhead

1 Toronto Board of Education, minutes, February 1981, p.120.

2 Dehli, Restakis, and Sharpe, "Rise and Demise of the Parent Movement in Toronto," p.218.

3 Toronto Board of Education, minutes, June 1982, p.541.

4 Johan Galtung (b.1930) is one of the founders of modern peace studies and a professor of

Peace Studies at the University of Hawaii, University of Witten-Herdecke, European Peace University, and University of Tromsø. He has published over fifty books, including *Human Rights in Another Key* (1994) and *Peace by Peaceful Means* (1995).

5 Barb Thomas, "Reflections on the Race Relations Program at the Toronto Board of Education: A Discussion Paper," Toronto, March 1984, p.4.

6 Kari Dehli and Ilda Januario, "Parent Activism and School Reform in Toronto," report prepared for the Ontario Ministry of Education and Training, Ontario Institute for Studies in Education, Toronto, October 1994, p.55.

7 Dehli, Restakis, and Sharpe, "Rise and Demise of the Parent Movement in Toronto," p.222. "Metro" was the umbrella group for the six boards of education in Metro Toronto. It negotiated with the provincial government around funding and received provincial money to distribute to the individual boards. It had a curriculum development foundation to co-ordinate curriculum projects with the boards and also ran specific projects, such as programs for the disabled. Members were appointed by individual boards.

## 5 Taking on the System

1 A.S. Neill, *Summerhill: A Radical Approach to Child Rearing* (New York: Hart Publishing, 1960).

2 The Toronto Board allowed for the establishment of alternative school programs with specific educational philosophies aimed at meeting the needs of particular groups of students within the publicly funded system.

3 The Women's Studies position was expanded to include both Women's and Labour Studies in 1984.

4 Toronto Board of Education, minutes, Dec. 13, 1984, p.1027.

5 Hitner Starr Associates, "Race Relations Program Review," Toronto Board of Education, December 1985.

6 Ibid., p.11.

7 Ibid., p.20.

8 Ibid., p. 40.

9 Ibid., p.49.

10 Ibid., p.61.

11 Ibid., p.57.

12 Ibid., p.89.

13 Ibid., p.107.

14 Ibid., p.109.

## 6 Backlash and Response

1 Toronto Board of Education, meeting transcript, May 29, 1986, p 2.

2 Ibid., p.9.

3 Two major Board committees vetted all issues before they went to the Board trustee meetings. The School Program Committee dealt with curriculum issues; the Personnel and Organization Committee handled issues dealing with human resources.

4 Details of the meeting come from an interview with Alok Mukherjee, who attended the event.

5 *The Toronto Sun*, June 18, 1986, June 23, 1986.

6 "Metro Morning," CBC-Radio, transcript, Toronto, June 17, 1986.

7 With a strong middle-class base and a membership skilled in committee and media work, Parents for Peace had developed a high profile at the Board. One of its major focuses was around Remembrance Day celebrations. The group wanted to turn the day into an oppor-

tunity for students to discuss alternatives to violence and war – infuriating both traditionalists (who believed the day was being hijacked) and some veterans' groups (who feared their sacrifices might be forgotten).

8 Simon's name was alternately spelled Nkoli.

9 Consultative Committee on the Education of Black Students in Toronto Schools, "Draft Report," June 1987, p.7.

10 Ibid., p.23.

11 Identification, Placement and Review Committees decided whether or not a student required special education.

12 Consultative Committee on the Education of Black Students in Toronto Schools, "Draft Report," p.39; emphasis added.

13 Ibid., p.43.

14 Ibid., p.45.

15 Ibid., p.10.

16 During World War II Japanese Canadians on the west coast were forced to leave their homes and were relocated to internment camps in the interior.

17 Consultative Committee on the Education of Black Students in Toronto Schools, "Draft Report," p.26.

18 Toronto Board of Education, minutes, April 28, 1988.

19 Maisy L. Cheng, "Visible Minority Representation in the Toronto Board of Education: Staff Changes, 1986," Research report no.183, Toronto Board of Education, May 1987.

20 Maisy L Cheng, "Who Seeks the Work? A Pre-Employment Pilot Survey," Research report no. 184, Toronto Board of Education, November 1987.

## 7 Power, Pedagogy, Curriculum

1 Enid Lee, *Letters to Marcia: A Teacher's Guide to Anti-Racist Education* (Toronto: Cross Cultural Communications Centre, 1985), p.9.

2 Joan Goody and Hugh Knight, "Multicultural Education and Anti-Racist Teaching," *English in Education* 19,3 (Autumn 1985), p.6.

3 Martin Francis, "Anti-Racist Teaching: Curricular Practices," in All London Teachers Against Racism and Fascism, *Challenging Racism* (London, 1984), p.97.

4 Lee, *Letters to Marcia*, p.8.

5 Simulation Training Systems, "Star Power," Del Mar, Cal. <www.stsintl.com>.

6 For the Colonialism game, Japanese Internment Role Play, and Chinese Head Tax game, see Tim McCaskell, *Toward Racial Equality: Materials for Secondary School Teachers* (Toronto District School Board, Equity Department, 1999).

7 Mary Ellen Goodman, *Race Awareness in Young Children* (New York: Collier Books, 1964).

8 Lev Vygotsky, *Thought and Language* (Cambridge, Mass.: MIT Press, 1962).

9 Lev Vygotsky, *Mind in Society* (Cambridge, Mass.: Harvard University Press, 1978), p.90.

10 Keith A. McLeod, ed., *Multicultural Early Childhood Education* (University of Toronto, Guidance Centre, Faculty of Education, 1984), p.13.

11 Louise Derman-Sparks, Carol Tanaka Higa, and Bill Sparks, "Children, Race, and Racism: How Race Awareness Develops," *Interracial Books for Children Bulletin* 11,3&4 (1980), p.9.

12 Ibid., p.8.

13 Ibid., p.7.

14 Elizabeth Parchment, "Effecting Change through an Elementary School Classroom," in "Anti-Racist Education in Practice: Experiences at the Toronto Board of Education," ed. Alok Mukherjee and Barb Thomas, unpublished manuscript, Toronto, p.78.

15 Joanne Maikawa-Roman, "Partnering in the Library: An Approach to Anti-Racist Work," in "Anti-Racist Education in Practice," ed. Mukherjee and Thomas, p.85.

16 Quoted in Lisa McNair, "Anti-Racist Education in Elementary Schools: What Does Being White Have to Do with It?" in "Anti-Racist Education in Practice," ed. Mukherjee and Thomas, p.67.

## 8 Great Leaps Forward

1 *Cindy: A Video for Anti-Racist Education*, directed by Oswaldo Garcia, Frameline Films, 1989.

2 The talk was later published in *Perspectives on Racism and the Human Services Sector: A Case for Change*, ed. Carl E. James (Toronto: University of Toronto Press, 1996).

3 For example: Wilson Head, *The Black Presence in the Canadian Mosaic: A Study of Perception and the Practice of Discrimination in Metropolitan Toronto* (Toronto: Ontario Human Rights Commission, 1975); *Equal Opportunity and Public Policy: The Role of the South Asian Community in the Canadian Mosaic* (Ubale Report), Toronto, 1977; *Now Is Not Too Late* (Pitman Report), submission to the Council of Metropolitan Toronto by the Task Force on Human Relations, 1977; Frances Henry, *The Dynamics of Racism in Toronto*, York University Research Report, 1978.

4 Karen R. Mock and Vandra Masemann, "Implementing Race and Ethnocultural Equity Policy in Ontario School Boards," Ministry of Education, Ontario, 1990.

## 9 Equity and Identity

1 Alok Mukherjee and Barb Thomas, "Anti-Racist Education in Practice: Experiences at the Toronto Board of Education" unpublished manuscript, Toronto, p.155.

2 Ibid., p.180.

3 Alok Mukherjee, Tim McCaskell, and Hari Lalla, *Did You Hear the One About . . . ? Dealing with Racist Jokes*, with illustrations by Carlos Freire (Toronto, Learnx Press, Toronto Board of Education, 1987).

## 10 A Single Spark

1 Stephen Lewis, letter to Premier Bob Rae, June 9, 1992. p.2.

2 Ibid., p.3.

3 Among the recommendations that drew the most heat: Lewis called for the reconstitution of a race relations and policing task force to assess the status and current implementation of previous recommendations, a systematic audit of police race relations policies, a strengthened police complaints commissioner and Special Investigations Unit, a requirement that police file reports whenever guns were drawn, beefed up race relations training, and an investigation into racism in other aspects of the criminal justice system.

4 Lewis, letter to Premier Bob Rae, pp.20-21.

5 Robert W. Runciman, MPP, news release, June 16, 1992, p.2.

6 Bernard Moitt, "Teaching African Heritage in Ontario Schools: Problems and Prospects," in *Educating African Canadians*, ed. Keren S. Brathwaite and Carl E. James (Toronto: James Lorimer and Company, 1996), p.190.

7 Suzanne Pharr, *Homophobia: A Weapon of Sexism* (Berkeley, Cal.: Chardon Press, 1988).

8 The talk formed the outline of his subsequent article in *Fuse* magazine: Richard Fung, "Working Through Cultural Appropriation," *Fuse*, 16,5&6 (Summer 1993).

## 11 Re-Evaluations

1 Paulo Freire, *Pedagogy of the Oppressed* (New York: Herder & Herder, 1970).
2 Mao Tse Tung, *Selected Readings from the Works of Mao Tse Tung* (Peking: Foreign Languages Press, 1971).
3 Ibid., p.100.
4 Michel Foucault, *The History of Sexuality*, vol.1, *An Introduction* (New York: Vintage Books, Random House, 1990), pp.92-93.
5 Stephen Richer and Lorna Weir, eds., *Beyond Political Correctness: Toward the Inclusive University* (Toronto: University of Toronto Press, 1995).
6 Kwame Anthony Appiah, *In My Father's House: Africa in the Philosophy of Culture* (New York: Oxford University Press, 1992).
7 Kwame Anthony Appiah, "Beyond Race: Fallacies of Reactive Afrocentrism," *Skeptic* 2,4 (1994), pp.104-7.
8 In the summer of 1992 I did research on this subject that ended up as a small booklet: Tim McCaskell, *A History of Race/ism*, Equity Department, Toronto District School Board, 1996. The booklet is available in the "Resources" section of the AMENO (Antiracist Multicultural Education Network of Ontario) Web site <www.ameno.ca>.

## 12 War of Attrition

1 Toronto Board of Education, minutes, Jan. 23, 1992.
2 Carol Tator, Frances Henry, and Winston Mattis, *Challenging Racism in the Arts: Case Studies of Controversy and Conflict* (Toronto; University of Toronto Press, 1998), ch. 7.
3 Toronto Board of Education, Policy Statement on Class Bias, minutes, June 24, 1993, pp.538-41.

## 13 The Good Fight

1 *The Toronto Star*, February 8, 1993, p.A1, "Students Joining War on Racism."
2 Peggy McIntosh, "White Privilege and Male Privilege: A Personal Account of Coming to See Correspondences through Work in Women's Studies," Working paper no. 189, Wellesley College Centre for Research on Women, Wellesley, Mass., 1988. The working paper was subsequently excerpted in a widely circulated article: Peggy McIntosh, "White Privilege: Unpacking the Invisible Knapsack," *Peace and Freedom*, July/August 1989, pp.10-12.
3 Peggy McIntosh, "Interactive Phases of Curricular and Personal Re-vision with Regard to Race," Working paper no. 219, Wellesley College Centre for Research on Women, Wellesley, Mass., 1990.
4 Ibid., p.5.
5 R. Herrnstein and C. Murray, *The Bell Curve* (New York: Free Press, 1994). The book proposed that a "cognitive underclass" associated with race had emerged in the United States.
6 See Carla Rice and Vanessa Russell, *EmBodying Equity: Body Image as an Equity Issue* (Toronto: Green Dragon Press, 2002).
7 George J. Sefa Dei, "Listening to Voices: Developing a Pedagogy of Change from the Narratives of African-Canadian Students and Parents," in *Educating African Canadians*, ed. Keren S. Brathwaite and Carl E. James (Toronto: James Lorimer and Company, 1996), p.33.
8 Diana S. Ralph, André Régimbald, and Nérée St-Amand, eds., *Open for Business, Closed to People: Mike Harris's Ontario* (Halifax: Fernwood, 1997).
9 Tim McCaskell, *Resources for Anti-Racist Education* (Toronto: Equity Studies Centre, Toronto Board of Education, 1996). This collection of exercises, discussion plans, case

studies, and role plays was reissued as *Toward Racial Equality* by the Equity Department of the Toronto District School Board in 1999.

10 *The Toronto Star*, April 5, 1996, p.D2.

## 14 Under Siege

1 Toronto Board of Education, minutes, June 27, 1996, p.538.

2 Toronto Board of Education, minutes, March 28, 1996, pp.174-79, April 24, 1997, pp.275-85.

3 These programs were listed in a report presented in April 1997 by Lloyd McKell, the Board's community services officer, on behalf of the African Canadian Student Affairs Committee; the report highlighted the work of the Consultative Committee on the Education of African Canadian Students and the Organization of Parents of Black Children. Toronto Board of Education, minutes, April 24, 1997, pp.322-25.

4 Toronto Board of Education, "Meeting the Special Needs of Students in the Toronto Board of Education, Research and Assessment Department, April 1997.

5 John B. Davies, "Taking Responsibility for Improving Schools: A Plan for System Improvement," Office of the Director of Education, Toronto Board of Education, October 1995.

6 Maisy Cheng and Maria Yau, "Secondary School Students' Characteristics, Needs and Experiences: Some Highlights Based on the Detailed Findings of the 1997 Every Secondary Student Survey," Academic Accountability Department, Toronto District School Board, June 1999.

## 15 Blueprints for an Invisible Future

1 Pharr, *Homophobia: A Weapon of Sexism*, pp.53-64.

## 16 Thermopylae

1 Jasmin Zine, "Negotiating Equity: The Dynamics of Minority Community Engagement in Constructing Inclusive Educational Policy," *Cambridge Journal of Education* 31,2 (2001).

2 Doreen Fumia, "Competing for a Piece of the Pie: Equity Seeking and the Toronto District School Board in the 1990s," Ph.D. thesis, University of Toronto, 2003.

3 Leah Rumack, "NDPer Not into Gay Equity," *Now*, March 25-31, 1999, p.18.

# Index